ESOPUS 15: TELEVISION

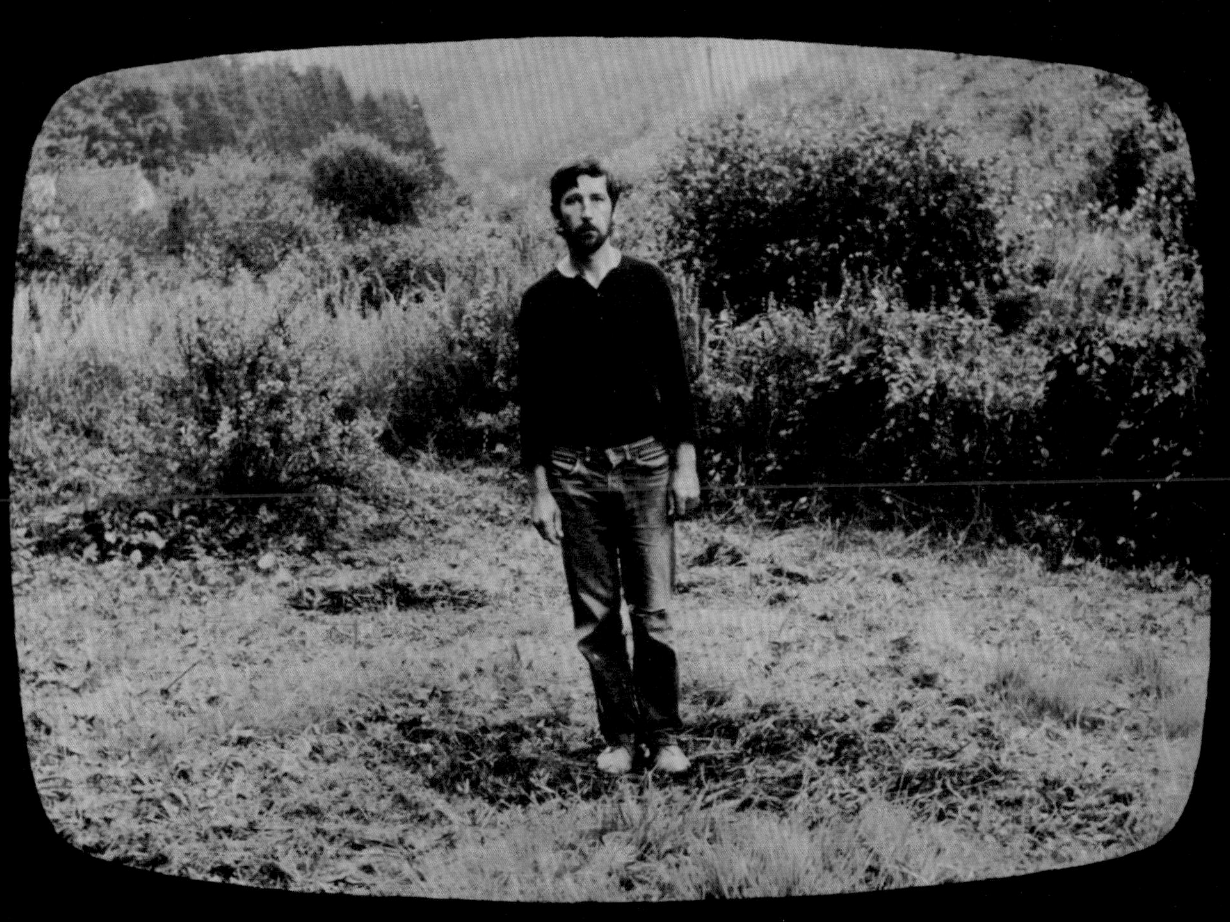

EDITOR'S NOTE

As most of you know, *Esopus* has kept advertising off its pages in order to provide a direct, noncommercial interface between artists and readers. You might find it ironic, then, that we have devoted an entire issue to television, a medium that for much of its existence has endeavored to do exactly the opposite. Put simply, television programming was created to sell products, a fact made glaringly obvious by the titles of many early shows (*Camel News Caravan*, *U.S. Steel Hour*, *Schlitz Playhouse*, etc.).

Of course, creativity flowers in unlikely contexts, and the history of TV, however commercially saturated, is filled with remarkable artistic accomplishments. This issue of *Esopus* celebrates a fair share of that work, with contents covering everything from the golden age of the medium in the 1950s to offerings from the present day—and even into the future, in the case of our "What Would You Like to See on Television?" invitational. Nearly every genre of the small screen is explored here, from sitcoms to soap operas, from reality shows to network news, from nature documentaries to telefilms.

As with television itself, though, advertising is never far removed. Some contributions address it directly, like artist Alex Bag's storyboards for imaginary TV commercials, but the topic is brushed up against in virtually every piece in the issue, whether in the interview with veteran soaps director Larry Auerbach, who recounts the product giveaways he was required to fold into show narratives in the 1950s, or in the materials reproduced from episode 124 of Norman Lear's pioneering series *Mary Hartman, Mary Hartman*, in which the title character has a nervous breakdown on live television as she babbles on about car-care products and waxy yellow buildup.

It's obviously difficult to approximate the experience of viewing television in a print format, so the issue you hold in your hands is only part of the story this time around. We'll be mounting a show this fall at Esopus Space, our exhibition and performance venue here in New York City, featuring videos by the three artists who created projects for the issue. We'll also include links on our website to video clips from much of the work discussed here. And there will be a series of screenings, concerts, and other events related to *Esopus 15* at Esopus Space and elsewhere throughout the winter. We encourage you to check *www.esopusmag.com* or our Facebook page for more information.—*Tod Lippy*

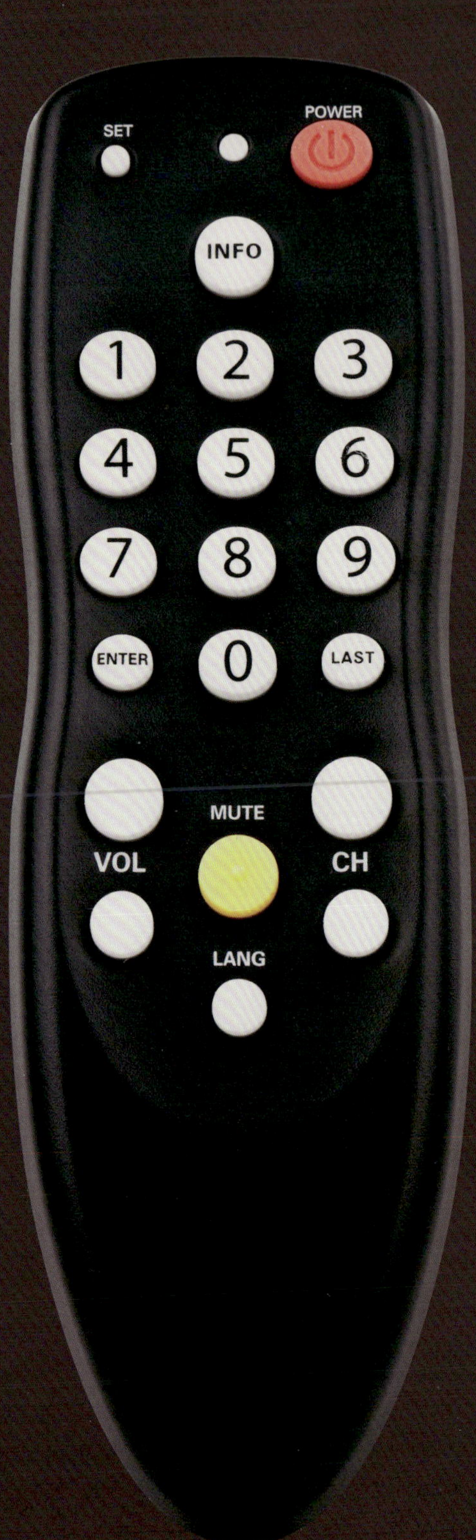

SET
POWER
INFO
1
2
3
4
5
6
7
8
9
ENTER
0
LAST
MUTE
VOL
CH
LANG

CONTENTS

CONTRIBUTORS

Born in 1930 in Oxford, England, **Keith Arnatt** lived and worked in Wales until his death in 2008. His conceptually driven, photo-based artwork was informed by a persistent sense of humor as well as a general search for the invisibility of the artist. Over the years, Arnatt investigated the dynamics of portraiture (as in "The Visitors," a series of portraits of tourists) and studied subjects such as garbage, rotting food, and his wife's comic household notes, often undercutting his own work with parodies of other established artists. The Photographers' Gallery in London held a major retrospective of Arnatt's work in 2007.

Larry Auerbach was born in 1923 in Mount Vernon, NY. His career-spanning work as a soap opera director helped cement the genre as a popular entertainment form in the United States. Beginning in 1951, Auerbach was the director of the CBS daytime drama *Love of Life*, a series that, during its 28-year run, initiated the careers of actors such as Christopher Reeve, Bonnie Bedelia, and Warren Beatty. He then went on to direct a number of other soaps, including *All My Children*, *As the World Turns*, and *One Live to Live*, for which he won a Daytime Emmy Award in 1984. Auerbach received the Directors Guild of America's Robert B. Aldrich Award in 1991 and was named a DGA Honorary Life Member in 2004.

New York–based **Alex Bag** received her B.F.A. from Cooper Union in 1991 and has since become a significant figure in contemporary video and performance art. Her videos—critical and ironic studies of television and media culture—have been exhibited in such venues as the Whitney Museum of American Art, the Andy Warhol Museum, the Museum of Modern Art, P.S. 1, Tate Modern, and New York's Elizabeth Dee Gallery (which also represents her). Bag has performed at the Knitting Factory and Threadwaxing Space in New York, and lectured at Yale University, Parsons School of Design, and CalArts. She received a grant from the Foundation for Contemporary Arts in 1995.

Claire Barliant earned her M.A. from the Center for Curatorial Studies at Bard College in 2004 and her B.A. in comparative literature from Smith College in 1997. The Brooklyn-based writer has contributed to the publications *Afterall*, *Artforum*, *ARTNews*, *Art on Paper*, *Modern Painters*, and *The Village Voice*. Barliant has also worked as a freelance editor for a variety of publications, as well as for the Museum of Modern Art, the Whitney Museum of American Art, and for the author Wayne Koestenbaum and the poet Bruce Hainley.

New York City native **Dara Birnbaum** attended Carnegie Mellon University and the San Francisco Art Institute before beginning a career-long and highly influential investigation of television and mass media in art. She has received a number of distinguished grants and awards throughout her career, including a Harvard Special Jury Prize in 1998, the TV Picture Prize in 1991, the Louis XIII de Remy Martin Award of Excellence, and the American Film Institute's Maya Deren Award for Independent Film and Video Arts in 1987. Represented by the Marian Goodman Gallery in New York, Birnbaum has exhibited widely in the United States and abroad, in venues such as the Centre Georges Pompidou in Paris, Tate Modern, the Whitney Museum of American Art, and the Museum of Modern Art. Most recently, her work was honored with a major retrospective at the Stedelijk Museum voor Actuele Kunst in Ghent, Belgium, which traveled to the Museu Fundação Serralves in Oporto, Portugal, earlier this year.

Michelle Elligott is Museum Archivist at New York's Museum of Modern Art. Elligott coedited *Art in Our Time: A Chronicle of the Museum of Modern Art*, cocurated MoMA's "1969" exhibition, and has published and lectured widely.

Rainer Werner Fassbinder was born in Bavaria in 1945 and lived and worked in Germany and New York until his death in 1982. Widely considered one of the most influential members of the New German Cinema, Fassbinder was extremely prolific throughout his relatively brief career and was a central figure of auteurist filmmaking throughout the 1970s. Working as director, producer, and actor, he completed 40 feature-length films, three short films, two television series, and 24 stage plays in less than 15 years. Though critics in Germany failed to recognize the merit of his work until he had begun to receive international acclaim, he went on to receive a number of honors, including a Baden-Baden Teleplay award for his television series *Katzelmacher*, the Cannes FIPRESCI Prize for *Ali: Fear Eats the Soul*, Gold German Film Awards for *Despair* and *The Marriage of Maria Braun*, and countless other festival prizes.

Born in Belgium in 1962, **Johan Grimonprez** currently lives and works in Brussels and New York, where he teaches at the School of Visual Arts. His first film, *dial H-I-S-T-O-R-Y*, premiered in 1997 at Centre Georges Pompidou and Documenta X in Kassel, Germany. Focusing on televised representations of airplane hijackings in the 1970s, it served as a meditation on the tensions between fact and fiction in the formation of historical narrative. In 2005, Grimonprez completed the film *Looking for Alfred*, which won the International Media Award (Germany) that year as well as the European Media Award in 2006. His latest work, *Double Take*, appeared in 2009. Grimonprez, who is represented by Sean Kelly Gallery in New York, has exhibited at Tate Modern, the Fruitmarket Gallery in Edinburgh, Scotland, and the Whitney Museum of American Art.

New York–based **J. Hoberman** earned his B.A. from SUNY Binghamton and his M.F.A. from Columbia University. He began writing for *The Village Voice* in 1977, where he holds the title of Senior Film Critic. Hoberman is also a frequent contributor to *The New York Times* and *Film Comment* and has published widely on experimental film. In 2008, he was honored with the Mel Novikoff Award at the San Francisco International Film Festival in recognition of his contributions to film studies.

Michael Patrick King was born in Scranton, PA, in 1954, and has lived in Los Angeles and New York since 1980. King began work in the entertainment industry performing stand-up comedy before going on to write for a number of television series, including *Murphy Brown*, *Cybill*, and *Will & Grace*. In 1998, he was hired as a writer on HBO's *Sex and the City*; King eventually directed a number of episodes and ultimately became co-executive producer of the series, which garnered him two Primetime Emmy Awards. King went on to serve as writer, director, and producer of *Sex and the City* and *Sex and the City 2*, the two feature films spawned by the popular series. King's directing work on *The Comeback*, the short-lived HBO series he cocreated with Lisa Kudrow, garnered him another Emmy nomination in 2006.

Born and raised in Encino, CA, **Lisa Kudrow** received her B.S. in psychobiology from Vassar College. She began her career by performing in various improvisational-comedy troupes, most notably The Groundlings in Los Angeles. After taking on smaller roles in television comedies such as *Cheers* and *Mad About You*, she won the part of Phoebe Buffay on the hit NBC series *Friends*. Her work on the sitcom garnered her a Primetime Emmy Award, a Screen Actors Guild Award, and an American Comedy Award. Kudrow has since acted in a number of films, including *Analyze This*, *The Opposite of Sex*, and *Wonderland*. She was nominated for another Emmy for her portrayal of Valerie Cherish in *The Comeback*, the HBO series she cocreated with Michael Patrick King. Kudrow is a currently a producer of NBC's *Who Do You Think You Are?* and is cowriter, coproducer, and star of the Internet series *Web Therapy*.

Norman Lear was born in 1922 in Connecticut and attended Emerson College before serving in World War II from 1942 to 1945. He began his television-writing career for *The Ford Star Revue* in 1950, and wrote later for comedies such as *The Martha Raye Show* and *The George Gobel Show*. In 1958, Lear cofounded Tandem Productions with Bud Yorkin. The company produced several films, including *Divorce American Style*, whose screenplay, written by Lear, was nominated for an Academy Award in 1967. Tandem's first TV series, *All in the Family*, ran for nine seasons on CBS and earned four Emmy Awards. It was followed by a number of other successful and often groundbreaking comedies, including *The Jeffersons*, *Maude*, *Good Times*, *One Day at a Time*, and *Mary Hartman, Mary Hartman*. In addition to his work in television, Lear has pursued a number of social causes. In 1981, he founded People For the American Way, a nonprofit organization devoted to the protection of civil liberties. Lear received the National Medal of Arts from President Bill Clinton in 1999.

Mame McCutchin received an M.A. from New York University's Cinema Studies program and was most recently host of *Artland: USA*, an HD television program about art and architecture that ran on the Ovation channel. McCutchin, who lives in New York, has written for *Daily Candy* and *Star* magazine; she is also a licensed NYC tour guide and a stand-up comedian.

A graduate of Dartmouth College, **Jean Passanante** acted in television and film and worked as a theater and literary agent in New York before she began writing for the daytime series *One Life to Live* in 1993. She was eventually promoted to head writer at the show before assuming that role at *All My Children*, *Another World*, and, from 2005 until its cancellation this September, *As the World Turns*. Passanante, who is based in New York, recently returned to *One Life to Live*. She has been honored with two Daytime Emmy Awards and three Writers Guild of America Awards.

Angus Trumble is Senior Curator of Paintings and Sculpture at the Yale Center for British Art in New Haven, CT. His books include *A Brief History of the Smile* (Basic Books, 2004), and *The Finger: A Handbook*, which was published in May of 2010 by Farrar, Straus and Giroux.

—*Compiled by Andrew Daly Frank*

ESOPUS

NUMBER 15: TELEVISION

Editor
Tod Lippy

Program Associate
Keriann Kohler

Interns
Logan Sebastian Beck
Andrew Daly Frank
Alexander Iezzi
Jacqueline Lash
Nicholas Pierce

ADVISORY BOARD

Joe Amrhein, Charles Burnett, Mary Ellen Carroll,
Daniel Clowes, Walter Donohue, Steven Heller,
Pamela A. Ivinski, Gareth Jones, Julie Lasky,
Scott Menchin, Stephen Motika, Mike Powell,
Jim Shepard, Christopher Trela, Dean Wareham,
E. Glen Weyl, Joshua White

SPECIAL THANKS

David Hariton, Marjorie and T. Edward Lippy,
Sam Amidon, Matthew Arnatt, Peter Becker,
Karina Daskalov, Beatrijs Eemans, Epson America,
Meg, Peter, and Thomas Galletti, Claudia Gonson,
George Kondogianis, Rose Lord, Juliane Lorenz,
Leon Neyfakh, Tim Saltarelli,
David Sparer/Canon USA, Chris Young

SUBSCRIPTIONS

One year (2 issues): $24 U.S. ($44 Can./$60 Int.)
Two years (4 issues): $45 U.S. ($82 Can./$115 Int.)

To subscribe, order single issues,
make a donation, or find out more about *Esopus*,
visit our website:

www.esopusmag.com

Or contact us at:

The Esopus Foundation Ltd.
64 West Third Street, #210
New York, NY 10012
phone: (212) 473-0919
fax: (212) 473-7212
e-mail: *info@esopusmag.com*

Distributed in the U.S. by R.C.S. and D.A.P.
and internationally by Central Books Ltd.

Printed in Canada by Westcan Printing Group

Esopus is proofed on Canon printers

ISSN 1545-9306

ISBN 978-0-9815745-4-7

Esopus accepts unsolicited submissions;
see our website for guidelines.

© 2010 *Esopus* magazine and the contributors

All Rights Reserved

ACKNOWLEDGMENTS

Esopus is published by the Esopus Foundation Ltd., a 501(c)(3) nonprofit organization that provides an unmediated forum through which creative people can connect directly with the general public.

The magazine never includes advertising or commercially driven content and is priced well below its actual cost of production so that it can be accessed by a wide range of readers. We therefore depend on support from individuals and organizations to sustain our efforts. Please consider making a contribution to the Esopus Foundation Ltd.: All donations are tax-deductible to the fullest extent of the law and will be noted both on this page and on our website, *www.esopusfoundation.org*.

The Esopus Foundation is grateful to the following individuals and organizations for their recent support:

$15,000
The Greenwall Foundation
The New York State Council on the Arts

$14,400
New York City Department of Cultural Affairs

$12,000
The Andy Warhol Foundation for the Visual Arts

$7,500
Peter and Carmen Lucia Buck Foundation

$5,000
The Lily Auchincloss Foundation
Marjorie and T. Edward Lippy

$2,500–$4,999
John Travis

$1,000–$2,499
Elizabeth Bartman and Andrew Solomon
Kjestine Bijur
Melva Bucksbaum
Foundation for Contemporary Arts
Meg Galletti
Steven L. Holley
Karen Holtzman
Elaine and Steven Masket
Louis Menand
Saul and Hila Rosen

$500–$999
Susan Almrud
Felicia and Keith Anzel
Brandon Chalk
James Cottrell
Linda Goldstein
Google Matching Grants
Jack and Nancy Larson
Sylvia Plimack Mangold
Puffin Foundation Ltd.
Frederic C. Rich
Edward Ruscha
Christina Shellen and Jeff Malmberg
Jonathan Zenios

$250–$499
Meg Armstrong
Laura Berick
Patricia Bitondo
D. Kevin Dolan
E.J. Farhood

$250–$499 (cont'd)
Stéphane and Alison Block Gerson
Ryan Greenlaw
Buck Henry
Alex and Ada Katz
Joel Kelly
Kenneth F. Koen
Werner Kramarsky/Fifth Floor Foundation
Stephen Motika
Jody Pollard
Ron Rifkin
John and Martha Sarno
Jan Scholes
Alison Simmons
Melissa Stern

$100–$249
Roz Bernheimer
Gay Block
Martin Brest
Joachim Brunckhorst
Barbara M. Cassidy
William & Sandra Christenberry
Dianne Connelly
Elizabeth Hope Cushing
Daiva Dambrauskas
Susan Daniels
Monroe Denton
Ellen Ellickson
Julian Fisher
Martin Fox
Phil Froncek
Logan Hauenstein
William Johnson
Dr. Miles E. Kuttler
Michael LaHaie
Roberta Lazarus
Sara Levi
John Limon
Russ Allison Loar
John Nutt
Christine Ogata
Peter Recker
Jock Reynolds and Suzanne Hellmuth
Ira Sachs
Kyle Sasse
Jose Scheinkman
James Taylor
Amy Villarejo
John and Christine West
John Valery White
Patricia Whitman
Justin Wray

Up to $99
Ben, Alix & Etta Aase
Scott Bednar
Neil Billingsley-Michaelsen
David Brown
Vincent Crapanzano
Paul Dalen
Marcus Denker
Stephen Douglas
Don Eicher
Mark Faigenbaum
Angela Foster
Michael Fuchs
Joseph Fusaro
George Ganat
Carolyn Ganus
Neil Goldberg
David Goldes
Drew Greenwald
Anna Grimm
Bruce Hanson
Margaret Harris
Marli Higa
Bridget Irish
Jason LaBumbard
Julie Lasky
Sara Levi
John Levin
Andreas Matern
Billy Mayer
Irene Oppenheim
Isaac Overcast
Chuck Pratt
Heather Rasley
Carol Reed
Adam Rowe
Lucette Runsdorf
Megan Satchell
Roland Schrebler
Wes Shull
Rebecca Smeenk
Nick Sprague
Amy Taubin
Fred Tomaselli
Alexandra Vassilaros
Charles Wylie
Eric Yealland

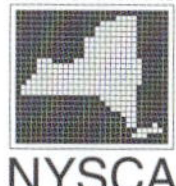

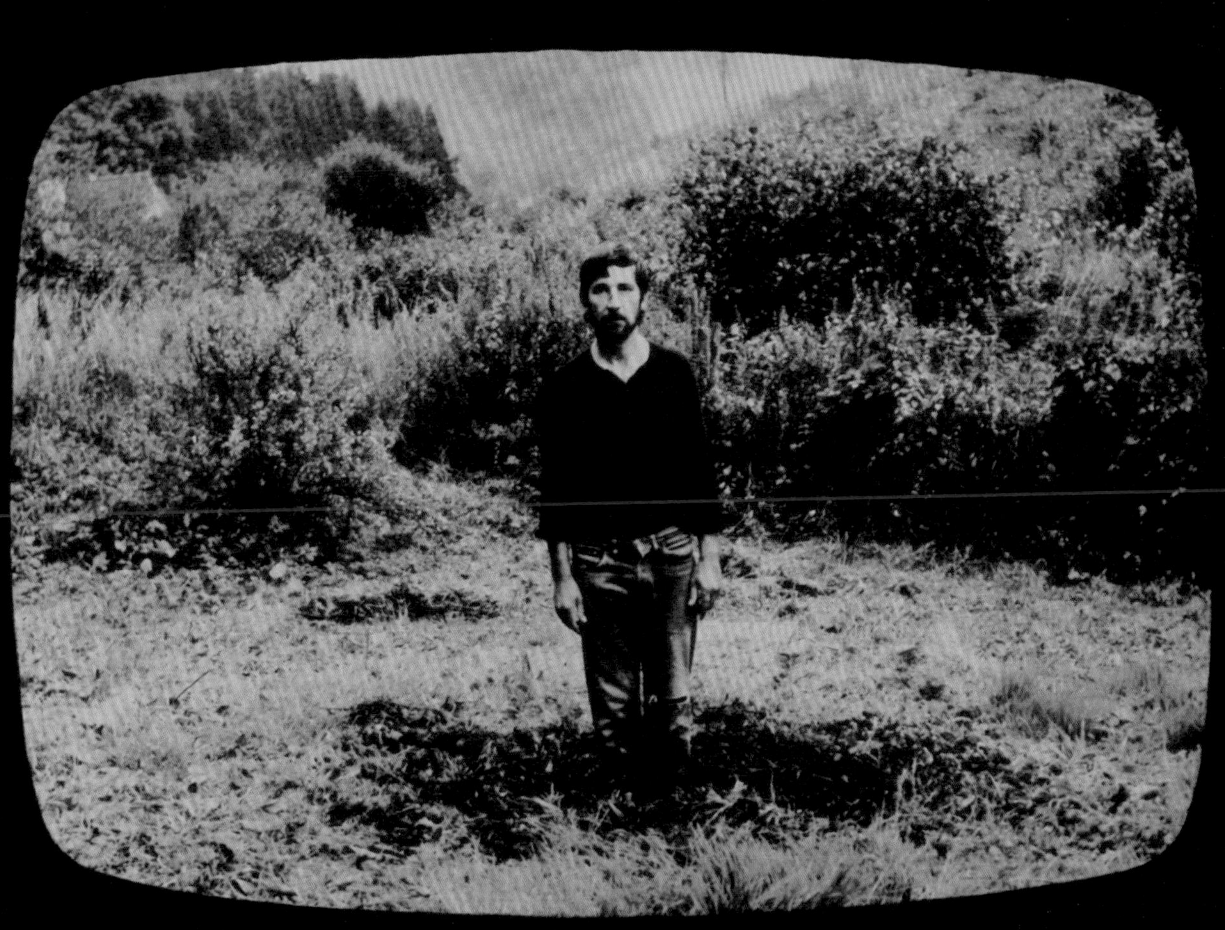

May 3, 1977

Dear Mr. Lear,

I am writing regarding your most outstanding production, Mary Hartman, Mary Hartman. I was dismayed to learn it is coming to an end but I understand how much pressure Louise, Tom, and the others must be under. I was seriously considering picketing Channel 11, but after thinking it through I came to a more profound conclusion. M.H., M.H. is in the relative field of existence. Although I think I'll die without it I must keep in mind that nothing in the relative can be completely fulfilling and last forever.

I see you as the truly enlightened man you are. M.H., M.H. had a purpose. I feel its purpose was to shine light on our ignorant states of existence. Alot of people who dislike the show, dislike it, in my opinion, because deep down they realize they are watching themselves in action. These people say it's far-fetched and stupid but they won't admit that that's the way we all are.

In conclusion, I would like to say, "THANK YOU" for shining some light on my dull existence and enabling me to have a hell-of-a-good time at 11pm Monday - Friday.

With great appreciation,

Linda Natale

Linda Natale, Linda Natale

P.S. If you ever need any support with the show and maybe getting it back on the air, please feel free to call on me.

EPISODE 124
THE MAKINGS OF A MELTDOWN

Mary Hartman, Mary Hartman was a surreal soap opera–cum-sitcom produced by Norman Lear and starring Louise Lasser in the title role that ran for only two seasons, from 1976 to 1977. By the end of the first season, it was a runaway hit. Airing at 11 p.m., five nights a week, the half-hour-long show resonated not only with mainstream viewers but also the intellectual and cultural elite: Academics panegyrized the show's satire of a consumer-driven society; jazz musicians Charlie Haden and Ornette Coleman released an album, an homage to the series, titled *Soapsuds, Soapsuds* in 1978.

Episode 124 was the perfect denouement to a show that was resolutely of its time, which chose to reflect current events while other sitcoms strove for a generically timeless, i.e., "classic," quality. That *Mary Hartman, Mary Hartman* was, well, *so* '70s makes it garishly fascinating to contemporary audiences. The American Indian Movement, hostage crises, Gore Vidal, Betty Ford, televangelism, gay rights, and, of course, feminism, are just a few of the quintessentially 1970s phenomena or figures the series touched on. Most compelling, though, was the way *Mary Hartman, Mary Hartman* critiqued television. Take, for example, the season finale: After having been dubbed "America's Typical Consumer Housewife," Mary is interviewed by David Susskind and three strident pundits. Unable to endure an interrogation about her shopping and sexual habits on live TV, not to mention that her marriage is falling apart, her 13-year-old daughter has run away from home, her grandfather is a flasher, and countless other indignities brought upon her by the show's genius writers, Mary has a meltdown.

The meeting notes and story breakdowns for the episode reproduced on the following pages shed some light on the mechanics behind this famous scene. Lasser's performance of the meltdown was so convincing that many viewers thought she was improvising. But these documents prove that it was scripted, down to the relentless and excruciating questioning that leaves Mary so severed from her identity at the end of the episode that she can only helplessly repeat her own name, "Mary Hartman, Mary Hartman, Mary Hartman," ad infinitum.

Last year, I had the opportunity to interview Norman Lear about *Mary Hartman, Mary Hartman;* a transcript of that interview appears below.—*Claire Barliant*

Claire Barliant: *Mary Hartman, Mary Hartman* enjoyed mainstream success—the show's star, Louise Lasser, was featured on the covers of *People* and *Rolling Stone* dressed as Mary. Yet it also developed a cult and academic following among viewers who were looking for something different or more offbeat. I was wondering if those dual successes surprised you at all.

Norman Lear: I don't think they surprised me, which isn't the same thing as saying I was not expecting to be surprised. What was interesting was that it seemed to be accepted on two levels. The people you're talking about got something that the average viewer did not get: They got the subtext. And then there was a greater subtext. I myself didn't realize how strong this greater subtext was until within the last year.

Can you describe that a little more?

Yes, I can. My concept for the show was that we were going to look at an average American blue-collar housewife and see how she was being impacted by the media. How the 24/7 of television, magazines, and the beginning of what is now a raging celebrity culture would impact her. Somebody recently put the last scene of the first season of *Mary Hartman* on YouTube. In it, there were three media talking heads—a feminist, a media critic, and a consumer advocate—along with David Susskind, playing himself, who were interviewing Mary, because she had just been chosen as "Housewife of the Year" by some publication. And these people, who represented the media, harangued her. The entire episode was probably 20 minutes, and she went crazy. She was driven fucking nuts by the media. I didn't realize how complete that subtext was. I was thrilled. The breakdown was…I've never seen a better performance ever, anywhere.

Louise Lasser does such a fantastic job playing Mary. How did she come to be cast in the role?

An agent read the script and brought her to me. In effect, he *really* cast her. Once I met her, I mean, you know, *[laughs]* there was only one.

Critique of consumerism is a major part of the show. For example, in the episode you were talking about, the pundits are grilling her about her susceptibility to commercials. And during the show she's always trying out new products, as in the famous opening scene where she is asking her sister whether she can see waxy yellow buildup on her floor.

She's doing that two minutes—or maybe it's 20 seconds—after having learned that a family of five and their eight goats and two chickens had been slaughtered around the corner.

Right. *[laughs]* When I watch the show now, I can't help but think that if it were on today, those moments would be product-placement opportunities.

[laughs] Yes, they would.

Do you have any thoughts about the direction in which TV has gone since? Is it what you expected?

You know, I can't say I'm smart or prescient enough to have predicted it, but I certainly was aware of its beginning, when advertising started convincing people that they couldn't believe their own eyes if an ad told them to believe something else. We certainly were ahead of the curve in that regard.

It seems like a revolutionary topic for a show at that time. In fact, there's a lot of material on the show that is very racy—for instance, the frank discussion of impotence—that seems ahead of the curve. Is that partly to do with the fact that the show aired late at night?

Well, it was on late night, but it was also on independent stations. Stations that carried it became known as part of the "*Mary Hartman* network." If you were running it, you were part of the "*Mary Hartman* network" because it was the only thing on the air that distinguished your station on a national level.

Can you talk about the distribution method? It's very unusual.

When we started out, we couldn't get arrested. We just couldn't get it on the air. There were only three networks and then the independent stations. I don't think we said, "Let's establish our own network." What happened was there was a NATPE (National Association of Television Program Executives) convention in L.A., and we couldn't sell it—we hadn't sold any. A couple of weeks in advance of this NATPE convention, we decided to have a dinner on the lawn at my home, and we invited all of the

guys who bought for the stations. I know Ted Turner was there, and a couple of stars—just some glitz to get them to come. We had a great turnout, and we had dinner on the lawn with my wife and daughters hostessing. The reason for making a point of that was that I wanted them to see this was a great family with two feet on the ground. The next morning we had a breakfast, with Ron, the promo man, trying to sell *Mary Hartman*. And here's what happened: Most of these guys showed up, and an older guy who was a dean among these guys stood up and said, "I want that show for my station." And the others followed, and that was how we broke through.

Can you imagine using a similar strategy to get something that subversive on the air now, or is it easier to turn to other models, like YouTube, for example, that offer alternative distribution?

Well, there certainly are new forms of alternative distribution. I don't know if it could happen. I'd like to try it.

Have you thought about making a show and putting it online?

Yes, we're working on a couple of things. You remember *Fernwood Tonight?* The conceit is that *Fernwood Tonight* has been on the air all these years in Fernwood, Ohio, and someone rediscovers it: "Oh my gosh, it's still there. They're still running it."

I read an autobiography by Ann Marcus, the main writer for the show, and when she writes about her experience working with you on the show, it is a little contentious. I'm sure you know about all of this. She claims that the show went downhill a little bit after you took her off of it. I was wondering if you had any comment on that?

It did go downhill. It might have been because Ann was just marvelous—she was stalwart, and exceedingly creative, and she brought in two other writers. The three of them were the mainstays. But it went downhill also because Louise was exhausted. So the combination of Ann's departure, which was meaningful, coincided with the situation with Louise.

It's interesting how many women there were behind the show.

That was true throughout our company. Women are my life. I have five daughters. I never did a show that was produced by dozens of guys, as these things go, that wasn't really produced by a woman.

***Mary Hartman, Mary Hartman* has had a second life since the issue of the DVD a couple of years ago. Do you have any thoughts on how future generations might view the show?**

First of all, in the long history of acting, there was only one Louise Lasser: She had a style and she caught something so enormously unique that it will always be impressive. Second, what we were dealing with was basically the human condition, and if there were allusions to things happening at that moment in time, they were in context—they were part of issues that never go away. So I would think it would be as interesting anytime. You know, I didn't have any problems with *Mary Hartman,* but when I did *All in the Family,* the network fought hard to not have us talk about Nixon, for instance—not discuss topical things—because they were hoping for a long afterlife for the series. They were sure that people would not be interested in subjects that had no current relevance. But as it turned out, that didn't matter.

RIGHT: First of six pages from the transcript of a story meeting with Norman Lear and Louise Lasser on April 9, 1976, concerning the end of episode 124.

NL: "TYPICAL AMERICAN HOUSEWIFE (OF THE YEAR)" - For Mary.
     After Cathy suggests her or the station decides to talk
     to her, somebody comes to her house to interview her.
     She's being interviewed at a time when Tom is an alcoholic,
     when she's got a problem with Heather, when other things
     are happening in the family. It's a tangent, a slightly
     bent STET scene. Instead of Mary doing a monologue,
     the person is asking exciting, involved, interested
     questions about her family and Mary is trying to answer them,
     but she's not able to talk about her drunk husband, etc.
     What Mary is doing is making it seem like things are fine,
     but she's talking around and around the things that we know --
     like Tom is an alcoholic, Heather ran away three times
     (by the way, that's happening too). Louise is also suggesting
     that in this interview there may be two people there, well,
     let's keep it one actor, and the person has a tape machine
     going which scares the shit out of Mary and is constantly
     taking polaroids which always forces her in the middle of
     trying desperately to keep a brave face -- she has to suddenly
     smile for a polaroid that's being snapped to her right when
     she's looking to her left.

     This material that the local station is taping is sent to
     New York where local stations from all over the country

have been asked to send the tape. Now I don't know whether Louise is intending this, but I see a scene in New York where two executives have just looked at the tapes of forty housewives. One of them refers to that Mary Hartman in Fernwood and says that he thinks she'd be great. The other one says, "Great! The woman is a near-hysteric.   I mean, something's wrong there. Some problem." And the other guy says, "But look at the balance -- you've got two happy housewives, and this one..." In other words, one guy is trying to profit on the fact that he thinks he has seen a woman in distress. And that's how she gets from their standpoint to the show.

LL: I think also on the show, she is the only "typical American houswife." Everyone else -- in the interview she'll say --

NL: Depending on how many interviews we do, the first interview with the Fernwood television station we may have covered. Maybe there's a second interview before or after they see her tape in New York, depending on how many scenes we need to carry this line. But after they see her tape in New York maybe there's a second interview, because they send somebody to Fernwood. And when she's asked questions about her typical housewife activity, she says she doesn't do anything. She just kind of gets up in the morning, and she mops sometimes,

and sometimes she does the oven, sometimes she does
the oven more than once, and sometimes she has to open
the refrigerator to get eggs, and then she closes it.
And they think it's great. Whatever she says, they think
it's absolutely great, and typical, typical, typical.

The television scene in which she has the breakdown
will now come out of New York. That will give it even
more size. And we will have seen how the process worked.
Forty women were selected out of tape that was prepared
from their local TV station and viewed in New York. Then
it was narrowed down to three women. I want to see you on
a show with two women who are perfectly well.
HOLD EVERYTHING! Louise is saying that when we get to that
television show in New York, we will know what the process
was because we will have seen the scene in New York where
they select Mary as one of the three. And then _finally_
they select her as the one. She's on the tube alone in a
David Susskind-type presentation where off-stage there is
an audience and we may hear a question asked, and onstage
is the whole family -- the whole family will be in the show.
Just to talk about the _set_ for a moment - to avoid a big set -
we can do this in front of drapes, as a lot of the talk shows
are done, with three men who are asking questions of Louise,
of the "Typical American Housewife." The family's in the

audience. We can film the family in the audience against
any other kind of backdrop, even like the recording studio, just
a few rows of chairs and an indication of other people.
They don't have to be taped at the same time, so we don't
have to have a complete set with 180 degrees to shoot.

It's a David Susskind kind of show. As a matter of fact it
can be David Susskind. I'm sure he'd be happy to come out
here and do it. It's David's kind of show, and then you can
do it from Fernwood and you won't expect to see his set
because David Susskind has come to Fernwood to the home
of the Typical American Family. That'll make the fact that
the family is there much more easy to take, too. They didn't
all fly to New York and that, because they really can't
afford the trip. So Susskind has come, it's a national
hook-up, and he has come to Fernwood having found the
Typical American Housewife, and the family's in the audience.
On the panel with him are two very strong female liberationists.
One is a Margaret Mead kind of person, an anthropologist,
a very strong lady. The other one is a Bella Abzug or
a Gloria Steinem kind of person. They're both _very_ strong
ladies. And another one is an author who's written some
great books, like _Fear of Flying_, Erica Jong, full of sex
and female liberation sex. One of the things that Mary asked
them _not_ to discuss on the show is sex. Not that she's

uptight about it at all. It's just that her daughter's going to be in the audience and they don't talk about those things in front of her daughter. And not on family hour. And David Susskind says, "But this is going to be on at ten o'clock," and she says, "In my house that's family hour. We don't have an hour that isn't. <u>All</u> hours are family hours. Six o'clock is family hour. Four-thirty in the morning -- family hour! You never know when Heather's going to have cramps."

Think about this gang -- the possibility of Mary having gone to New York alone with Susskind and the family isn't in the audience because they really wouldn't all go back there, they can't afford that. And the fact of her isolation alone, having left her little hotel room and come to the Susskind studio and the big city with the big lights and all of those things all alone may make the breakdown -- I think the breakdown <u>is</u> more interesting that way.

LL: I do too.

NL: Let's do that. In New York and alone. And let's see the family by cutting to them around the television set. Same feeling.

There's a scene for Mary and the priest where she's trying to pray in a Catholic way. She's tried everything else, and she's asking him how you do it. Maybe she's gotten some beads from a friend, and she's asking the priest how to count them and could he please put some water on her head. She brings him a glass of water, and he starts to drink and she says, "No, that's not to drink. Just touch me on the head." And here then she brings him a cracker, a graham cracker because she didn't have a wafer.

Louise is suggesting a wonderful scene. It could be more than a scene. It could be a scene and a thread through a lot of other things. Mary has all kinds of crazy gourmet foods and other things stashed. She's eating a great deal. She has chocolates, everywhere, and things she's never eaten before like cumquats, she didn't even like to say the word before. And she's stuffing herself. There's a good scene in that and possibly an attitude for a number of scenes.

<u>THE END</u>

ccs

coming in with a dithering Martha and pooped Grandpa, who just wants somepeanut butter and some prune juice. George wants everyone to calm down. It;s not the end of the world. Yes, it is, says Martha -- she's been disgraced, she's been held over for trial, they had to put up the whole Winabago fund for her bail ... and now on top of everything Billy's gone! George is sure the police'll find him! Grandpa isn't and frankly he's glad. Martha's disconsolate. It was bad enough them all being arrested, expecially Billy for assulting Willard Armitage, the spokesman from the Bureau of Indian Affairs, by pelting him with rotten tomatoes, but now that Billy's escaped from Fernwood City Jail, they'll really throw the book at him. Here she is, an adopted child who's finally found her true father, a full-blooded Choctaw, only to have the man arrested and charges preferred against him so that he'll probably spend the rest of his life behind bars. They find the note from Cathy. Martha too upset even to take it seriously, until Grandpa says it's probably got that priest involved somehow. Martha feels faint. George says there's no time for her to pass out. It's almost seven thirty. Time for America's Typical Consumer Special, starring their daughter, Mary Hartman. They turn on the set.

<u>CUT TO: TV STUDIO</u>

David Susskind welcoming America to an intimate look at itself, it's hopes, it's dreams, it's frustrations, and it's buying habits. Behind him in shadow a seated figure with braids. He goes on to explain the format of the show,

25

the real-life film they'll be seeing, the panel of experts,
and America's Typical Consumer herself ... whom he now introduces. Mary Hoffman. Hartman, the seated figure corrects,
as the lights come up around her, Mary Hartman.

#124

<u>ACT ONE: TV STUDIO, ON THE HEELS OF IV, #123</u>

David face to face with Mary, who's got a coast to coast
smile going for the viewers at home. Introductory chit-
chat, no, she's not nervous, yes, she's enjoying NY, yes,
she's a typical tourist. And into a short personal history
just to get the ball rolling. (Won't you tell us something
about yourself, Mary?) And the picture we get is pretty
much the way the makers of Johnson's Wax would have it.
Kind of post-Pepsi Generation coping, seeing the bright
side, middle American morality glossing the rough spots.
But somehow the information on David's fact sheet doesn't
seem to be jibing with the picture Mary's trying to paint.
As he probes, she starts becoming nervous. No, she's not
actually separated; she and her husband are just no longer
living together, though they have much in common and enjoy
the same aspects of the good life. No, she and her daughter
do not fight; they just have differences of opinion. What
does her daughter want to do when she grows up.? She doesn't
know. But then why should she? She doesn't know what she
wants to do when she grows up either. David cuts to the
film (with Hugh's voice-over), and we see bits and pieces

of Mary's week, intercut with Mary's reactions. Breakfast
from #116, coming home from shopping (same episode), Mary
dusting with Heather from #117. And all the personal traumas
that have been weaving through her days. Mary looks uncomfortable. She didn't realize they'd be using so much
of the personal things and so little of her "consumerism."
The footage grinds on, Mary sinking lower and lower in her
chair.

ACT TWO: SHUMWAY KITCHEN
George and Martha and Grandpa watching as David breaks
for a commercial. Martha's upset; she doesn't like the
way Mary looks. George thinks his daughter looks fine, her
dress, her braids. But that's not what Martha means. She
means the look on Mary's face; she looks like she's going
to be sick. And Martha'll bet anything all that prying and
personal questions is not what Mary expected. But then she
doesn't know why Mary agreed to the show in the first place.
She certainly wouldn't have done it, all all their dirty
linen for all the world to see.

CUT BACK TO: THE TV STUDIO
David introducing his experts, who are now faced off against
Mary and commenting round-table-style on the film they've
just seen. They are not kind and treat Mary pretty much
like a lab specimen. She shrinks, she squirms. No, it's
not like that. Her life is fine, her household is well-
managed, her child is happy.

CUT TO: CHICAGO MOTEL ROOM

(Re-dress of Fernwood Motel Room? With TV) Loretta and
Merle and Jimmy Joe watching Loretta's friend; Loretta
upset. She knows this isn't going the way Mary expected.
Merle sending Jimmy Joe out of the room, so he and Loretta
can talk. In fact, this trip to Chicago isn't turning out
the way Loretta expected. So far there's been no work on
her act for the Revival and Merle seems very vague about
all his plans. He'll confess, says Merle. He did get her
here under false pretenses. What false pretenses? He's
not all that hot about her singin', but he is about her.
Loretta's startin' to feel mighty nervous. Merle locks
the door, just so they won't be disturbed. Disturbed from
what? Loretta wants to get back to the TV show, the commercial's over. But Merle has other ideas of what they oughta
get to. He's crazy about Loretta, has been ever since he
first met her. And Jimmy Joe's crazy about her too. And
they can both see how she feels about them. Merle moving
in for a clinch. He wants her. They're right for each
other. A beautiful woman like Loretta doesn't need some
bald old man with glasses. He kisses her, she struggles.
He presses. She tries to get out of the room. He acts
like she's playing, and continues, pins her against a wall.
She grabs a lamp and beans him. He falls. She's scared.
She tries to get him to stand up, nothing. No response.
Panicked, she calls Charlie (TWO-WAY) Charlie, help me!
I'm in trouble.

ACT THREE: THE TV STUDIO

Where Mary's under heavy fire from the panel of experts.
Does she feel her life is being controlled by Madison
Avenue? Does she get her money's worth from the goods
and services she buys? Does she have a satisfactory sex
life? Mary's trying to keep the discussion on a family
hour plane and be polite all at the same time. For the
most part she feels the products she buys -- do her sexual
fantasies now seem different than the ones she had before
she was married? Actually, she responds, kitchen and food
products are somewhat more satisfactory than clothing goods,
but of course that has to do with style. Shirley's pinning
her on her failed hopes and lost ambitions. Is the male's
role as head of the house a detriment to the emerging woman?
Mary talks about car care products. Does she believe in the
liberation movement? She talks about products for bedroom
and bath. Is she concerned about the quality of education
and how her daughter will be able to cope with a changing
world? Absoluitly. Does she worry about her daughter's
sex life? Or is her attitude more like the First Mama's?
Mary's getting frazzled. What about her husband's drinking
problem? What about extra-marital sex? Mary tries to give
second hand Ann Landers Reader's Digest comments with allowances,
of course, for the kinds of passion evoked by Rich Man, Poor
Man. Tucker McMarshall pins her. Is she trying to say
that all her opinions are second-hand? That she can't re-
late to ideas in terms of her own experience? Mary gets
wound up for one last-ditch defense of her life. She has
opinions, she has idea, she has feelings, and she is in

control of her fate. She did not crack under the threat of VD
or indecent exposure or homosexuality down the block.
She has stood strong in the face of anti-semitism, auto
wrecks, fibroid tumors, and mass murder. She can even
cope with the fact that her real great-grandfather who has
been located through adopto-Find is a Choctaw Indian. She
believes in herself, she believes in the future, she believes
in the United States of America. If only the mail would come
on time, but you see, it doesn't, and then of course there's
the planes -- the flight patterns should be changed back,
or maybe it's the working conditions in large factories,
like the one in which her semi-estranged husband used to
work. Or maybe it's consumer boycotts, or waxy yellow
build-up or adultery or sexual diamonds and therapists
-- maybe it's everything! Maybe everything is just too
much! Maybe television is too much! Maybe all these people and cameras and sponsors and families and electronic
everything is just too much. David tries to bring everything back into focus. Is Mary saying that she has trouble
maintaining her identity in the face of modern living?
Is she unliberated, asks Shirley? Is she unprotected against
the interests of big business, asks Norman? Is she buffeted
into numbness by the media, asks Tucker. Yes, screams Mary!
she'll confess! Yes, to everything. All the failures, all
the mistakes! The world has tried to make life wonderful
and she's loused it all up. She's guilty! Are they still
on the air? She's hopeless? Can they come back tomorrow?
She doesn't know what to do! To do, to do, to do .....

<u>ACT FOUR: HOSPITAL ROOM WALL</u>

Mary sitting on a chair in a hospital gown, motionless, silent. Around her voices. Hospital administrators getting sign-in information from George and Martha, Tom's concern, Heather wondering where she'll go to live -- a nurse explain- the set-up at the hospital, another doctor giving a very guarded prognosis. The nurse calls to Mary, come along now. That's right, I'm Mrs. Gimble. Do you want to tell me your name? Mary, almost catatonic, muttering: Mary, Hart- man, Mary Hartman .... The confusion around her continues. Perhaps her mother interjecting something about the trouble Loretta's in. None of it seems to reach Mary, who just sits, every few seconds muttering Mary Hartman, Mary Hartman. Doctors conferring about possible treatment. Tom crying, apologizing for everything. Grandpa wondering if it could have been Billy Twelvetrees disrupting all their lives .... And where's Cathy? They haven't seen her since they found her note. Heather's hungry. Medication coming, a room arranged for. Maybe just a couple of weeks, maybe months. Mary completely tuned out, just her voice droning inter- mittantly. Mary Hartman, Mary Hartman ....

<u>END OF SEASON</u>

hears. It's almost time for Mary's show on tv. She had no idea it was so late. She's gotta go since Merle doesn't have a set here and besides, she should be home for Charlie. Merle says he wants her to stay because they have something more important to do. Loretta politely disagrees. There ain't nothin' more important than watchin' Mary's show even though she's mad at her because she said such negative things about Merle and her goin' to Chicago. But she's still her best friend and she dearly wants to watch her in this triumph... of bein' America's Typical Consumer. Merle prevents her from going by locking the door and pocketing the key. He doesn't want to frighten her, he simply wants to talk to her.

<u>CUT TO: TV STUDIO</u>

David Susskind welcoming America to an intimate look at itself, it's hopes, it's dreams, it's frustrations, and it's buying habits. Behind him, in shadow, a seated figure with braids. He goes on to explain the ofrmat of the show, the real-life film they'll be seeing, the panel of experts and American's Typical Consumer herself ...whom he now introduces. Mary Hoffman. Hartman, the seated figure corrects, as the lights comes up around herp Mary Hartman.

<u>FRIDAY, #124</u>

<u>ACT ONE: TV STUDIO, IMMEDIATELY FOLLOWING ACT 4, #123</u>

Same as original.

<u>ACT TWO: HAGGERS L.R., NIGHT</u>

Charlie, watching Mary's show, wondering where Loretta could be. DOORBELL. Loretta musta forgot her key again, says Charlie, going to the door. He opens it, but doesn't see anyone because it's Jimmy Joe who only comes up to his

knee. Charlie thinks something awful's happened to Loretta.
Not yet, says Jimmy Joe and explains how he was supposed
to go to the movies and sit through twice, but he got to
hearing a Voice on the bus which told him to come here
instead. He's worried about his Pa's weakness and sinning
and what he said about Mrs. Haggers .. like how she's gonna
be his mother and his Daddy's wife when that can't be because
polygamy is disallowed in the Bible and coveting another
man's wife, too, and if Mr. Haggers would like him to
quote chapter and verse, he'll be glad to. Charlie is
staggered. His mouth drops open ... then he rushes out
the door.

CUT TO: MERLE'S MOTEL ROOM

Incorporatin' much of what was on p. 27 of original, only
rememberin' that we are not in Chicago. And .. when you'uns
git to the end ... stop at ...a beautiful woman like Loretta
doesn't need some bald old man with glasses. He kisses her,
she struggles, and screams. POUNDING ON THE DOOR AND CHARLIE
SHOUTING ...OPEN UP!! Merle gets a gun; Charlie kicks the
door open. Merle aims the gun at Charlie; Loretta grabs
for him; Charlie dives towards them. The gun goes OFFFFFFF!!
And we go to BLACK before we know who's been hit.

ACT THREE: TV STUDIO

Same/s original.

ACT FOUR: HOSPITAL ROOM WALL

Same as terrific original ... only nitpick .. if Martha
should say ...'don't tell her about Loretta and Charlie' --
which keeps that mystery alive.   And .... oh yes ... at
the very end, the voices of her family drift away as they
all leave. Mary is alone with Mrs. Gimble, the nurse,

who takes her under the arm, helping her up. 'Shall we go
along to.our room now?' Mary, docile and expressionless,
goes with her. They exit room, come to a locked corridor
door, with a wire-reinforced window. Nurse Gimble knocks
at the door. A hospital guard opens the door. Mary passes
through with the nurse. We now see the guard. It's ....FOLEY.

FADE OUT.

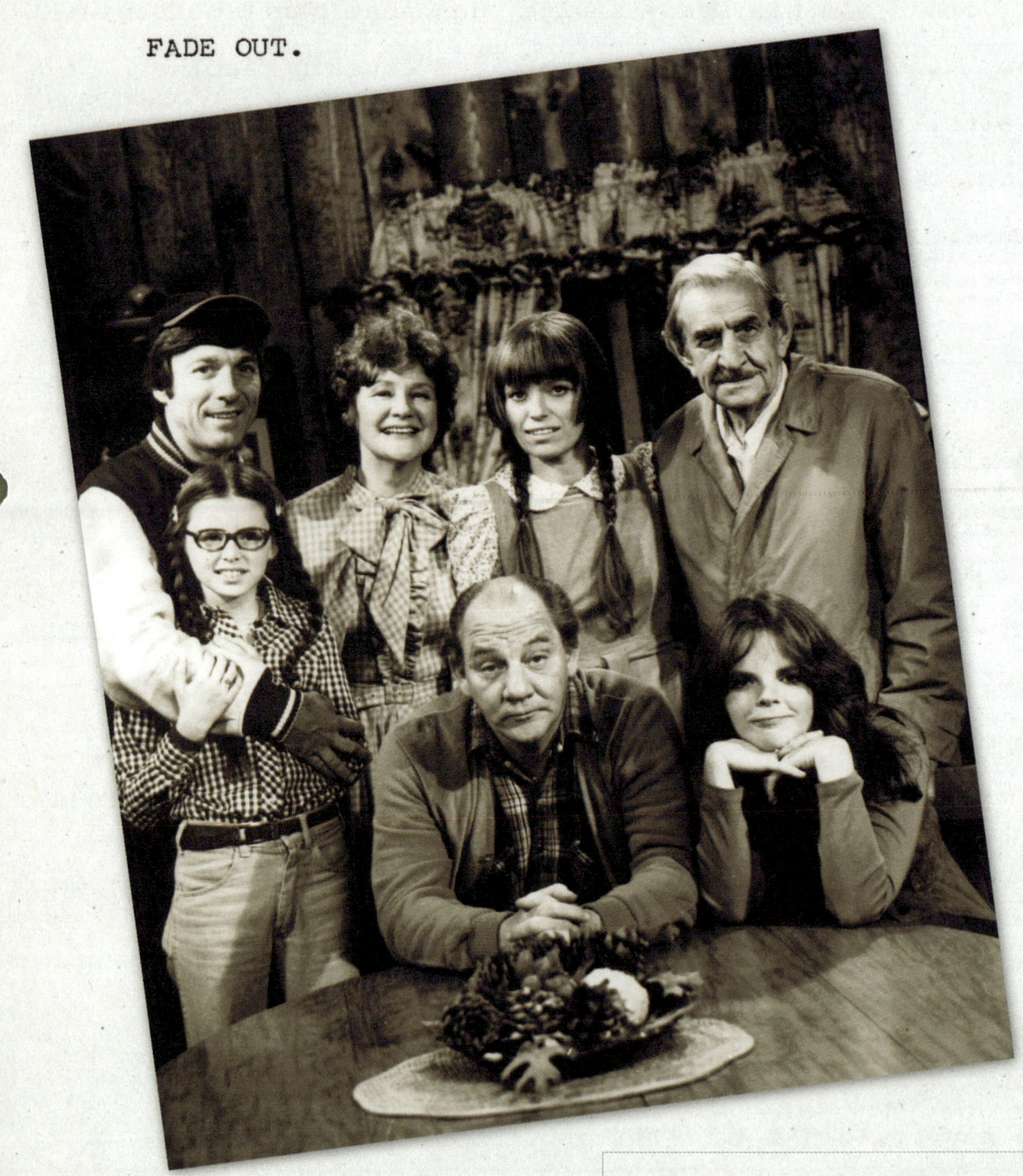

ITEMS REPRODUCED HERE:

p. 9: Letter from Norman Lear's archives, May 3, 1977

pp. 13–18: Pages from transcript of story meeting on April 9, 1976, with Norman Lear and Louise Lasser concerning the end of episode 124

pp. 19–25: Pages from story breakdown for episode 124

pp. 26–28: Pages from revised story breakdown for episode 124, with changes made to act two and act four.

p. 28: *Mary Hartman, Mary Hartman* cast photograph

Reproductions courtesy of Act III Communications (©Sony Pictures Television)

SKYJACKERS SERIES   JOHAN GRIMONPREZ

STILLS FROM *dial H-I-S-T-O-R-Y*, 1997

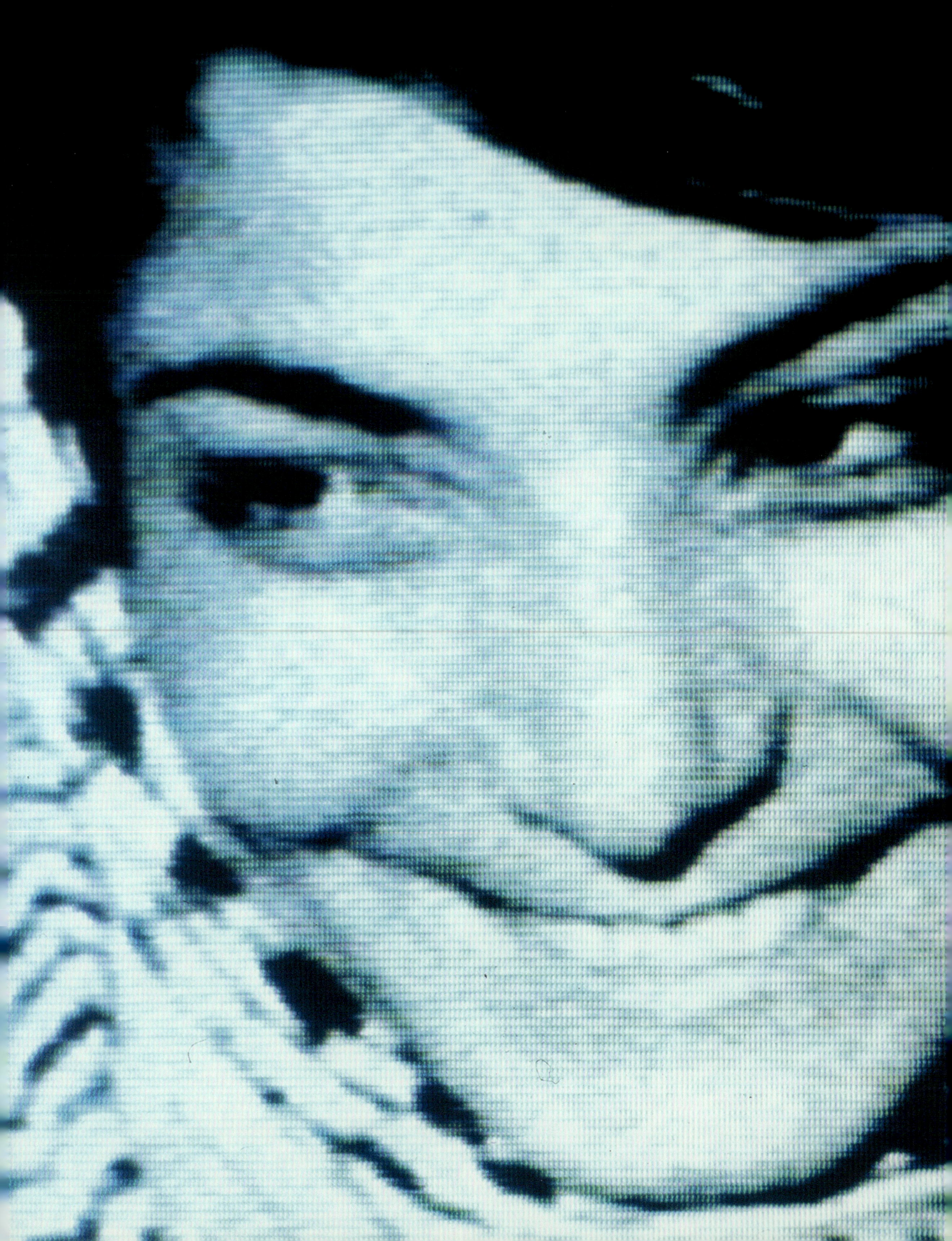

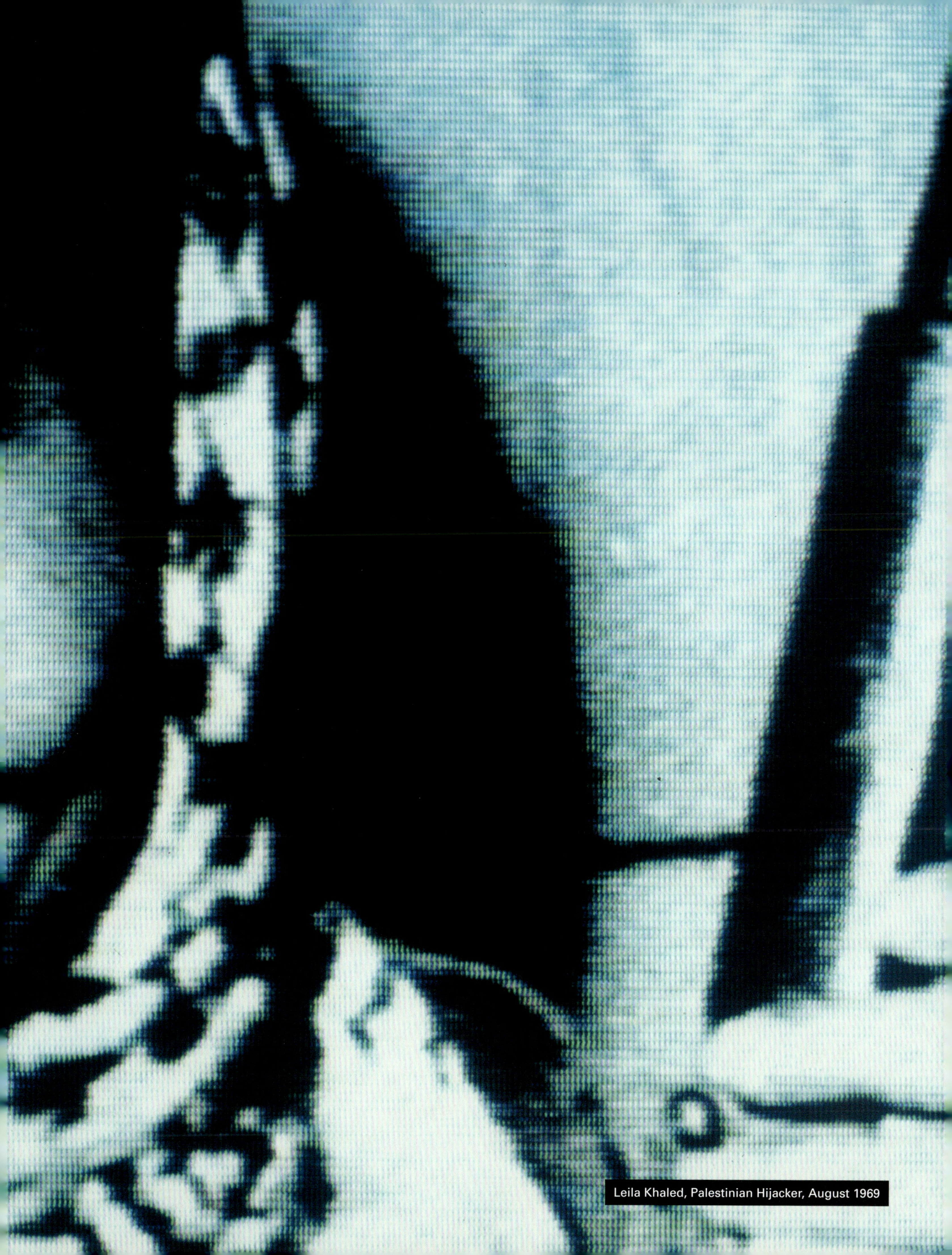

Leila Khaled, Palestinian Hijacker, August 1969

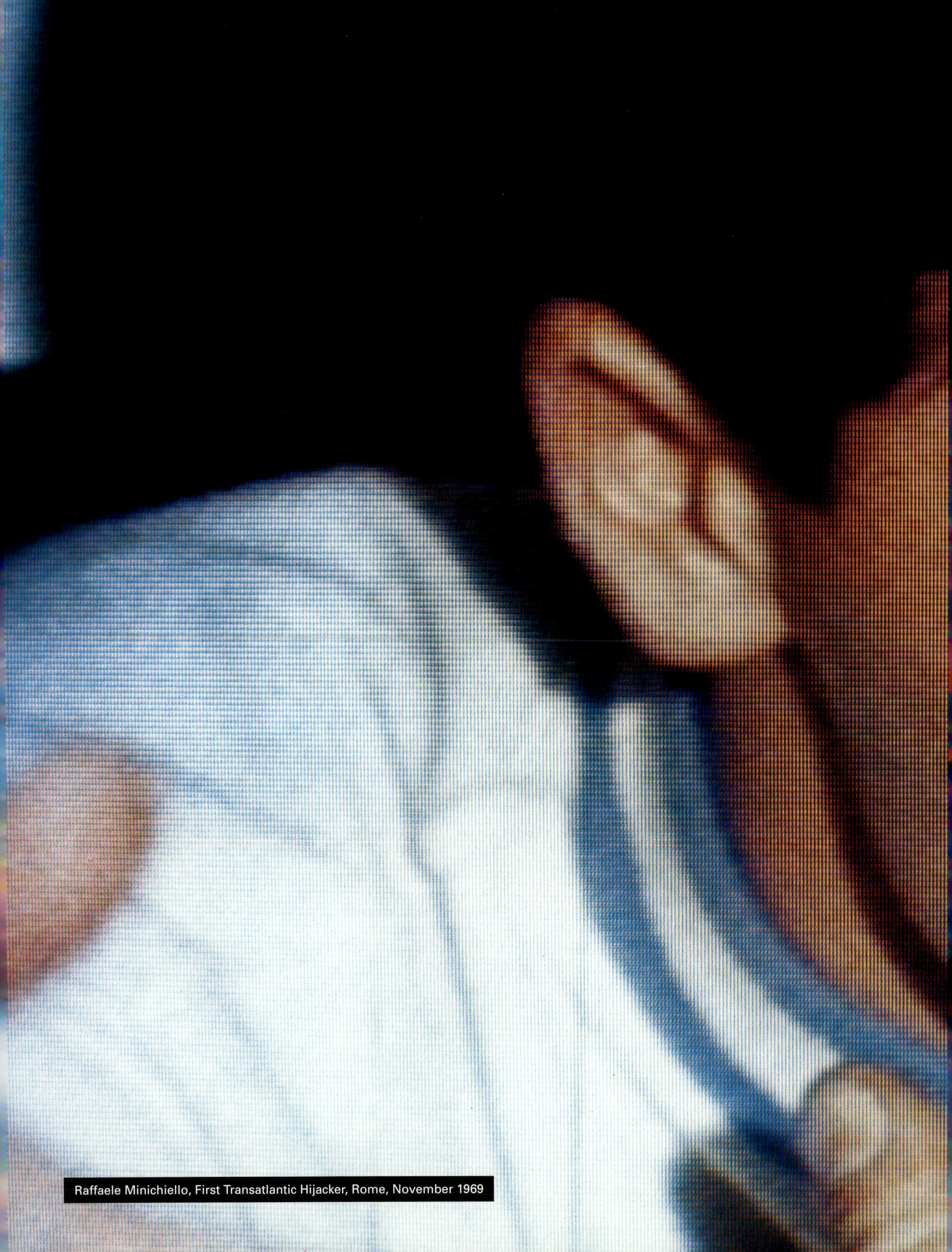

Raffaele Minichiello, First Transatlantic Hijacker, Rome, November 1969

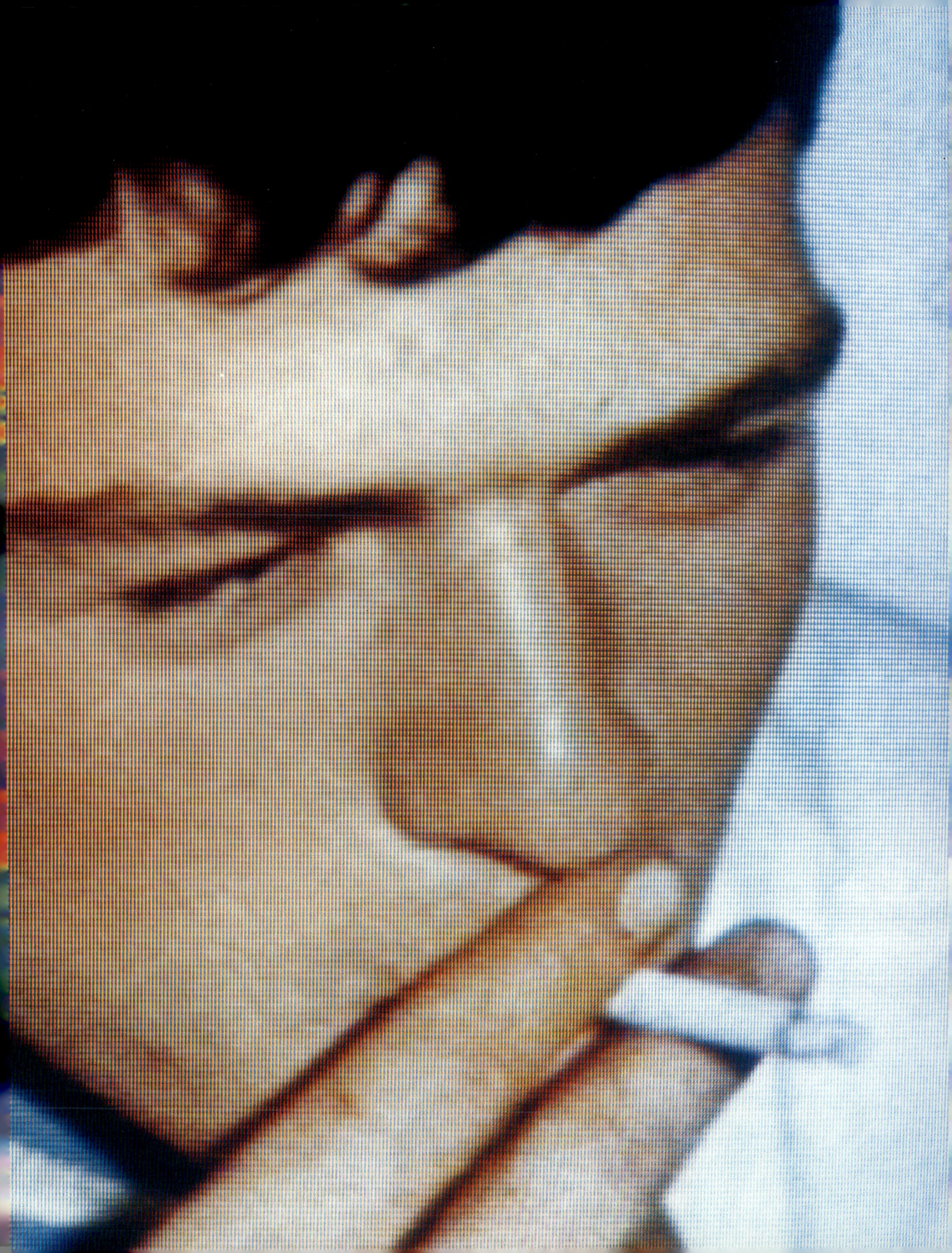

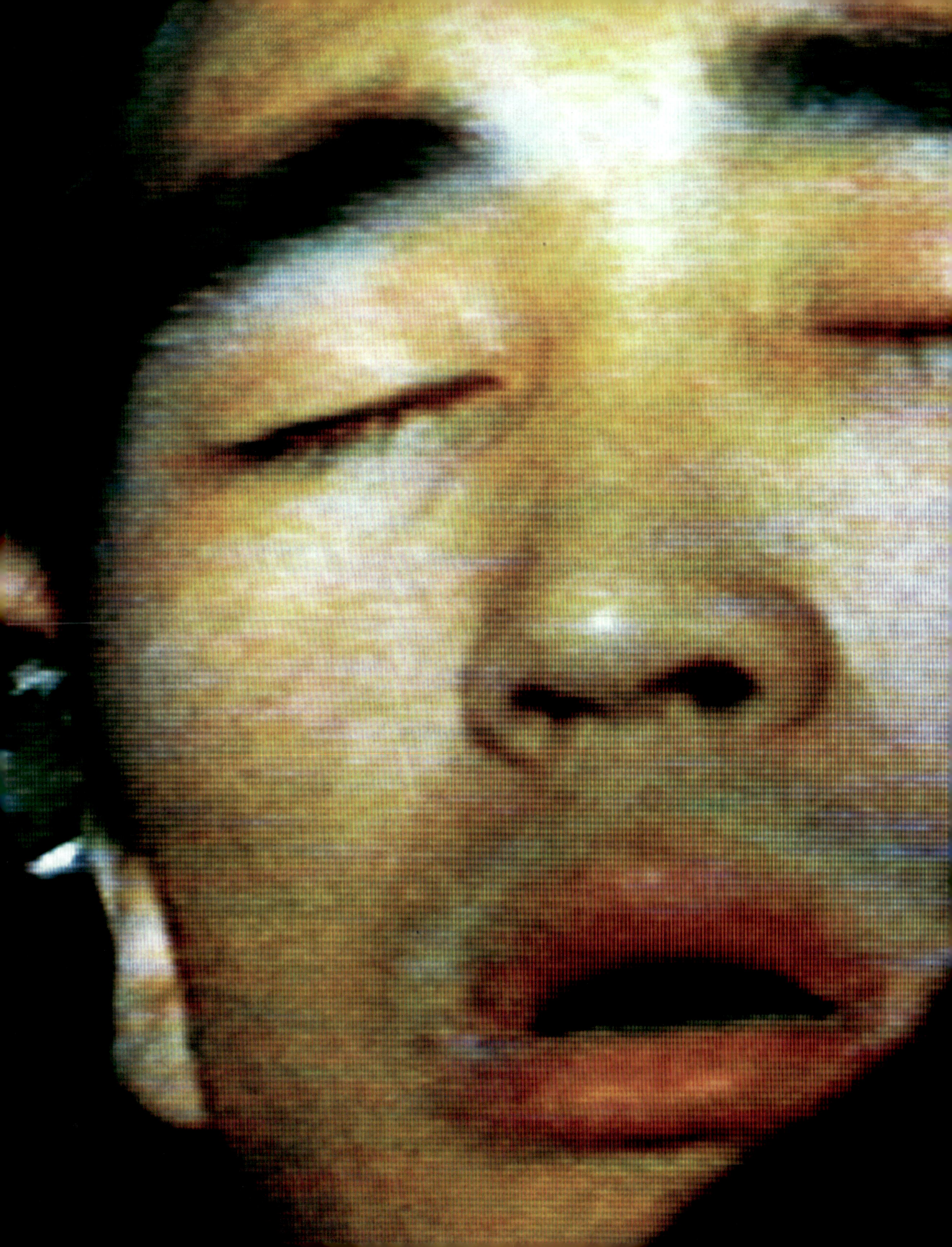

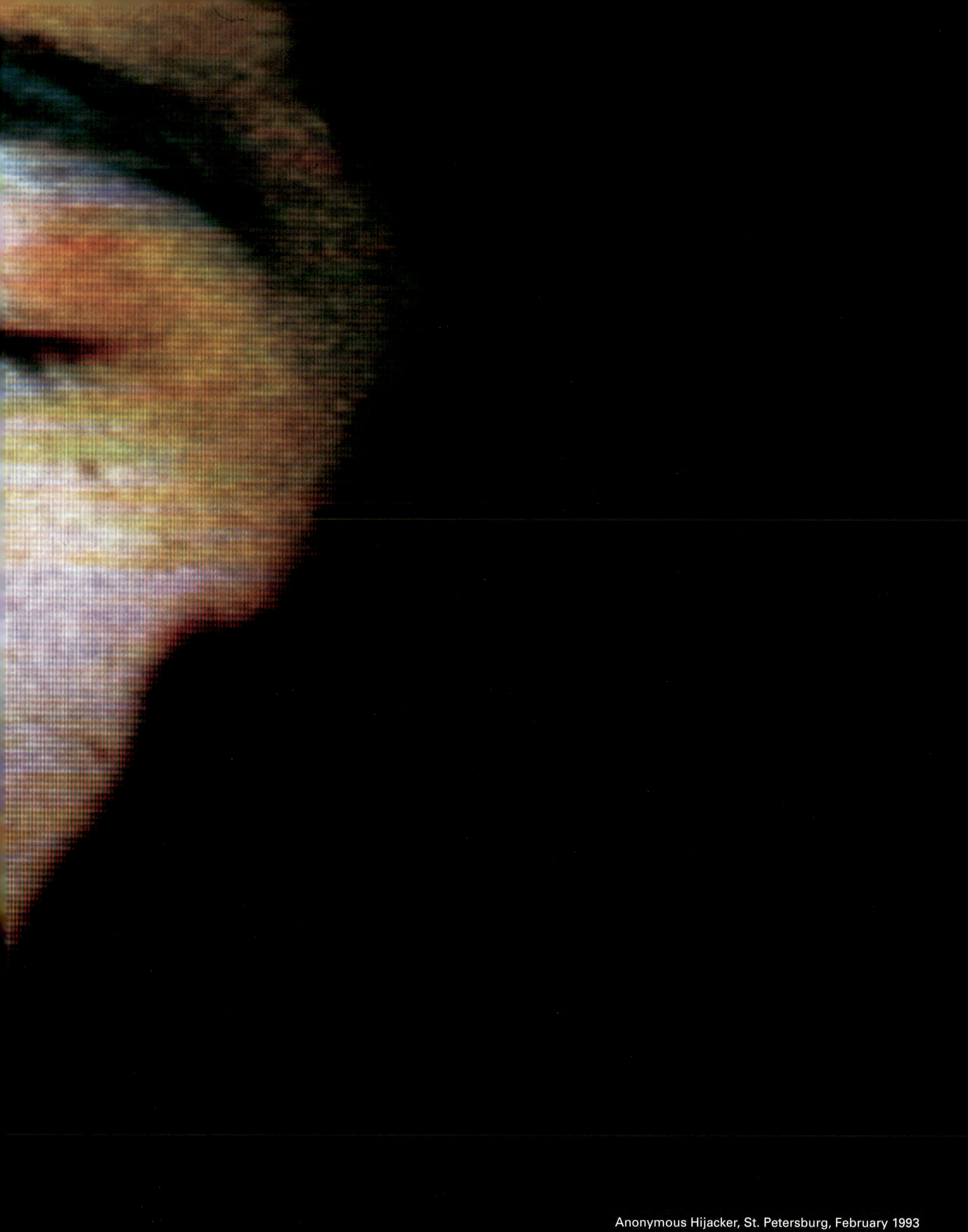

Anonymous Hijacker, St. Petersburg, February 1993

INS

COMM

HB

ERT
ERCIAL
RE

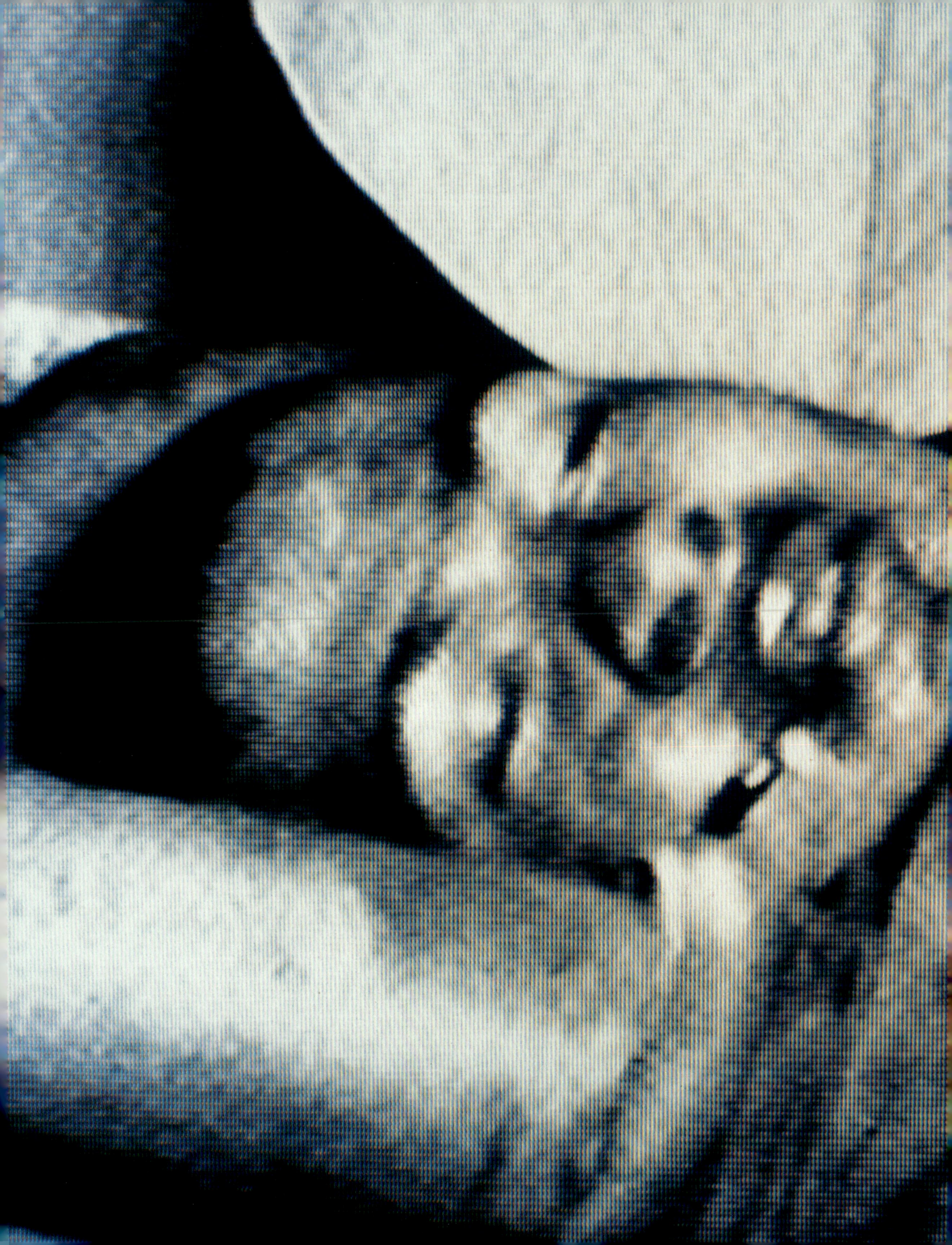

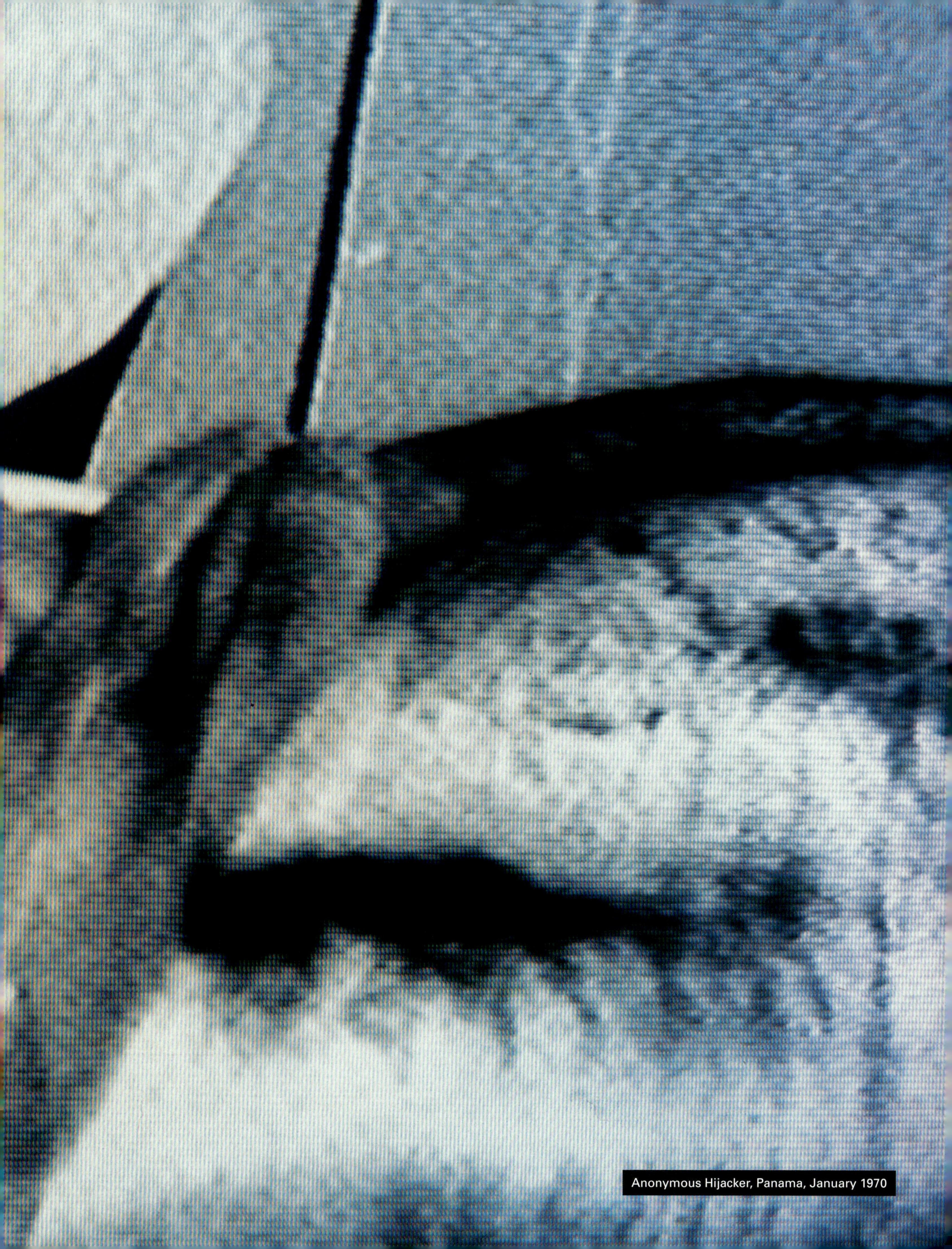

Anonymous Hijacker, Panama, January 1970

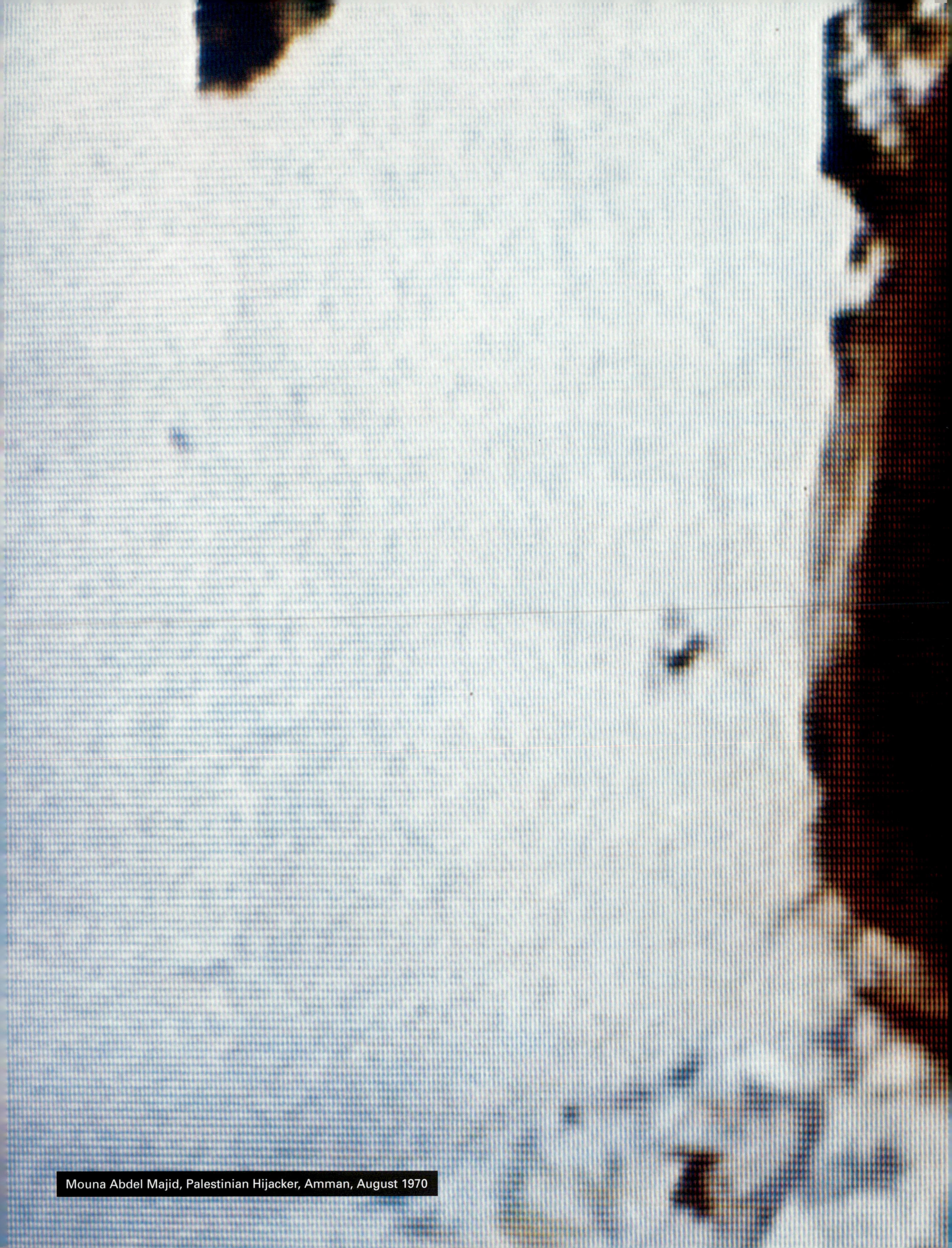

Mouna Abdel Majid, Palestinian Hijacker, Amman, August 1970

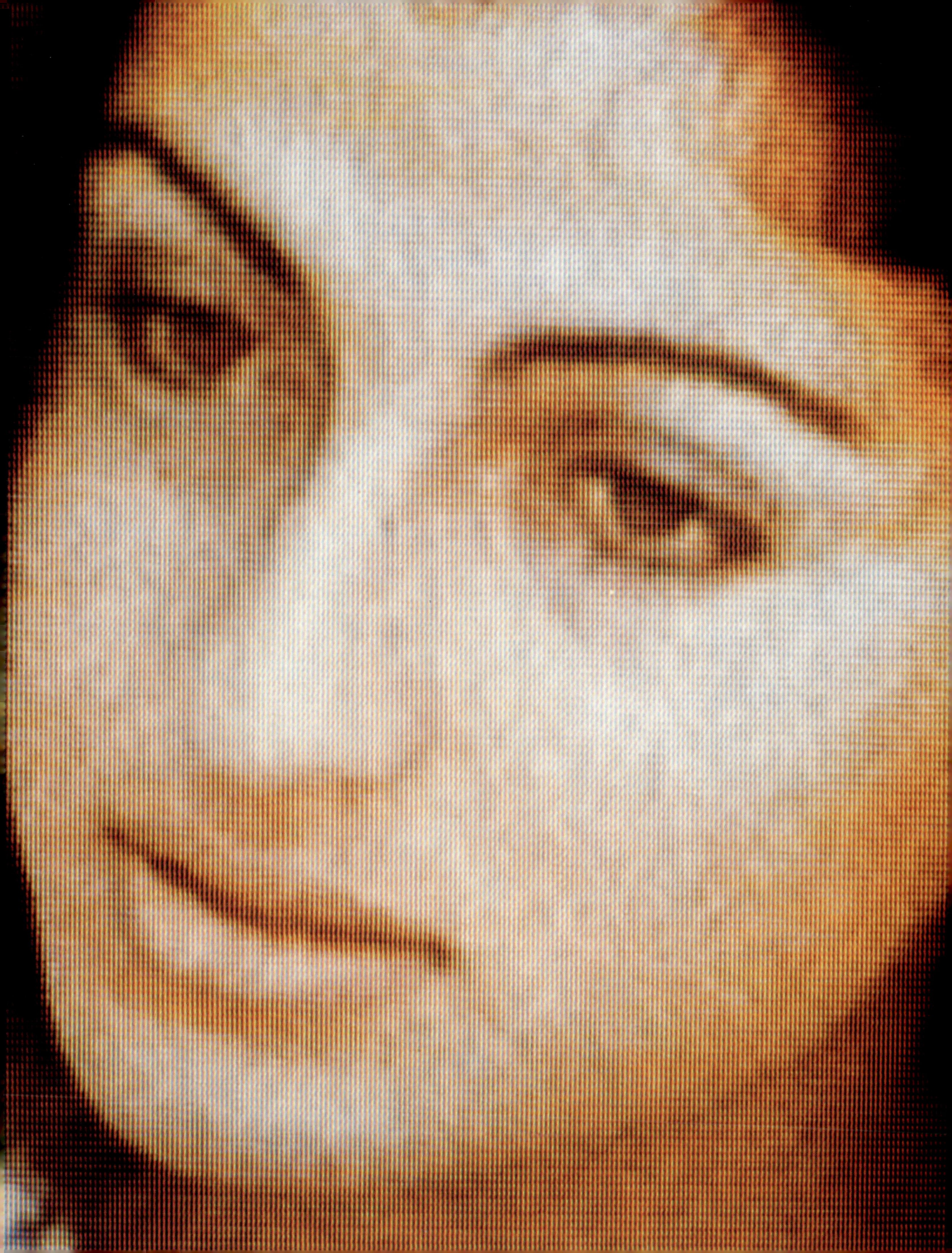

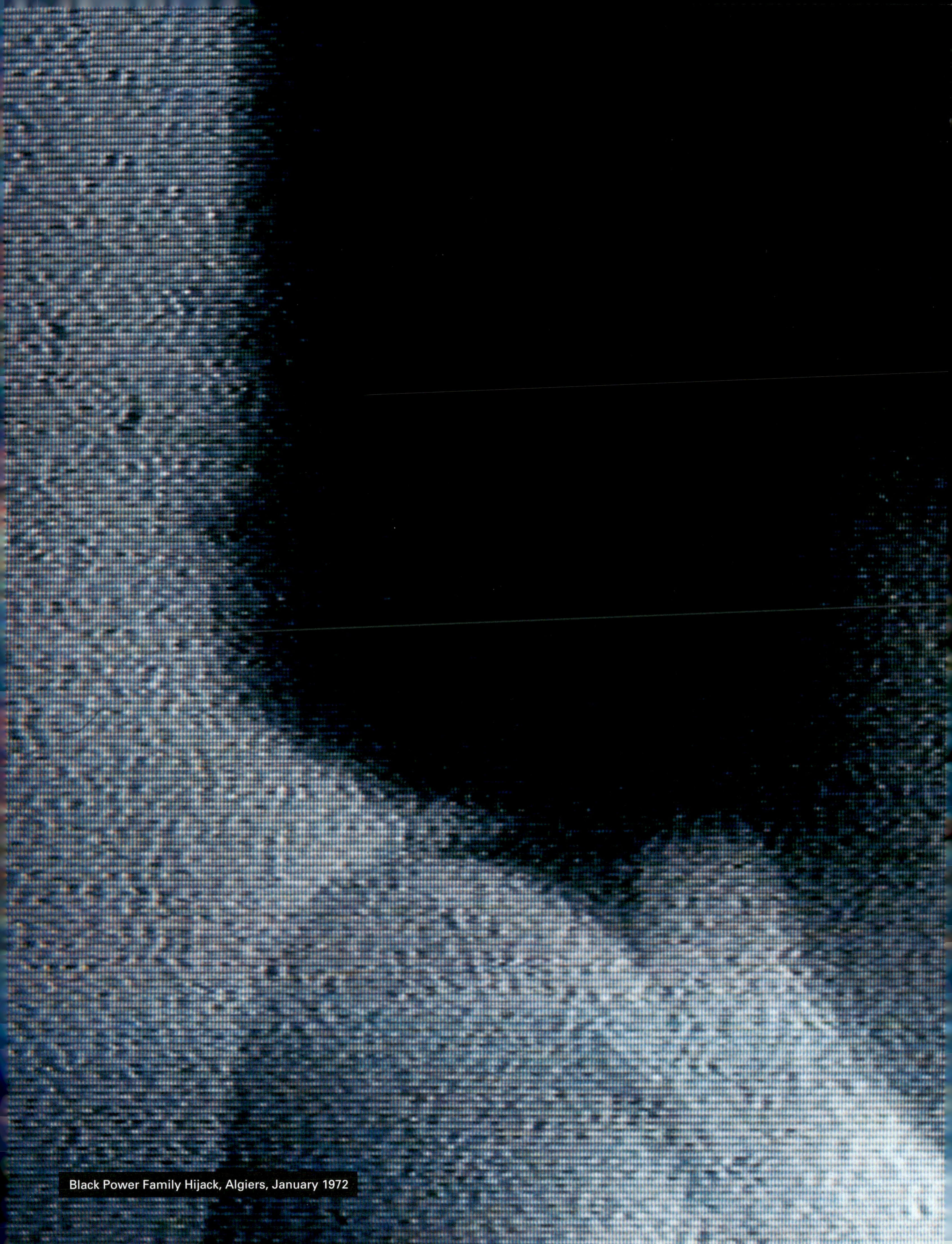

Black Power Family Hijack, Algiers, January 1972

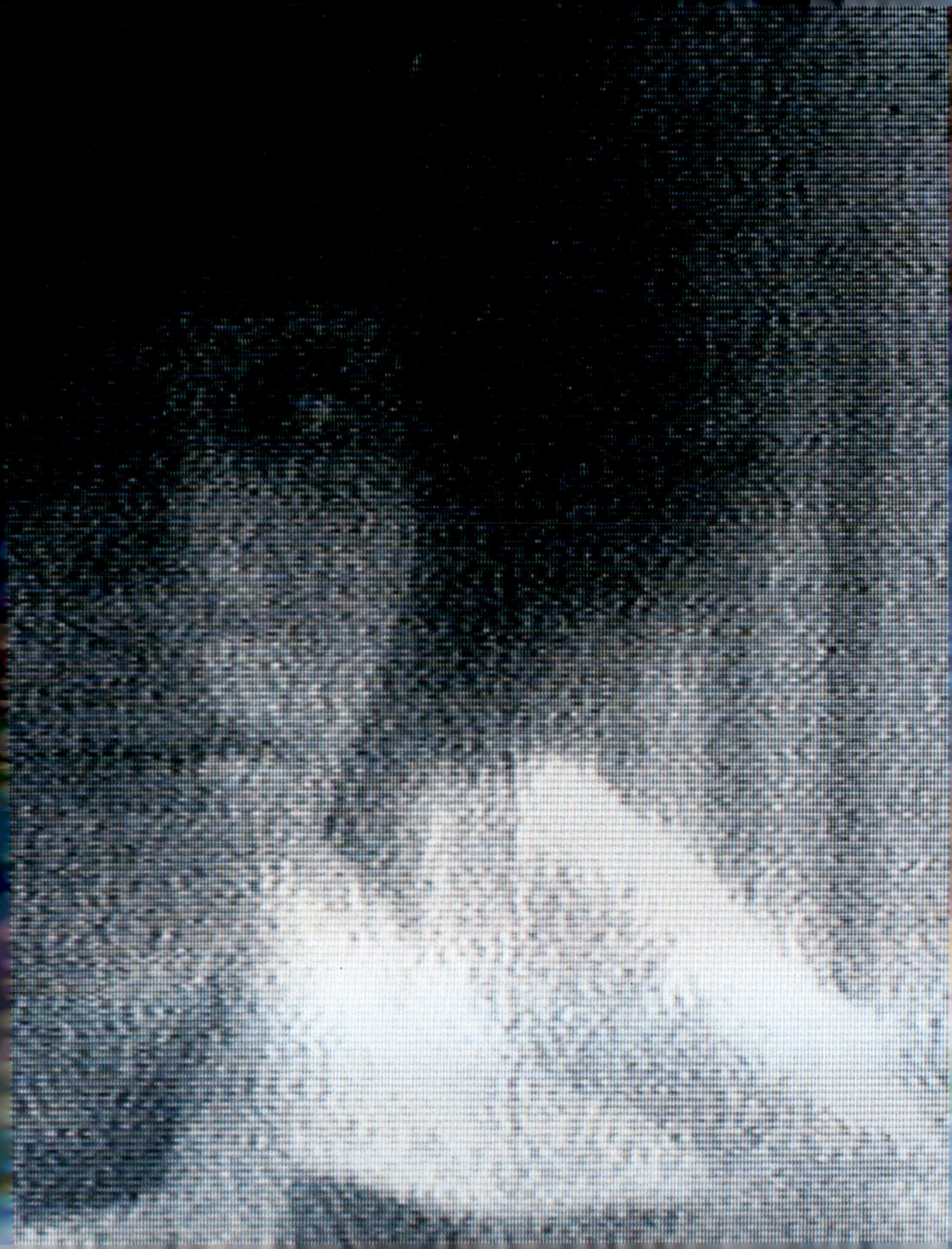

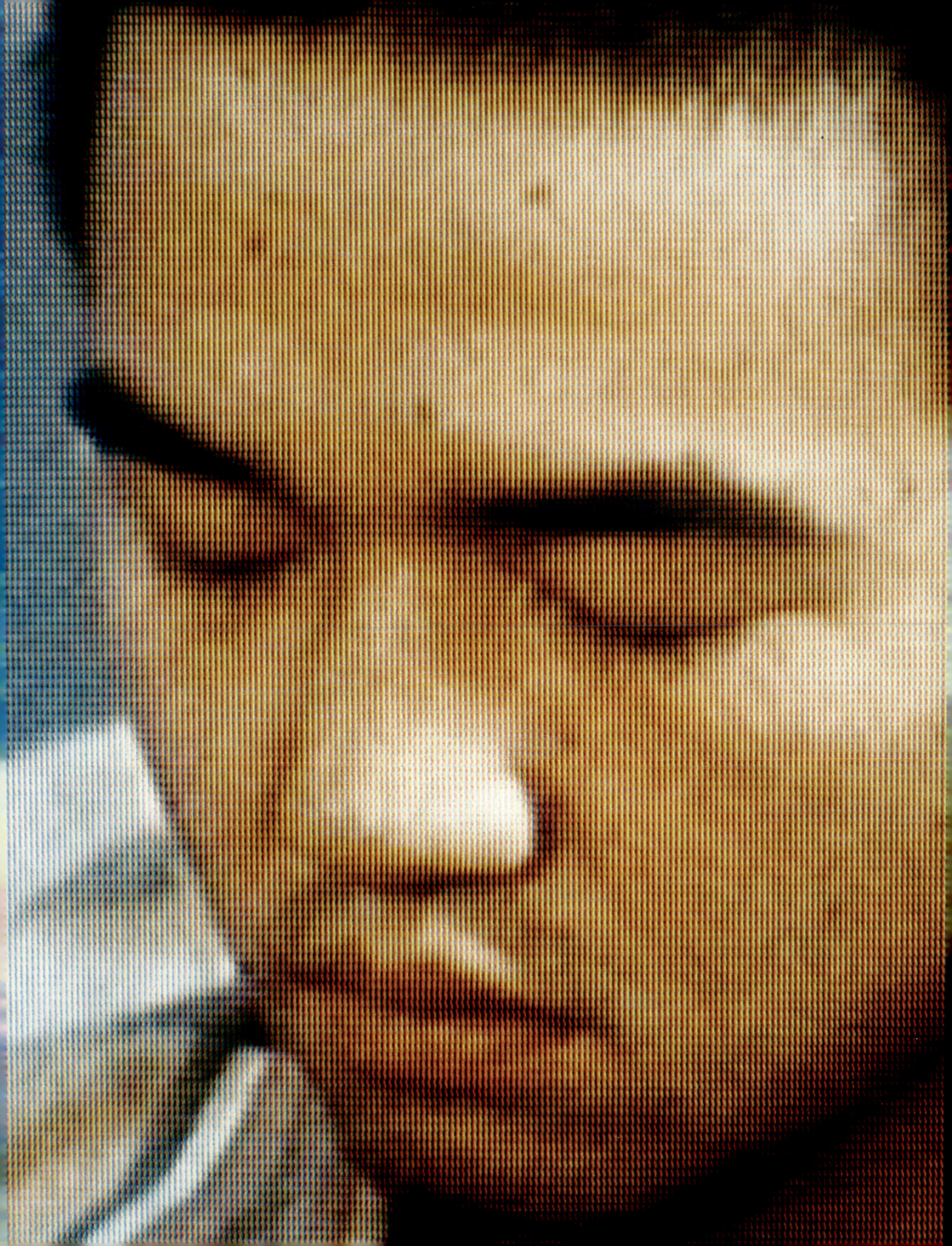

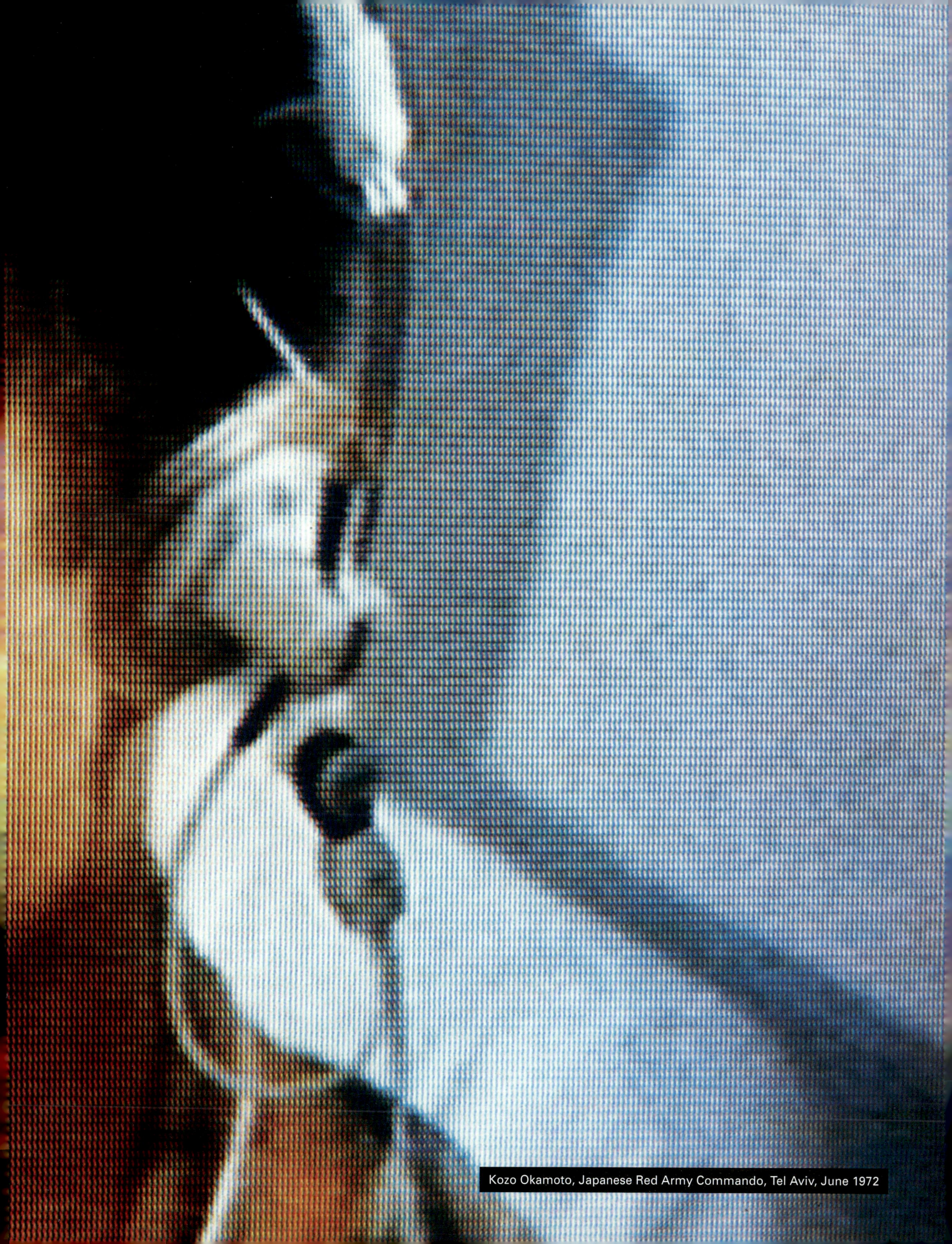

Kozo Okamoto, Japanese Red Army Commando, Tel Aviv, June 1972

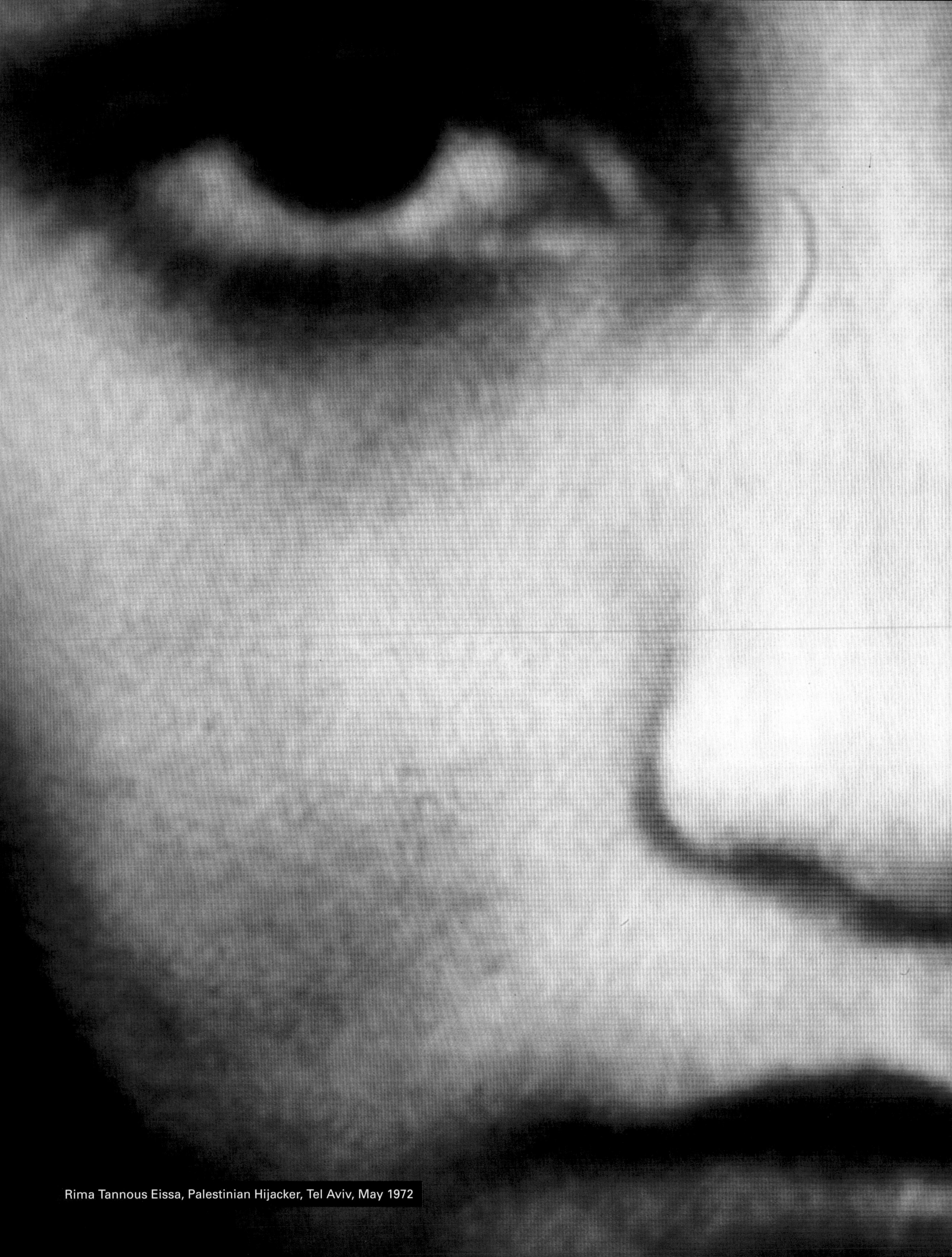

Rima Tannous Eissa, Palestinian Hijacker, Tel Aviv, May 1972

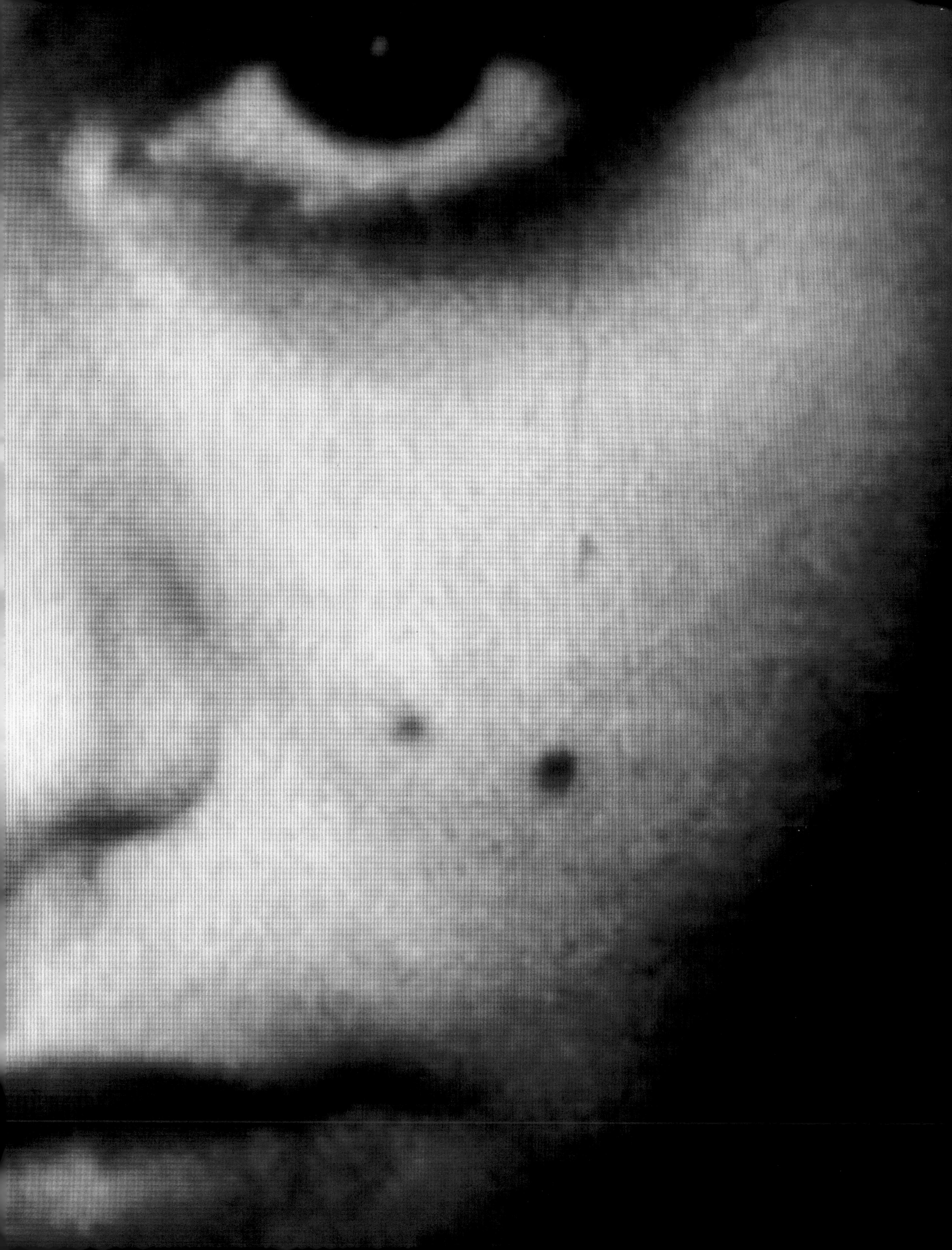

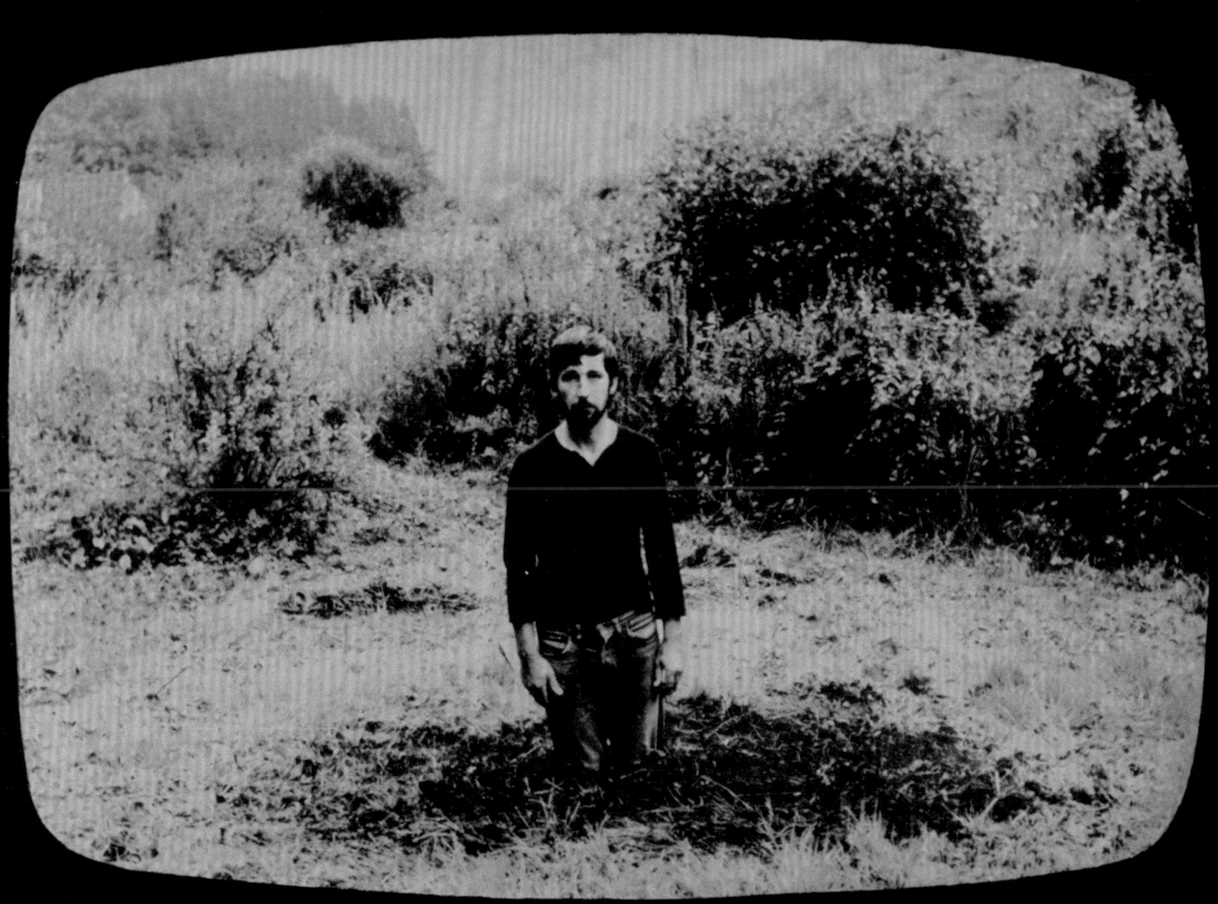

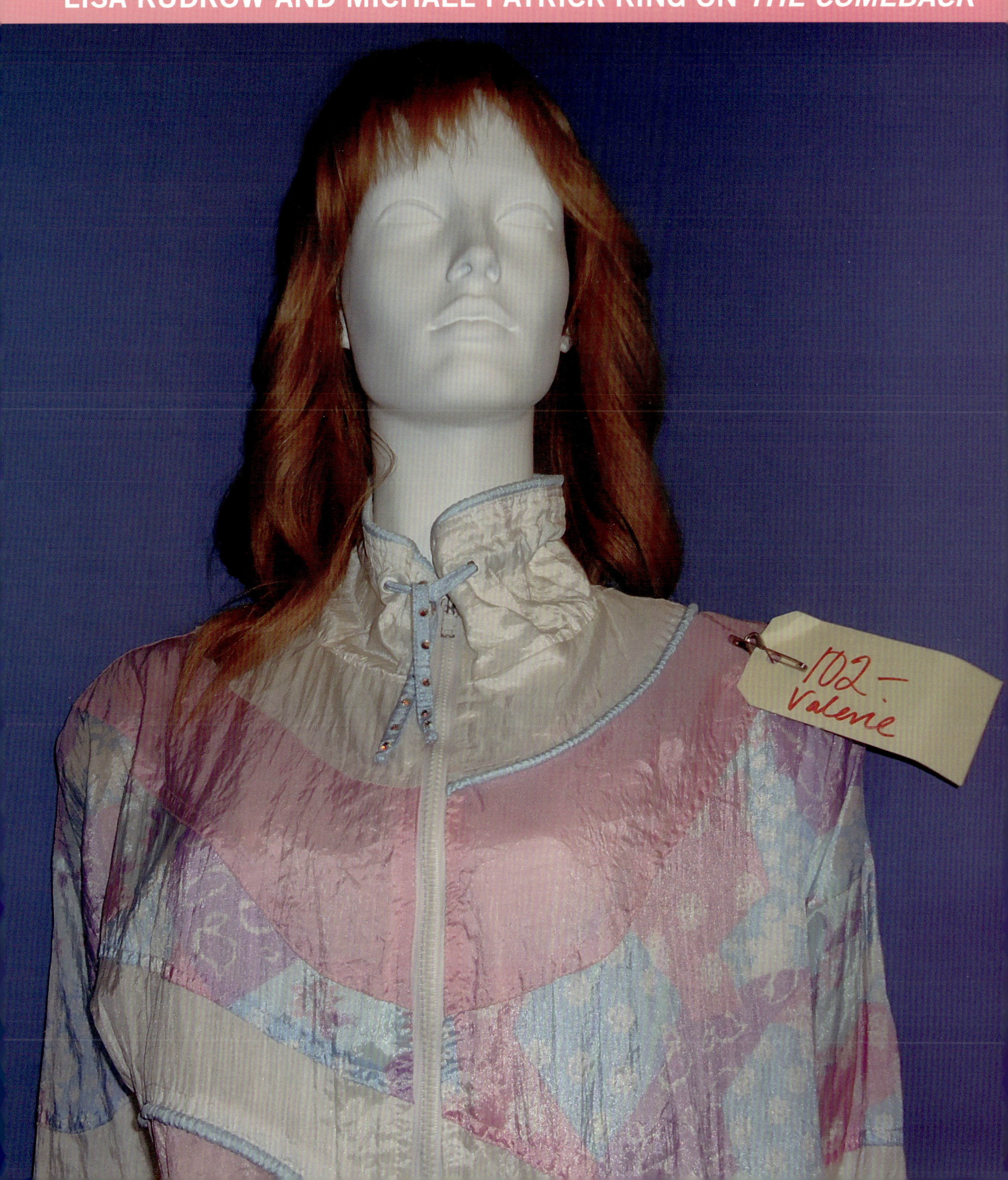
NOT IT ANYMORE
LISA KUDROW AND MICHAEL PATRICK KING ON *THE COMEBACK*
102 —
Valerie

Lisa Kudrow and Michael Patrick King have each left indelible marks on television: Kudrow for her winning portrayal of the character Phoebe on hit NBC sitcom *Friends* (1994–2004), and King as a writer, director, and eventual co-executive producer on the HBO series *Sex in the City* (1998–2004). But their most remarkable contribution to TV was something they conceived of and worked on together: the short-lived HBO series *The Comeback,* which ran for only 13 episodes in the summer of 2005. The show revolves around the unforgettable character of Valerie Cherish (played brilliantly by Kudrow), a faded sitcom actress so determined to regain her celebrity she agrees to be the subject of a reality show documenting her return to television (playing the thankless role of "Aunt Sassy" on a sitcom called *Room and Bored*). A penetrating and often brutal satire of reality TV, sitcoms, and show business in general, *The Comeback* received three Emmy nominations, including best actress for Kudrow and best director for King, despite being canceled after only one season. Kudrow and King were able to speak with *Esopus* this summer; a transcript of the interview, along with an assortment of artifacts from the show's conception and production, appear on the following pages.

Tod Lippy: Lisa, didn't the character of Valerie Cherish originate with a sketch you did when you were part of the Groundlings improvisational-comedy troupe in L.A.?

Lisa Kudrow: It was actually a character monologue: an actress on a talk show who was phony and self-serving. That was it.

Michael Patrick King: An unnamed Valerie...

LK: I called her "Your Favorite Actress on a Talk Show." She talked about how she hadn't worked in a while, and it was all just spin, spin, spin. It wasn't much appreciated there because my sensibility didn't always translate to a big sketch-comedy context. *[laughs]* But that character was really just like a grain of sand compared to what Valerie is in *The Comeback.* When you take an idea like that to Michael Patrick King, he whips it into this gorgeous character.

Let's talk about that process a bit. My understanding is you both knew each other before you worked together on this...

MPK: My friend John Stark was at the Groundlings, so I had seen Lisa do things there, and I was aware of her very unique energy. I once saw her do a sketch as Audrey Hepburn on a fishing show, which was not an accurate Audrey Hepburn, but that wasn't the point: It was the most absurdly brilliant idea. And of course I had a crush on Lisa because it's impossible not to. Later on, we were both working on the Culver lot—Lisa was on *Mad About You* and I was running my first show—a failed sitcom with Shelley Long that I had been brought in to fix, and as it turns out, you can't fix stuff sometimes—and Lisa and I would get together and complain about showbiz.

LK: I don't think I was complaining. I think I was thrilled at this point.

MPK: I'm not saying we were bitching—it was more funny. Like—"what's going to happen to me today?"

LK: Right. "What a brutal business this is." We had heard tell of it...

MPK: And then, years after that, we had the complete opposite of that relationship. We were in this weird grown-up show busi-

ness relationship at the Golden Globes at our separate tables every year.

LK: I would literally have to move out of the way so that all of the *Sex and the City* people could get up to receive the awards they beat *Friends* out for every year. *[laughs]*

MPK: It was this amazing and strange knew-each-other-in-different-time-periods thing. We had always had an emotional connection, and now we were playing these other parts. Then one day Lisa called me up and said, "Let's have lunch," and we went to the Beverly Hills Hotel.

LK: Actually, our agents called each other.

MPK: Oh, the agents called! That's right—we were both done with our respective shows, and they wanted to get the two of us together. And at lunch, Lisa said, "I have this idea..."

LK: No, the first thing was—

MPK: I don't remember.

LK: You don't remember! *[both laugh]* We sat down, and we looked at each other and said, "So, it's good to see you...." And Michael said, "I have to tell you, I really don't see myself doing a sitcom, and I don't really see you in this, like, shiny multi-camera thing." And I said, "No, I really don't have an interest in doing another show. The only thing I could ever see myself ever doing"—and then I started telling him this very vague, not-at-all-fleshed-out idea of an actress who is so desperate to be in the limelight that she agrees to be in a reality show called *The Comeback*. And we sat there for four hours.

MPK: Once we started talking, it literally just flew, didn't it?

LK: Oh my god, I think we pitched it two weeks later. It was ridiculously fast.

Who did you pitch it to?

MPK: Well, we knew it was going to HBO because that was where I had some heat and power, and everybody wanted Lisa at that time. I'm not kidding you—everybody wanted Lisa. The idea that she was returning to television a year after *Friends* was a big deal. So we pitched it to Carolyn Strauss at HBO. I think the thing that made her laugh the hardest—and I knew it would—was the idea that in the pilot, Mark, her husband, is noisily defecating during Valerie's personal video diary. *[both laugh]* In the meeting, Lisa actually did the video diary improv—it wasn't scripted yet—and I would make these farting noises, and Carolyn laughed. I'm telling you, from then on, we just railroaded it down their throats. [Read King and Kudrow's pitch notes on pp. 61–64.]

So you hadn't written a pilot script at this point?

MPK: No, we wanted the idea to be bought first. It was hard for HBO, quite frankly—all egos aside—to get it.

LK: No, they didn't get it. I think they actually said it out loud at one point: "You know what, we don't fully get it, but go ahead."

MPK: It was hard for them not to say yes to us, because we were bound and determined.

LK: And you were Michael Patrick King.

MPK: Well, I had come off of a hit, and Lisa had come off a hit, so it was hard for them to say no. And Carolyn has a great sense

     RIGHT: First page of the shooting script for episode one

of humor, so she understood the dark stuff. But I don't think they understood the whole concept.

LK: It's very hard to describe.

MPK: And then when we wrote the pilot, we had a blast.

Can you talk about your writing process a bit?

MPK: Lisa is a brilliant, brilliant writer. Brilliant and also ruthless. She's not at all indulgent. As we were writing the pilot, she would be cutting things as they were coming out of her mouth: "No, we don't need that." It's this fantastic stuff, and I'm typing it, and before she even finished the sentence, she'd say, "No, it's too long, we don't need that either." We always knew the Valerie stuff was going to be funny, but then we came up with the idea of the sitcom, *Room and Bored,* that Valerie gets the "Aunt Sassy" part on, and things really took off.

The crucial thing Lisa contributed to the pilot—in addition to everything else—is something I would never have come up with on my own. It's a small but significant idea: the water leak in the house that Valerie ignores after being warned about it by her housekeeper. Lisa kept saying from that scientist part of her brain, "There's a leak in the wall that she's ignoring because of her career." What was so smart about it was that it was the beginning of the germ of the idea that if you pay too much at-tention to show business, your personal life will collapse out from under you. You will literally gut your home. It's very subtle, and it's only there on a kind of subliminal writing level. But the thought that Lisa, underneath it all, put into the series was that this choice would destroy Valerie's house. And she's more than happy to have her home destroyed, because she cares more about her career.

LK: Right, so even when the wall in her house is in shambles, the thing that breaks her heart is the fact that her pictures from showbiz have been damaged.

MPK: The things she cherishes the most. That reminds me of that whole other idea we had there—Mark gets one little spot on the wall for his Rotary Club plaque. *[both laugh]* So anyway, yes, we wrote the pilot together, and when it was finished, we were very happy with it. It's unlike any other pilot you've ever seen because it's just Valerie talking to the camera for the whole first section. And I remember that people couldn't figure out if it was funny.

LK: Right.

MPK: And then when Lisa read it at the table, everybody laughed.

LK: That was during the auditions for the other actors. That

```
INT. VALERIE'S HOME/ KITCHEN- DAY

An upscale kitchen in a Beverly Hills home.  CLOSE ON:
Valerie Cherish (39) pretty with red hair.  She is looking
directly into the camera, smiling.

                    VALERIE
          So, this is my comeback.
               (beat)
          Let me try that again.
               (beat)
          This is my come-- See, the camera's
          going in and out -- Is that --?

The camera ZOOMS in close on her face; way too close.  We see
tiny age lines around her sparkling green eyes, the CAMERA
zooms back out.  JANE (30) the reality show producer speaks
from off-camera.

                    JANE (O.C.)
          It's always going to be moving.
          Just keep going.


                    VALERIE
          Yes, I know that -- I just didn't
          know if I should wait for it to
          settle.
               (beat; nothing)
          Okay, so this will be moving --
          that's right -- because this one...

She points to a tiny camera hanging on the ceiling.

                    VALERIE (cont'd)
          ... Is stationary.
```

was the first time anyone at HBO had heard it. And they were pretty happy.

MPK: Up until then, there was this vague concern: "Is it going to be funny?" And that's because it's not written "jokey." It's all character stuff, like all of the weird Valerie pauses and stuttering. When we were actually shooting the series and Lisa was on a break, we'd ask her to come into the writing room—she was there a lot, considering the fact that she basically never left the camera—and it was my job to type in every vocal tic and grammatical mistake while Lisa went on a run, speaking as Valerie. I would make sure it came out exactly as Lisa said it, down to the stuttering and the dashes. I was like a Nazi in there—

It sounds almost like you were taking dictation.

MPK: We actually looked into getting a court stenographer, because I wanted the dialogue exactly as it was pouring out of Lisa. It was too expensive, though. And then, part of Lisa's brilliance as an actor was that she was able to commit it to memory—almost like Morse code. She would use all of these mannerisms as anchors, and they would get her right back into character. As an actress, she paid very close attention to the writing.

LK: Most of the time. *[laughs]*

This series aims its satirical sights at two television genres: One, of course, is the sitcom, which we'll talk about more in a moment. The other is reality TV. I remember reading somewhere that you had gotten hold of some bootleg tapes of raw footage from one of the reality shows, and that these ended up being your "way in" to the unusual format of the series.

MPK: That's right, and we had even hired a couple of writers who had worked on reality shows as well. Those tapes gave us access to the boringness of unedited reality-show footage, and we fell in love with the idea that the actual story was in the stuff that Valerie thought would be cut from the final series because of that boringness. What interested us, a lot, was this kind of Stockholm syndrome situation with Valerie and Jane, the producer of the reality show. We knew that Lisa was going to be on camera, and we wanted to find ways to show the cracks in her performance versus the real thoughts she was having while being constantly filmed. We came up with the idea of "leaking" people from the outside—Jane, the cameramen, the sound guy—into the frame. This was important, because we didn't just want to do a parody of a reality show; we wanted to put in the foreground the behind-the-scenes manipulation and the cruelty. Once we realized we could use this unedited-footage approach, it just became really interesting to us, because then you can see everybody that is in the show. But it was that boringness—the endless hours of unmanipulated footage—that we thought would be interesting to show. That's why we decided to start each episode with the color bars.

It essentially allows the viewer to become an editor, which turns the experience of watching these episodes into a very suspense-filled exercise. You're constantly thinking, "Are they going to use that line they just tricked her into saying in the final show?

Are they going to squeeze in that humiliating fall she just took?" **It makes you kind of squeamish as a viewer, but it also allows you to take a more active role, at least conceptually.**

MPK: Right. The macro thought for us was that this footage maybe represented the very first assembly of a junior editor that would then be given to the other editors. Even the way it starts, with that annoying, alienating color-bar sound. I have to say, we really knew what we were doing in terms of what we wanted people to feel.

It presents enormous challenges as far as narrative exposition is concerned, though, right? Valerie is virtually never off-camera.

MPK: It was very tricky. I don't think there's ever been a show on television where another character doesn't say at some point, "Boy, *she's* in a bad mood today..." There was never a moment of exposition behind the scenes, because Valerie was hyperaware of everything, and she never left the camera. So as a writing team, we had to figure out how to have everything happen in front of the camera, with her always somewhere in the frame. It was a big puzzle, and it cost us a lot of figuring-out time.

LK: That's why it was so important for Michael to direct the pilot and the second episode. And he would have done more if there were time, but he had to do everything else.

MPK: When you're running a show you usually get to do the first two, because at that point the scripts are caught up. And then if you're lucky, you get to do one in the middle—I did the red-carpet episode—and then the final one. But the idea was that she was always the center, and then the camera will swing too far in one direction or the other and you catch the writers, for instance, glaring at her. Jimmy Burrows, the TV director, who plays himself in several episodes, said to me, "You running six cameras at once, I don't know what the hell you're doing." We had a lot of cameras going, to get the sitcom, the backstage, the handheld. It was a really interesting puzzle.

Did you create storyboards?

MPK: Ever since doing *Sex and the City,* which was a very expensive film show, I have always done storyboards. But then when we worked with great guest directors, like Greg Mottola and Michael Lehmann, there was never a storyboard approval. They had to be creative and figure out their own way to do it within this very specific landscape that we had already set up. It had to be about the stories happening behind her, behind her, behind her. Like an Escher print, almost. The unraveling behind her that she can't see. But you see it. You almost see the fuse being lit over her head.

One of the most amazing moments along those lines is in the second-to-last episode, when Jane offers to speak with the writers about giving Valerie more lines in order to promote the about-to-premiere reality show. In the foreground, Valerie sits with her hairdresser, Mickey, while we can just barely make out Jane and the two writers, Paulie G. and Tom, out of focus

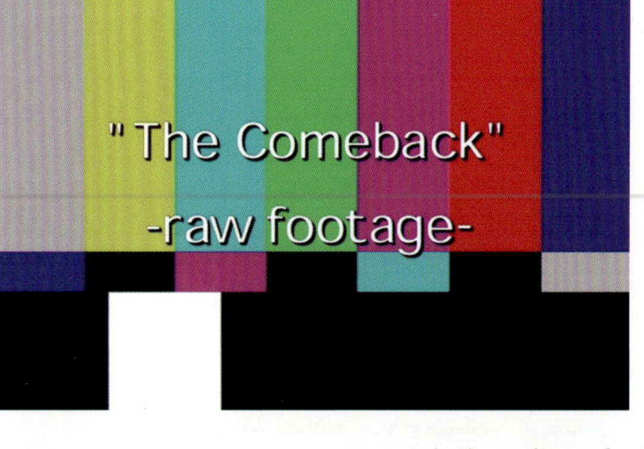

 ABOVE: Opener for every episode of *The Comeback* (All images ©Home Box Office Inc.)

in the background. While Jane and the writers are engaged in this intense shouting match, Valerie is extolling the virtues of Mickey's heirloom tomatoes. It's so layered, because we—and, of course, Valerie and Mickey—are hearing what's going on, but Valerie is desperately trying to distract us, and herself, from what is being said. It's an important moment, because it manages to pack so much information—about character and story—into the frame.

MPK: You know, it's so great to hear you say it's important, because we thought it was hilarious. It was so alive. We were giggling all the time and laughing. You know what I mean? Even though the gravitas was there, we thought it was really funny. At the start, people said it was too harsh, and I said to Lisa at one point, "This is a documentary. Everything I'm writing, I know for a fact is true, true, true."

Michael, you worked as a writer on _Murphy Brown, Cybill,_ and a number of other shows, and Lisa, obviously you had your many years on _Friends_ and on other sitcoms before that. How did you conceive of _Room and Bored,_ the sitcom in the series? And how did you come up with the scene from _I'm It!,_ Valerie's sitcom from the late 1980s/early 1990s featured in episode four?

MPK: I didn't direct episode four, but I did direct the _I'm It!_ section—I was like, "No, I'm in there. I know this world." I love that _I'm It!_ scene with her, when they're doing that crass Tracy/Hepburn–esque thing and she closes the guy's tie in the file drawer. "Oh, come _here,_ you!" How many times have you seen that on TV? That crazy, multi-camera coverage when she goes to the door, and the camera goes with her, and then that fake, awful pathos moment when they finally kiss.

And what I love about it is Valerie watching it. This was her peak. She's actually convinced herself that that was a Sam and Diane moment. And she looks over at Mickey, and he gives her that beaming look. That's the dream—that's what sitcoms are. Her hair, the suit, the fake office set, the sight gags—

LK: It seems like at a certain point in television history, that's all you needed: people who looked a certain way and were able to memorize lines.

And a pumped-up studio audience.

MPK: Yeah. And I have to tell you this, having been in many development meetings with actresses that I wound up not working with who thought they were going to be sitcom stars. There is one thing that every actress always says: "I'm really good with physical comedy."

That's a line given to Valerie in the show.

MPK: That's the line used by every actress who is insecure about an innate comic rhythm. You would never hear Lisa say that—in fact, you'd hear Lisa say the opposite.

LK: "I want stunt pay." _[laughs]_

MPK: But they all say that. So for us to put that _I'm It!_ shtick

with the computer keyboard and the tie getting caught in the file drawer—it was important, because that's what paraded around in television as comedy for a while.

LK: Also, women couldn't be flawed in the way that men are, because it was seen as insulting. You were putting them down. They always had to be—

MPK: Cute but flummoxed.

LK: Right. It wasn't sexist; it was overcompensating for sexism. But that essentially meant that the female characters in these shows couldn't even be interesting.

MPK: So, yeah, we decided to include that scene from _I'm It!_ to show her heyday, and also as an excuse for her to trap Gigi, the new writer, in her dressing room for a writers' meeting. "I'm going to get this girl on my side."

LK: Right, I need someone in that room writing for me.

MPK: "Aunt Sassy's bitch," in the other writers' words.

Speaking of Aunt Sassy, can you talk about coming up with _Room and Bored?_ It's so perfectly rendered—and perfectly awful—that it feels like something you might catch on the WB.

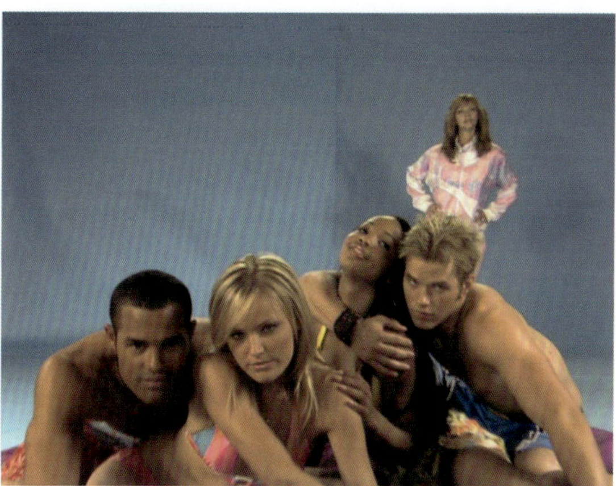

MPK: Or the CW, or maybe even Fox at one point. What we took from all of those kinds of shows was the colors of the set, the design, the surfboards on the wall. I mean, come on! _[both laugh]_ And I think there's a little bit of the _Friends_ set in there—that brightly colored stuff. We decided to set the sitcom in California and put in the fake ocean backdrop. Most important, of course, was the sex. Because that's what replaced that corporate vibe in sitcoms from the 1980s and early 1990s, like what you see in the _I'm It!_ scene we wrote. Now it's all about partial nudity, the audience oohing and aahing when they kiss—shit like that. We worked hard on the dialogue and setups for _Room and Bored,_ to the point where "I don't need to _see_ that!"—Valerie's signature line—

The "clam," as you referred to it in one interview...

MPK and LK: The clam!

LK: That's what Michael kept saying: "We've got to have that clam." And I didn't know what he was talking about.

MPK: I'm going to brag now. "Clam" is a term Peter Tolan and I came up with when we were working on _Murphy Brown._ [Show creator] Diane English asked us to read a bunch of spec scripts, and I said to Peter, "Have you noticed that every script has a line like, 'I came back from lunch and got sick—I must have had bad clams.'" And he said, "Yeah, there must be a lot of bad clams out there." So we decided that any recurring joke that can be found in pop culture's lint drawer is a clam. The current clam, by the way, is "Wait for it...!" Anyway, the original clam we had in there for Aunt Sassy after she opens the door and finds the two kids making out was, "Why don't you two get a room?" And then Lisa and I thought we could do better than that: "We have to come up with our own clam, something that sounds like a sitcom line." And we came up with "I don't need to *see* that!"

LK: "Note to self—"

MPK: Right. "Note to self: I don't need to *see* that!" Right. "Note to self" was the clam.

LK: It was a clam and a hook. *[laughs]*

MPK: With an extender! But yeah, we both know that whole sitcom world really well. And then we had such fun casting it. And we had rehearsals with the kids where we wrote entire scenes that never aired so that they had a better sense of what they were doing.

LK: I want to say one thing, though, because I would hate to have any confusion about what we did on *The Comeback* and my feelings about *Friends*. None of this was informed by *Friends*—that was a really great experience, and [show creators] Marta Kauffman and David Crane were always generous and collaborative with the actors. I'm not sure what happened in the writers' room. I think we all know that there was some tension, and that maybe they felt a little differently about the actors. I knew that stuff existed, and always felt like, on other shows especially, there is this tension between the actors and the writers. The actors are getting all the attention and accolades, and the writers are just told, "Stay in your room and write this stuff for me. And by the way, where is it? Why isn't it ready?" I think writers get a little, well, sad about that.

MPK: Having not been around *Friends,* and having no awareness at all of what that writing room was like, my experience has been very different. I have been in a couple of writing rooms—not *Murphy Brown*'s, by the way, because that was like the Harvard of sitcoms. But before and after that, I'd been involved with shows where—I'm just going to go on the record here—the writers hated the actresses. They just hated them. There was something about an actress of a certain age—at least in the rooms I was in—that bugged people.

These were just male writers, or female writers also?

MPK: Well, there's a fine line. The writers that I thought were most lethal were guys. And then it would get down to a more specific complaint, like "She can't do my jokes." This often happened at sitcoms where somebody wound up in charge who wasn't, for some reason, a comedy person. "The joke was good." "No, she couldn't do it." It was a constant war. This led to one of my favorite scenes in *The Comeback*, the cookie "rape" scene, where Valerie stops by the writers' room late at night with cookies, and they're making brutal fun of her. In my writing rooms, I've never allowed that to happen. It's just not good. I believe you have to be in love with the people you're writing for.

LK: It's worth mentioning that it always gets more tense when the show's not a big hit. *Sex and the City* was at the top, and *Friends* was at the top, so everyone was pretty happy. But when all of these egos—and it's not like writers don't have them too—

start getting a little nervous and threatened and scared, I think there's no more dangerous an animal than a writer. *[laughs]*

MPK: And then there is the split between the two types of writers, which is embodied in *The Comeback*: Tom, who is the sycophant who will literally bend over backward because he has a house in Toluca Lake and a wife and kids and wants a career, and Paulie G., who's probably truly gifted but is stuck in a cul-de-sac, tied to his writing partner, and ultimately, to Valerie Cherish.

LK: It's a case of the artist being paired with "Get along to go along."

MPK: And I actually understand all of those people. I understand Paulie, I understand Tom and I understand Valerie. It was an interesting kind of lethal combination—a death pact.

LK: Also, it's worth mentioning that the writers who worked on *The Comeback* had experiences in many other writers' rooms, and none of this seemed foreign to them. In fact, it made all the sense in the world to them.

Valerie Cherish has got to be one of the most memorable—and complex—characters ever to appear on television. She has

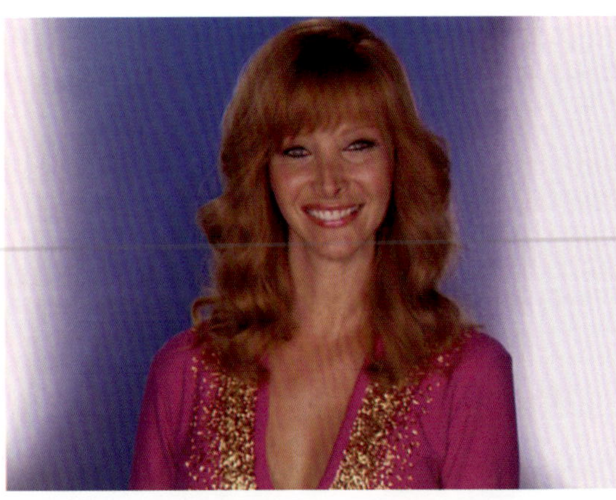

a funny line early on in the series when she chastises Chris, one of the younger actors on *Room and Bored*, for "playing to the camera," but the irony is that Valerie is always playing to the camera and is always desperate to come off well, even if it means throwing someone else under the bus in the process. I'm reminded particularly of the scene in the Palm Springs episode when she is recognized by the gay couple on the street who are huge fans of hers. When Jane presents them with release forms to sign, the younger guy declines nervously because he isn't out to his family, but Valerie is so desperate to have a scene with adoring fans in the show that she convinces him to sign it anyway—in the guise, of course, of encouraging him to be true to himself.

MPK: But also in that Palm Springs episode is the only moment when she chooses Mark over showbiz. That's our big "Valerie gets it" moment. *[laughs]* I just started thinking about another scene in that episode, when Mark and Valerie, who've both taken sleeping pills because the people in the room next door are having an all-night party, wake up and realize they've missed their chance to get the good chairs by the pool. The film crew knocks on their door, and Valerie with her crazy raccoon-smeared makeup opens the blinds, and you see Mark's bare ass as he's sleeping on the bed behind her. *[both laugh]* That's the balance I love. That we actually have that crazy mania, and then at the end of the episode, she puts those sunglasses on, not letting the audience see her eyes, and says, basically, "I choose Mark." She chooses Mark's need to hear the Cheap Trick song over her need to be on a reality show. It's the beginning of a turn.

Lisa, your portrayal of Valerie not only brings out the humor we talked about earlier but also imbues her with a humanity that makes her at times feel almost like a character in a tragedy. Alessandra Stanley in *The New York Times* called the series

    ABOVE: An over-lit Valerie (Lisa Kudrow) tapes an interview segment for her reality show.

"the saddest comedy on television," and she's right. I couldn't watch more than three episodes at a time—it's really draining, as hilariously funny as it is at the same time.

LK: Especially those first two episodes.

MPK: I think Lisa's performance is like no other performance I've ever seen before. In terms of the complicated layers that you're not being told you're experiencing, but you are subliminally feeling.

It's interesting how often the viewer's relationship to the character of Valerie changes. At one moment you feel sorry for her, then a scene later you're exasperated with her, then she does something that makes you really revile her. And then, before you know it, you love her for some hilarious insight she offers.

MPK: What you just said, that's everything. That's what we became fascinated by. That you could actually portray a human being in the midst of doing a comedy reality show. A character who is so complicated and so changeable that you change while you're watching her.

In the "Valerie Demands Dignity" episode, Valerie becomes anxious after she sees an *Entertainment Weekly* cover story with the headline "Is Reality TV Dying?" She starts to worry that the only way the show will be a hit is if she humiliates herself. She has a great line: "People do not want to see Valerie Cherish brutalized!" Of course, that's exactly what they want to see—and more to the point, it's what we're seeing constantly in the series. One minute we see her crawling up the aisle of a plane experiencing intense turbulence, the next she gets dog poop in her hair, then in another scene she falls, scraping her knee, in a desperate dash to make it to an interview with a *TV Guide* reporter. It's horrifying but also hilarious. Again, I think that probably has to do more with your performance, Lisa, than anything else.

LK: Thank you for the nod to it possibly being about a performance, but no, it's the idea of a person thinking they're in control of something as random and chaotic as life. That's always hilarious to me. And then on top of that, working with manipulative producers on a reality show with a very definite agenda, and thinking you can somehow control that. That's really funny to me.

MPK: Right, like whenever she gives the "time-out" sign with her hands to Jane and the film crew. Even in this tornado, she has to have a moment where she's saying no, even if it's clear that she has absolutely no power.

LK: She's also living in another time. She hasn't caught up to the fact that there's no such thing as propriety anymore. The ironic thing is that people have seen so much reality TV that the show might be received a little bit differently now. When we did this, it was, like, season two of *The Amazing Race.* To me, that was the height of humiliation—vomiting and crying on TV—

MPK: Or eating bugs on *I'm a Celebrity, Get Me Out of Here.*

LK: We felt the show had to be brutal, because one of the things we were trying to shine a little light onto, even if it's in a subtle way, is that even though these people who sign on to these shows are human beings, they've essentially decided to become brands—that's the big word now. And by doing that, they're actually throwing away their humanity, you know? It's as if that's not important. What's important is, how much can

you get paid to show up at a party? I see interviews with reality stars who say things like, "I don't like what's happening to my character." It's their name, their husband, their child, their address—that's not a character, that's *you. [laughs]*

Reality TV has certainly become more extreme since the show was shot. The stakes have gotten so ridiculously high that you end up with situations like that of the couple in California who staged the "runaway balloon" hoax with their six-year-old son, who then vomited on two different morning news shows after his parents asked him to lie about it.

MPK: Well, of course, Valerie had a double vomit.

That scene, which occurs in the second-to-last episode, when Valerie finally gut punches a drunk Paulie G., is worth an entire interview on its own.

MPK: That's the one moment where Lisa and I almost came to blows. She was fully on board with the vomiting, wearing the cupcake costume, everything—and then when we were filming it, every time we did a take, some innate actress-survival-Darwinian skill *[Lisa laughs]* would make her turn her mouth away from the camera.

Lisa, you didn't want to be filmed actually vomiting?

LK: I really thought no one would want to *see* that. *[laughs]*

MPK: She wasn't opposed to the vomiting, but she didn't want it to be shown. You know, you see the vomit hit the floor as she turns away from the camera. And I kept saying to David Steinberg, the director for that episode, "I didn't see the vomit come out of her mouth." And I would keep coming out onto the set and saying, "Lisa, I didn't see the vomit." She's in a giant cupcake with a cherry on her head, and every time she did it she would still turn her face away and vomit. I came back in again and she glared at me and said, "You're here *again?* You're brave!" And I said, "I'm here to represent Lisa Kudrow the writer. She's on board with the vomit coming out of Lisa Kudrow the actress's mouth."

What did you say to that, Lisa?

LK: "You're a sadist!"

MPK: She was also saying "Shit. Fuck. Shit. Fuck!" And then I walked away, and in the next take she directed her head right toward that camera and vomited. And I was delighted.

Lisa, do you think it could be that it's easier to write a scene in which someone humiliates themselves than to actually play it?

LK: I didn't feel humiliated—that wasn't it. I just didn't feel like anyone should be subjected to watching vomit come out of anyone's mouth. It's too vulgar, or at least that's what I thought. Since that happened, of course, all I see on TV are people vomiting from the front.

MPK: Listen, Snooki got punched in the face on *Jersey Shore* and it became a hit because of it. I saw Khloé Kardashian give her sister a Brazilian bikini wax and they pixilated her blistered vagina. Pixelated her vagina! The difference between *Kourtney & Khloé Take Miami* and *The Comeback* is that in the former, somebody cut away the humanity and the humiliation from the show that ended up on the air, and we didn't cut away from it.

I could actually see a scenario where Valerie would consider the Brazilian, because that's where we are now. It's good reality-show stuff.

LK: Yeah. *[As Valerie:]* "You gotta be flexible...." *[laughs]*

MPK: I could see a scene where Mickey says, "Red, that's going too far," and she says, "Well, Mickey, I'm competing with Khloé. They got very big numbers for that. And Jane, you're not going to see it, right? You're going to pixelate it?"

LK: She can rationalize anything.

MPK: "If you're not going to see it, can't I just keep a thong on? Can't we fake it?" *[both laugh]*

Jane, the producer, is such a seminal figure in the whole structure of the show. As with Valerie, the viewer's feelings about her constantly shift. She's cold and clearly manipulative, but there are times when it's clear she's actually moved by something Valerie has said or done—in a few instances, the camera even catches her tearing up. It gives the viewer the chance to hold out a bit of hope that the "nice" side of Jane will prevail when the reality show is finally put together.

LK: Well, you know, the truth of these shows is that the producer just shoots it and then hands in the material. It's someone else who's doing the assembling. But Jane does "guide" Valerie—

MPK: She's very canny. "Oh, you don't want to do that, Valerie? Okay, I'll just call Ben Silver, the studio exec, and tell him you're not on board." Or when Valerie asks Jane to turn off the camera, and she says, "No, we can't." Just the idea of saying "no" to Valerie creates an energy that's going to make for good reality TV. You see Valerie swallowing and trying to figure it out: "What am I going to do with a 'no'?" Jane was really important, because she was the firestoker, and Valerie needed a push and a pull. And the fact that she was a woman was important, too.

There's that wonderful scene between them near the end of the last episode, after Valerie's *Jay Leno* appearance, when Jane spontaneously hugs Valerie. I read somewhere that that was an undirected move on actress Laura Silverman's part.

MPK: Right, when Valerie's so excited about getting picked up, and Jane just jumps across and gives her hug. That line of yours is the one improvised line in the series, Lisa. Valerie says, "Well, look at that. She just cracked open." That breaks my heart.

We actually wrote that part with Laura Silverman in mind, because we wanted someone who was a "non-actress actress." That was very important for Jane, Mickey, and Mark. Those three characters needed to be completely believable, "real" people. We kept saying, "We want Mickey to be eccentric; we don't want an eccentric actor."

How did you find Robert Michael Morris, who plays Mickey in the series?

LK: Michael knew him.

MPK: He was my college theater teacher. Michael would write these incredibly emotional Christmas letters every year and send them out: "Well, I've got melanoma again, but they froze it." And I started telling Lisa about Michael. We wrote the part with him in mind, and then we saw a lot of actors for Mickey. We had to audition everybody, and we had to see how each would work with Lisa. But when Michael came in, it was a reality. And he brought Lisa a little fake diamond necklace.

LK: Which I wore every day. It was good luck.

The relationship between Mickey and Valerie is fascinating. It's almost like a comic version of the one between Petra and her assistant, Marlene, in Fassbinder's *The Bitter Tears of Petra von Kant*: basically a sadomasochistic dance. Valerie tends to put Mickey through hell, but he still adores her, and she depends on him, too. Michael, I think in one interview you called him "Valerie's airbag."

MPK: It's an interesting dynamic in that he annoys her, but he also buoys her up. Without him, she wouldn't be able to make it, because he's almost mirroring back the person she wants to be—or the person she was. It's a case of the star and the sycophant. And then there is another complicated level that's only briefly alluded to in the show, and that is that he's eating the shit because he needs the health insurance. You know what I mean? He needs the job, so he's not quite just a victim; he's also pushing her to continue, because there's not another job for him in all of Hollywood. There just isn't. Not with that hairdo he does for her, or those big curlers. They're both keeping each other's heyday alive.

Perhaps they get along so well because they're both so self-deluded. There is a very funny scene in which Mickey is mortified when one of the young actors on *Room and Bored* offers to set him up with a male friend of hers: He can't understand how anyone would guess he were gay.

MPK: He's from a different time. They both are. And they're both from the end of that time, so now they're living in this different context. He's thinking that because he hasn't said it, it doesn't exist. And she's thinking she's a star because she has a hairdresser who follows her around town.

LK: I love the look on the face of Dan Bucatinsky, who plays Valerie's publicist, when Mickey announces he's going to come out—"Come out of what?" *[laughs]*

MPK: He's just another great deluded character.

One of my favorite characters in *The Comeback* is Juna [played by Malin Ackerman], the young actress in the sitcom with Valerie. She's adorable, sweet, a little naive—

MPK: She's true.

LK: Right, and everything is going her way. She doesn't have to fight for anything.

MPK: She's a golden child. It was really important to us in the writing that Juna be good—

ABOVE: Valerie (Lisa Kudrow) and her hairdresser, Mickey (Robert Michael Morris)

LK: So that you're not allowed to hate her.

Is she there to serve as a reminder to Valerie of what she can never be?

MPK: Well, she represents the effortlessness with which some people move through life, versus the struggling so many others have to undergo. Making Juna a nice person was important, because you know, show business isn't all snarky. Every now and then there is someone who is lovely and wonderful and who does come to your chocolate-fountain party. And that created another level of struggle for Valerie, because she couldn't write her off. She's in a beauty pageant with someone who actually is Miss Congeniality. I love Juna, and Malin Ackerman was flawless.

LK: She was.

Mark, Valerie's husband, is the most "centered" character on the show, which might have to do with the fact that he's the only one not in show business. Can you talk about how you came up with him? Was there any real-life referent?

MPK: Lisa, you should talk first about Mark and Valerie as husband and wife, and how important that was.

LK: Well, I thought it was important not only that he be a good guy, but that he be successful. It's important that she's not doing any of this because she needs the money. This quest of hers has nothing to do with her having to pay a mortgage. And he's this guy who's only mildly interested in what she's doing. As long as whatever it is she's doing doesn't interfere too much with his life, it's going to be okay.

MPK: He also gives her complete permission to be, I would say, a "lazy wife." Do you know what I mean? She always orders out for dinner, and he's fine with it. There's a very Beverly Hills aspect to it all.

LK: But I also like that they each have their independence. She sees them as sort of a modern couple. Yes, he doesn't insist that she cook. But she is the one who prepares his lunch and takes care of him and makes sure he's not too put out. Like arranging car pools for his daughter, Francesca, when she goes to New York. The key was that Mark couldn't be needy. A little selfish at times, but not needy.

MPK: It was another interesting part to cast, and there weren't a lot of options.

LK: Well, at first we thought he should be a lot older. She just married this very successful guy, and it's not a love thing.

MPK: But then we wanted to have someone who thought of her as a catch, and someone she actually could catch, because she's a genius about surviving. She saw the career dip and suddenly she was married to a guy who has money, and who also sees her still as a star. Damian Young came in many times when I was casting *Sex and the City,* and he was always too complicated for any of the one-off guys we would have on that show. He was too interesting to be the idiot, and he was too handsome to be the ugly guy, and he was too real to do a cartoon turn. So we were thinking, "Who's handsome, and yet real? Who's ap-

propriate, and who's dry?" That was the most important thing. He needed to be dry. Effortless. Present. Valerie was such a hummingbird, so we wanted a low vibe from the husband so that together as a couple they're tolerable. And then Damian read and we all loved him.

The other thing that's really important about their relationship is that she sexes it up for him. She might not cook, but she likes to wear those tight-fitting dresses. So when they put her in that baggy Aunt Sassy tracksuit, it really is a humiliation.

One of the reality cameras is mounted on the ceiling in their bedroom, and they seem to be making fairly frequent trips into the bathroom to have sex—one of these off-camera episodes is featured as a funny voice-over at the end of one episode.

MPK: We wanted to make sure that there was a sex vibe to Valerie, because she was being categorized by others as not sexual. She has a sex life, and the tragedy is that, because of her age, on sitcoms, she's basically dead, which explains all the terrible jokes about Aunt Sassy's "big beaver" coat. There is a vital woman there who is being desexualized because of what the network says is sexy.

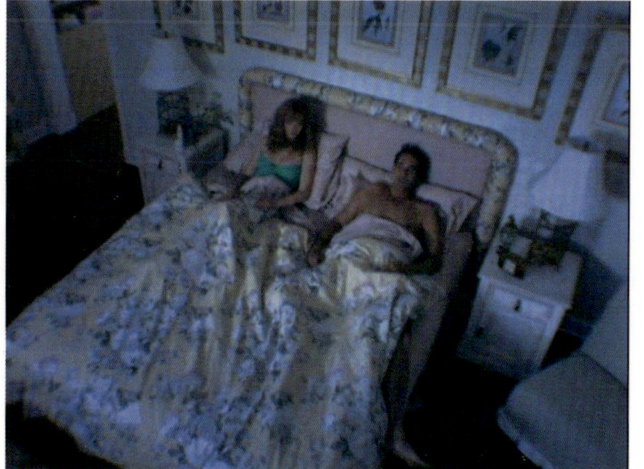

Speaking of the network, I was curious to know if all of the unidentified people—and there are quite a few—at the table readings for *Room and Bored* were meant to be from the show's network.

MPK: They're network executives, junior executives, studio execs. Everyone who is paid to be there to laugh too loud when something is working, and give too many notes when it isn't.

This is typical for any kind of television series?

MPK: Not for a filmed show. It's unique to a show like *Room and Bored,* when there is an actual sound that's supposed to come out of an audience that registers whether it's funny or not. For sitcoms that I've been on—*Cybill, Good Advice, Good Sports*—there's always someone there from the network to laugh at the good parts and to give you notes when there are no laughs.

LK: For a big, big hit, those table reads are not as populated, because there aren't really notes.

MPK: Right. On season three of *Friends,* it's really hard to give Marta Kauffman and David Crane a note, because it's like, "Oh, don't worry, we'll fix that." But there's a lot of worry when you're starting a new sitcom that network people are going to make you do something that won't necessarily be good for the show.

LK: You haven't yet had a chance to prove that you can fix a problem.

MPK: And the other thing is, everybody wants to make sure that it works, because everybody's livelihood is tied to it. So it made perfect sense that those first couple of episodes of *Room and Bored* would be greatly populated, because the show is starting and people are like, "We got this thing on the air, now let's move forward."

The second or third episode on any sitcom is brutal, because you work a long time on the pilot, and then suddenly, you're like, "Oh, this is really it." Even on *The Comeback*. When we were filming the Palm Springs episode, I was editing the third episode. There's that scene near the end where Valerie goes to the Ivy to meet Juna, and she's just sitting at the table waiting for Juna, who's late. Valerie awkwardly eats a piece of bread, checks her watch—it goes on for what feels like forever—and I had a moment of complete panic. Lisa talked me off the ledge. She said, "No, it's exactly what it's supposed to be. Sometimes it should be inert and it should be about nothing. It's enough." But I started to get the vapors! Even I didn't know if that was enough.

LK: It was enough.

MPK: Lisa was standing outside at the Parker Palm Springs with her hair in a towel, and she said to me, "It's exactly what we wanted it to be." I mean, thank god you have a partner in those situations.

LK: But the thing was, when the network saw that third episode, they loved it. Remember?

MPK: Right, they were like, "Oh, *this* is what it's about."

Another aspect of the series that was really pitch-perfect were all of the product-placement moments, particularly in the Palm Springs episode, where Valerie and Mark are given a Lincoln Navigator but are then accompanied on the trip by a PR person from the car company who keeps insisting they insert "the Navigator" into every comment they make about the car.

MPK: At around that time I began noticing this on reality shows. You know, you're watching *Top Chef* and you're thinking, "Why I am looking at the stove?" "Why are there all of these shots of the Tupperware?"

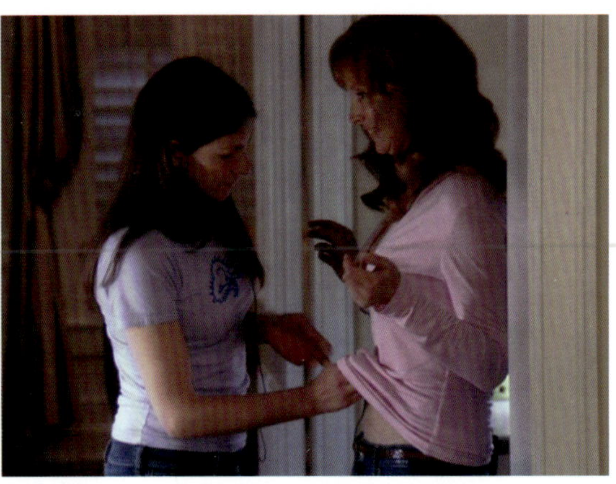

LK: But we'd also hear stories from people working on scripted shows, where it was like, "Oh god, we have to figure out how to work in this product because they're going to underwrite a lot of the budget."

Did you ever have to deal with this on the other shows you've worked on?

MPK: When *Sex and the City* was on HBO there was never any product placement. As a matter of fact, people said to me, "Trojan must have given you a lot of money," since we had a shot, for example, of Samantha opening her cabinet and grabbing the rubbers. I said, "No, not at all, I just wanted the most instantly recognizable condom." I just don't like it on a show when people are drinking fake Diet Coke, you know? With the fake swirls of color on the can? One of the great joys of writing *Sex and the City* came in knowing I could actually write, "She's on the runway in a Gucci outfit," as opposed to, "She's on the runway in a Fafoofoo from Paris outfit." Which makes everything seem so fake to me. Same thing on sitcoms: When people are drinking swirly colas, it drives me crazy. But since *Sex and the City,* product placement has become a big deal. It's a huge revenue stream on reality shows, which is why we used it. Even in the second episode, Valerie is given a huge basket of hair product for Mickey to use before the upfronts.

That's one of the few times she won't give in to the demands of Jane and the show.

MPK: I said to Lisa when we were filming it, "Do not say 'no' right away. Take as long as you possibly can before saying it." It's great—you can see the wheels turning, you see every thought—"Am I going to get yelled at?" "Will this damage me in some way?" Her head is practically vibrating! And then she finally says, "No. No. Sorry." But it's the longest pause ever. So all of this came from reality shows, not from anyone telling me to put anything in. We were ahead of the curve on that one.

Not only on that one. I read somewhere that you two were amazed to find Madonna sporting Valerie's hairstyle after the show aired.

LK: Oh, we couldn't believe that!

MPK: We couldn't believe it. We were flattered, because—

LK: How could you not be?

MPK: Madonna was trying to work it as retro style, but Valerie was wearing it without thinking it was retro, it was just style. *[both laugh]* If we were still on the air, that would be a great moment for Valerie: "Madonna stole my hair. She stole my hair. I was first."

Do you think this show could have been made for network television?

LK: No.

MPK: No. It apparently couldn't even be made for HBO. It is too complicated. Also, the nightmare of cutting to a commercial in the middle of raw footage would have destroyed the tension we were trying to create, which would usually break near the end when we would use all that really great music to close the show. That was the only salve we gave the audience; you get to see a slightly more polished end.

LK: Right, like you were actually watching a TV show!

MPK: But up until then there is no music, no credits, no break. We wouldn't have been able to do it.

LK: No, and also the pacing...

MPK: Right, the timing was important. A half-hour show on network TV is now 20 minutes when you factor in commercials, and that extra 10 minutes is the stuff that makes you love Valerie. The character stuff, and the luxury of watching paint dry. The non-energy of not moving it along was basically the antidote to a network show.

And it was probably also important to have the option of showing nudity and using curse words, for instance, which heightened the "raw footage" feel.

MPK: Well, I'll tell you that even in the simplest, simplest edit, a network would have told us that Mark could never say that he and Valerie had tried cocaine—which is a significant, significant part of their backstory. I know we would have gotten a note about that on network TV. And the other, much more general

   ABOVE: Valerie (Lisa Kudrow) gets miked by Jane, the reality-show producer (Laura Silverman).

note we would have gotten—the ultimate network note about a female character—would have been: "Is she likable?" You would have heard it from everyone. "Is she likable?" "Do we like her?" "Is she likable?" "Will the audience like her?" And that question can't exist for a character like Valerie Cherish, because the answer is "yes," "no," "yes," "yes," "no"…

LK: And just off the page, it's "no."

MPK: So there you go. Without Lisa's performance, off the page, it's "no." Because there's no energy, no sadness behind the eyes, no investment. Like when she really loses herself dancing during Juna's concert at the Viper Room. The one moment she actually forgets about the camera. And what did we do? As she comes back to earth, she sees Mark dancing with another woman.

Valerie calls it "dirty dancing."

MPK: Right. It's the only moment she lets go, and all hell breaks loose. *[both laugh]*

So now for the big question: Why do you think this show only lasted one season on HBO?

MPK: I have theories.

LK: I do too.

MPK: First of all, you have to understand that it was the greatest mystery and disconnect for Lisa and me. It wasn't even like we had the normal emotional infrastructure that happens when something gets canceled. It's almost like we were in a Jean-Paul Sartre play—"I don't understand anything that's happening…." The direct evolutionary line that I can draw, having worked at HBO before, is that their M.O. is "quality, not ratings." They're not in the ratings game, they're in the quality game. The only manifestation of quality at the beginning of a series is critical response. So if *The New York Times* says that *The Comeback* is a significant, important new type of television series, that puts you on a track that is quotable—and comforting to a show-business machine. And I think our first wave of critical responses—with the exception of, as I like to say, "the Pulitzer Prize–winning Tom Shales of *The Washington Post*," who really got it—didn't include enough snobby quotes. And I do say snobby, because there were plenty "Lisa Kudrow is a genius" comments.

LK: But they all came back later and wrote more favorable pieces—

MPK: They all turned around.

It's funny you mention that, because when I was doing research, I was fascinated to find that reviews of the series when it was airing were generally much less enthusiastic than later reviews of the DVD. And these came from the same publications. What does that say to you?

MPK: I know what it says. People have so little faith that there is an actual method to the madness. When they saw the first or second episode, they thought, "They can't keep this up—this is

so off the track I'm not even sure there's a thought behind it." Angela Tarantino was our publicist at HBO, and after I showed her the pilot, she said to me, "Uh, it's really good. We're going to have to educate them as to how to talk about this." And we never accomplished that, as much as we tried. The reality was that out of the gate, people had never seen anything like this character before. It's like in life, where you only really start to understand someone's sense of humor after you've gotten to know them for a period of time. So at first, people were kind of stunned, and then by the final episode, they got it.

LK: In my mind, people weren't going to "get it" until some point well into the second season. To me, that's why we were at HBO, because that's where you can do that. I mean, all of their biggest hits were shows that for the first couple of episodes or even seasons you kind of went, "Wait, what is this? How do I even categorize this?" I think it's the same with anything new and different. Conan got horrible reviews when he first started on late night. But that's who he was, and he didn't go anywhere, and then everyone went, "Oh, okay, we get it!" That's what I was expecting, and it actually took off even more than I ever expected it to in the first season.

MPK: Also, Lisa was not Phoebe.

LK: And you weren't delivering *Sex and the City.*

MPK: It was kind of a bait-and-switch situation, because people thought that they were in for the greatest, funniest, sexiest show, because that was our brand.

LK: Something else was happening. HBO had just come off of *Sex and the City,* and everyone was still waiting for the next season of *The Sopranos,* and the network had done a few industry series—*Entourage* and *Unscripted,* the George Clooney show—which weren't reviewed well at all. People were starting to wonder aloud about what HBO was doing with all these "inside-industry" shows, and then *The Comeback* came out. So I think it was HBO's turn to get a little flack.

How far into the series were you when you found out it wasn't going to be renewed?

MPK: We didn't find out until the series was over. I remember going into HBO—I actually dragged Lisa in with me—right before we shot the Palm Springs episode. I said to them "I'm going to be very bold right now and tell you the truth: It's going to turn around, and if you pick us up now, there will be fuel behind this. If you say there will be a second season of *The Comeback* right now, everything will change. Lisa will get nominated for an Emmy"—which she did anyway, although my feeling is she would have won if it had been renewed. I even said, "Get us off Sunday. Create a new night: Monday. Call it 'Monday, Monday' and play The Mamas and The Papas song, make it kind of sad. 'You think your boss is bad? Here's Valerie Cherish.'"

LK: *[laughs]* Right, I forgot about that—that was great!

MPK: Lower the expectations. Make it an off-Broadway night. Stop trying to make it be Carrie Bradshaw and Mr. Big in Paris.

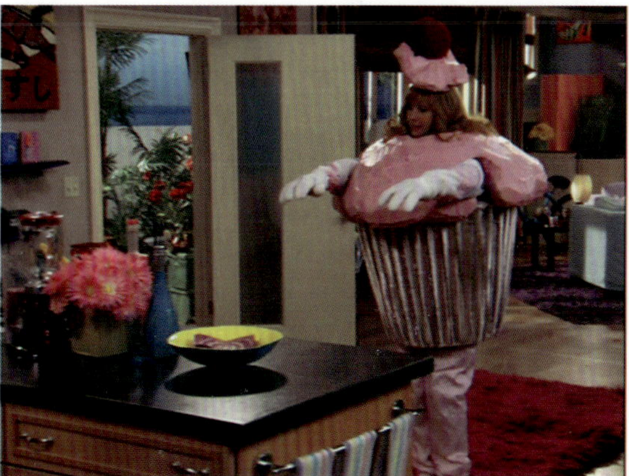

It can't be that, yet or ever...that took six years to build. Put it on Monday—"Rainy Days and Mondays" as the theme song—go with a darker, sadder vibe, and let it find a small audience.

But for some reason they didn't buy it. I could have gone in there and pitched the second season like crazy: This is what we're going to do—you'll love it. We'll never paint ourselves into a corner—it's Lisa and me. But it didn't happen.

LK: There were other powers at work that we don't know about, obviously. The quality was there, the ratings were actually fine for a first-season show. It had done better, as I recall, than *Entourage* in its first season. So essentially, there wasn't anything where you could definitely say, "Here's why." And what I heard later from people who were at HBO at the time was that they went back and forth every day on whether it was going to get picked up or not.

Do you think the critique of the TV industry was off-putting to some people?

LK: I do. The interesting thing to me was that artists—writers, directors, actors—loved it and could not believe it had been canceled. Executives and business types would look at me and say, "Wow, yeah, I guess it was just too brutal." Or "I guess it wasn't funny enough." Or "I guess the ratings weren't good enough." But it was funny to see how those two different types responded to the cancellation. The executives had to justify it: "It can't have been wrong, because they did it." *[laughs]*

MPK: I've gotten some "We shoulda" calls since then. I loved it when *Entertainment Weekly* named it one of the top 10 shows of the decade. *Newsweek* called it one of the 10 funniest comedies of the decade, but *Entertainment Weekly* called it one of the top 10 shows of the decade. *The Sopranos* was number 1, and we were number 10. It was a nice validation, as were the three Emmy nominations.

LK: What I'm noticing also is that it seems to be gaining popularity with college-age kids.

MPK: It is truly an original, and I have to tell you that we had such a great time on this, and we were a great team. And to this day, we still call each other up and say, "What if Valerie did this? Or that? Should we?"

LK: We might not be done.

Lisa, you've been working on the terrific *Web Therapy* series on the Internet—would you consider something along those lines?

LK: I don't know. We talk about what it could be, but you know, we don't own it. *[laughs]*

MPK: It's a very interesting situation, because the idea of Valerie in the world is like a creative wellspring. It never goes away. The idea of an unsatisfied person who's not going gently into that good night represents an endless opportunity for comedy—and tragedy.

Would you two be willing talk a little bit about some of the ideas you had for the second season if the show had been renewed?

MPK: Well, off the top of my head, we thought that Valerie's fame would give her more power. And that she would therefore probably get rid of Paulie G. and promote Gigi to the show runner—and then Gigi would become a monster. And I can tell you that Mickey was going to get bad porcelain veneers. And leave his boyfriend for a young man. And we had a great idea for a drifting-away Mark.

At the close of the final episode, when Valerie is signing the vomit bags with her likeness on them in the *Leno* parking lot, you see Mark suddenly realizing what this newfound fame is going to do to Valerie, and by extension, to their relationship.

LK: Right.

MPK: We always thought about doing an episode where we get to see Valerie and Mark's wedding. We decided they had a ski wedding, and she wore a white parka.

LK: In Aspen!

MPK: They got married on the slopes. It was completely correct for her. Just a photo of them on skis getting married.

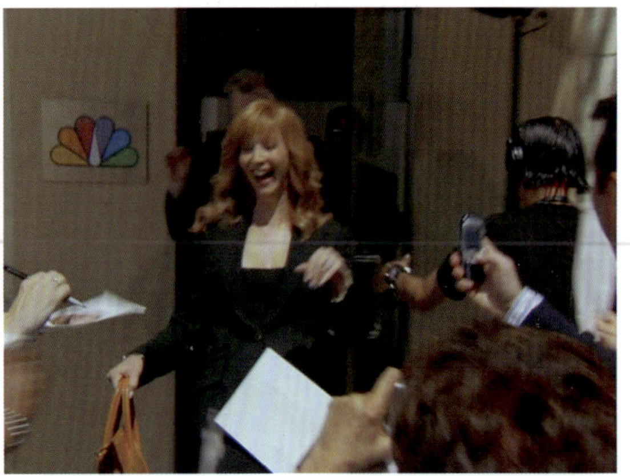

LK: And we really wanted to introduce the character of her father, who is this grumpy guy. The kind of person who would trip and then blame her.

MPK: That's what my father did. At my sister's wedding, he tripped on his own feet walking her down the aisle and he looked over at her and said: "Jesus *Christ,* Ellen." *[both laugh]* So we thought he would be a fun and painful character. But the second season was really going to be about the rise of Valerie's power. And how, even with power, the ambition just starts to destroy her.

LK: It would never be enough. Even if she ends up in a movie with Nicole Kidman, she's still not going to be invited to the same parties.

MPK: The reason that we had absolute confidence that we could continue doing *The Comeback* was that Valerie would never be satisfied with what she had. Celebrity is a race against time. I'm sure even Nicole Kidman has days where she says, "What happened?" The spotlight will not stay on you, whoever you are. And our übersophisticated thought was that Valerie would eventually gain some sort of awareness about this, but to what level, we weren't sure. We even talked about her leaving Hollywood and going to a different city.

LK: We wanted her to go to New York.

MPK: Right. Here's the thing about the character of Valerie: I can say to myself, "What is the worst, most tragic situation I can think of?" And then I put Valerie in it, and I immediately start thinking about what she would say that would make me laugh. It's the same with every bad situation you can think of: If you put Valerie Cherish in it, and think about her trying to get her head around it, it's funny.

Raw Footage: The Lisa Kudrow project

A scripted reality show that follows a former B level sitcom star from the mid-1990's on
her come-back trail as a supporting player on a new mediocre sit-com. The episodes of
Raw Footage are made up of the raw footage being shot for a fictional reality show called
"The Come-Back" which chronicles the life of this deluded tragic comic "star" as she
makes her way through her sad life living in Beverly Hills while pinning all her hopes
and dreams on the success of the new mediocre sit-com filled with much younger, sexier
actresses. We watch each week as she attempts to "spin" all the "on camera"
humiliations captured on this journey and hide her true nature from the ever-watchful eye
of the reality camera.

It's a show with-in-a show about making a bad show.   It looks with a lacerating and
knowing eye at the brutal world of B-level celebrity, sitcoms and a sinking woman.

Because the conceit of the show is that we are seeing "only the un-edited raw footage" …
We are able to show the personally revealing and ugly behind the scenes behavior of
people behaving as their true selves. At the end of each episode of Raw Footage we see a
30 second tease for the soon to be aired reality show. It's all the raw footage edited
down by the reality show producers to show to slant the aspects of the Star's life that
week.

A show that works on three reality levels:

The star's actual reality
Her "spinning" of her reality for the reality show.
The reality shows edited slant of her reality.

The character is tragic/comic for a number of reasons:

She thinks she's more talented that she is.
She thinks she's nicer than she is.
She thinks she knows "sit-com" formulas.
She thinks she's still famous.
She thinks she's has only a "window" of fame left.
She's desperate for a comeback
She's a woman aging in Hollywood.
She's in a sex-less dead end marriage.
She's invested in all the wrong things in her life… except real estate.

Season One: Raw footage:
Pilot:
Lens cap uncovered: "So, this is my big comeback". Zoom in; too close, and then out.
(Perhaps "sticks" separate every scene, use the clap as punctuation. Hard in and out)

Producer relentless prompting: Say who you are. She is thrown, they know who she is…
but she gets she has to make everything super clear. I'm I was the star of "I'm It". Tell
us about "I'm It". Thrown again, she recovers, well I could show you. Follow me. She
moves out of the kitchen. She leads us through hall. The cameraman hits his back on
wall. Jars camera, first glimpse of crew around her, (This established the not no
slickness of a new reality crew before they know the environment.) She is concerned that
that is unusable; they tell her its all-raw footage only of percentage of this will make it on
air. She is enlightened: Such a new way of working.
 She takes us to her "it wall". See her framed TV guide covers, People choice award.
She speaks into the lens, they tell her not to. That's not how reality works. She is
prompted to explain what this is all is. She tells us it's a reality show called The Come
Back, which will trace my "comeback" as I audition and hopefully get a part on a new
WB sitcom. The Comeback. She puts " The comeback" in quotes, as she tells us she
never really went anywhere, she's still here… but that's the hook they needed.
Her husband makes a brief, uncomfortable appearance, not interested in on camera
experience. She laughs it off" Business man." The producer pushes her along: what's
today all about? She tells us it's the morning of her final call back audition, for a new
sit- com on the WB called: Room and Bored. B-o-r-e-d. The shows about four women
and one man, who all live in a big condo at the Newport Beach. She tells us she's up for
the part of Laney, the sexy, funny woman whose name is on the lease.
Hairdresser (old caftan queen) from "It", enters, wants to do her signature "it" hair.
He hasn't worked since it went off and is a little desperate.

Car ride; her concerned about the lower angle of lens of camera is seat next to her. Asks
about maybe getting some of those higher hung Taxi cab Confessions cameras.
Hairdresser picks at her hair from back seat of her Mercedes. No drive on at studio gate.
Can't get in Studio gate. Guy doesn't know who she is. She used to work here. Asks for
Charlie? Charlie? Either she has to park or Charlie rescues walk or her.

If she walks, we see her outfit, good shoes. Maybe points out where her parking space
used to be.   Bungalow. Some one recognizes her: Hi, I love you. It puffs her up
before audition.
Or
She plays it like a fan, turns out it was "It's" production manager. Who is still working
on the lot.

Enter the audition and sees two other real TV actresses (Markie Post, Crystal Bernard)
waiting with their own film crews. Is surprised and thrown that she's not the only one
being followed. Never thought about it. The producer tells her they have to have there

back covered: only one of them is going to get it.   Realizes that's she auditioning for two shows.
 She rallies and approaches the actresses. They are much less enthusiastic about the process, forced into by their agents, and insist that She turn her camera off, like they forced theirs to do. She doesn't and they won't talk to her.

She is about to sign contracts before she goes in and the casting director tells her, there is a problem and she has to call her agent. She does and discovers they want her to lower her price, reason: they also have Markie and Crystal both interested.   She eats the humiliation and scratches out the figure and writes in the new one on camera.

Goes in, comes out. It felt good.   Not validated by desk.   Soon, I'll have a space.

Personal confession at home: Faux: Talking about her hopes.

Waiting for the call.   The nerves.   The message is yes.   She is thrilled.

First table read.
        She meets and discovers that all the cast members are young and sexy, but her. They are psyched to meet a star and "loved" It" when they were young.

        Meet writer/executive producer, reality TV chip on his shoulder. Not too happy about: " Reality" taking away my kids college future away, but hey… the network wants you here. And if this thing gets picked up, it'll be good promotion." She says: When. When this gets picked up. Think positively." He looks at her like she's an asshole. It's the first moment he has an inking of what his week will be.

A pop of the rehearsal. She comes home in a business suit and briefcase and discovers: everyone making out in bathing suits and says: "Get a room! " She does a take

Re-write meeting: Bait and Switch scene. He tells her she now the aunt who lives upstairs. No one bought an old woman living in the condo. Er- Old-er. She argues, that she was hired to be someone a professional not someone's aunt. She tells her he's trying to find a way to cement her into the show; so, she owns the building and rents to her niece. She's Aunt Sassy. Do I at least work still? Am I a professional? No, we need you at home so we can put you in more stuff.. She argues "In it" I was a Young Urban professional and they found a way to keep me in every scene. He argues this isn't a workplace comedy. He wants her to have a reason to use her every time he needs her. She's the owner. You own apartment buildings, right? A few. See, we're building this from your own life.   I'm not an aunt. You're a hot sexy Aunt. Let's find it together.

Costume fitting, bad tracksuit. He said: I'm a hot sexy aunt. The script says: running suit. She suggests: Juicy couture. You don't have a juicy ass.   She puts him in his place

Personal confession at her vanity mirror in big bathroom. Middle of the night, tomorrow is the filming. These things happen. Justifying going on.   The Husband walks behind her on way to bathroom and farts.

Show night:: Her intro before show, last curtain call, people applaud. She shines, familiar turf. Very happy.

Scene: "Get a room" in bad track suit… Audience laughs.   Moving on: She asks to do another one.   The director is satisfied: She burlesques, for the audience: Pleeeeeeease! The audience applauds. We see a little of her cute act "it" fake star power surface.

After filming, hugs cast good-bye; the director comes up to her. Want to talk in private, cameras won't shut off, takes her behind flat. Producer says Keep running, always keep running.   We hear him calls her on the power trip. On it I was allowed to – He cuts her off, You're not it anymore.   She walks back out and recovers on camera, joking: get a room.

She gets the automated call that her show is picked up. Calls agent; Trust wanting to make sure, they are flying her hairdresser. Nope. Thrilled to New York. No one will pay for her hairdresser to go. She decides to fly him herself.

Backstage   at Up Fronts. Hearing announcements of all network reality shows. Not to mention our one sit-com. Show gets a room clip. They announce cast, not her.   She is thrown, did they say my name? Should I go out, I got the laugh in the clip. . Hairdresser encourages her to go out. She runs out a little too late, just as the other cast members are turning to come back in. She is alone, lost in the spotlight, it goes out.

Outside, smoking alone, caught. Anxiety filled wondering if she looked like a fool. Realizes the camera has found her. She says; No, I don't smoke. I don't smoke on camera. We won't use it necessarily use it, raw footage. She holds it bellow the frame. Some agent type person passes by and says: Good look… looks like another winner for you!   It cheers her

Promo for the Comeback: Skewed reveal the most juicy, unflattering moments.

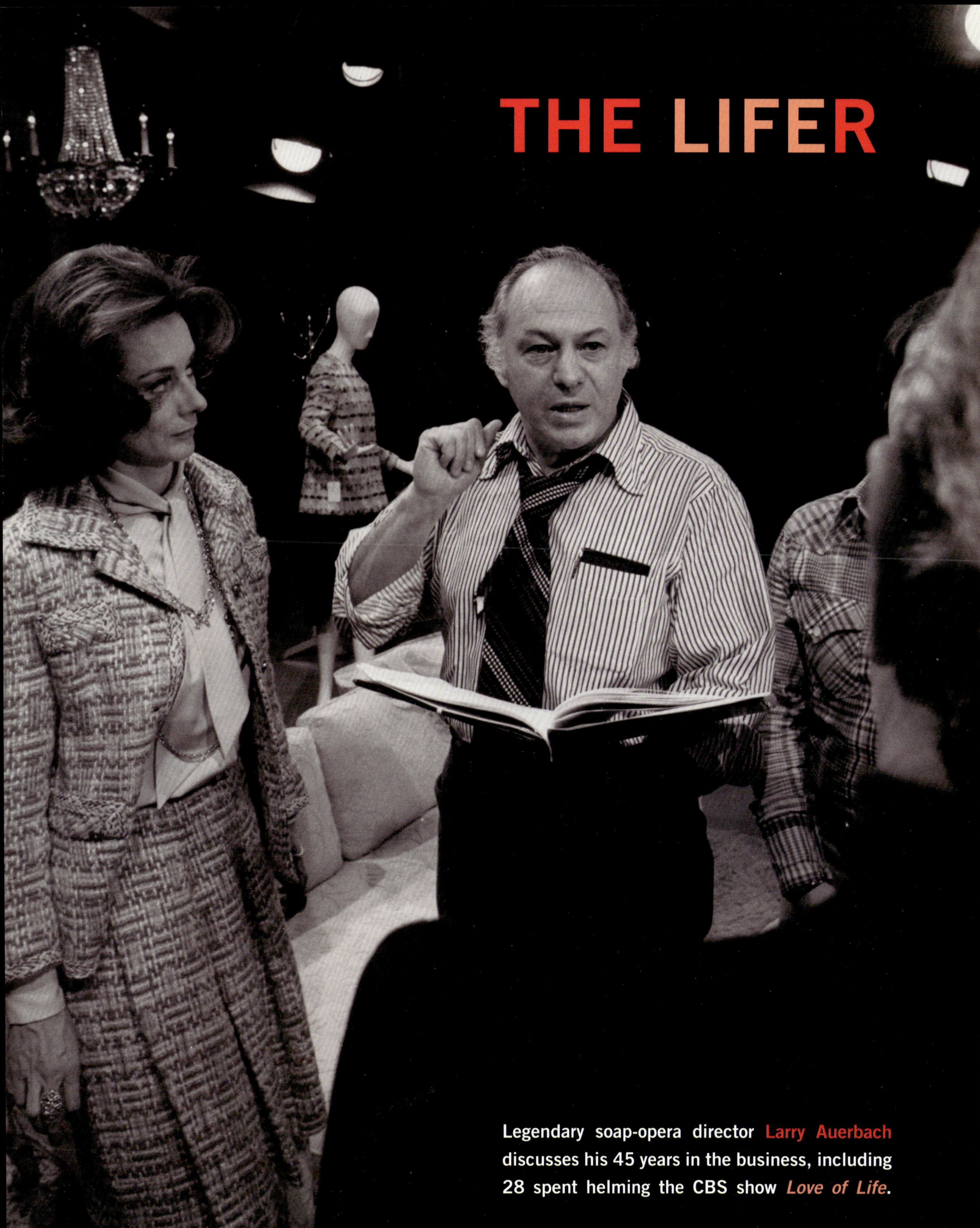

Legendary soap-opera director Larry Auerbach discusses his 45 years in the business, including 28 spent helming the CBS show *Love of Life*.

According to Wikipedia, "It's possible that Larry Auerbach has directed more dramatic television than any other American director (approximately 3,000 hours)." Nearly every one of those hours has been devoted to soap operas, so it might also be fair to assert that no other person knows daytime drama as well as he does. Auerbach, who is now retired, has been justly rewarded for his expertise: The director received a Daytime Emmy award in 1985 for his work on the ABC soap *One Life to Live,* and was also the recipient of the Directors Guild of America's Robert Aldrich Award in 1991. In 2004, the DGA named him an Honorary Life Member, a designation he shares with an elite group of filmmakers that includes Charlie Chaplin, Frank Capra, and Walt Disney. In early August, Auerbach agreed to offer *Esopus* readers his recollections of and frank opinions about working in soap operas for nearly a half century.

Tod Lippy: From what I understand, you pretty much jumped right into broadcasting in Chicago after a stint in the army and a degree from Northwestern University's speech school...

Larry Auerbach: Well, I graduated in June of 1947, and in January of 1948, I got a job writing copy at a radio station in Burlington, Vermont. That was 40 hours a week for 40 bucks, subsidized by the government because I was a veteran. One of my instructors at Northwestern had been Art Jacobson, a moonlighting executive from NBC Chicago. In the spring of 1948, NBC needed somebody to cover the daylight-savings network. I had kept in touch with Jake, and he sent me a telegram asking if I'd be available for a summer job at NBC. In 1948, most of the country was still on standard time; it was only the metropolitan areas that were on daylight-savings time. So everything was recorded on great big disks and played back an hour later to the standard-time network. This was done out of Chicago, and they needed somebody to be out there and supervise the process since those big disks gained or lost a second or two every half hour. Because the NBC chimes controlled the network, everything had to be exactly on time. So an announcer—often it was Hugh Downs—and I sat in a control room, and at the proper time I would give Hugh, or whoever was assigned, a cue, and he would push the button to ring the chimes. At the end of that summer there was an opening at NBC, and they kept me on. Eventually, Jake went over to television and brought me with him. It's a classic example of being in the right place at the right time.

This was just as TV was beginning to find its footing, right?

Oh, yeah. This was 1950, what is now considered the golden age of television. Dave Garroway was doing his program in Chicago, with Bob Banner directing. Dan Petrie was directing *Studs' Place,* with Studs Terkel, which I was the stage manager on. And I was the first director of *Mr. Wizard,* which was a science program for kids. It was a wonderful time, and everything was live. What you got on the air was whatever you had on camera in the studio, and that worked very well. If there was an error, then there was an error. You had to cover it the best you could.

Hawkins Falls, which I'm pretty certain is considered to be the first television soap opera, was being produced in Chicago around that time. Did you work on it at all?

Ben Park was the producer and director on that, and I was one of several stage managers. As a matter of fact, we actually did some location work for it, which was very unusual at the time because the equipment didn't really facilitate it.

How did you get from Chicago to New York?

My father was very ill, so I took a leave of absence and came home to New York. While I was here I thought I would look for work. I went to see Dan Petrie, just to chat, and he said that Roy Winsor, whom I had worked for in Chicago, was now in New York and had been made head of television and radio at an important ad agency, the Biow Company. He said, "You ought to go see Roy; I hear he's going to do a couple of soap operas." So I went to see him, and he put me in touch with the guy who was going to be producing *Love of Life,* a guy by the name of Green. And I wrote him a letter thanking "Mr. Grey," and he didn't like that much, so I didn't get to do the pilot. *[laughs]* As it turned out, they weren't happy with the pilot, so Roy called me one day and said, "You're starting next week." We went on the air with the first show on September 24, 1951, and our last show was in January of 1980—28 years later.

When *Love of Life* started, each episode was 15 minutes, which was the same length as the radio soap operas that had been around for some time.

That's right. And they were in black-and-white.

There is one of these from 1953 available online, and I had a chance to watch it the other day. In it, the show's protagonist, Vanessa Dale, is told by Beanie, her "bad" sister Meg's son, that the man she is interested in is being pursued by Meg.

[laughs] Oh, you really watched.

I found the economy of means to be really compelling: three short scenes, two characters each, and each taking place on a different, but very basic-looking, set.

Actually, we often had more than two people in a scene, but the budget allowed for only a certain number of performances per week. Therefore, if, say, Vanessa's contract guaranteed the performer three performances a week, that had to affect how many other people we could cast during the week. I don't think the writers actually had to count, but someone would keep track to make sure the budget didn't get out of whack.

We shot the show at the Liederkranz Hall, which had originally been the headquarters for a German singing society, so it had good acoustics. CBS took it over in the '40s and made radio, or perhaps recording, studios out of it. Later on, they put four small television studios in there. It was on 56th Street between Park and Lexington, next to the Library for the Blind, but it has since been torn down.

There were two studios on the first floor up the stairs from the street, and two studios on the floor above it. Every piece of scenery and furniture had to be hand carried in by the stagehands. And there was only one studio in which you could fit a car, and it had to be winched in up a ramp. So if I wanted to use a car, I had to do it at a time when that studio wasn't being used for *Search for Tomorrow,* which was another soap Roy Winsor had started for Procter & Gamble. Later on, he came up with *Secret Storm.*

My understanding is that American Home Products basically created these two shows—much like Procter & Gamble had created *Guiding Light*—as a vehicle for selling its products.

  PREVIOUS PAGE: Larry Auerbach gives notes to actress Tudi Wiggins on the set of *Love of Life* in the mid-1970s.

That's essentially right. American Home sponsored them, but hired Roy to create them.

The episode I watched opened with a Chef Boyardee ad, and then, at the end, there was an aspirin ad, I believe for Bayer—

No, it would have been Anacin.

That's right. So these types of ads for American Home Products always bookended every episode?

There were two 30-second and two one-minute commercials in every 15-minute program.

At this point, who actually owned the show? CBS, or American Home Products?

Basically, American Home owned it and just bought the time from CBS to air the show. Eventually, CBS licensed it from American Home—as I recall, American Home didn't want to carry the full weight anymore, and I believe CBS eventually owned it all and sold off commercial spots.

Can you describe a typical day's worth of production?

Well, first I would get the script. I would go over it, and then we would have a lot of rehearsal, which doesn't happen anymore. We would start rehearsal in the afternoon of the day before. It would take three hours, as I remember, and we would schedule the performers to come in as needed—if someone was in every scene, they'd be there all afternoon; otherwise, they'd be there just part of the time. After we had that rehearsal and had done the physical blocking, I would go away and work out all of my camera positions.

How many cameras were you using?

Three cameras. And no zooms in those days. Each camera had four lenses. So I would notate all of my camera stuff in the script, and then we'd come in the next morning and have another hour of dry rehearsal in the morning. After that, we'd go into the studio and have a camera blocking, a run-through, and a dress rehearsal, and then we'd air the episode. That was the preparation when we had a 15-minute, black-and-white, live show. And when it went to a half hour in the '60s, we kept pretty much the same schedule, but if I remember correctly, by then we had gone to videotape, so we were no longer shooting live. And then the next step was color, in the late '60s.

How many writers were working on the early episodes?

The first writer for the show was John Hess, and he did it all himself. My relationship with him was somewhat removed, because the producer, who worked in the office and worried about the budget, was the one who always worked with the writer. I would see John at a meeting or something—I might have some suggestions here and there, but my contact was limited. I'm sure you know about Irna Phillips. She was considered the doyenne of soap operas, and she had originally come out of radio. Basically, every word that flowed from her pen was gold, and you didn't dare touch it, because you'd turn it into lead. Fortunately, I never had to work with her. As I'm told, Irna would sit and watch each show, and as soon as it was off the air, the phone in the control room would ring and she would present her notes, comments, and criticisms to the director. I wouldn't have been able to put up with that, and I didn't have to, fortunately.

There was some talk at one point that Roy was going to bring her in to do *Love of Life,* and I said to him, "You'll have to stand between her and me."

I felt there was a difference between the written word and the spoken word, and sometimes it came out of the actor's mouth better if we changed a word or two or four. I felt that as long as we kept the writer's intention—kept the story going per the outline—if it came out more realistically or believably, it was worth doing. So to that extent, I've had some input into the writing. I've often felt that writers should sit there and read out loud what they wrote. I mean, this is a verbal medium, after all.

But the writer was never on the set?

No. It was just the actors and the stage manager.

How about you?

I directed from the control room, with monitors for every camera. During rehearsal I might very well go out onto the floor and talk to one of the actors. Between takes, which is something we had the luxury of only when tape became available, if there was anything that wasn't working, or you wanted to adjust a movement or something, I could either ask the stage manager to convey it to the performer or go out on the floor myself. But generally speaking, communication between the performer and the director would be through the stage manager, who was always on the set. And there were usually two stage managers on every show after the shows went to an hour. The first stage manager was more or less in control of the floor, and the second would help out with the extras or the heavy action scenes, or wherever needed. On *Love of Life,* we had only one stage manager.

Can you describe the control room for me?

There were monitors for every camera, and a technical director who was doing the switching, an audio man responsible for monitoring the sound, and a video guy handling the video signal from the cameras. There was also an associate director who would sit to my right and make notes, since he or she was doing most of the editing. And then there was a production associate sitting in the back, doing timings and taking down my notes to performers, particularly during a rehearsal. I would spew out note after note after note, which the poor PA would have to write down, and then between rehearsal and taping, I'd go out to the floor and the PA would have the notes, which we would then pass along to each actor. You know, "You turned just a little bit too soon." And of course, in the early days, when you had to get on the air and off the air, or even when you were trying to make the taped material meet time constraints, it was very important for the PA to keep you apprised of time. You had to be very aware of scenes speeding up, which meant the show would be short, or stretching, which meant you'd end up with too much material. Today they don't care about that; they just cut it. When it was live, obviously, timing was essential. If you didn't finish, you were finished!

It sounds like you really thrived on these limitations, which sound pretty formidable.

Yeah. Because the pressure to get it done was stimulating. You had to deal with what you had to deal with. If I had a camera go out, I'd have to work around it. That's number one. Also, when you got done, you were done. Once we started taping shows, and the shows became more expensive to produce, supervision increased. It was no longer about getting it done. It was a slog, because there were people looking over your shoulder constantly. The material became much more complicated, and there was a lot more of it. Today, it's just awful—the days can get very long, and in some ways, you're basically just a traffic manager. So, yes, I would like to have kept it to the "shoot live, do it, walk out of here and start again tomorrow" model.

You know, when I first started out, I thought, "I'd like to go to Hollywood and make a movie." After I'd directed soaps for a number of years, though, all I could think to myself was, "I could never work that slowly." I just couldn't do it. Spend four hours on one shot, screwing around? Do it, get it in the can, and let's move on. And I was happier when I was the only director.

From what I understand, that's pretty unusual for soap operas.

That's right. I was the only director for a long time on *Love of Life.* In my case, it changed pretty much when we went to color. And the reason it changed was that Roy Winsor used it as an excuse to get me a raise. He went to the sponsor and said, "This is much too complicated now with color; we can't ask Larry to do this five days a week. We're going to give him the same money and he'll do only four days a week." So that's how I got a second director—as a raise. *[laughs]*

Eventually, when CBS took over the program and we began to have more supervision, the producers felt that I should do three days a week and somebody else should do two.

How did the CBS takeover manifest itself on the set?

Well, they were present. They were looking over your shoulder; they were making suggestions. As long as you had people who had been in the business, who were competent, that could be helpful—however annoying. But when you began to get people who hadn't been in the business, who came from god-knows-where, and who thought that as long as they were there, they had to do or say something, it was terrible. I had one unpleasant so-called executive producer who had come from Hollywood and film and didn't know the first thing about "live on tape" television—it was awful.

What did they want from you and the show?

They wanted to keep their job. I always felt they wanted to be a director but didn't want to take the risk of sitting in the chair and having to actually do it. It was a lot easier to say, "Oh, that shot's no good. Take it from over there." Sometimes it was just easier to say okay rather than stand there and argue about it. They came in without having done the preparation and with this preconceived idea that they had better say something today.

But didn't American Home have suggestions in the earlier days too, or were you and the writer given pretty much free rein?

I don't think American Home ever got involved. They left it to Roy Winsor and the Biow Company, and later just to Roy when he had his own company. All they were interested in were the numbers. The head writers did do a long story outline. Later on, they did a week's outline, and then when we began to have subwriters, they would do even daily outlines. But it was basically Roy and the writers—John Hess, Don Ettlinger, or whoever—they all sat down and worked out these story arcs and then would work from that. American Home really was interested in only two things: how much it cost and what the audience was

like. They were a huge company. They were a major, major advertiser, just like Procter & Gamble. Not as big, but the same idea. And they owned the program, which doesn't happen today.

That reminds me of something else you don't see anymore: In those days, you couldn't have competing products in the same 15 minutes of advertising. Today, you know, a Chrysler ad is followed immediately by a Ford ad.

Speaking of ads, that early episode I saw seemed to run uninterrupted from start to finish. Were there were no commercial breaks when the shows were only 15 minutes long?

Actually, there were breaks for commercials. You must have seen an edited version. There were the four I mentioned earlier—two 30-second ads and two one-minute ads in each episode, and in the early days, they were done live in the studio. We had a commercial set also. Don Hancock, who was the announcer, would do a commercial for Anacin and a commercial for BiSoDol or whatever the agency scheduled. Don would hold up the product and then give his pitch. I'd have to break one of my three cameras from the drama scene to get to the commercial set, and once that was under way, I'd have to get the product "beauty shot" on a second camera, then reverse the procedure to get back to the story material.

Were any of these products ever "placed" into the actual show?

Interesting you should ask that. Not the products, but we had giveaways. You could send in a box top from Anacin with 25 cents and get, for example, a packet of seeds from Mother Dale's garden. Suddenly American Home would decide they wanted to give a premium, and the writer would have to include that in the story. One time they decided they were going to give away perfumed earrings. They were little tiny cagelike earrings that had small pieces of cotton in them, and you would put perfume on the cotton balls. For a box top and 50 cents, or whatever, viewers could get their own pair. So Meg was in jail, and her boyfriend brought her these wonderful earrings, which of course we would have to get a beautiful close-up of. As a matter of fact, I was told that even at 50 cents, American Home made money on the deal. *[laughs]* That kind of thing happened maybe twice a year.

Three different actresses played the role of Vanessa Dale in *Love of Life* over those 28 years it was on the air. I know this is a fairly common phenomenon on soaps, especially long-running ones. Was that difficult to navigate around as a director?

Like everything else in those days, you just dealt with it. When Bonnie Bartlett was unable to come to a contract agreement with Roy Winsor, we shot her going to bed on Friday, and on Monday, we shot Audrey Peters waking up in the same spot.

Speaking of actors, *Love of Life* had a pretty incredible roster of talent on the show over the years, including Warren Beatty, Roy Scheider, Christopher Reeve—

Well, Christopher, who was at Juilliard at the time, actually played a regular character on the show: Vanessa's son, Ben. Beatty and Scheider were there only for small parts.

Didn't Frances Sternhagen appear on the show also?

Oh, Franny Sternhagen, she played several different characters over the years. She's a wonderful lady, by the way.

    RIGHT: Opening credits from *Love of Life* spanning its 28 years

Was there a certain collegiality between you, the actors, and the other production people off the set?

There was a certain familial feeling in the earlier days because we were all in the pool together. I think that some of the actors befriended one another, and we would occasionally decide to have a cast-and-crew party somewhere, but we didn't really hang out together. At least I didn't—I had to go home and do my homework: There were always scripts to read, story plans to review, and camera blocking to do.

When did you do the actual camera blocking for the show?

Well, the camera blocking followed the physical blocking of the actors, and that came from working in the rehearsal hall. So the camera work was done after the physical work, when I knew where all of the actors were going to be and could see how they were interacting: "Now, what am I going to do with my cameras..." The lighting was done in the morning because we had a lot of rehearsal time in the studio. Eventually, when I was working in the hour format on a show after *Love of Life* was canceled, everything became much more complicated. The sets were bigger and more complex, and the input of the director into the design of the sets became more and more minimal. We'd walk into the preproduction meeting or the studio and would essentially be given the set, which is a bunch of shit.

So in the earlier days, you had input into the set design?

Oh, yeah. I worked with a wonderful set designer named Lloyd Evans on *Love of Life.* He also designed stuff for the New York City Opera. Lloyd and I would meet all of the time. Set design on a soap opera is important, and when you have one director and one designer, it's a very cooperative kind of venture.

As you've noted, so many things related to technology and the production process changed over the course of your career. How did the dramatic societal changes of the '60s and '70s impact *Love of Life?* The series certainly had its share of divorces, extramarital affairs, and the like.

Well, as society began to be more accepting, we were able to do a little bit more. We no longer had to do what the movies had been required to do with love scenes, for instance—you know, one foot on the floor all the time. Certainly there were things happening in society that a writer could pick up on and use.

Did you ever get a script and find its material to be problematic? Or would that have already been taken care of in the meeting with the producer?

That would have been taken care of before it got to me.

Did you ever get a script to shoot and find it inappropriate, or at least not credible in some way?

I was never particularly concerned about appropriateness. I got plenty of scripts that I didn't like. *[laughs]* I was more concerned about whether I could swallow what the script was about. I mean, these people were writing 260 shows a year! You ask a guy to sit down and knock out 260 of these a year and it's not going to be Shakespeare.

It must be pretty draining, though, to have to work with material you don't like—I would imagine it would be tough for the actors as well.

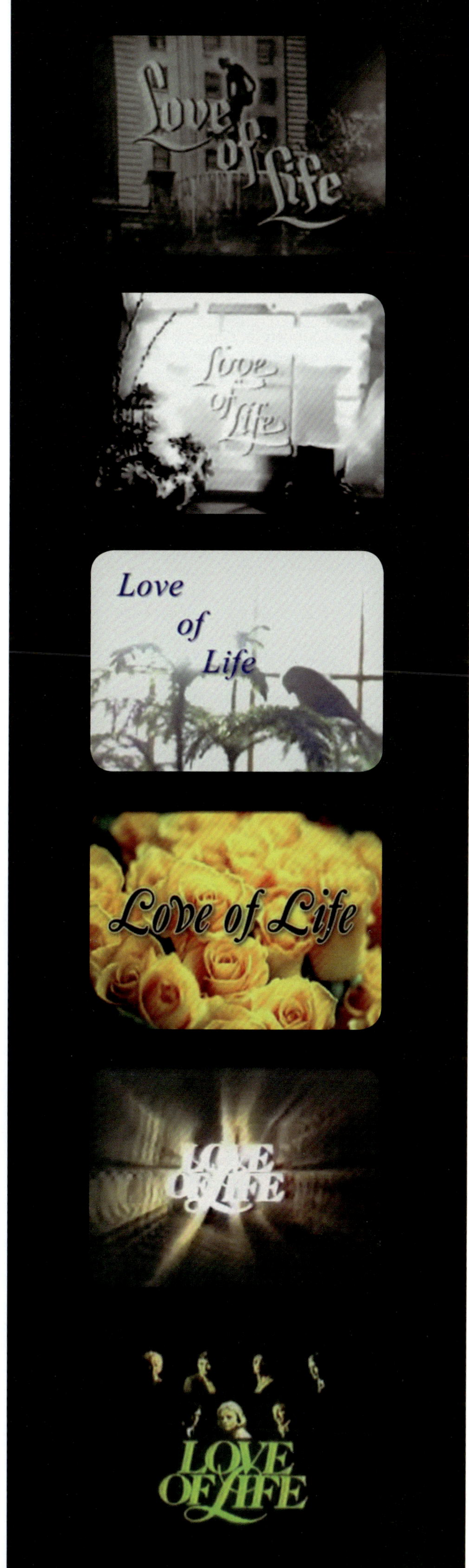

You know, you signed a piece of paper and you said you were going to do your job, so you just try to do it as best you can. Make it better if you can. I mean, you bitch and complain, but you get up and go in and get it done. It was a lot of material. You know, when the shows went to an hour, you would be shooting 70-, 80-, even 90-page scripts in a single day.

Did actors memorize lines, or were teleprompters used?

We didn't use them at first, and then eventually we got them. The first ones held rolls of paper, and every once in a while, the roll of teleprompter paper tore and you would be able to hear this ripping sound off-camera. Then at some point we got video teleprompters. On *One Life to Live,* the producer Paul Rauch eventually dispensed with the teleprompters because you would too often catch the actors looking at them. There was one guy who did this constantly—he also happened to be a rotten son of a bitch. He'd be in a scene with another actor who would be having this intense moment of communication with him, and he wouldn't even be making eye contact—he'd be looking for his line on the teleprompter. So Paul, who was a difficult producer but a very good producer, dispensed with them, and the actors had to learn their lines. I don't know if they're used now or not.

You know, the more I hear, the more it strikes me that the whole soap-opera genre is some kind of test of human endurance. Writing this enormous volume of new material, memorizing and performing it, shooting it, etc., day after day after day. There seems to be nothing else like it in the entertainment industry.

It's very difficult. But I think it's worst for writers. I don't know how they last, to tell you the truth. And as a matter of fact, they don't. Writers migrate from one soap to the other more than directors and performers—except maybe for the day players.

Soap-opera fans can be pretty passionate about their shows; did you ever run into any of this while you were directing?

No, I didn't get any of that. I would get reports back from the actors, who would be accosted on the street—*accosted* being the proper word in a couple of instances. Bonnie Bedelia was on *Love of Life* for a long time, and I'm pretty certain it was she who told me about a fan coming up to her at a bus stop and slapping her in the face because her character had been ugly to Vanessa on the show. So, yeah, fans got really involved—they considered the performer's character to be the real person.

Why do you think *Love of Life* was canceled in 1980? You have said before that you suspected CBS's decision to move it to a four p.m. time slot in the late '70s was one important factor.

I think that had something to do with it. I also think the last writer CBS chose, who had failed on other shows beforehand, had something to do with it. And I got the sense that CBS—I mean, this is only a guess, as I wasn't privy to this stuff—wanted the time slot back.

The final episode closes with a shot of you walking through the sets of the show on an otherwise empty soundstage, turning off the lights as you leave the studio. In the background, we hear Tony Bennett's "We'll Be Together Again." It's a nice moment.

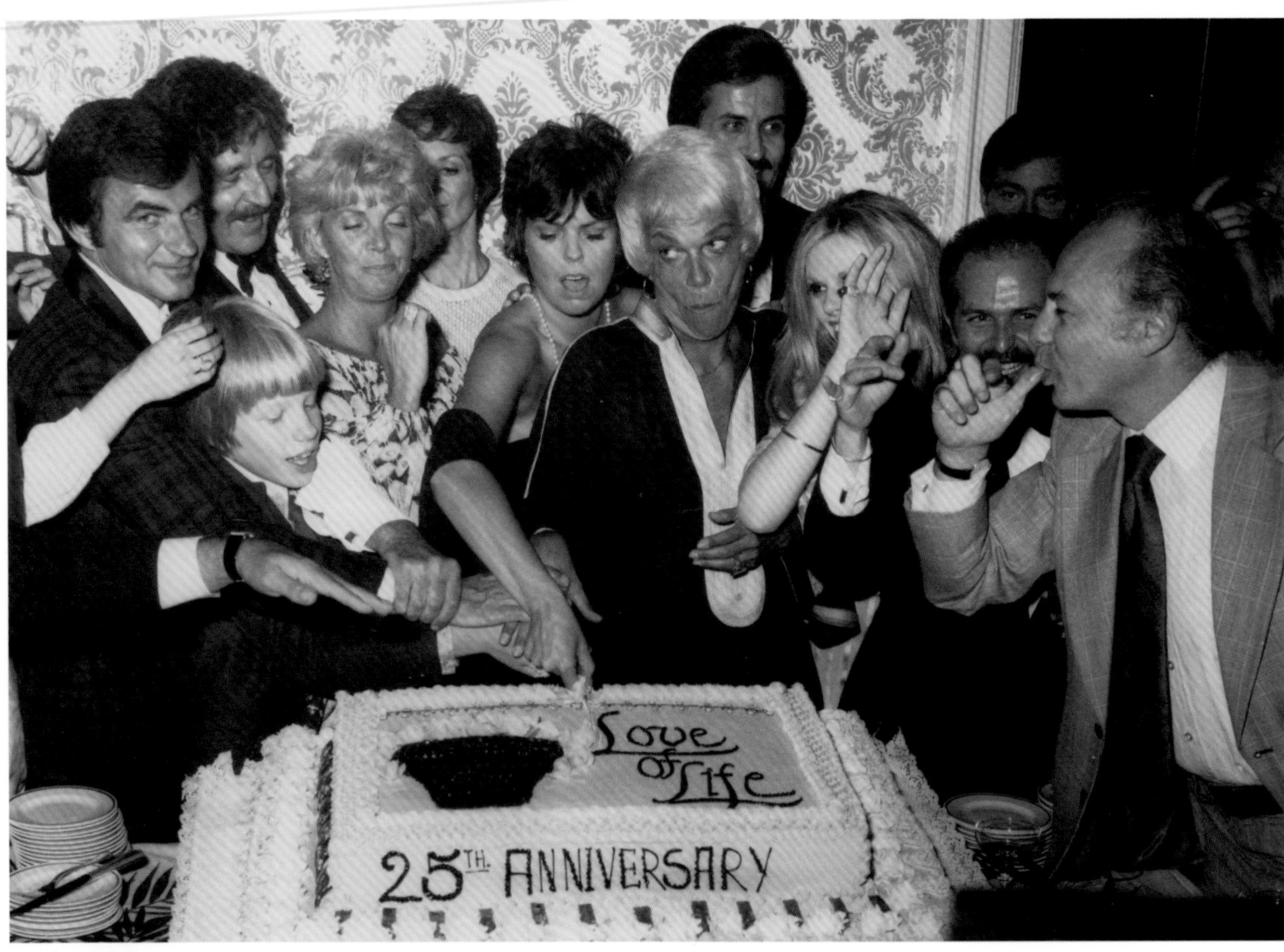

   ABOVE: Members of the cast of *Love of Life* (with Auerbach at far right) celebrate the 25th anniversary of the show.

Somebody else may claim authorship for that last scene, but I'm pretty sure it was my idea to walk through and turn the lights out at the door.

It serves as a reminder that soap directors don't normally play a very visible role, making the genre not the best home for the auteur theory. As you mentioned, there are usually several directors working on any given show, and of course it's important to keep a certain sameness to the presentation of the material. That said, do you think there is any way to distinguish your work from that of other directors on the soaps you've worked on?

I don't think so—especially today, when everything is so edited. If you managed to look at the tapes and you knew who directed that day, you might be able to discern something once in a while. You might notice, for instance, that there are a lot more close-ups in one episode than another.

Were close-ups something you were partial to as a director?

I had a theory about close-ups, particularly in the early days. You know, we were working for very small screens. If you go to the theater and sit in the back, and there are three people on a dramatically lit stage with some furniture, your mind is able to somehow create the proper size relationship with the performers. But if you're looking at an actor on a small screen in your living room, your eye is also unconsciously aware of the furniture and other objects in the room, and it diminishes the size and impact of the person on the screen. If I want to grab the attention of the viewer, I need to make sure the characters are large enough to be noticed. So in those earlier days, when we were restricted to those small screens, I wanted the close-up. The wide shot, the two shot, were less important. Today, when the screens are so much larger, it's different.

But I don't think you could look at a show and say, "Oh, that's a Larry Auerbach show, or that's a Gary Donatelli show." Particularly now, when nobody does a complete episode anymore. On any given day, one director will do some scenes for a particular show, and the next day, another director will do another group. It's a mishmash. In order to save money, they'll fill the studio with sets—say, on a Monday—and shoot all the scenes that are supposed to take place in those sets in the next week or so. Then they'll strike those sets, put up others, and shoot all the scenes taking place in those on Tuesday. So there could be four different directors' work in one particular episode.

I don't know how it is today, but I was always careful to read all of the scripts, which in itself took a lot of time. And I would talk to a director from whom I was going to pick up a scene to find out where he was leaving the actors and where I was going to pick them up. And then I would call whoever was going to take over that scene from me to give them the same information, so he or she could continue with minimal interruption.

My guess would be that soap-opera actors are probably great with continuity issues, since they've inhabited their characters for such a long time and at such a consistent pace.

Absolutely. That's a big help. Somebody like Susan Lucci from *All My Children,* she knows the character of Erica Kane better than any writer or any director around. She's been doing it longer than anybody. Although with some actors, that can be a hindrance too. An actor who is stubborn might say, "But my character would never do that!" That's shit—the character does what the writer wants him to do.

After *Love of Life* ended, didn't you go almost immediately to *All My Children*?

That's right. I worked there with a wonderful producer named Jørn Winther—he was a guy who really knew how to produce a soap opera, and he was a good director. After *All My Children* I went to *One Life to Live,* and when I had a chance to renew my contract, I intentionally declined to do so, because I didn't like the way I was being treated. I also worked as a fill-in for *Another World* and *As the World Turns.*

And you never wanted to pursue other kinds of directing?

Sure! *[laughs]* I thought about it. As I said, I eventually decided shooting a movie would just be too goddamn boring. And I don't know too many directors who've made that leap. Peter Levin, who directed soap operas here in New York, went to L.A. and had some success doing episodic television, but it's a rarity. Part of it, of course, is that soap operas always have a stigma.

Why do you think that is?

Well, because the material doesn't reach great heights. There has always been a feeling that soaps aren't worth paying very much attention to. You know, people think if you're grinding something out every day, it can't be worth that much. So soap-opera people have always been looked down upon—not actors so much, but writers and directors. But I defy anybody who has shot a movie to come in and try to do a one-hour soap opera in one day in a studio. To deal with that many pages, to deal with the sets—to get it all done in eight hours.

In the past couple of years, several of the surviving long-running soaps—*Guiding Light, As the World Turns*—have gone off the air, and the feeling is that more—and perhaps all—will follow. Why do you think the genre appears to be on its last legs?

It's several things. Economics. Audience. And, of course, technology. Life has changed. First of all, the number of women at home during the day has decreased precipitously. And instead of being able to get only three networks, now you get 103, so the availability of material for the eyeballs to rest on is so much greater. I used to go to a cleaners in Mamaroneck, and the woman who ran the counter there told me she had two VCRs going all the time at her house during the day. Over the weekend, she would watch all of her soaps. Today, nobody cares that much. People don't need a relatively simple story when they can rent or buy a DVD anytime, or for that matter, just go on the Internet. Also, it's expensive to produce these: It's no longer about simple sets with a little wainscoting and a piece of black velour. There are location shoots, stunts. It's gotten to be like making a movie every day.

In the '50s and '60s, we had something like 16 soap operas shooting in New York; now we've got one left: *One Life to Live.* How long that will be around, I don't know.

Your last gig in soap operas was in 1995. Do you miss it?

Well, I'll sometimes occasionally dream about being in the control room and not being able to get on the air. *[laughs]* But no, I don't miss being in that world, particularly as it is today. I'll tell you what I really miss: I miss being back in radio. I wasn't there very long, but I loved it. You had to get in there and you had to do it. If there was a problem, fix it right now, because there is no tomorrow. Just like live TV: Have a real rehearsal, get in the control room, do it, and move on. That I miss.

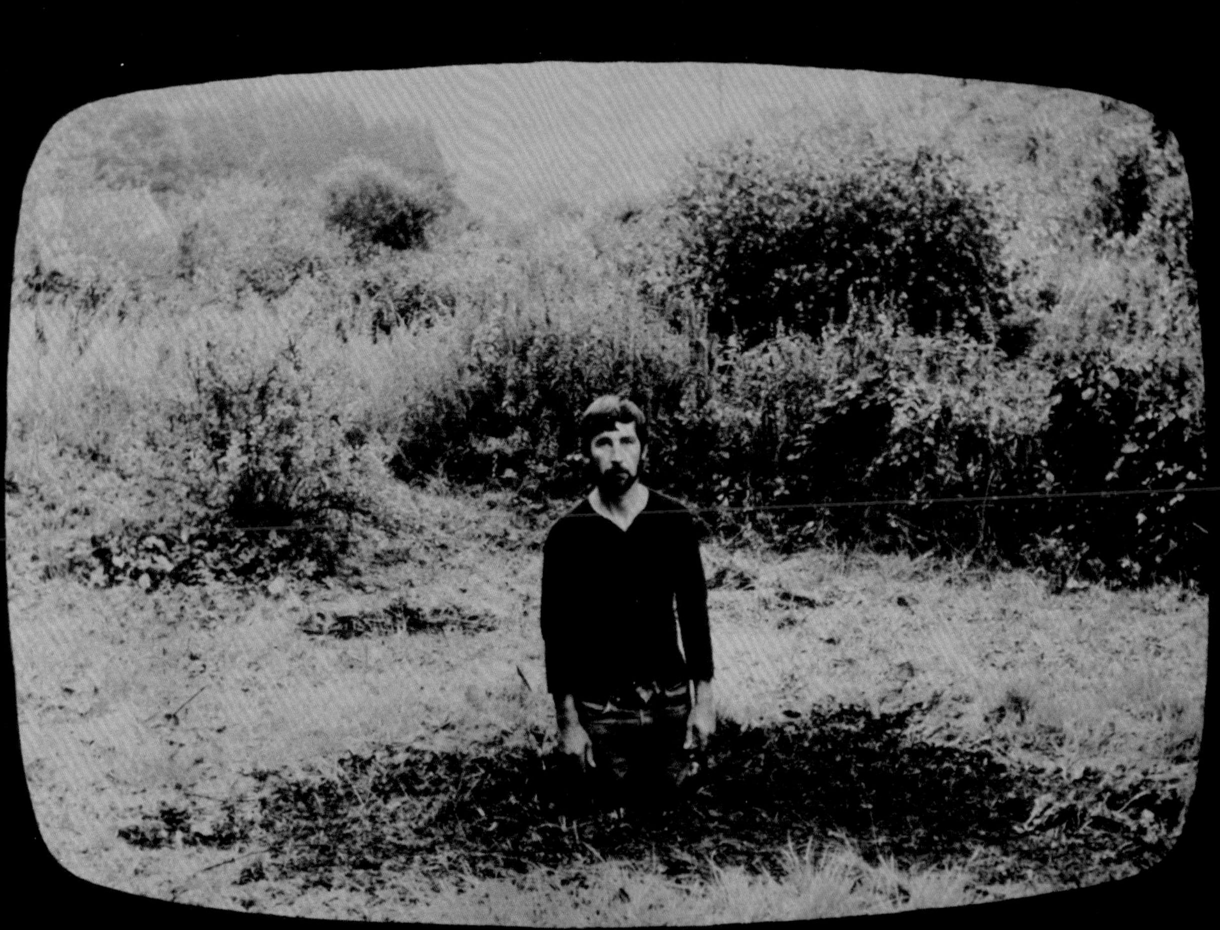

The End of the *World* as We Know It

By Jean Passanante

I was gripping my pinot gris, elbowing my way to the little crab cakes, when a squarely built woman with helmet hair and downturned mouth planted herself in my path.

"Is Ellen coming back for Nancy's memorial service?" Her tone was accusatory, and slightly threatening. But there was no way around it. I had to break the bad news. No, Ellen wasn't slated to attend Nancy's memorial.

The woman (I'm calling her Marge) was offended. "Why not? She'd definitely want to be there. And anyway, she lives in Oakdale."

Well, no, Marge. Ellen doesn't live in Oakdale. Ellen doesn't live anywhere. Ellen is not a real person. And Oakdale isn't a real place. Oakdale, Illinois, exists only in the fictional geography of the daytime-TV serial drama *As the World Turns*, whose extraordinary life ended in September of 2010 after a 54-year run.

In fact, the character called Ellen had been written off the show many years before. But it's possible that the sixtyish Marge, who had paid good money to attend this tribute to *As the World Turns* at the Paley Center for Media Studies, had spent more time in the company of Ellen and the other characters on *As the World Turns* than with members of her own family. For years Marge lived through Ellen's tortured adolescence, witnessed her marital disasters, and celebrated her eventual success in love. For all I know, Marge's friendship with Ellen was the most enduring personal relationship in Marge's life. So just try telling Marge that Ellen isn't real.

When I started writing for *As the World Turns*, the show was already more than 40 years old. Many of the characters still on the air had been created decades earlier. Before I started work, I received what is reproduced in excerpted form on the following pages: a binder full of information about all the characters, including each one's blood type, allergies, marriages, e-mail address, phone number, favorite foods, and cherished personal mementos, as well as a list of their friends, lovers, and enemies. It was daunting to write for a show with so much history, so lovingly preserved.

The first episode of *ATWT* aired live on Monday, April 2, 1956. It was penned by the formidable Irna Phillips, principal architect of television soap operas, a genre that would captivate its largely female audience and dominate the daytime airwaves for the better part of the 20th century.

Episode one introduces the Hughes family: Nancy and Chris, the parents; Penny and Don, the older teens; and Bobby, the youngest child. The central conflicts are efficiently and immediately introduced, providing the springboard for years of story.

Nineteen-year-old Don, we learn, is dating Janice, who at 20 is considered an older woman. Scandal will ensue. Penny, at 16, is disgruntled and rebellious. She plays her *Zambesi* record over and over again on the Victrola, and she deliberately musses her hair, presumably to annoy Nancy, her mother. Things are tense between Penny and Nancy. An elder sister, Susan, has recently died. Penny is haunted by a memory of a grief-stricken Nancy wailing, "Why did it have to be Susan?" thus signaling Penny's belief that her mother preferred Susan and will never love Penny as much.

Later, we meet the aforementioned Ellen, Penny's best friend. Ellen's parents are separated, a source of confusion and shame for Ellen. More scandal will ensue. Still another story thread is introduced in which tightly wound housewife Nancy and her mellower lawyer husband Chris hope to persuade Chris's farmer father to sell his property and move to Oakdale.

Bopping genially through the episode is the baby of the family, Bobby Hughes, who is apparently too young to have problems of his own. His function in episode one is comic relief, including the dispensing of insult humor to his older siblings, such as, "Aw, dry up."

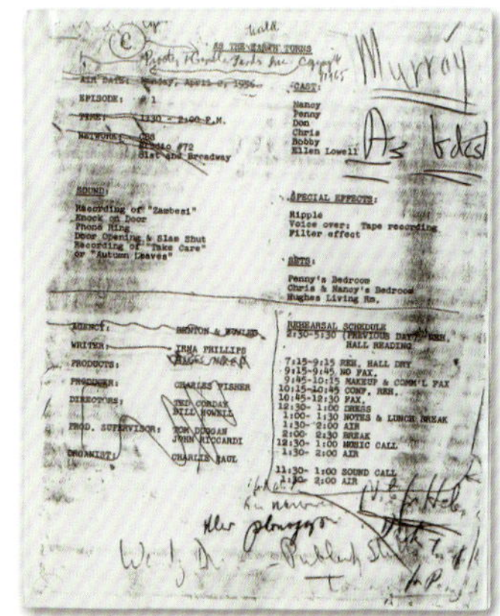

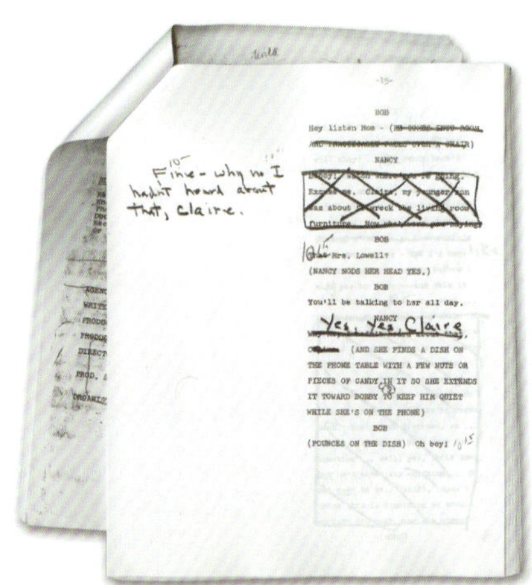

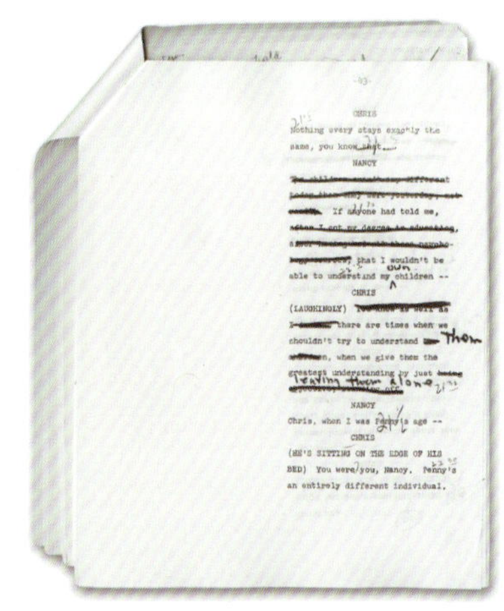

73

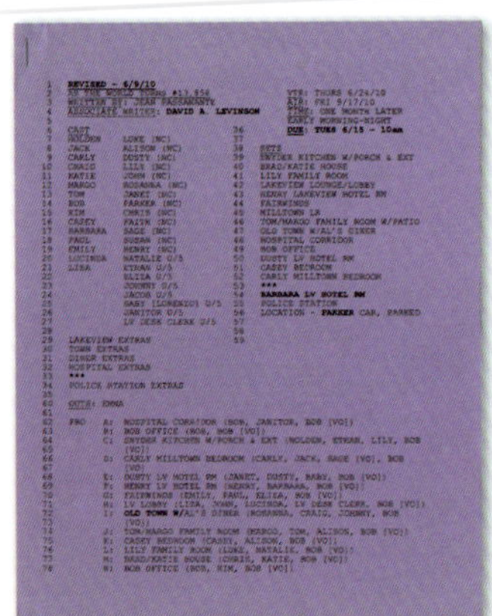

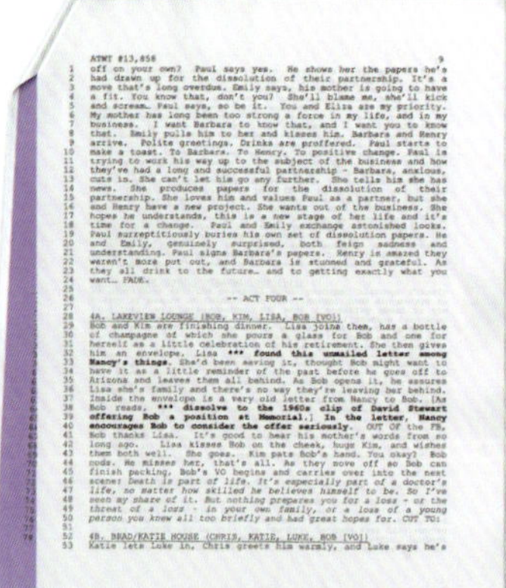

Fast-forward 54 years. I was co–head writer of *As the World Turns* on the gray day when the cast, crew, and staff gathered on the studio floor as executive producer Christopher Goutman broke the news that the show was canceled. Viewership had eroded (as it had with all the soaps), budgets had been slashed, and, after the cancellation of *Guiding Light* the previous year, we knew the end could come. CBS seemed less and less interested in staying in the soap-opera business, and Procter & Gamble, which owned the show, seemed powerless to do anything about it. But at the studio, we were shocked nonetheless. Episode 13,858 would be the last episode and the final chapter in the story, and I would have to find a way to sum up 54 years.

The one thing I knew was that the end of the show had to honor its beginnings. Sadly, Helen Wagner, who played Nancy Hughes and spoke the first words of the show back in 1956, had unexpectedly died only a few weeks before the last episodes were taped. Happily, little Bobby Hughes had grown up on the show and evolved into a "tent-pole" character. Dr. Bob Hughes was now a physician and chief of staff at Memorial Hospital; he was a trusted friend, adviser, husband, father, grandfather, uncle, ex-husband, son, etc. Though not a perfect person (thankfully—perfection is death to drama), Bob was in some ways the moral center of the show, and my partner Lucky Gold and I decided that Bob would frame the show's conclusion.

One actor—Don Hastings—played Bob Hughes for the last 50 years. I have vague memories of my two immigrant grandmothers in the 1960s, honing their English language skills watching Bob's romantic tribulations with Lisa, his restless, narcissistic vixen of a first wife. I couldn't have been less interested in the marital foibles of grown-ups at the time, but my reaction was not typical. The romance of Bob and Lisa, with Lisa being played by Eileen Fulton up until the last episode, was a ratings juggernaut.

By the time episode 13,858 rolls around, Bob has been married at least five times. Kim, the love of his life, has been his wife for 25 years, or approximately two-and-a-half times longer than the typical American real-life marriage. They have a son, Chris, a pediatrician. (Chris was born on the show about 24 years ago, but he appears to be at least 30. This mystery is explained by a fan-invented phenomenon known as SORAS: Soap Opera Rapid Aging Syndrome.) Bob has had some health problems, and Kim would like him to think about retiring.

Bob's retirement became the metaphor for the end of the show and Thornton Wilder's *Our Town* its inspiration. A reflective, omniscient Bob takes a final stroll through the hospital before moving out and moving away. Like the stage manager in Grover's Corners, Bob conjures and describes Oakdale and its citizens in their extraordinary ordinariness. Just as Bob has borne witness to so many births, courtships, marriages, and deaths among the show's populace, so has the audience. Now, for Bob and for the audience, it's time to let go.

As the World Turns' remarkable longevity is part of what defined it. In fractured and frantic times, those who watched and loved the show since its early days found continuity and community that was perhaps absent in their so-called real life.

The marathon demands of serial storytelling (and the limitations imposed by network executives, actor vacations, firings, pregnancies, etc.) are such that inevitably, stories are repetitive, elongated, absurd, and occasionally just plain bad. At other times the stories can be vital, relevant, exhilarating, and even transcendent. The serial storyteller has a unique opportunity to show the consequences of characters' actions from multiple points of view over an extended period of time. It's no wonder the viewers embrace the characters with unusual fervor and make them part of the fabric of their own life.

I'm proud to have played a small role in the show's long history. It's hard to imagine how any audience will ever again spend so much time in the company of a group of television characters, or get to know those characters so intimately, as have the fans of *As the World Turns*. The loss of the show will leave a deficit in the lives of many. But as it happens—magically—in the final image of the series, the world will keep turning all the same.

ABOVE: (top) Page one of the script for episode 13,858; (bottom) cover and interior page of the revised breakdown

ATWT CONTINUITY

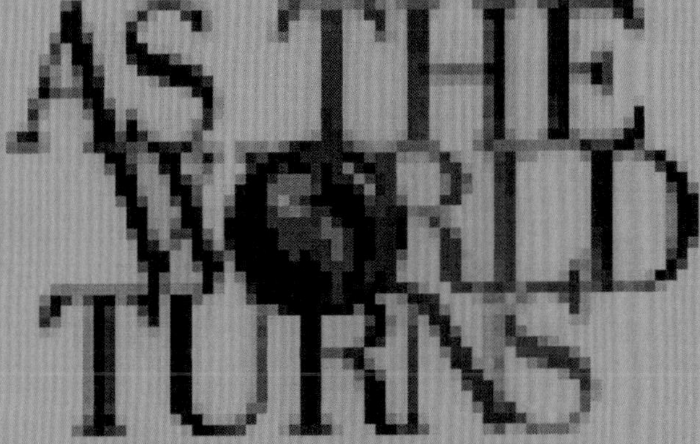

CONTINUITY BINDER

UPDATED 11/25/02

CONTINUITY DETAILS – BRIEF VERSION

Parents/Children: (**bold** current characters, *italic* recurring-only characters)
(NOTE: Women's last names are <u>current</u> as they are most commonly thought of, <u>not</u> necessarily what their legal name is or was when child was born)

Molly Conlan & **Holden Snyder**/Abigail Williams (adoptive parents: Diana & Mitchell Williams)

Lyla Montgomery & Bart Montgomery/**Craig Montgomery** & Cricket Montgomery

Lyla Montgomery & Casey Peretti/**Katie Peretti Frasier**

John Dixon & *Lyla Montgomery*/ **Margo Hughes**

John Dixon & Rosemary Kramer/ Ian 'Duke' Kramer

John Dixon & **Kim Hughes**/Andrew Dixon

John Dixon & *Iva Snyder*/Matthew John (MJ) Dixon

John Dixon & **Barbara Ryan**/Johnny (John, Jr.) Dixon (deceased)

Lily Snyder & **Holden Snyder**/*Faith Snyder* (a.k.a. Melinda Hamilton after switched at birth) & Natalie

Lily Snyder & *Damian Grimaldi*/**Luciano Eduardo 'Luke' ~~Grimaldi~~ Snyder**

Lisa Grimaldi & **Bob Hughes**/**Tom Hughes**

Lisa Grimaldi & John Eldridge/Scott Eldridge

Lisa Grimaldi & Michael Shea/Chuckie Shea (deceased as child)

Kim Hughes & **Bob Hughes**/**Christopher Hughes** & Sabrina Fullerton Hughes

Margo Hughes & **Hal Munson**/Adam (Hughes) Munson

Margo Hughes & **Tom Hughes**/*Casey Hughes*

Bob Hughes & Jennifer Hughes/Frannie Hughes (see above for others)

Tom Hughes & Vietnamese lady/ Lien Hughes (see above for others)

Hal Munson & Lynda Graves/Nikki Munson

Hal Munson & **Barbara Ryan**/**Will Munson**

Hal Munson & **Carly Tenney**/**Parker Joe Munson** (originally thought **John Dixon** real father)

Nancy Hughes & Chris Hughes/Donald, Penny, **Bob Hughes**, Susan (deceased)

Barbara Ryan & *James Stenbeck*/**Paul Ryan** (see above/below for others)

Barbara Ryan & Darryl Crawford/Jennifer Munson (see above for others)

Emma Snyder & Harvey Snyder/*Iva* (adopted from Jared Carpenter), *Seth*, Ellie, *Caleb*, **Holden**, and Meg Snyder

Iva Snyder & Josh Snyder (aka Rod Landry)/**Lily Snyder; Rose D'Angelo (identical twins)**

Holden Snyder & Julie Wendall Snyder/**Aaron Snyder** (see above for others)

Dolores Snyder (Pierce) & Burt Snyder/**Jack Snyder**

Emily Stewart & **Tom Hughes**/*Daniel Stewart Hughes*

Susan Stewart & Larry McDermott/**Alison** (McDermott) **Stewart** (using Emily's donated egg)

Susan Stewart & Dan Stewart/**Emily Stewart**

Carly Tenney & **Mike Kasnoff**/Nora Kasnoff (died during premature labor)

Lucinda Walsh & Jacobo Esteban/*Sierra Esteban Reyes Montgomery*

Lucinda Walsh/**Lily Snyder** (adopted, disaffirmed, reconciled); Bianca Marques (adopted)

Craig Montgomery & *Sierra Esteban Reyes Montgomery*/Bryant Montgomery (deceased) & **Lucinda Marie (Lucy) Montgomery**

Joe D'Angelo & Anna Marie Romano D'Angelo/**Rose D'Angelo** (adopted)

Jake McKinnon & Vicky McKinnon/Bridget & Michele McKinnon (twins)

Mr. & Mrs. Roger Frasier/**Simon Frasier; Celia Frasier** (presumed dead)

Jessica Griffin & *Duncan McKechnie*/**Bonnie McKechnie**

Cricket Montgomery & Cody Sullivan/Billy Ross

<u>CONTINUITY DETAILS – BRIEF VERSION</u>

<u>Current Spouse/Previous Spouses, how marriage(s) ended:</u>

Dr. John Dixon: none/Carly Tenney (divorced); Barbara Ryan (divorced); Karen Haines Stenbeck (divorce?); Ariel Aldrin (divorce?); Dee Stewart (divorced); Kim Reynolds (divorced)

Lily Snyder: Holden Snyder/Diego Santana (shot/killed at wedding); Damian Grimaldi (presumed dead in plane crash/went off to monastery); Holden Snyder (divorced); Derek Mason (killed in exploding cottage he set up for her)

Katie Peretti Frasier: Simon Frasier/none

Margo Hughes: Tom Hughes (separated – renewed vows)/none

Lisa Grimaldi: none/ Martin Chedwyn (arrested, not truly valid marriage – though technically never referred to as annulled); Eduardo Grimaldi (killed by Orlena Grimaldi); Earl Mitchell (killed in line of duty for Interpol); Whit McColl (murdered); Grant Colman (divorced); Michael Shea (murdered); John Eldridge (divorced, now dead); Bob Hughes (divorced)

Bob Hughes: Kim Hughes/Miranda Marlowe (divorced); Jennifer Ryan (killed in accident); Sandy McGuire (divorced); Lisa Miller (divorced)

Kim Hughes: Bob Hughes/ Nick Andropoulos (died); Dan Stewart (died); John Dixon (divorced); Jason Reynolds (died)

Hal Munson: **Emily Stewart**/Barbara Ryan (divorced);Carly Tenney (divorced); Barbara Ryan (divorced); Barbara Ryan (divorced); Lynda Graves (divorced)

Holden Snyder: Lily Snyder/Lily Snyder (divorced); Angel Lange (divorced); Emily Stewart (divorced)

Tom Hughes: Margo Hughes (separated – renewed vows)/Carol Deming (divorced); Natalie Bannon (divorced)

Lucinda Walsh: none/James Stenbeck (divorced); John Dixon (divorced); James Walsh (died); Martin Guest (suicide); Jacobo Esteban (divorced; now dead)

Emily Stewart: **Hal Munson**/Holden Snyder (divorced)

Jack Snyder: none/Julia Lindsey (divorced)

Ben Harris: none/Denise Maynard Dixon (illegitimately via Rev. Horner)

Isaac Jenkins: none/none

Molly Conlan: **none**/Jake McKinnon **(killed)**

Nancy Hughes: none/Dan 'Mac' McClosky (died – Alzheimer's); Chris Hughes Sr. (died)

Carly Tenney: Jack Snyder/Winston Lowe (while married to Brad, John; now deceased); Brad Snyder (divorced); John Dixon (divorced); Hal Munson (divorced)

Barbara Ryan: none/Craig Montgomery (divorced); Hal Munson (divorced); John Dixon (divorced); Hal Munson (divorced); Hal Munson (divorced); Gunnar St. Clair (Stenbeck) (presumed dead); James Stenbeck (divorced)

Susan Stewart: none/Larry McDermott (divorced); Dr. Bruce Baxter (annulled); Dan Stewart (divorced)

Jessica Griffin: none/Duncan McKechnie (marriage annulled – Shannon returned alive)

Emma Snyder: none/Harvey Snyder (died)

Simon Frasier: Katie Peretti/Conchetta Maria Concepcion; Monique Ferrara; Eleanor; Ilsa

Craig Montgomery: none/Barbara Ryan (divorced); Sierra Esteban Reyes (divorced); Betsy Andropoulos (divorced)

Bonnie McKechnie: none/none

Lucy Montgomery: none/none

Aaron Snyder: none/none

Alison Stewart: none/none

Rosanna Cabot: none/none

Mike Kasnoff: none/none

Chris Hughes: none/none

CONTINUITY DETAILS – BRIEF VERSION

Last-known location/disposition of previous characters:

Edith Hughes: (Bob's aunt) Married Dr. George Frey and moved to Seattle. (within 1956-1960)

Penny Hughes moved to England and married Anton Cunningham (within 1971-1975). She was seen for Nancy's 80th birthday party.

Pa Hughes: Married Irma Kopecki and left town. (1975)

Joyce Colman: "returned from the dead," confessed to shooting Don, no charges were pressed. (1980)

Grant Colman: Decided to not remarry Joyce. He moved to San Francisco. (1981)

Don Hughes: Left town to marry and join Mary Ellison in Laramie. (1981)

Brad Hollister made love with Dee Stewart, but she turned on him (given his greed and deception about the silver mine). He left town. (1981)

Dee Stewart: Left for a job with Flair magazine in NYC. (1983)

Cricket Montgomery and Ernie Ross married. They moved to California with their newborn daughter (Suzie) and Cricket's son, Billy. (1983)

Miranda Marlowe: Swept off to Paris by her old flame, Antoine Bisset, away from husband Bob Hughes. He got divorce from her on grounds of desertion. (1983)

Karen Dixon: Left Oakdale, leaving Dusty with John. (1984)

Jeff Ward: Offered a job at a hospital out of town. He, Annie Stewart, and their quadruplets (Nancy, Maria, Lowell, & Gregory) left town. (1984)

Diana (McColl): In Witness Protection Program (re: gambling syndicate operated on her yacht). (1985)

Gunnar St. Clair: Supposedly killed when his balloon crashed in the Australian outback. (1985)

Kirk McColl: Moved to NYC to pursue journalism. (1985)

Lord Stewart Markham Cushing: Married Marcy Thompson and moved to England. (1985)

Denise Darcy: (former Simply Barbara model) In jail for murdering Tad Channing. (1986)

Marsha Talbot: In jail for killing Douglas Cummings. (1986)

Steve Andropoulos: Left Betsy and Dani to start over in Greece when his business faltered. He is currently in prison for life on drug trafficking charges. (1986)

Dr. Rick Ryan: Fled to the Caribbean after the truth came out re: Sabrina Fullerton Hughes. (1987)

Dusty Donovan: Hired by Lucinda to work for Walsh Enterprises and sent off to London office. (1988)

Meg and Josh Snyder: Moved to Waco, TX. (1989)

Duke Kramer: Joined Lien out at Rutgers, he was going to attend medical school, in the wake of Casey Peretti's death. He and Lien have since broken up. It is currently unclear where he is now, though the current thought is that he went back to his boxing days, and stayed in N.J. (1991)

Gavin Kruger: In jail for the murders of Carolyn Crawford, Frank Wendall, Philippe and Nicole. (1992)

Frannie Hughes: Joined Sabrina at her clinic in Montega after learning that Jennifer was Barbara and Darryl Crawford's daughter via an affair. (1992)

Darryl Crawford: Returned to Des Moines with his daughter, Carolyn Dana. (1992)

Marcy Breen: Left town, pregnant with Linc Lafferty's child. (1992)

Ellie Snyder: Took a job with Meridian in NYC (after Kirk divorced her over her abortion). (1992) Last seen in 1994, canceling on Julie and Caleb's wedding, since company sending her to Zurich.

Lyla Montgomery Peretti: Left Oakdale on a singing tour. (1993) Living in California now, she broke her hip and was incapacitated in Spring 2000. Visited briefly for Xmas 2000 to convince Katie to end marriage to Simon.

Iva Snyder: Moved to Washington, D.C. with her new husband, Jason Benedict, and her son M.J. (1993) Has visited Oakdale at various times from 1998-2001.

Seth Snyder and Angel Lange Snyder: Moved to NYC and Seth pursued a writing career. (1993) Back in 1994 for Caleb/Julie's wedding. Seth returned in 2001 for Holden and Luke's memorial service.

Royce Keller: Had his alternate personalities Roger and Dooley fused into his. He jilted Emily at the altar and left for Singapore on an architecture project. (1994)

Courtney Dixon: Divorced Andy Dixon and rejoined her brother, Sean Baxter, in Switzerland. (1994)

Revised 11/25/2002

<h1 style="text-align:center"><u>CONTINUITY DETAILS – BRIEF VERSION</u></h1>

<u>Blood Types:</u>

A+: Rose D'Angelo, Lily Snyder, Holden Snyder, *POSSIBLY Faith Snyder*
A-: Andy Dixon, Luke Grimaldi (Snyder), Damian Grimaldi
B+: **Julia Lindsey**
B-:
O+: *POSSIBLY Faith Snyder, NOT Chris Hughes, NOT Craig Montgomery, NOT Lucy Montgomery, NOT Margo Hughes*
O-: Jack Snyder, Pilar Domingo, *NOT Chris Hughes, NOT Lucy Montgomery, NOT Margo Hughes*
AB+: Lucinda Walsh, John Dixon, Sierra Esteban Montgomery, Duke Kramer, Dahlia Ventura
AB-: Hope (Snyder) Maynard (Dixon), Kim Hughes, Denise Maynard Dixon

Prosecutors: **Acting D.A. Evelyn Hart (After Marshall stepped down**/first seen for Molly's murder case)
Roger Carter (in Gary Rady's case)
Carol Leslie (on Emily's murder trial)

Judges: Mark Chen (Abigail's murder trial of Nick Scudder)
Judge Charlie Clark (issued warrant for Fairwinds after Jessica pressured him)
Judge Blanchette (issued order to let Molly wear wire to Nick's night of murder)
Judge Morris (Barbara/Craig's arbitration re: WorldWide stock bought w/ BRO funds)
Randall Franklin (Craig's attempted murder trial)
Marc Horowitz (Ben's adoption of Curtis Thompson)
Karen Swenson (Simon's case re: crashing through Lucinda's foyer)
Andrews (granted Tom joint custody of Daniel with Emily)
Covelli (judge that Tom sought to get injunction against WOAK's stalking PSA)
Hathaway (John's suit re: gross negligence against Denise to get custody of Hope)
Rydell (<u>Peoria</u> judge, decided case to return Hope to Denise from foster care system)
Arthur Terell (<u>Peoria</u> judge, friend of John Dixon's. Arthur's wife: Edith)
Madeline Rosen (in Carly/John custody hearing re: Parker)
Arlen Jessup (on Gary Rady's case, Ben's racism trial vs. Oakdale PD)
Henry Shaw (Lily's murder trial; Molly's hearing; friend of Lucinda's)
James Blanchard (Margo's murder trial)
Strongwater (Carroll Cty. judge, presided over Katie/Simon wedding; Tom knows)

Other lawyers: T. Marshall Travers (Barbara's lawyer re: Carly/Emily/Rose kidnapping case; **D.A. after Jessica, falsely prosecuted Paul Ryan; stepped down after exposed as working for Stenbeck)**
Sheridan Blake (James' lawyer)
Corinne Lee (Assistant District Attorney)
Jay Inwald (Legal Aid lawyer for Leo Thompson)
Cass Winthrop (Craig's catch-all, Carly's custody, and Jack's divorce lawyer)
Noah Beachman (Chicago lawyer, expert in grandparents' rights, hired by John re: Hope)
Arthur (Gary Rady's defense counsel)
Bryan Parsons (Carly's custody case lawyer)
Greg Lauritz (Lily/Holden's lawyer re: Hope)
Harry Moss (Rose's public defender)
Rick Hamlin (Barbara's divorce lawyer in 2nd divorce from Hal)
Jessica Griffin (John's custody case lawyer, Denise's consulting lawyer re: Hope, Lily/Holden's customary lawyer, appointed D.A.)
Fred Greer (sleazy lawyer, last known client was Tonio Reyes)
Tom Hughes (owner of Hughes & Hughes; Lucinda's, Lily and Holden's lawyer)

CHARACTER DESCRIPTIONS/COMPANY CONTINUITY DETAILS

NOTE: All entries in **bold** are revisions/additions/deletions. Compare to previous version.

Characters:

Character:	Rosanna Cabot
E-mail address:	**Rosanna@CabotMotors.com**
Nicknames called:	Rosebud (by Carly Tenney), **Cabot (by Craig Montgomery)**
Date of birth:	
Address:	**Fairwinds, 100 Stone Ridge Road, Oakdale, IL 60324** c/o Lakeview Towers, 1440 Lakeview Road, **Suite 1214,** Oakdale, IL 60324 **also has an apartment in NYC, a condo on St. Bart's**
Telephone number:	**555-3963**
Parents: Mother:	Sheila Washburne Cabot (deceased)
Father:	Alexander Cabot (deceased)
Siblings:	Carly Tenney (½-sister, Sheila mother) Peter Cabot Lauren Cabot
Siblings living in Oakdale:	Carly Tenney
Relationships:	**Craig Montgomery (engaged)** Scott Eldridge Mike Kasnoff (engaged, she broke it off upon learning he slept with Carly) Evan Walsh Hutch Hutchinson
Career:	Heiress (inherited $600 million from Alexander Cabot (of Cabot Motors)) Sits on Board of Directors at the Wentworth Academy for Girls, located in WI
Companies Owned/run:	Cabot Motors **Monte Carlo (formally BRO)**
Special Talents:	**Brown Belt in Jujitsu.**
Servants (personal/professional):	Staff of people including personal assistant and trainer **Henry Coleman (personal spy); Dr. Schiller (gynecologist)**
Miscellaneous notes/ Most recent story notes:	Nemeses: Carly Tenney, Molly McKinnon, When Carly returned in 1997, she found out that Rosanna had imposed new restrictions on the trust fund: not only could Mike Kasnoff not be the father, but she must be married to the father when the baby is born, which must be prior to Jan. 1, 1999. When Rosanna found out that Parker was actually Hal's son, and not John's, she revoked the trust fund, and set up another one for Parker, to be administered by Hal. She also took back everything that was garnered by way of the fraudulently acquired trust fund. Rosanna returned to Oakdale in the aftermath of Carly's abduction and Hal's incapacitation to gain temporary custody of Parker to help care for him. **She even put up $1M for Dr. Weston's capture. When Carly returned, Rosanna willingly gave back Parker.** **Rosanna and Craig started flirting, each for multiple reasons. While they're attracted to each other, each is using the other with a Carly-centric goal in mind: Rosanna to wreak revenge from when Carly stole Mike, and Craig to make Carly jealous enough to want him back. Gradually, though, Rosanna and Craig are finding real feelings for each other.** **Kasnoff returned to town in the summer of 2002 and Rosanna quickly went to work on wreaking his budding relationship with Molly but to no avail – thus far. In an effort to appease Craig, Rosanna bought out BRO and handed it to Craig who renamed it Monte Carlo. In handing over BRO, Rosanna created a "Carly Clause" which stipulates that if Craig has an affair with Carly he loses control of BRO. After Hiring Henry to spy on Carly, Rosanna got info that Carly slept with someone the night before her wedding and believed it to be Mike. Eventually, Craig copped to being the one who slept with Carly the night before her wedding. Rosanna promptly broke up with him, but when Craig showed up and supported Rosanna when she got a hysterectomy, their relationship went on the mend. Rosanna asked Craig to marry him and after much soul searching, they were engaged. Soon after, Rosanna found out that Craig had been lying about sleeping with Carly, but Craig professed his love and Rosanna moved in with him and Lucy to Fairwinds. Rosanna has become a confidant for Lucy, who after losing her memory in an accident, is having trouble finding someone to trust.**

NOTE: All entries in **bold** are revisions/additions/deletions. Compare to previous version.

Character:	Molly (Peterson) Conlan McKinnon (a.k.a. Cherish Forever)
E-mail address:	Molly.Conlan@WOAK-TV.com
Nicknames called:	Cuz (by her cousin, Carly Tenney), Moll (by Nick Scudder, and Jake McKinnon, Carly)
Date of birth:	October 14, 1969
Address:	**7 Millstone Road, Franklin Lake, IL 60323 (Lucinda's Cottage)** Palm Court Apartments, 12 Hudson Court, Oakdale, IL 60324 (penthouse apt.)
Telephone number:	555-6424 **(Lucinda's Cottage)** 555-5253 (penthouse apt.)
Other relatives:	Carly Tenney (cousin – unknown how; Carly is Rosanna Cabot's ½ sister)
Married to:	Jake McKinnon (10/3/01)
Relationships:	**Mike Kasnoff (first tells Mike she loves him 1/07/03, breaks up with him after finding out Carly slept with him) ; Chris Hughes** Andy Dixon (engaged, he broke off when she admitted sleeping with Reid); Brad Snyder David Stenbeck (engaged, harshly jilted her the night he sank the Valetta); Jack Snyder Nick Scudder (landed her in jail – she was driving "get away car" of armed robbery) Holden Snyder Mike Harrington (1st crush)
Affairs with:	Reid Hamilton (a.k.a. David Stenbeck) (while engaged to Andy Dixon) Holden Snyder (seduced him while he was engaged to Lily)
Children:	Abigail Williams (born & forcibly given up for adoption, June 27, 1985 – father Holden Snyder – adoptive parents: Diana & Mitchell Williams)
Legal troubles:	Fraud re: Parker's paternity scam (disclosed 8/99, not yet put on trial – basically dropped) Money laundering (arrested, charges thrown out re: spending Holden's ransom money to David found by her/Brad) Accessory to Armed Robbery (in getaway car when boyfriend held up store – released early)

Career:	Current: News anchorwoman, WOAK-TV
	Former: PA, WOAK-TV (also Katie's temporary back-up) – convinced by Jake to quit
	     Columnist, The City Times
	     Weather girl, News anchor, WOAK (resigned after Chris/Molly photos appeared)
	     Talk show host WOAK "In Your Face"
	     Advice columnist City Times (Cherish Forever)
	     Author – "Love's Revenge" book published by Lucinda, totally altered
	     Waitress (in bar where she met Nick Scudder originally)

Medical Conditions/Blood Type:	Faked retrograde amnesia Coma after falling down stairs after argument with Abi re: Chris/Molly affair (Feb–April '00)
Nicknames calls others:	Cuz (calls her cousin Carly Tenney); **Rozilla (Rosanna Cabot)**
Miscellaneous notes/ Most recent story notes:	Devastated by the loss of Jake and the twins, and feeling helpless and useless to Abigail, Molly first spiraled into drowning her sorrows with alcohol, then decided to just run away to NYC. While there, she became friends with Mike Kasnoff, who helped straighten her out. Once she discovered who he was, she returned to Oakdale. **Mike followed her back to Oakdale and wore her down until she was open to the possibility of them becoming a couple. However Rosanna interfered, sending him to Venezuela on a construction gig. Molly and Carly figured it out and informed Mike and he quickly returned. With the possibility of Mike leaving town for work again, Molly made an anonymous donation ($ 1.75 million) to fund the Hospital's burn unit and arranged for Mike to the contractor on the job. With Henry's help, Rosanna exposed Molly, and Mike broke it off with her. That night, Mike found Carly broken hearted and they made love. The next day Mike forgave Molly and they happily attended Carly and Jack's wedding. Later Carly told Molly that she had been unfaithful to Jack the night before their wedding, but didn't tell Molly she was with Mike. Eventually Craig copped to being with Carly the night before her wedding and when Carly became pregnant, Molly suspected it was with Craig's baby.** **Carly did her best to keep her affair with Mike a secret, but eventually Jack found out. Mike went to Molly and confessed to the one night stand and Molly was devastated. A drunk Jack found Molly in a Lakeview hotel room, and Jack and Molly fell into a sudden passion filled tryst – though the did not make love. Mike arrived and mistook them for lovers.** Note: She has a fear of the dark from when her father used to lock her in a dark closet

CHARACTER DESCRIPTIONS/COMPANY CONTINUITY DETAILS

NOTE: All entries in **bold** are revisions/additions/deletions. Compare to previous version.

Character:	**Margo Montgomery Hughes**
E-mail address:	Margo.Hughes@opd.town.oakdale.il.us
Address:	724 Pinewood Lane, Oakdale, IL 60324
Telephone number:	555-9432 and 555-6746 (cell phone: 217-555-2355)
Parents: Mother:	Lyla Montgomery
Father:	John Dixon (assumed Lyla's husband Bart was her father until full adult, when Lyla admitted in court that John was her father, hence she calls John by his first name, never "dad")

Siblings:	Johnny Dixon (½ brother, John father, died 12/3/97)
	 M.J. Dixon (½ brother, John father)
	 Katie Peretti Frasier (½ sister, Lyla mother)
	     Husband: Simon Frasier
	 Ian "Duke" Kramer (½ brother, John father)
	 Andrew Dixon (½ brother, John father)
	 Cricket Montgomery (½ sister, Lyla mother)
	     Husband: Ernie Ross -- have daughter, Suzie
	     Has son, Billy, from affair with Cody Sullivan
	 Craig Montgomery (½ brother, Lyla mother)
	     Wife: Sierra Esteban Reyes (Lucinda's natural-born daughter)
	     Children: Bryant and Lucinda Marie ("Lucy")

Siblings living in Oakdale:	Katie Peretti Frasier, Craig Montgomery
Married to:	Tom Hughes (6/3/83, separated 5/19/99, renewed vows 1/14/00)
Relationships:	James Stenbeck
Affairs with:	Alec Wallace (while separated from Tom) Hal Munson (while separated from Tom circa 1988, conceived Adam)
Children:	Casey Hughes (with Tom Hughes, born 2/14/91) Adam (Hughes) Munson (with Hal Munson, born 9/8/88, aged to turn 16 on 9/8/98)
Children living in Oakdale:	Casey Hughes
Legal troubles:	2nd degree murder (convicted of killing Alec Wallace; freed prior to sentencing when Georgia Tucker finally confessed to self-defense shooting) Murder (confessed to killing Diego Santana – later helped prove that Kirk Anderson killer)

Career:	Current: Detective, Oakdale PD (orig. partner with Hal, then Jack)
	 Former: Private Investigator (while on suspension from Oakdale PD)
	     Tom's (legal) assistant
	     Stablehand (loves horses)
	     Barbara's private nurse (hired by James)

Medical Conditions/Blood Type:	**Living Donor Liver Transplant recipient (from sister Katie)** **Hepatitis C (contracted from Elroy Nevins rape in 1992, but was dormant for years) & Liver cancer** Suffered Post Traumatic Stress syndrome following crash of Kingsley-Malta jet, after Diego Santana shooting, and after rape by Elroy Nevins Raped in 1992 by (HIV+) Elroy Nevins and accomplice, Ficket. Margo finally tested HIV-. Temporarily deaf in 1985 after incident during gambling ring sting. Have had 3 miscarriages. **Blood type: NOT O (since John is AB+)**
Miscellaneous notes/ Most recent story notes:	Nemeses: James Stenbeck, **Barbara Ryan** **Margo has become increasingly worn down with each successive case added to her load: Hal's disappearance, the kidnappings of Carly, Emily and Rose, Jack being held prisoner by Julia, and Dahlia Ventura trying to implicate Simon in multiple crimes. This helped mask some of her worrisome symptoms. Finally, she was forced to undergo some tests, which resulted in being diagnosed with Hepatitis C. Though resistant to the diagnosis at first, she finally realized that she must have contracted it in 1992 when Elroy Nevins raped her. As a result of the Hepatitis, she developed liver cancer, curable in her case only by a liver transplant. Katie volunteered to donate half her liver to Margo. The transplant was a success.** **While resting at home, working unofficially, Margo tracked down James in Mexico, poised to return to town. When James did, Margo led the investigation in Brandy's murder and suspected James, although Paul was initially charged – but eventually exonerated.**

CHARACTER DESCRIPTIONS/COMPANY CONTINUITY DETAILS

NOTE: All entries in **bold** are revisions/additions/deletions. Compare to previous version.

Character:	**James Stenbeck**
Date of birth:	**October 31, 1947**
Parents: Mother:	Greta Aldrin
Father:	
Siblings:	Ariel Aldrin
Married to:	Lucinda Walsh (11/18/98; divorced by mail 1/17/00) Karen Haines (blackmailed him into marriage since she found out he wasn't true Stenbeck heir; divorced when James went broke) Barbara Ryan (divorced)
Relationships:	Emily Stewart Monica Lawrence Corinne Lawrence Margo Hughes
Affairs with:	
Children:	Paul (Stenbeck) Ryan David (Allen) Stenbeck (a.k.a. Dr. Reid Hamilton)
Children currently living in Oakdale:	**Paul Ryan**
Legal troubles:	You name it, he's done it – murder, weapons dealing, drug trafficking, money laundering, etc.
Career:	Criminal
Servants (personal/professional):	Amber (last known henchman, only one ever left alive)
Medical Conditions/Blood Type:	Returned from the dead several times
Miscellaneous notes/ Most recent story notes:	Nemeses: All of Oakdale After the whole incident at the spa had spun out of control, Rose had returned to Oakdale, and Carly survived the fun house, James turned in Weston in order to get flush with the $1M reward money Rosanna put up. He used some of it to restore Barbara to her beautiful, unscarred self. He then confronted Barbara with the need to eliminate the last remaining loose end, Emily. Rather than kill Emily, Barbara conspired with Emily and stabbed James in the gut so they could both escape his wrath. James survived, and even referred one of his attorneys (T. Marshall Travers) to Barbara's case. **Once Paul discovered that Marshall had previously represented James, he formulated the theory that Marshall was running for DA so when elected he could take drop all charges against James in Oakdale. His pursuit to stop Marshall had him linking up with Bonnie and together with Isaac, Simon and Henry, they bugged Marshall's hotel suite. In the process Paul caught Marshall and Jessica in the midst of a tawdry affair. Threatening to expose Jessica, he blackmailed her into finding out info on James' whereabouts. Jessica eventually conceded the election for DA to Marshall.** **James returned again on Halloween of 2002 to reclaim his love, Barbara Ryan. That night James framed Paul for murdering Brandy Taylor and Marshall prosecuted. James offered to get Paul off if Barbara would agree to go away with him, but Paul convinced her not to give into James.** **Bonnie never gave up on Paul and with the help of Isaac she uncovered Marshall's past and found out that he had a 15 year-old daughter named Neia Bellaguese and Jessica used that and his conscience to get Marshall to admit to falsely prosecuting Paul, and he was exonerated. Feeling Barbara's love was lost, James put up little protest when he was arrested and then shipped off to a maximum-security prison.** **Note: Speaks Mandarin Chinese**

CHARACTER DESCRIPTIONS/COMPANY CONTINUITY DETAILS

NOTE: All entries in **bold** are revisions/additions/deletions. Compare to previous version.

Character:	**Kimberly Sullivan Reynolds Dixon Stewart Andropoulos Hughes**
E-mail address:	Kim.Hughes@WOAK-TV.com
Nicknames called:	
Date of birth:	
Address:	10 Yardley Place, Oakdale, IL 60324
Telephone number:	555-2473
Parents: Mother:	Frances Sullivan
Father:	
Siblings:	Jennifer Sullivan Hughes (died)
Married to:	Dr. Robert Hughes (4/12/85, separated, renewed vows 12/19/91) Nick Andropoulos (died) Dan Stewart (died, brain tumor) John Dixon (divorced while pregnant with Andy) Jason Reynolds (died – she was widow when she first came to town)
Relationships:	
Affairs with:	Bob Hughes (while he was married to her sister!)
Children:	Christopher Robert Hughes (with Bob Hughes, born 9/2/86 – in 1998 aged to turn 18) Andy Dixon (with John Dixon, via "marital rape," born 9/9/76; aged to turn 16 in 1985) Sabrina Fullerton Hughes Crowley (with Bob Hughes cheating on wife Jennifer, born 12/14/65)
Children currently living in Oakdale:	**Christopher Hughes**
Legal troubles:	People at Kim/Bob wedding reception were all put in a holding cell, since a gambling sting happened on the boat simultaneously with their reception. No charges were filed against any of the guests. Tried to protect Frannie by confessing to killing Doug Cummings, but the evidence didn't bear out her story. Later discovered that Marsha Talbot killed Doug in a jealous rage.
School attended/attending:	
Career:	Current: Host, "Patterns", WOAK Co-owner WOAK-TV (Acting Station Manager, too) Former: Receptionist at Lowell, Hughes & Colman
Companies owned/run:	WOAK (co-owns with Lily Snyder)
Medical Conditions/Blood Type:	Bone marrow donor for Hope (Snyder) Maynard – Denise/Andy's biological daughter Aortic Stenosis, required heart valve to be replaced in 1997 Emergency gall bladder surgery (in early '70s) Marital rape by John Dixon (early 1970) Victim of attempted rape by Cliff (don't know last name) Blood type: AB-
Nicknames calls others:	Sweetie, Kiddo, Toots (calls anyone, depending on her mood/context)
Miscellaneous notes/ Most recent story notes:	Nemesis: Dr. Susan Stewart (mostly truce now) Kim is one of the bedrock, model citizens of Oakdale. You can always expect her to be straightforward with an honest opinion, like it or not. Though she has a "high-minded" set of morals, she's not one to denigrate another that doesn't follow that set. She'll attempt to convince them of the error of their ways. When Dr. Bob had his affair with Susan, Kim was deeply hurt/betrayed. It took a long time for her to trust Bob again. A few years ago, she finally buried the hatchet, effectively forgiving Susan, and dropping the grudge against her. On rare occasions, though, Kim gets a twinge of resentment when she sees Bob/Susan together, friendly. Kim put aside the past and asked Molly to become the news anchor again, to help the sagging ratings since Katie's fiasco and firing. While assisting Adam and Abigail investigate certain aspects of the "mystery woman" who they theorized killed Nick Scudder, Kim was assaulted and knocked unconscious, her purse and incriminating videotapes stolen. Kim/Bob song: "Can't Help Loving That Man of Mine" Favorite flower: Apricot rose

OAKDALE ADDRESSES & PHONE NUMBERS

NOTE: Oakdale is situated in northern Illinois, **in Lee County**, about 50 miles southwest of Rockford. **Luther's Corners is 11 miles west of Oakdale.** It is just south of I-88, and has U.S. highways 30 and 52 running through it, and State highway 26 also running through it. As established on-air, Oakdale is 50 miles west of Bay City along I-88, so more than 50 miles west of Chicago. Oakdale also has a river running through it (at least on the edge of town), which has at least two islands, each of which has a castle, one being Duncan McKechnie's ancestral castle where the Earl Mitchell Center is located.

NOTE: The area code for Oakdale phone numbers should be 309. The area code for cell phones should be 217.

Residences and Phone Numbers:

Rosanna Cabot	**Fairwinds, 100 Stone Ridge Road, Oakdale, IL 60324**	**(555-3963)**
John Dixon	c/o Lakeview Towers, 1440 Lakeview Road, Oakdale, IL 60324	(555-3821)
Simon/Katie Frasier	**c/o RR #25, Box 17, Oakdale, IL 60324**	**(555-7466)**
Jessica Griffin	65 Central Avenue, Oakdale, IL 60324	(555-6832)
Lisa Grimaldi	835 Pearl Street, Penthouse, Oakdale, IL 60324	(555-1420)
Ben Harris	1520 Russell Street, Apt. 6, Oakdale, IL 60324 (w/ Curtis)	(555-3622)
Bob/Kim Hughes	10 Yardley Place, Oakdale, IL 60324	(555-2473)
Nancy Hughes (McClosky)	10 Yardley Place, Oakdale, IL 60324 (garage apartment)	(555-4726)
Tom/Margo Hughes	724 Pinewood Lane, Oakdale, IL 60324 (w/Casey & **Daniel**)	(555-9432 & 6746)
Isaac Jenkins	c/o Stratford Arms Hotel, 4861 High Street, Oakdale, IL 60324	(555-7525)
Mike Kasnoff	**7 Millstone Road, Franklin Lake, IL 60323 (Lucinda's Cottage) (555-6424)**	
Bonnie McKechnie	65 Central Avenue, Oakdale, IL 60324	(555-6832)
Molly McKinnon	**7 Millstone Road, Franklin Lake, IL 60323 (Lucinda's Cottage) (555-6424)**	
Craig Montgomery	Fairwinds, 100 Stone Ridge Road, Oakdale, IL 60324	(555-3963)
Lucy Montgomery	Fairwinds, 100 Stone Ridge Road, Oakdale, IL 60324	(555-3963)
Hal & Emily Munson	4 Patchin Place, Oakdale, IL 60324 (w/ **Daniel**, Will)	(555-7926)
Barbara Ryan	~~Fairwinds, 100 Stone Ridge Road, Oakdale, IL 60324~~	~~(555-3963)~~
Paul Ryan	Lakeview Towers, 1140 Lakeview Road, Rm 726, Oakdale, IL 60324	(555-7285)
Susan Stewart	182 Courtland Place, Oakdale, IL 60324 (w/ Alison & Daniel)	(555-7246)
T. Marshall Travers	office: 3 Worldwide Plaza, Oakdale, IL 60324	(217-555-8743)
	Lakeview Towers, 1440 Lakeview Road, Suite #3, Oakdale, IL 60324	
Lucinda Walsh	25 Old Stable Road, Ruxton Hills, IL 60324	(555-7424)
Lucinda's Cottage	7 Millstone Road, Franklin Lake, IL 60323	(555-6424)

Businesses:

Al's Diner	103 Washington Street, Oakdale, IL 60324	(555-3463)
<u>The Argus</u>	8058 Monument Avenue, Oakdale, IL 60324	(555-8222)

CHARACTERS' FRIENDS AND ENEMIES LIST*

Character	Best Friend(s)	Friend(s)	Negative Feelings Toward	Worst Enemies
Rosanna Cabot	**Craig**	~~Craig;~~ **Lucy**	**Molly; Mike;** ~~Lucy~~	Carly
Henry Coleman		**Simon; Katie; Lucinda; Magda**	**Craig; Lucinda**	
Rose D'Angelo	Mitzi; Paul; Emily; Carly	Lily; Matthew; Lucinda; Holden; Jack	Craig	Barbara; James Stenbeck
John Dixon		Barbara; Emma; Sierra	Isaac; Ben; **Chris**	James Stenbeck
Katie Peretti Frasier		Henry; Bonnie	Henry	Dahlia Ventura
Simon Frasier		Craig; Lily; Mac Renfrew; **Bonnie; Isaac; Paul**	Craig; Henry	Dahlia Ventura
Jessica Griffin	Ben	Margo; Tom; Lisa; **Marshall**		~~Marshall Travers~~
Lisa Grimaldi	Kim; Barbara; Nancy; Ellen Stewart	Lily; Isaac; Jessica; Charlotte Lindsey	Lucinda; Emily; Craig; Sierra; **Carly; Barbara; Brandy**	
Ben Harris	Jessica	Bob; Jack; **Mike**	John; Andy	**Marshall Travers**
Curtis Thompson Harris				
Casey Hughes				
Daniel Hughes				
Kim Hughes	Lisa; Barbara	Molly; Lily; Holden; Joe;	Emily; Henry; Carly; Barbara; **Brandy**	
Margo Hughes	Hal; Jack	Jessica; **Emily**	~~Emily~~; Barbara; **Brandy**	James Stenbeck
Nancy Hughes	Lisa; Ellen Stewart	Joe	Emily	
Bob Hughes		Susan; Ben	John	
Chris Hughes		Abigail	**John; Rosanna**	
Tom Hughes		Hal; Jessica	**Brandy**	
Isaac Jenkins		Lisa; Emily; Jack; Jessica	John; Craig; **Brandy**	
Mike Kasnoff		Carly; Molly; Lily; Ben; **Jack**	**Rosanna; Henry**	
Mitzi Matters	Rose	Paul; Jack	Carly	Craig; Barbara
Bonnie McKechnie	Isaac	Katie; **Ben; Paul; Simon**	**Marshall; Brandy**	**~~Marshall Travers;~~ James Stenbeck**
Molly McKinnon	Carly	Lucinda; Rose; Hal; ~~Mike~~	Rosanna; **Carly; Mike**	Henry; Donna; Marley

* Generally, relatives are not listed in this chart, nor are ex-spouses, etc., unless there is a particularly compelling reason to do so.

Revised 11/25/2002

CHARACTERS' FRIENDS AND ENEMIES LIST*

Character	Best Friend(s)	Friend(s)	Negative Feelings Toward	Worst Enemies
Craig Montgomery	**Rosanna,** ~~Carly~~	Lily; ~~Rosanna~~, **Carly**	Isaac; Jack; Rose; **Aaron; Alison**	Lucinda; Paul; Barbara
Lucy Montgomery	Aaron	Katie; Abigail; Alison; **Gloria Perez (friend from Montega)**	Alison	
Sierra Montgomery		Craig; John	Craig; **Rosanna**	
Emily Munson	Hal; Carly; Rose	Isaac; Craig; Paul; **Margo**	Lisa; Molly; Craig	Barbara; Lucinda; James Stenbeck
Hal Munson	Margo; Jack; Emily	Carly; Paul; Molly	Craig; **Alison**	James Stenbeck
Parker Munson		Jack; Craig; John		
Will Munson		**Alison, Luke, Aaron**		
Barbara Ryan	Kim; Lisa	John	**Marshall**	Emily; Lucinda; James Stenbeck; Craig; Carly; Rose
Paul Ryan	Rose	Emily; Lily; Hal; Jessica; Lisa; Mitzi; **Simon; Jack; Bonnie; Isaac; Henry**	Barbara; **Marshall**	Craig; James Stenbeck
Aaron Snyder	Lucy	Abigail; **Alison; Brady Rudd**	Alison	Craig
Carly Snyder	Molly; Emily; Rose	Jack; Hal; Jennifer; Abigail; Mike	**Henry**	Julia; Barbara; **James Stenbeck; Rosanna**
Emma Snyder		John; Joe	Carly; Molly	
Faith Snyder				
Holden Snyder	Jack	Molly; Joe; Rose		James Stenbeck; Damian Grimaldi
Jack Snyder	Holden; Margo	Hal; Ben; Isaac; Carly; Mitzi	Craig; **Mike; Carly**	James Stenbeck; Julia
Lily Snyder		Lisa; Craig; Rose; Paul; Simon; Mike	Damian Grimaldi; Barbara	
Luke Grimaldi (Snyder)		**Will**	Damian Grimaldi	
Alison (McDermott) Stewart		Isaac; Lucy; Aaron	Lucy; Craig; **Hal; Rosanna**	
Susan Stewart		Bob; Andy; John; Isaac		
Lucinda Walsh		John; Rose; Molly; Simon; Paul	Barbara; Lisa; Emily;	Craig; James Stenbeck

* Generally, relatives are not listed in this chart, nor are ex-spouses, etc., unless there is a particularly compelling reason to do so.

Revised 11/25/2002

OAKDALE NICKNAMES

Henry Coleman
Calls   Katie Frasier "Peretti" (<u>not</u> "Katie-bird" or any such variant)

Joe D'Angelo
Calls   Rose D'Angelo "BB" or "Bella Bambina"

Rose D'Angelo
Calls   Joe D'Angelo "Pop"
        Lucinda Walsh "Ms. Walsh" much more often than "Lucinda"
        Lily Walsh "Tiger Lily"
        Luke Snyder "Luciano"
        Isaac Jenkins "I-Man"
        Ron Shanks "Sugar Shanks"

John Dixon
Calls   James Stenbeck "Jimmy" (to be nasty)

Katie Peretti Frasier
Calls   Lyla Peretti "Mama"

Lisa Grimaldi
Calls   Lucinda Walsh "Lucy"
        John Dixon "Johnnie"

Curtis Thompson Harris
Calls   Ben Harris "Dad"
        Isaac Jenkins either "Uncle Isaac" or "Isaac" – situation-dependent

Casey Hughes
Calls   Margo Hughes "Mom"
        Tom Hughes "Dad"
        John Dixon "Grandpa"
        Lisa Grimaldi "Grandma"
        Bob Hughes "Grandpa"
        Kim Hughes "Grandma"
        Nancy Hughes "Gram"

Chris Hughes
Calls   Bob Hughes "Dad"
        Kim Hughes "Mom"
        Nancy Hughes "Gram"
        Abigail Williams "Daisy"

Kim Hughes
Calls   Nancy Hughes "Mom"
        Anyone "Kiddo" or "Toots" or "Sweetie" – situation-dependent

<h1 style="text-align:center"><u>OAKDALE NICKNAMES</u></h1>

<u>Margo Hughes</u>
Calls   Lyla Peretti "Mama"
          John Dixon "John" (NEVER "Dad")

<u>Bob Hughes</u>
Calls   Nancy Hughes "Mom"

<u>Tom Hughes</u>
Calls   Nancy Hughes "Gram"
          Bob Hughes "Dad"
          Lisa Grimaldi "Mom"
          Casey Hughes "Case"

<u>Isaac Jenkins</u>
Calls   Bonnie McKechnie "Duchess"

<u>Bonnie McKechnie</u>
Calls   Jessica Griffin "Mother"
          Duncan McKechine "Daddy"
          Jennifer Munson "Jennie"
          Isaac Jenkins "Ike"

<u>Molly McKinnon</u>
Calls   Abigail Williams "Abigail" more often than "Abi"
          Carly Tenney "Cuz"
          Rosanna Cabot "Rozilla"

<u>Craig Montgomery</u>
Calls   Lucy Montgomery "Lullaby"
          Rosanna Cabot "Cabot"
          Barbara Ryan "Bar-Bar"
          Parker Munson "My little Hombre"
          Aaron Snyder "Little Hairball" & "Little Fabio"

<u>Lucy Montgomery</u>
Calls   Craig Montgomery "Daddy"
          Sierra Montgomery "Mom"
          Lucinda Walsh "Gran" or "Grandmother" – situation-dependent (NEVER "Grandma")

<u>Sierra Montgomery</u>
Calls   Lucinda Walsh "Mother"

<u>Emily Munson</u>
Calls   Susan Stewart "Mother" or "Mom"
          Alison Stewart "Ali"

SPECIAL CHARACTER-RELATED NOTES

Below is a list of all the special items associated with certain characters, and their meaning, if any, as well as allergies and fears that are currently established. Please notify me of any additions that should be made to this list.

Character:	**Item**:
Molly McKinnon	Afraid of the dark; Class ring necklace given to her from Mike
Dr. John Dixon	Deadly allergic to scallops
Dr. Ben Harris	Stravinsky's "Firebird" (Ben/Denise "song")
Dr. Bob Hughes	Apricot roses (wife, Kim's, favorite flower) Son Chris' little league trophy for participation in office
Chris Hughes	Little league trophy for participation in father, Dr. Bob's, office F. Scott Fitzgerald (favorite author) Daisies (special flower sends only to Abigail Williams)
Daniel Stewart Hughes	Freddie the Frog (favorite toy)
Kim Hughes	Apricot roses (favorite flower)
Margo Hughes	African violets (Tom/Margo made love for first time in Africa) Owns mutt: Lucky "If You Say My Eyes Are Beautiful" (Tom/Margo song) Sauvignon blanc wine, Chesapeake Bay oysters, rack of lamb royale, "plain old" chocolate pudding (favorite foods, especially chocolate)
Tom Hughes	African violets (Tom/Margo made love for first time in Africa) Owns mutt: Lucky (lives at house) "If You Say My Eyes Are Beautiful" (Tom/Margo song)
Julia Lindsey	Jack hung a working swing out in front of Snyder farm house Afraid of thunderstorms
Denise Maynard	Tiny ballet slippers (remind her of her childhood dream of becoming a dancer) Stravinsky's "Firebird" (Ben/Denise "song")
Nancy McClocky	Diamond bracelet engraved by first husband, Chris
Jake McKinnon	Allergic to hay, cats, cucumbers, cilantro and plaster
Lucy Montgomery	Bike helmet given to her by Aaron
Hal Munson	"(If They Asked Me) I Could Write a Book" (Hal/Barbara song) <u>Lady and the Tramp</u> (favorite movie)
Barbara Ryan	"(If They Asked Me) I Could Write a Book" (Hal/Barbara song) Tulips (favorite flower) Duck (favorite food)
Carly Snyder	Made "JJ" a jacket embroidered with JJ on the front
Faith Snyder	Allergic to new antibiotic used to treat her ear infection
Holden Snyder	Carved wooden cat ("Ma'am") he gave Lily when young
Jack Snyder	Hung a working swing out in front of Snyder farm house for Julia
Lily Snyder	Carved wooden cat ("Ma'am") Holden gave her when young

Georgia Tucker	Elephant beanie (Samantha gave to her, with promise she'd never forget)
Lucinda Walsh	Allergic to cats
Abigail Williams	F. Scott Fitzgerald, favorite author
	Daisies (special flowers sent only by Chris Hughes)

<u>**Special/Favorite/How to Prepare Foods**</u>

Adam	Favorites:	Lunch: Bologna, cheese, potato chips
Abigail	Prepare:	Hot chocolate with tiny marshmallows
Aaron	Favorite:	Apple Pie
Barbara	Favorites:	Duck a l'orange
Bonnie	Favorites:	Drink: Peach Bellini
Carly	Special:	Chateau de Maraville (near-sex in wine cellar with Jack)
	Favorites:	Cranberry-orange muffin Crispy, greasy onion rings
	Prepare:	Coffee (milk, two sugars)
Craig	Favorites:	French Roast with sugar
	Hates:	Halibut
Emily	Prepare:	Coffee (cream, no sugar)
Emma	Favorites:	Movies: Shoot 'em up
Hal	Favorites:	Italian dinner a la <u>Lady & The Tramp</u> (favorite movie); Baked Trout
	Prepare:	Eggs over easy, rye toast, no butter
Henry	Prepare:	Coffee (drop of milk and dash of sugar)
Holden	Favorites:	Breakfast: Eggs Benedict
	Hates:	Cherry Vanilla ice cream
Jack	Special:	Chateau de Maraville (near-sex in wine cellar with Carly)
	Favorites:	Chocolate ice cream, chocolate chip cookies
	Prepare:	Coffee (cream and 1 sugar)
	Hates:	Tuna casserole (anything with tuna)
Jake	Bachelor dish:	Chicken Florentine
	Favorites:	(Pizza) toppings: Pepperoni, sausage, Molly
	Prepare:	Coffee (a little cream, two sugars)
James	Drink:	Rob Roy, double scotch, neat
	Favorite:	Halibut
Jennifer	Favorites:	Meal (by Hal): Fried chicken and waffles

Katie	Cure-all:	Cocoa w/ marshmallows
	Favorites:	Dessert: banana split
Lucinda	Favorites:	Candy: Champagne truffles
	Hates:	Halibut
Luke:	Favorites:	Peach & raspberry pie Meal: Chicken nuggets, French fries, cookies, chocolate ice cream, chocolate milk
Margo	Favorites:	Sauvignon blanc wine, Chesapeake Bay oysters, rack of lamb royale, "plain old" chocolate pudding; Oatmeal cookies
Molly	Prepare:	Coffee (black); Hot Chocolate with tiny marshmallows
Paul	Drink:	Merlot
Rose	Favorites:	Red Pistachios Orange juice (heavy on the pulp)
	Drink:	Rusty Nail

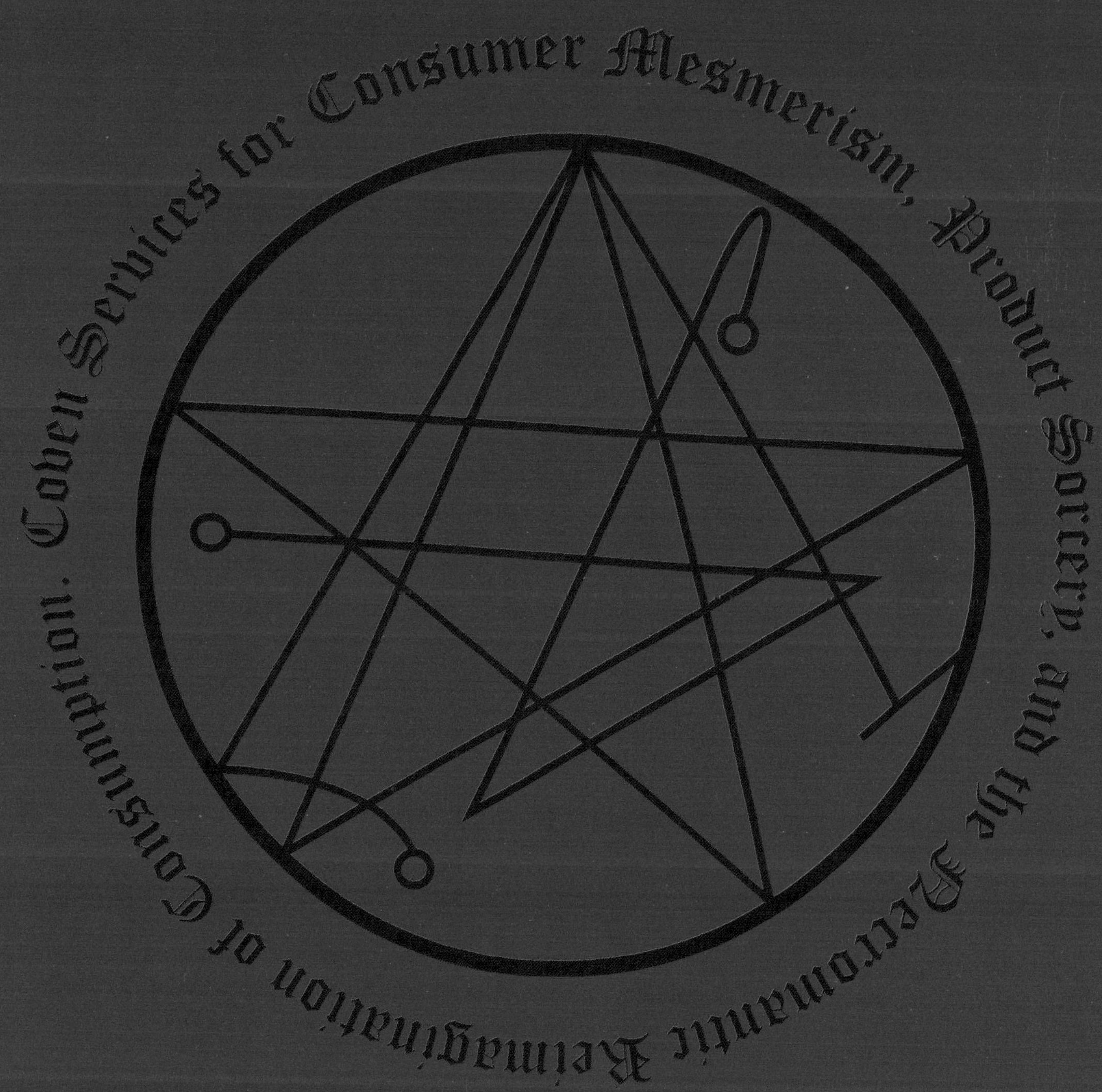
Coven Services for Consumer Mesmerism, Product Sorcery, and the Necromantic Reimagination of Consumption.

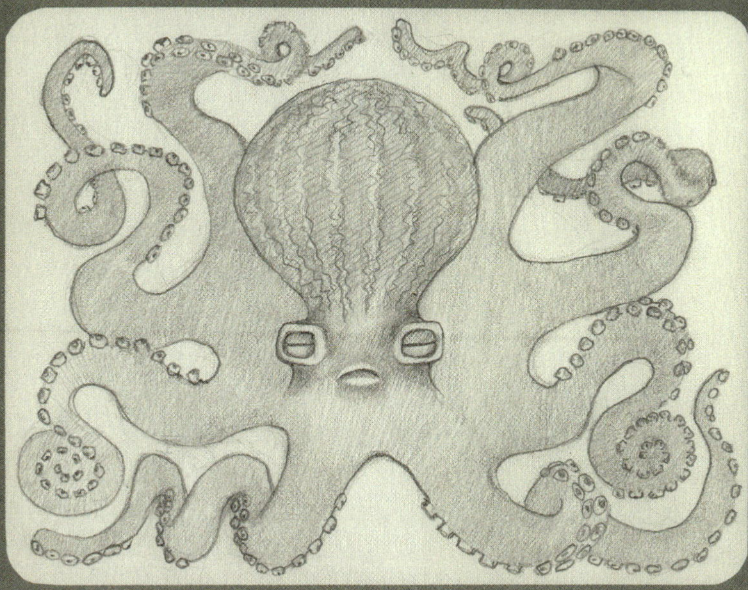

V.O.
"HELLO. I'M ELI LILLY.
I'M AS OLD AS TIME AND I HAVE MANY
POWERS. BUT TODAY, I'M HERE TO TALK
TO YOU ABOUT DEPRESSION."

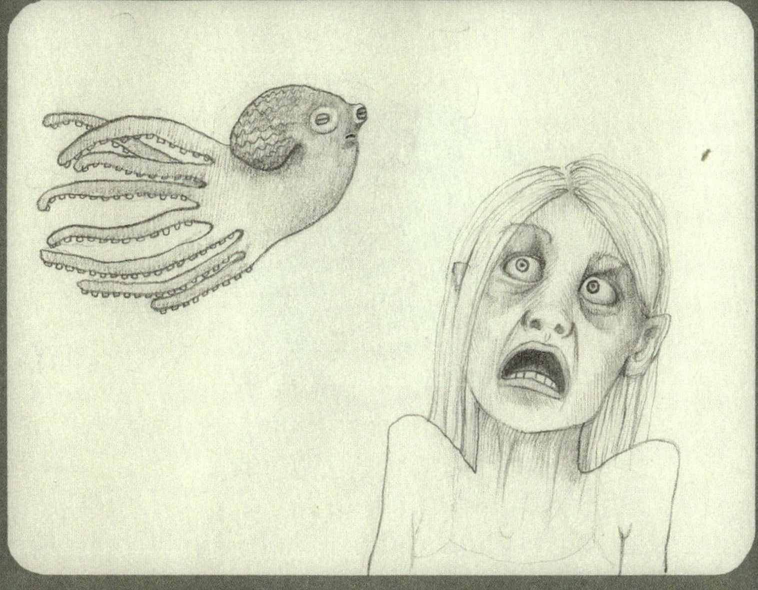

"MOST OF US HAVE EVERY RIGHT TO SUFFER FROM DEPRESSION. THIS WORLD IS A CRUEL, CRUEL PLACE. MOST LIKELY YOU "WORK" AT A JOB THAT YOU FIND TEDIOUS, DULL, AND ULTIMATELY POINTLESS FOR A PAYCHECK THAT'S INSULTING - AND NEVER-EVER ENOUGH TO AFFORD ALL THE PRODUCTS AND SERVICES THAT GIVE YOU ANY PLEASURE AT ALL - HOW MUCH PLEASURE CAN YOU EXPECT TO FIND IN OBJECTS ANYWAY? BEING DEFINED AND JUDGED BY YOUR PURCHASES IS A SAD FACT OF MODERN LIFE BECAUSE YOU KNOW YOU AMOUNT TO MORE THAN YOUR SHOES AND PURSE - ALTHOUGH SECRETLY YOU DOUBT EVEN THIS. YOU MAY JUST BE AN EMPTY SHELL PLODDING THROUGH LIFE HOPING NO ONE FINDS OUT."

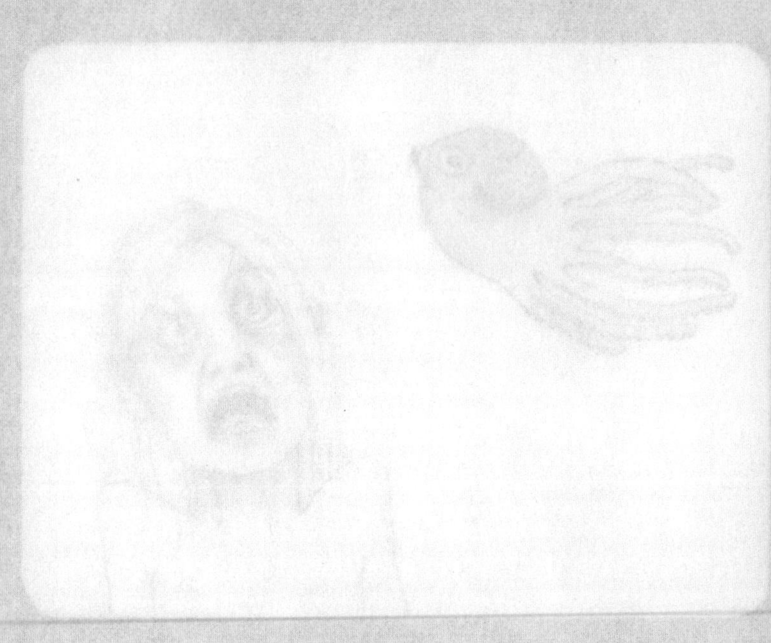

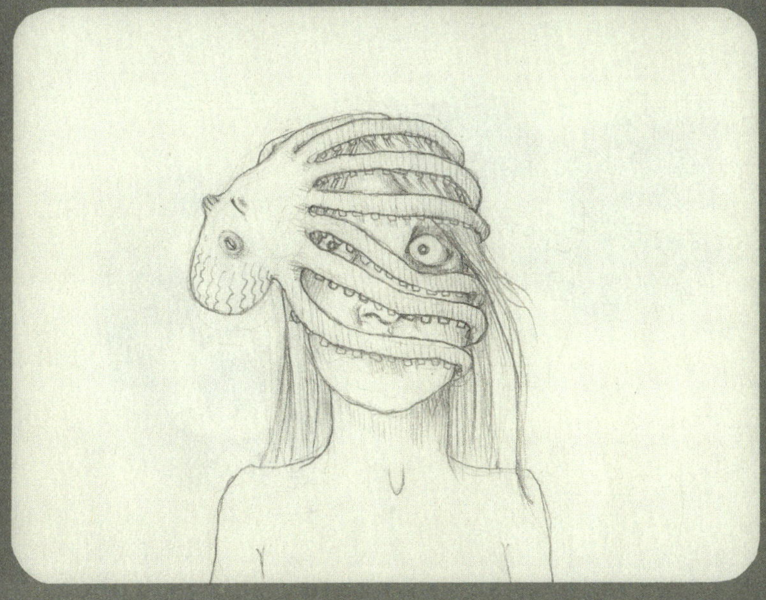

V.O. CONT.
"YOUR "FRIENDS" CAN'T HELP YOU. THEY DON'T CARE ABOUT YOU ANYWAY — BECAUSE THEY'RE HOPELESSLY ENTWINED IN THEIR OWN PSYCHODRAMA. AND THEY VICIOUSLY MOCK YOU EVERY TIME YOUR BACK IS TURNED.

"HOME" AS A CONCEPT USED TO MEAN COMFORT AND PRIVACY, BUT NOW IT'S JUST A LOCATION, CONSUMED WITH THE PRESENCE OF THE PERSON YOU SETTLED FOR, WHO SINGLE-HANDEDLY ROBBED YOU OF YOUR IDENTITY, SPACE AND TIME IN THE NAME OF "LOVE" MANY, MANY YEARS AGO.

"FAITH" OFFERS YOU NO SOLACE BECAUSE IT'S DIFFICULT TO BELIEVE IN A GOD WHOSE REPRESENTATIVES HERE ON EARTH FONDLED YOU AS A CHILD."

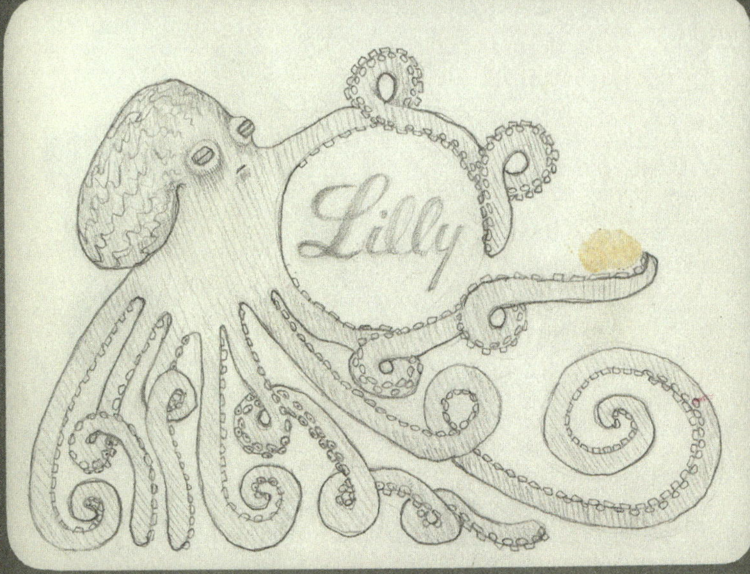

V.O. CONT.
"AND WHAT DOES THE FUTURE HOLD? SO MUCH MORE OF THE SAME WITH THE ADDED DISCOMFORT OF YOUR MIND AND BODY SLOWLY AND PAINFULLY DISINTIGRATING UNTIL ULTIMATELY, YOU DIE.

ISNT IT RE-ASSURING TO KNOW THAT YOU CAN RID YOURSELF OF ALL THIS PAIN AND ANGUISH WITH ONE LITTLE PILL?

PROZAC FIXES ALL THINGS BROKEN.

SIMPLY TAKE PROZAC ONCE A DAY, EVERY DAY, FOR THE REST OF YOUR LIFE, UNTIL YOU DIE, AND RID YOURSELF OF ALL UNCOMFORTABLE THOUGHT.

ASK YOUR DOCTOR ABOUT PROZAC, AND TELL HIM, ELI LILLY SENT YOU."

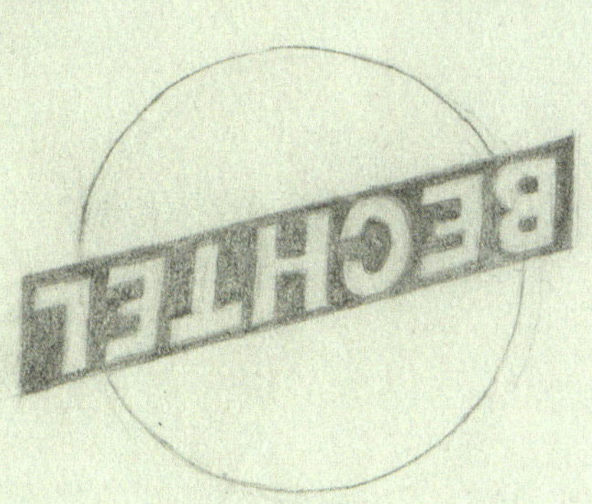

V.O.

"WHAT ARE THE CIRCUMSTANCES THAT BROUGHT YOU TO THIS PLACE AT THIS MOMENT IN TIME?
    WHAT ARE YOU LOOKING FOR?
    DO YOU REALLY EXPECT TO FIND IT HERE? NOW? ON YOUR TV SET!?
    WHEN WILL YOU STOP DEPENDING ON OTHER PEOPLE TO ENTERTAIN YOU?

WHAT ARE THE CIRCUMSTANCES THAT
REQUIRE YOU TO TAKE NOTICE OF YOUR
MOMENT IN TIME?
WHAT ARE YOU LOOKING FOR...?
DO YOU EXPECT...TO THINK OF
WERE A BOOK ON YOUR DESK...?
WILL YOU STOP READING AND
THINK PEOPLE TO ENTERTAIN YOU?

2.

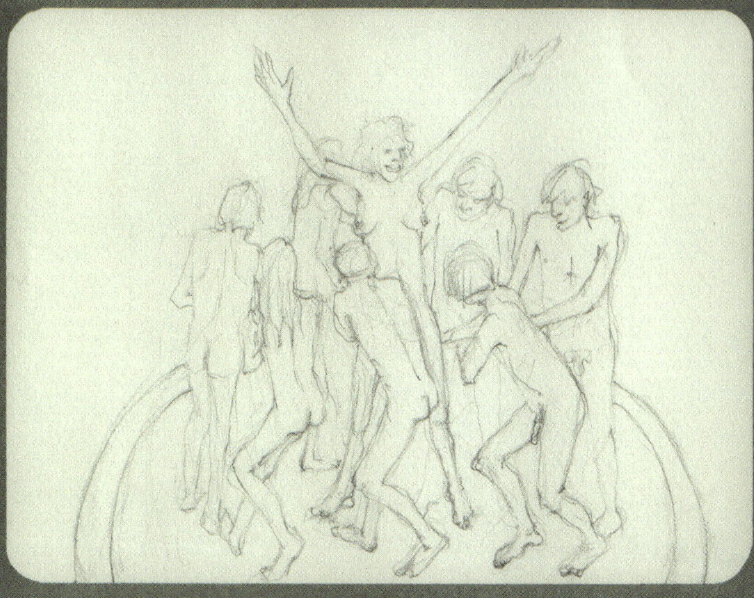

V.O. CONT.

"ALL HAIL THE REAL MAGIK OF CHANGE!
STAGNATION AND COMPLACENCY ARE
THE ENEMY OF THE PEOPLE!

DEATH TO THE SOUL CRUSHING TYRANNY
AND MIND-NUMBING OPPRESSION
OF BOREDOM!"

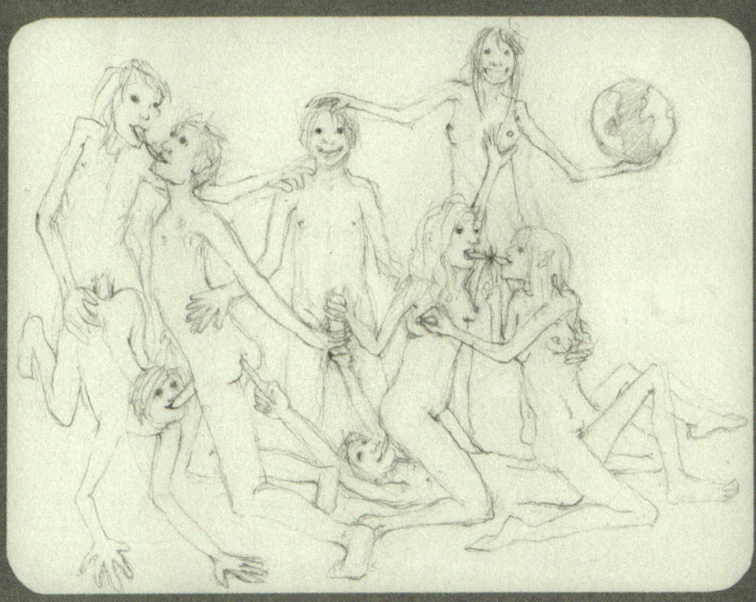

V.O. CONT

"FREE YOURSELF FROM GUILT AND
SHAME YOU'VE BEEN MADE TO FEEL
FROM BIRTH—AND MAKE THINGS
HAPPEN!
ANYTHING IS POSSIBLE. YOU HAVE THE
RIGHT TO MAKE DREAMS REAL!
YOU HAVE THE POWER TO CREATE
TOMORROW'S HISTORY TODAY!"

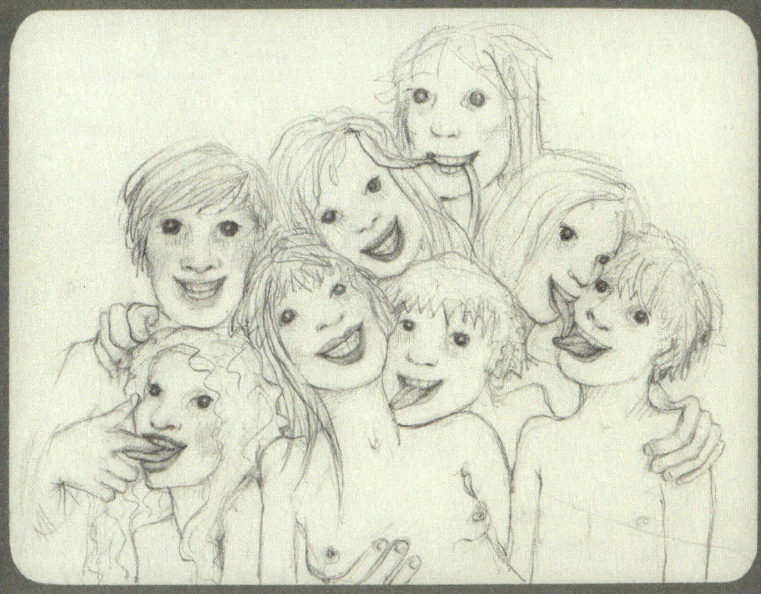

V.O. CONT.

"LOVE IS A WEAPON. USE IT AGAINST
THE CONFINEMENT OF LAW AND THE
RESTRICTIVE WILL OF THE STATE!

DON'T LET THE MODERN WORLD DISCONNECT
YOU FROM OTHER HUMANS!

YOU AND YOUR CIRCLE OF FRIENDS ARE SO
BEAUTIFUL AND STRONG! THESE ARE THE
PEOPLE WHO REALLY MATTER; WHOSE PAIN
YOU FEEL, WHOSE TRIUMPHS YOU'RE PROUD OF.

ALWAYS BE ON THE LOOK-OUT FOR PEOPLE
TO LOVE!"

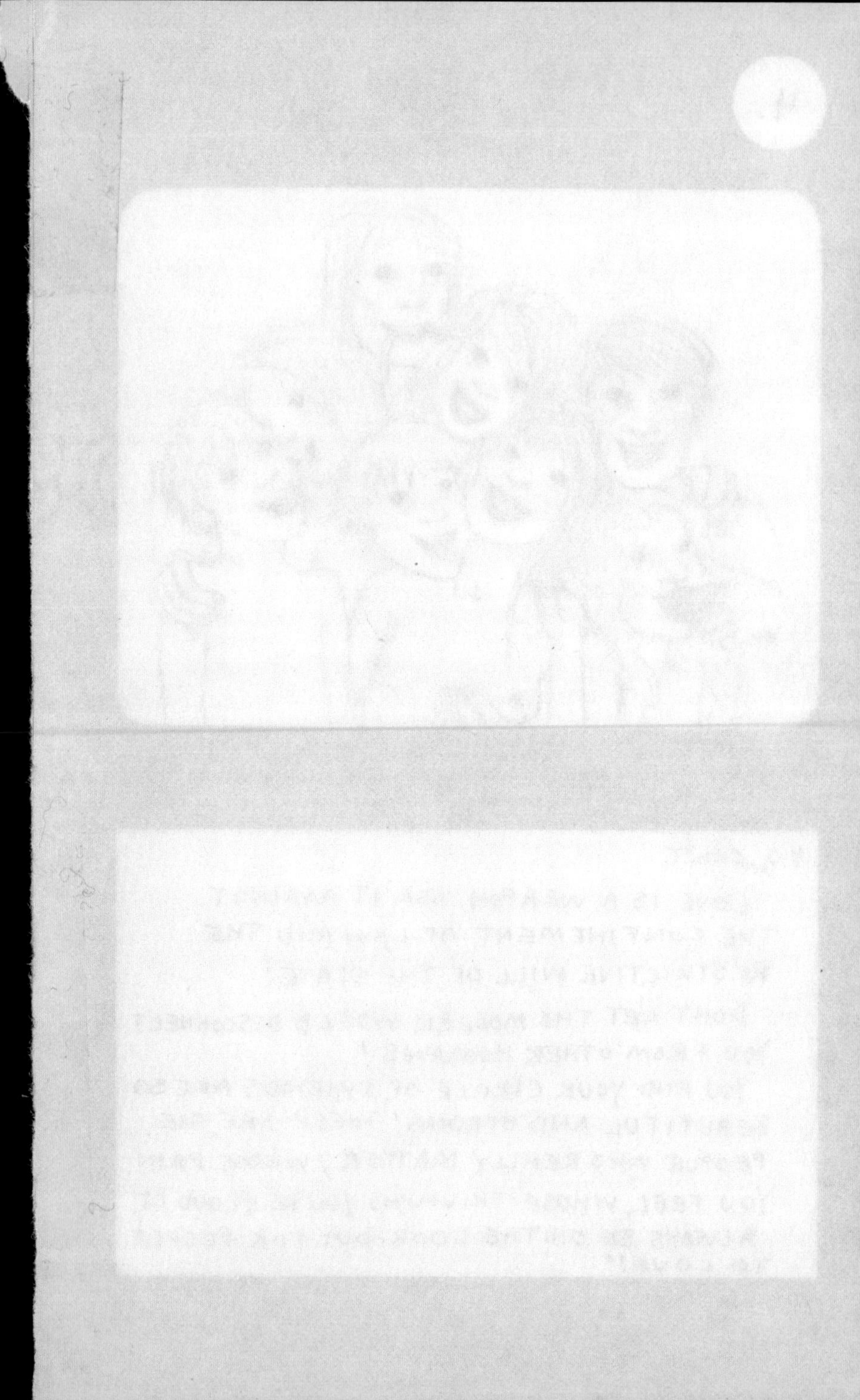

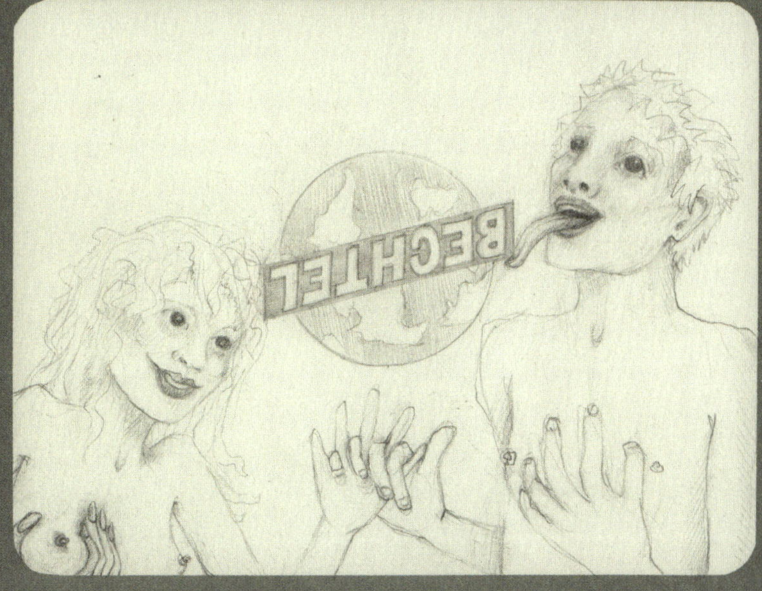

V.O. CONT.
"HERE AT BECHTELL WE COULDN'T AGREE
WITH YOU MORE.
WE'RE JUST LIKE YOU.
TAKING FULL ADVANTAGE OF OUR
FREEDOM AND RIGHT TO AFFECT CHANGE
IN A WORLD THAT NEEDS CHANGING.
LOVING OUR FRIENDS, THRIVING ON
THE POWER THAT HUMAN CONNECTION
GIVES US."

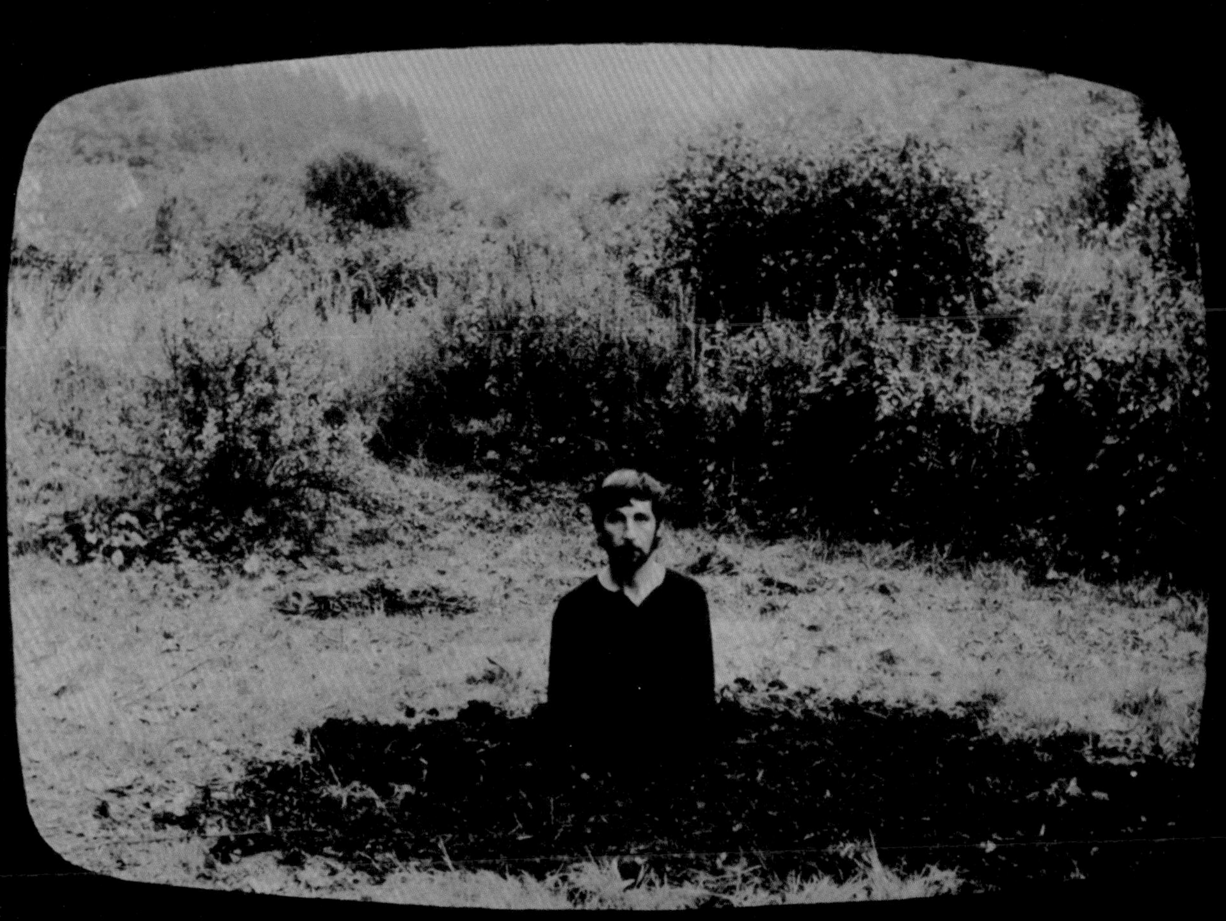

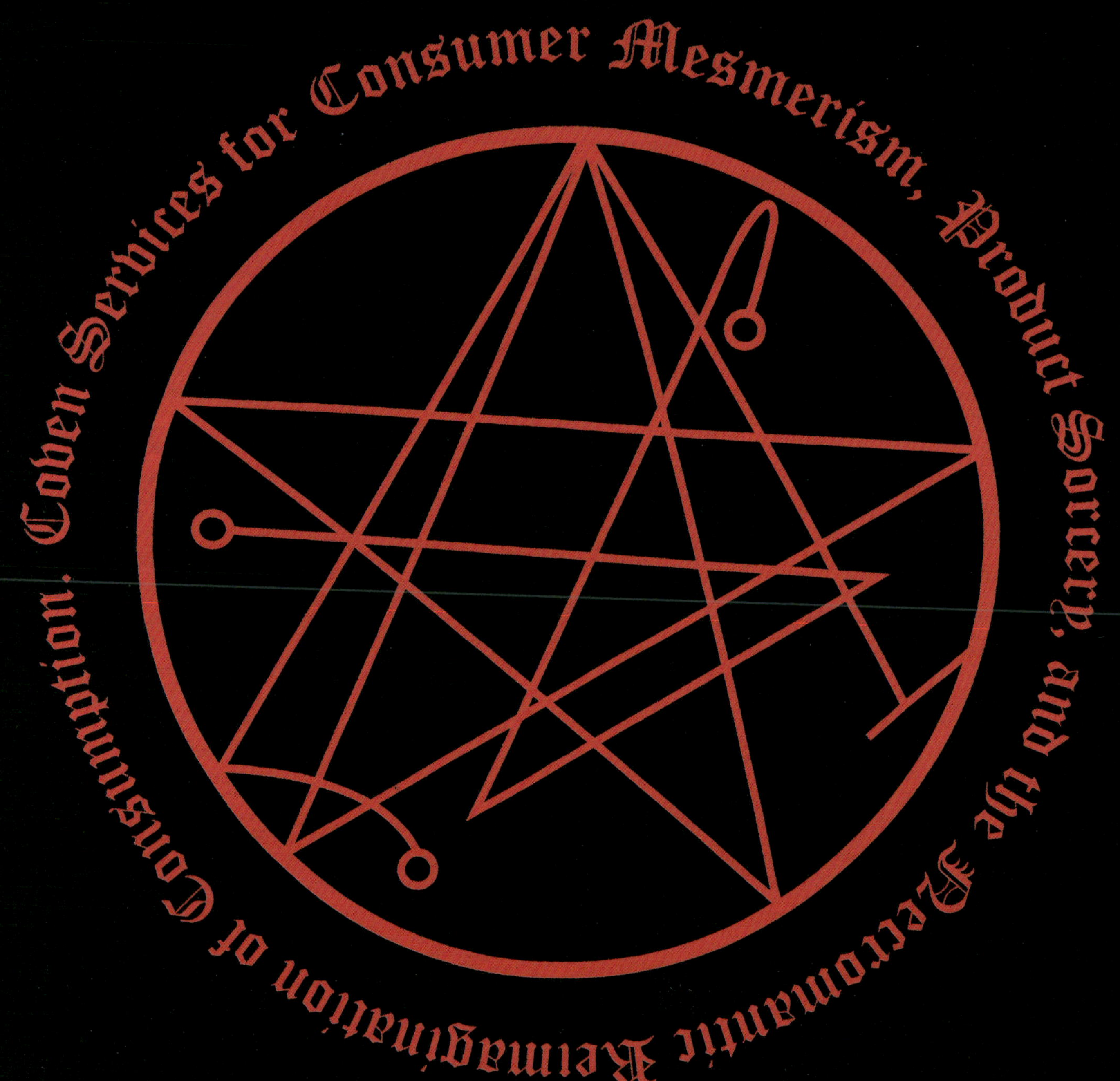
Coven Services for Consumer Mesmerism, Product Sorcery, and the Necromantic Reimagination of Consumption.

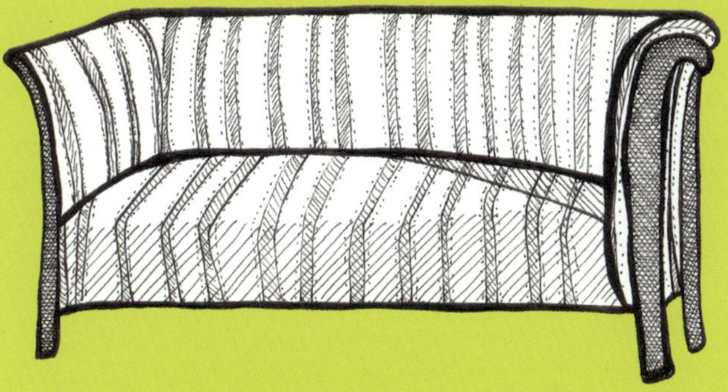
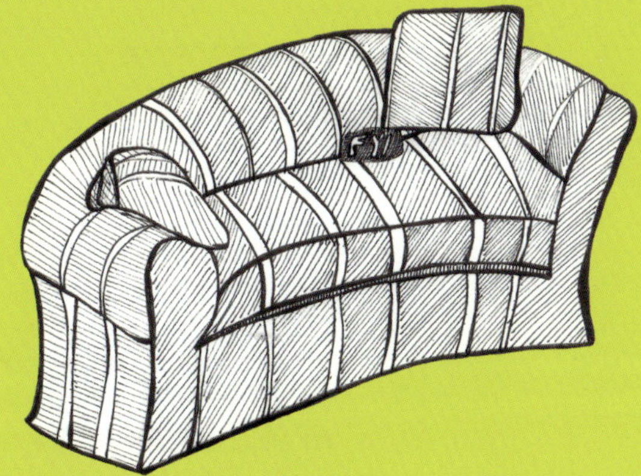

SEAT OF COMEDY

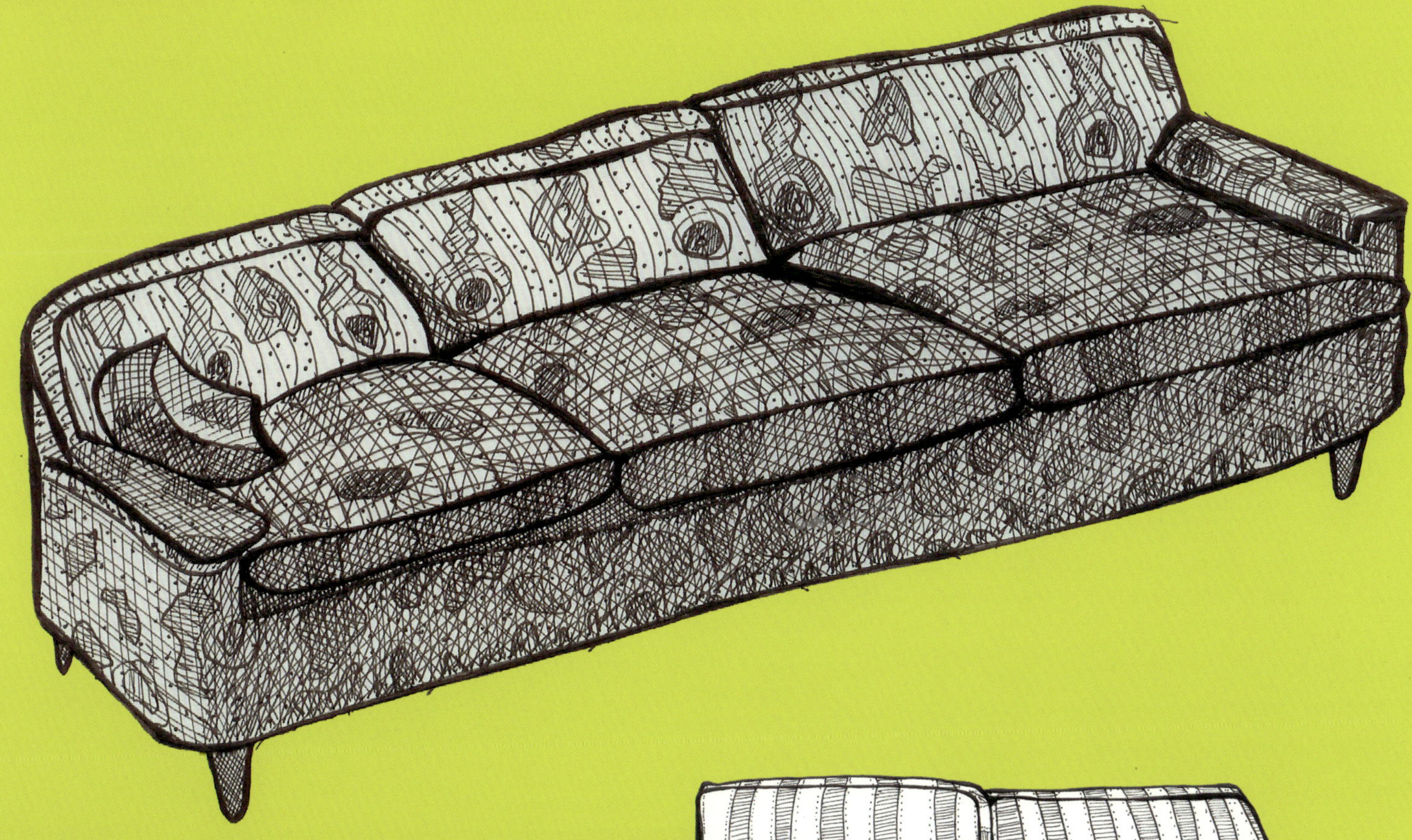

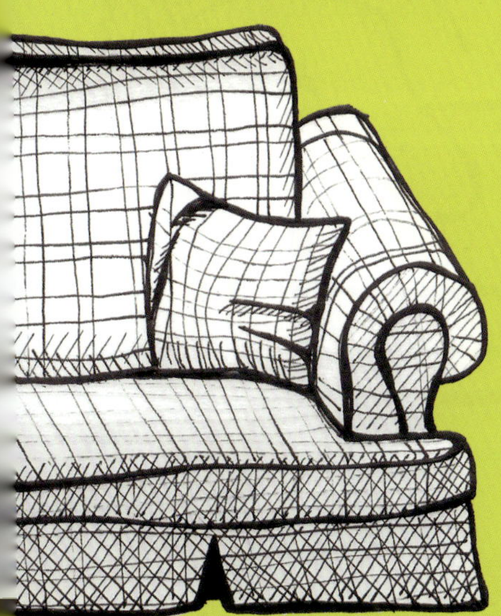

Text and drawings by Mame McCutchin

99

I was raised on—and to a certain degree, by—sitcoms.
When my parents were arguing about their impending divorce, I was watching George
and Weezy duke it out on *The Jeffersons,* followed by a marathon of Mr. Kotter and the
Sweathogs, the Fonz, Mork, and Mr. Roper. I ached to join these characters on their
couches as they sat together laughing, crying, and hugging one another. Whether it was
the swanky upholstered settee on *The Jeffersons* or *Laverne and Shirley*'s blue-collar
budget sofa, these couches emanated a sense of solidity as, week after week, wacky
plotlines threatened to pull families asunder (if only until the end of each episode).

I never quite shook my fascination with these sitcom sofas, and as I was nosing
about looking for a research topic for graduate work in cinema studies a few years ago,
I finally had an excuse to indulge it. After half a semester's worth of reading and viewing, along with all of the hours I had spent with my TV families as a kid, I felt vindi-
cated to discover how pivotal this one piece of furniture is to the sitcom genre. In fact,
I would argue that sofas are not just pieces of furniture in these shows; they are the
primary signifiers of class and family unity, and function as the anchors of identification for the audience.

Sofas first appeared in the living rooms of early family-oriented TV shows from the
late 1940s and 1950s such as *The Ruggles* (1949–1952), *Father Knows Best* (1954–
1960), and *Leave It to Beaver* (1957–1963). Much has been written about how these
early sitcoms—essentially created to sell the products of their sponsors—established
and maintained the myth of the "all-American" white suburban middle-class family. The Cleaver family from *Leave It to Beaver* is a classic and ridiculously enduring
exemplar of this mythical entity, so much so that the name *June Cleaver* has become
synonymous with *perfect housewife.* Also in the canon of unattainable domestic perfection is the Nelson family from the hugely popular *The Adventures of Ozzie and Harriet*
(1958–1966). And even earlier was *The Growing Paynes* (1948–1949), one of the
very first sitcoms to air in the U.S., which portrayed a working father, stay-at-home
mom, and young son who live in the suburbs. Historian Mary Beth Haralovich pegs
this mythic family as "a social and economic arrangement valued as the cornerstone
of the American economy in the 1950s." As I took a closer look at sitcoms from this
period and those that followed, I was struck by how the sofas in these shows provide a
consistent series of visual cues about how well the characters of any particular series
are living up to their end of that arrangement.

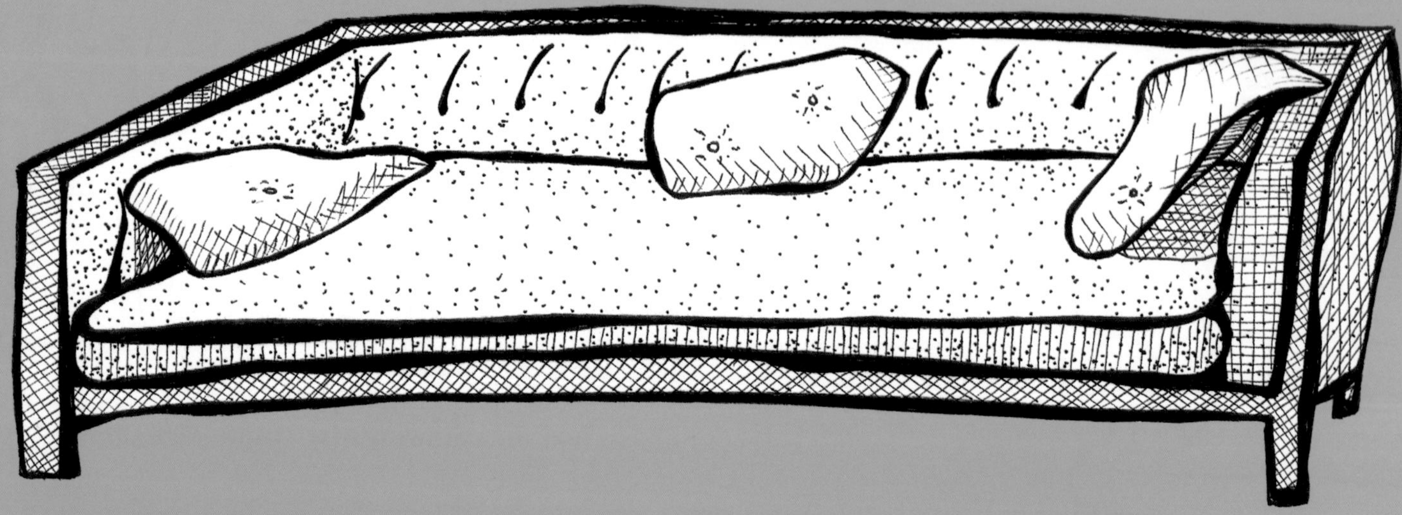

  PREVIOUS PAGE (CENTER): *Married...with Children*'s iconic sofa; ABOVE: The upscale couch from *The Jeffersons*

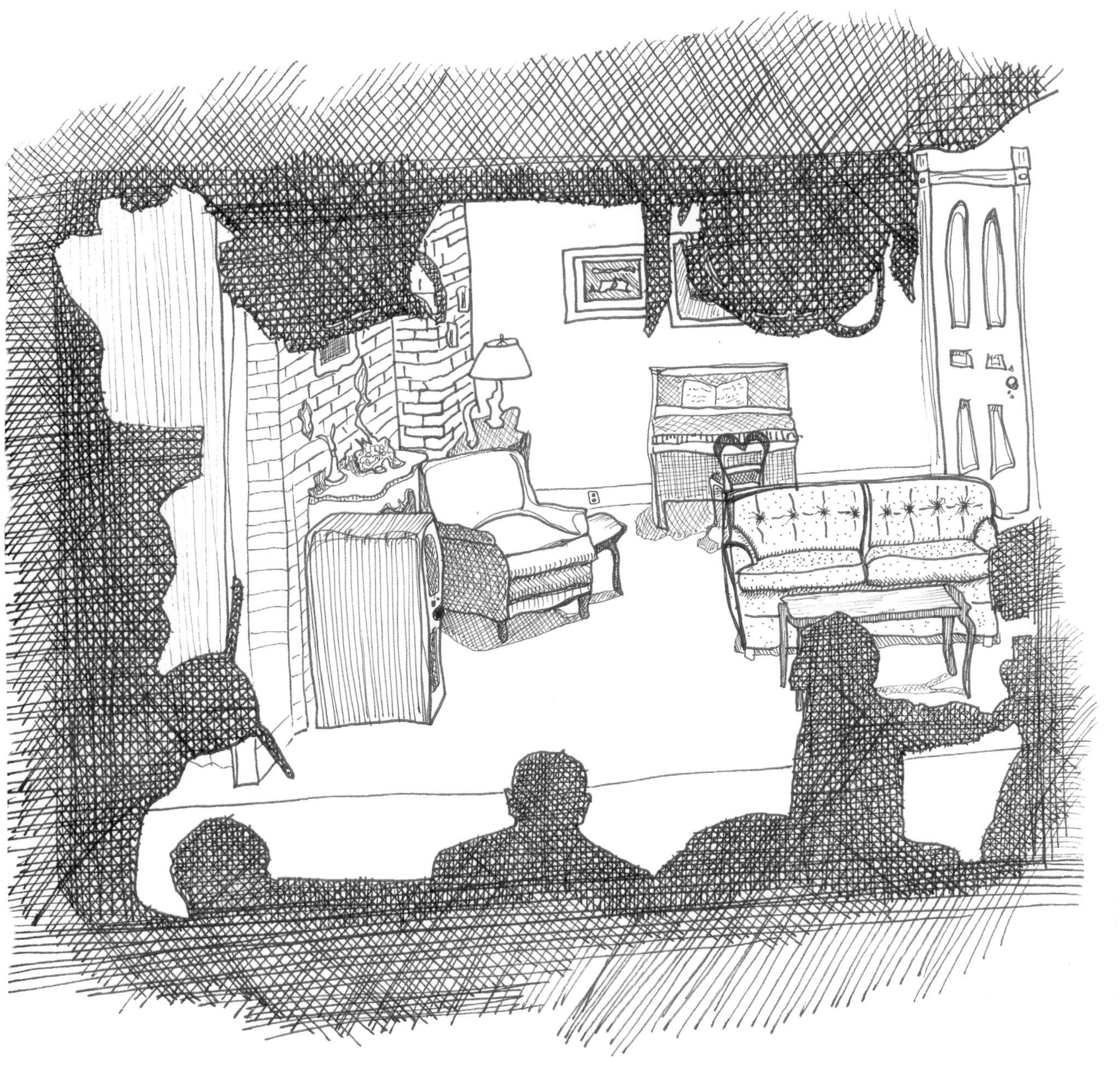

Most shows that depict solidly middle-class families, such as *I Love Lucy* (1951–1957), *The Dick Van Dyke Show* (1961–1966), and *Happy Days* (1974–1984), or, more recently, *Family Ties* (1982–1989), *Growing Pains* (1985–1992), *Married… with Children* (1987–1997), *Everybody Loves Raymond* (1996–2005), and *That '70s Show* (1998–2006), feature sofas that are squared off to the central camera in the three-camera setup that is pretty much universal to these shows (we have Desi Arnaz to thank for this convention). Essentially, viewers are being presented with a mirror image of themselves. This even happens on animated sitcoms. A particularly pointed example is the opening-credits sequence of *The Simpsons* (1989–present), which always ends with Homer, Marge, Bart, Lisa, and Maggie piling on the couch facing us to watch TV—a scene that surely reflects the hustle some viewers make to get to the set in time for the popular show's beginning.

Any variation on this theme almost always indicates trouble in mythical family land. On the set of *Will & Grace* (1998–2006), for example, there is a couch, but the small television in the room is placed in front of a stuffed chair located upstage, suggesting that there is no family—or to be more specific, no straight couple and their children—to sit on the couch and watch TV together. Indeed, the chair belongs to Will, who is gay and therefore forced into exile when he engages in that all-American activity of watching TV.

Sitcoms with a couch that is perpendicular to the central camera or positioned at an odd angle generally feature families that are dealing with difficult, fractured relationships. For example, the Bunkers' couch in *All in the Family* (1971–1979) is at a right angle to the camera and appears only occasionally, usually occupied by Archie's liberal daughter, Gloria, and son-in-law, Mike, with whom he is constantly at odds. Taking the prime position at center stage is Archie's worn armchair. In the eight-year run of the series, nothing about Archie's chair ever changes, reflecting the rigidity of his character and isolating him as an anachronism—basically, something to laugh at. The brilliance of the show's designers, writers, and its creator, Norman Lear, was in realizing that some of their viewers would not laugh at Archie; rather, they would laugh and identify with him—so they made sure that such viewers would do so only under threat of their own exile.

Also in exile is Martin, the unsophisticated father of Frasier Crane on *Frasier* (1993–2004). Frasier is an aesthete, which is clearly reflected in his apartment furnishings, so he and his uncultured father continually clash, a situation handily reinforced by the incongruity of Martin's old duct-taped Barcalounger sharing a room with Frasier's Coco Chanel–replica couch. Since he has faded as a patriarch, Martin is relegated to his own domain, where he remains as a source of continual annoyance to his children. Frank Barone, the father of Ray on *Everybody Loves Raymond,* serves as another example of the father-in-exile routine found in many domestic sitcoms (and, for that matter, at my in-laws' house).

And then there is *3rd Rock from the Sun,* which provides one of my favorite examples of the sofa as a litmus test for family unification. The clan of aliens doesn't sit on a couch; instead, they have arranged a row of single chairs next to each other. This, I would argue, reflects the fact that they are only masquerading as an American family and can't fully grasp the idea of togetherness. Interestingly, though, in *Harry and the Hendersons* (1991–1993), *ALF* (1986–1990), *Small Wonder* (1985–1989), and a number of other shows featuring solitary aliens, robots, or supernatural creatures, couches still have a prominent place on the set, squared off to the camera, because these shows all feature "regular" American families sticking together under extraordinary circumstances.

The position and appearance of couches on certain sitcoms not only points to the level of unity among family members, it also indicates a family's financial status, which is a key element for audience identification—or not. For instance, well-off sitcom families nearly always have a couch on their main set that goes unused. On *The Nanny* (1993–1999), the sofa, which is perpendicular to the proscenium, typically remains off-limits. It is light in color—an unrealistic and just plain silly choice for a family with young kids—and is often piled with so many pillows that there is no place to sit. While the main character, Fran, is welcome in family affairs and occasionally perches upon an arm of the couch, she usually sits in a chair or stands, symbolizing her status as an employee from another class. Similar situations can be found on *The Fresh Prince of Bel-Air* (1990–1996) and *Diff'rent Strokes* (1978–1985), which also deal with class lines.

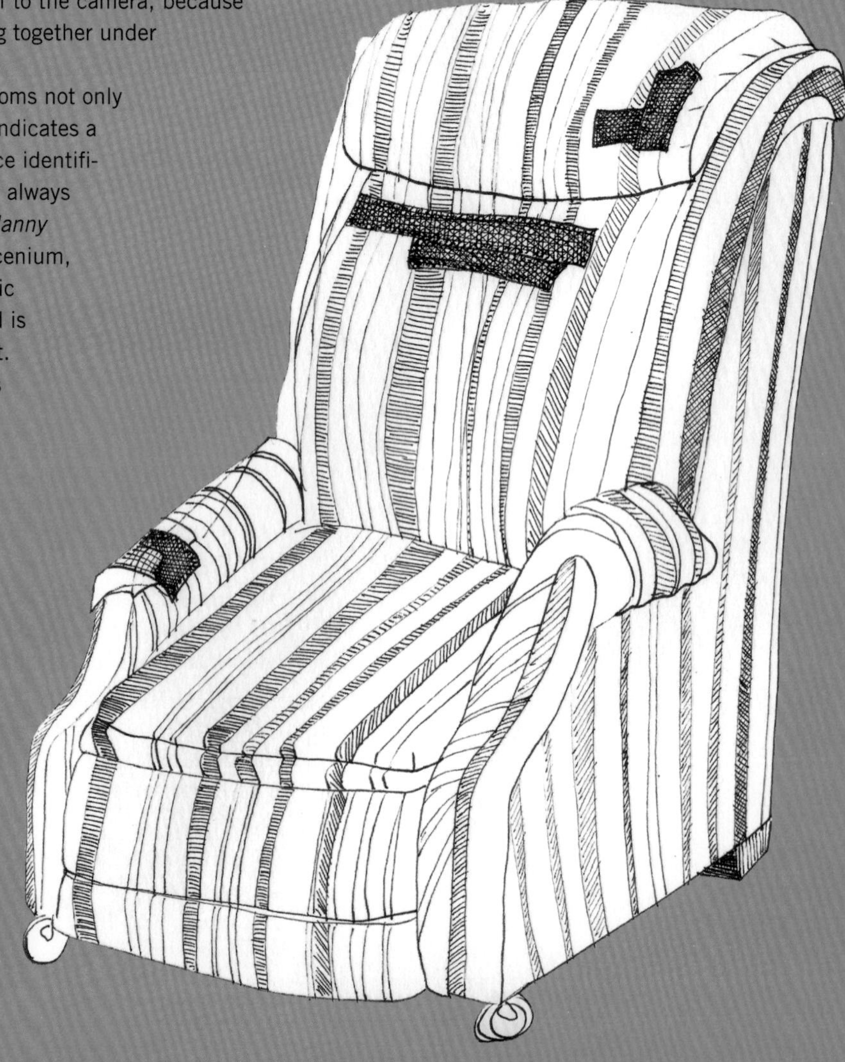

    RIGHT: Martin's duct-taped Barcalounger from *Frasier*

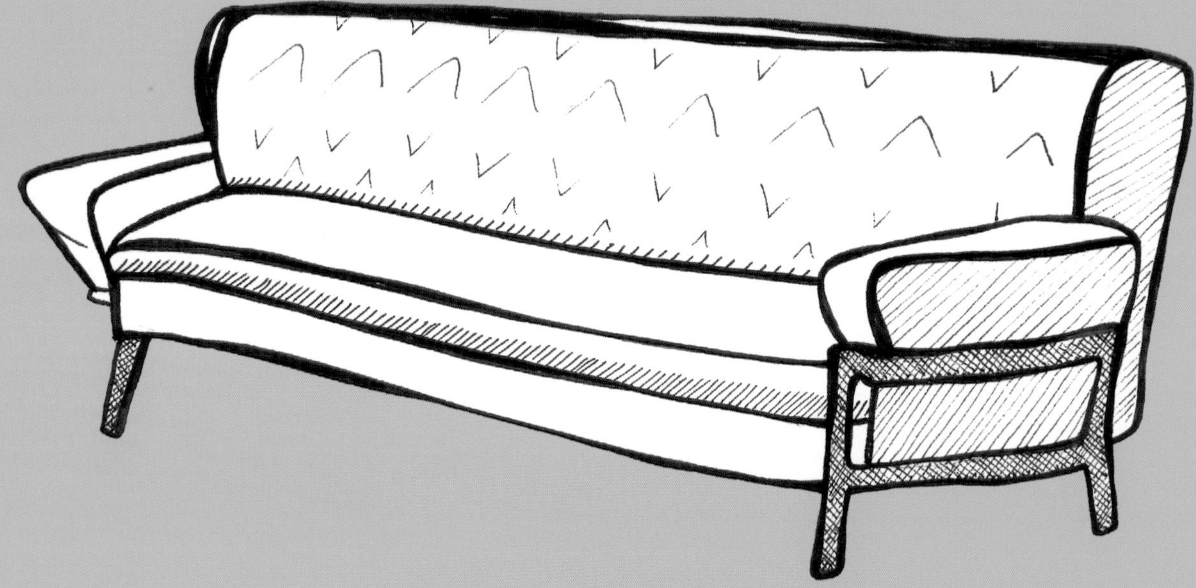

Yet another example of a wealthy sitcom family is the Clampetts, from one of my favorite shows, the wonderfully subversive *The Beverly Hillbillies* (1962–1971). Some episodes feature a sitting room with a couch, but most of the action takes place in the large kitchen, the main hall (with its grand staircase and chandelier), and the bank, where waiting-room chairs are the closest we get to seeing the characters seated together as a family. The lack of couch on this show seems to reflect the fact that the "family" is anything but nuclear: Consisting of characters named Granny, Uncle Jed, Cousin Jethro, and Elly May, the show defies viewers to figure out who is grandmother, uncle, or cousin to whom. In 1962, this couchless quandary no doubt made it difficult for viewers to identify with the family, but some have argued that *The Beverly Hillbillies,* like *The Munsters* (1964–1966) and *The Addams Family* (1964–1966), actually paved the way for shows featuring "nontraditional" families.

On the other end of the economic spectrum are characters like the Evans family of *Good Times* (1974–1979) and Fred and Lamont Sanford of *Sanford and Son* (1972–1977). On *Good Times,* the couch serves two purposes: It is a sofa on which people drop their coats and bags and sit, but it is also the pullout bed for the Evans sons, Michael and J.J. (In fact, when Janet Jackson's character, Penny, joins the show, she tells the boys that there's enough room for her to sleep there too.) This dual function of the couch—antithetical to the established each-child-in-a-bedroom legacy of those 1950s shows—made *Good Times* one of the earliest sitcoms to invite identification from nonwhite and/or poor households, and it did important work chipping away at the very idea of the mythical 1950s nuclear, suburban, white family. The couch on *Sanford and Son* is a beat-up affair draped with an old blanket. Since Fred Sanford sits mostly in his own chair (yet another example of an exiled elder with antiquated ideas), the sofa is more his son Lamont's domain. The fact that the ratty sofa is occasionally moved as part of the on-screen action, which is highly unusual in sitcoms, reflects Lamont's own aspirations for class mobility. Not surprisingly, it also functions as a disruption to any identification on the part of the audience.

Speaking of disruptions, I found evidence suggesting that any sofa replacement on a solidly middle-class family sitcom will result in automatic shark-jumping. In the final season of *Roseanne* (1988–1997), the Conner family won the lottery and bought a new couch—and that was good-bye to the show. *The Ruggles,* one of the earliest televised family sitcoms, featured a family that eventually moved from the Bronx to Long Island. They bought fancy new furniture for their fancy new house and, not surprisingly, that was the last we saw of them.

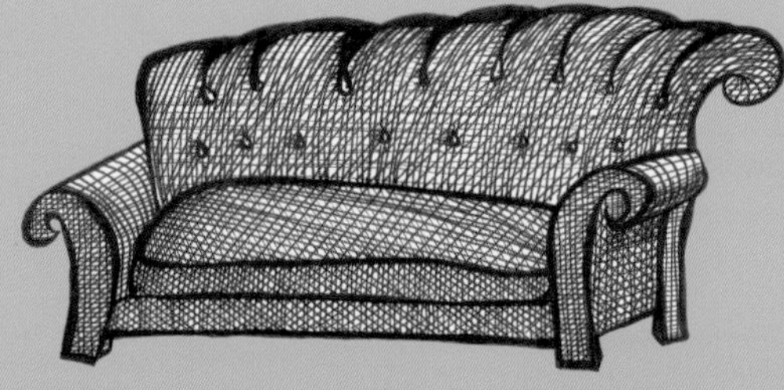

The significance of a couch purchase is underscored in a particularly resonant way in season one, episode two, of *Mad About You* (1992–1999), when the show's characters spend the entire episode buying a sofa. This shopping trip represents the sitcom's commitment to its viewership: By bringing the viewers along, they are inviting us to join them in choosing the piece of furniture that they—and we—will all share for the run of the show. Oddly, the couch they purchase in this episode ends up in the corner of the living-room set and is rarely used. Nevertheless, the gesture was very much appreciated.

Some sitcom sofas have become iconic. It is the rare TV viewer who wouldn't immediately recognize the crocheted afghan covering the Conners' couch on *Roseanne*, or the curvy orange sofa on the coffee-shop set of *Friends,* or the unfortunate upholstery on the *Married...with Children* sofa. But only one settee has attained the ultimate validation as a pop-culture artifact: In 2000, the U.S. Postal Service issued a stamp featuring the couch that served as centerpiece of the hugely popular series *The Cosby Show* (1984–1992). This oversized, slightly worn, inelegant couch, which appears to be out of place in a room filled with oriental rugs, oil paintings, and polished wood, communicates the notion that even amid the trappings of substantial wealth and higher education, family remains the most important thing. The relative modesty of the couch is visual shorthand for the fact that the Cosby family, despite the elevated legal and medical professions of Claire and Bill, subscribes to solid middle-class values. Set designer Garvin Eddy (who also designed the set for *Roseanne*) commented specifically on the Cosby's couch, asserting, "Some things have to be a little rough around the edges so you know that people actually live here."

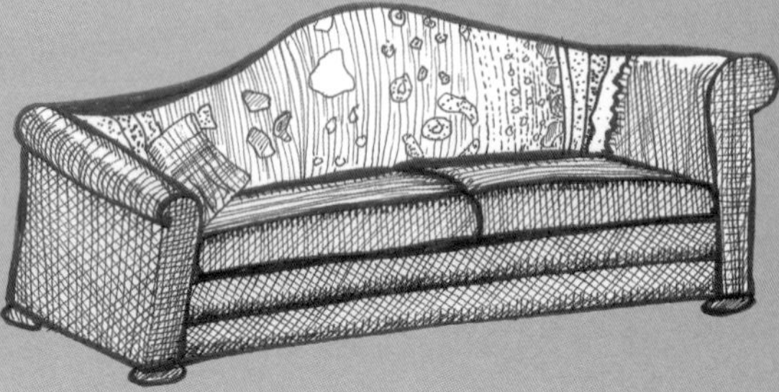

Growing up, I really wanted to be a member of the Cosby family—and I sort of thought they would have me. It seemed that breaking the news of a bad report card, or a fender-bender in the family car, would be easier to deliver nestled into that broad, comfy, and inviting couch. Completely squared off to the central camera, it evokes a sense of inclusion that transcends economics, race, and age. While most classic sitcom sofas do a fine job of offering stability and support in the midst of ever-crazier plotlines, the *Cosby* couch manages to suggest something else: Change may be unavoidable, but if a family sticks together, it is nothing to worry about. It can even get a couple of laughs.

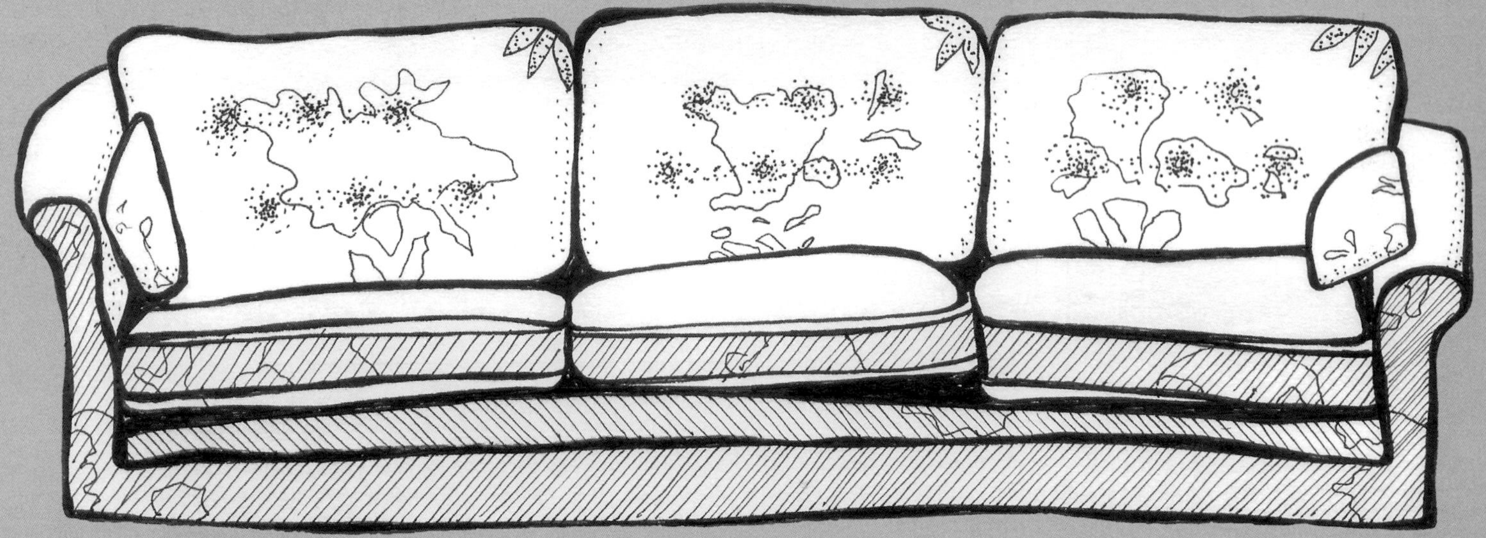

  ABOVE: *The Cosby Show*'s comfy couch; TOP RIGHT: the sofa from *Mad About You*

64
TELEVISION
SOFAS

Use the form included here (or download it from *www.esopusmag.com/files/64sofas*) to identify all 64 sofas. A complete set of correct answers wins a one-year subscription to *Esopus*.

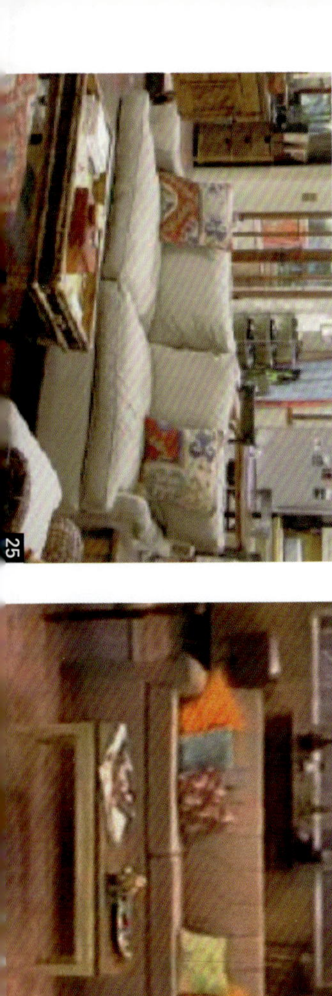
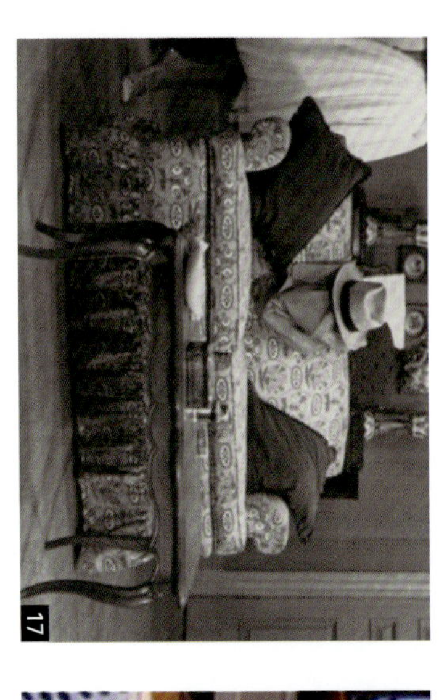
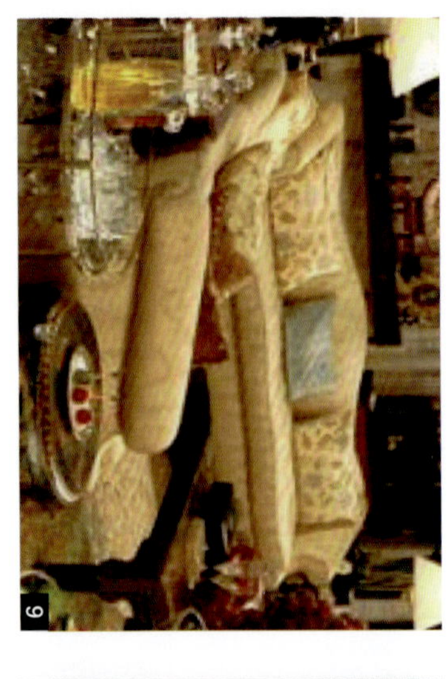
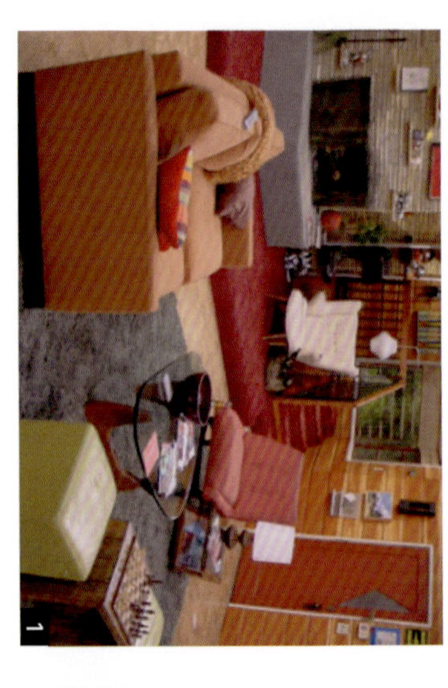
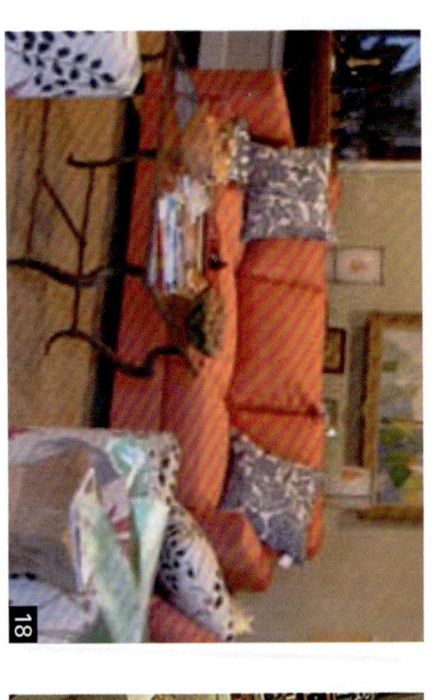
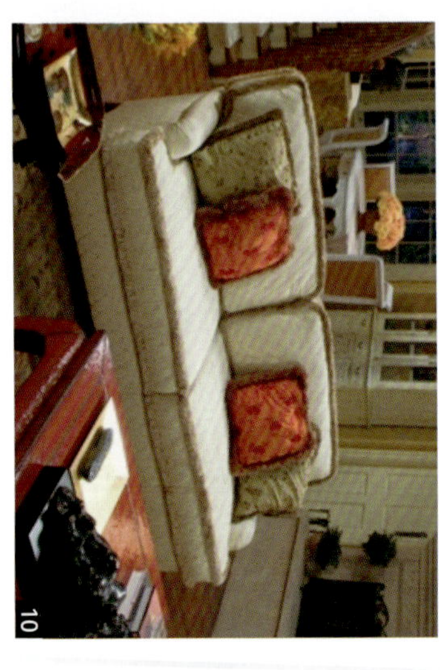
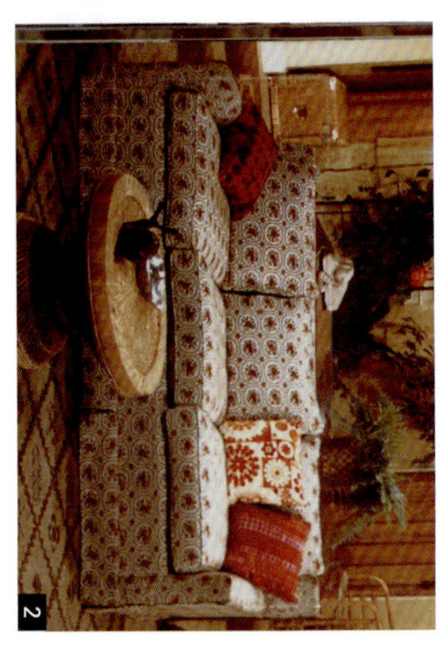
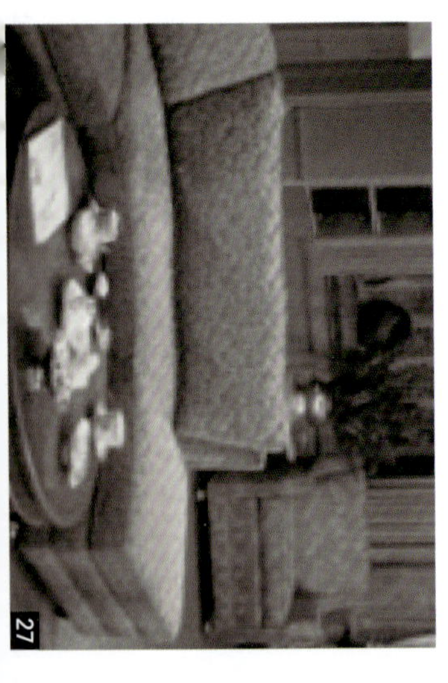
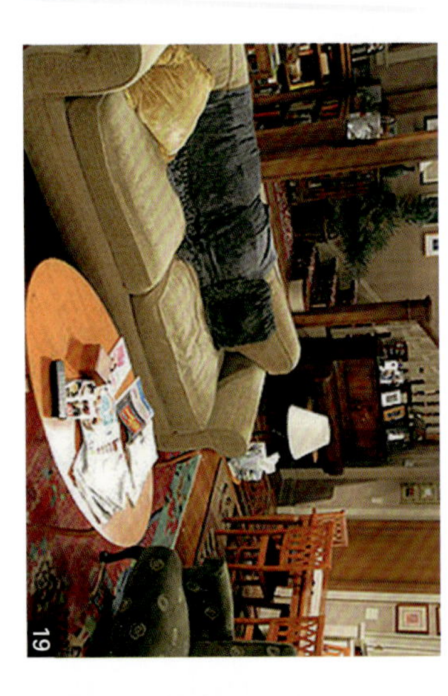
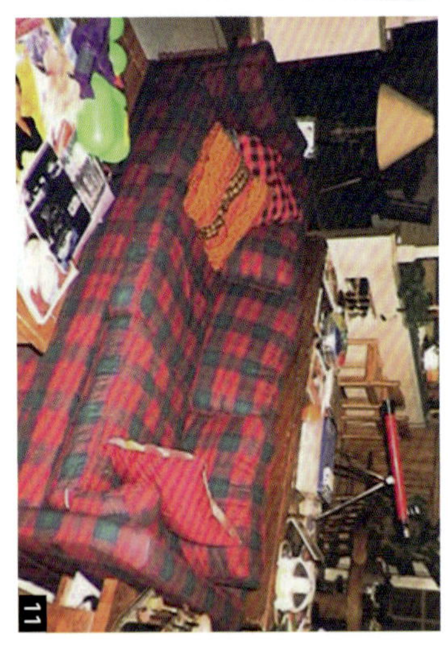
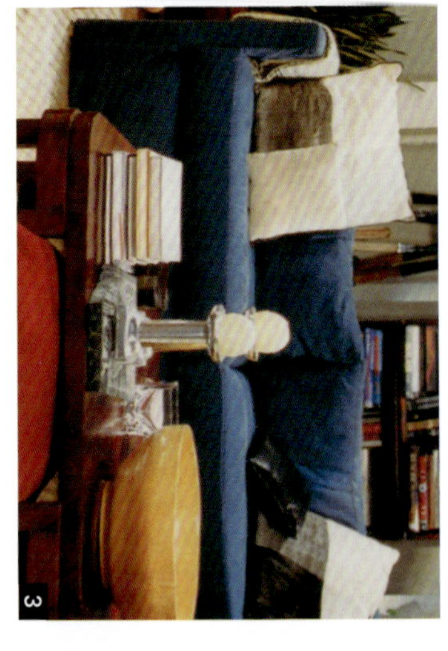
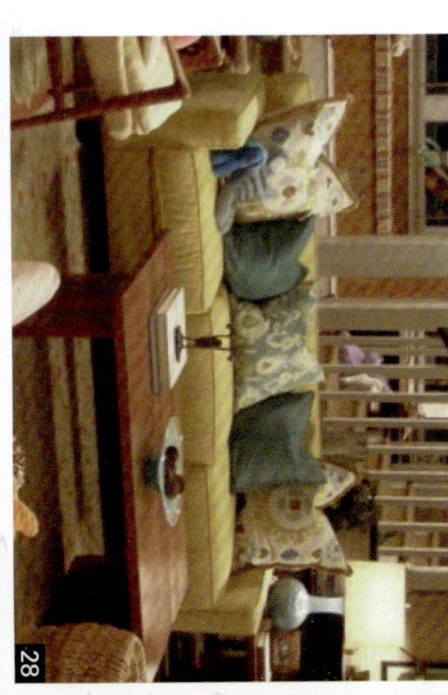
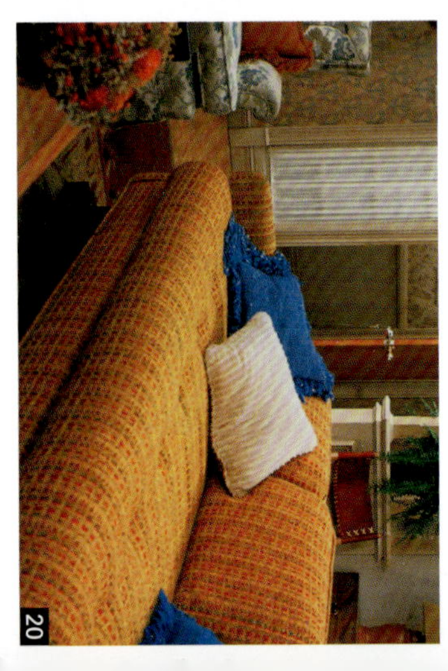
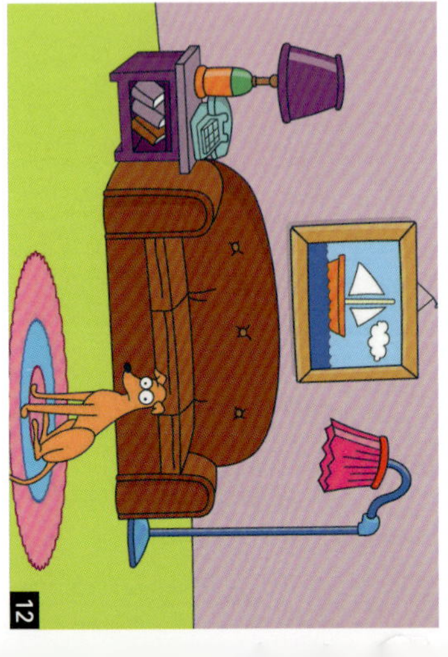
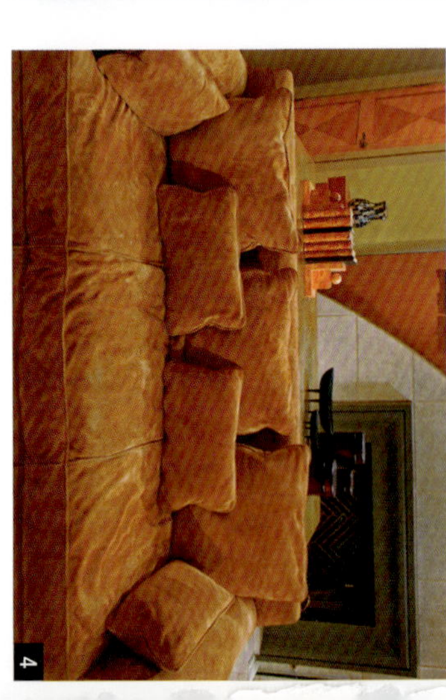

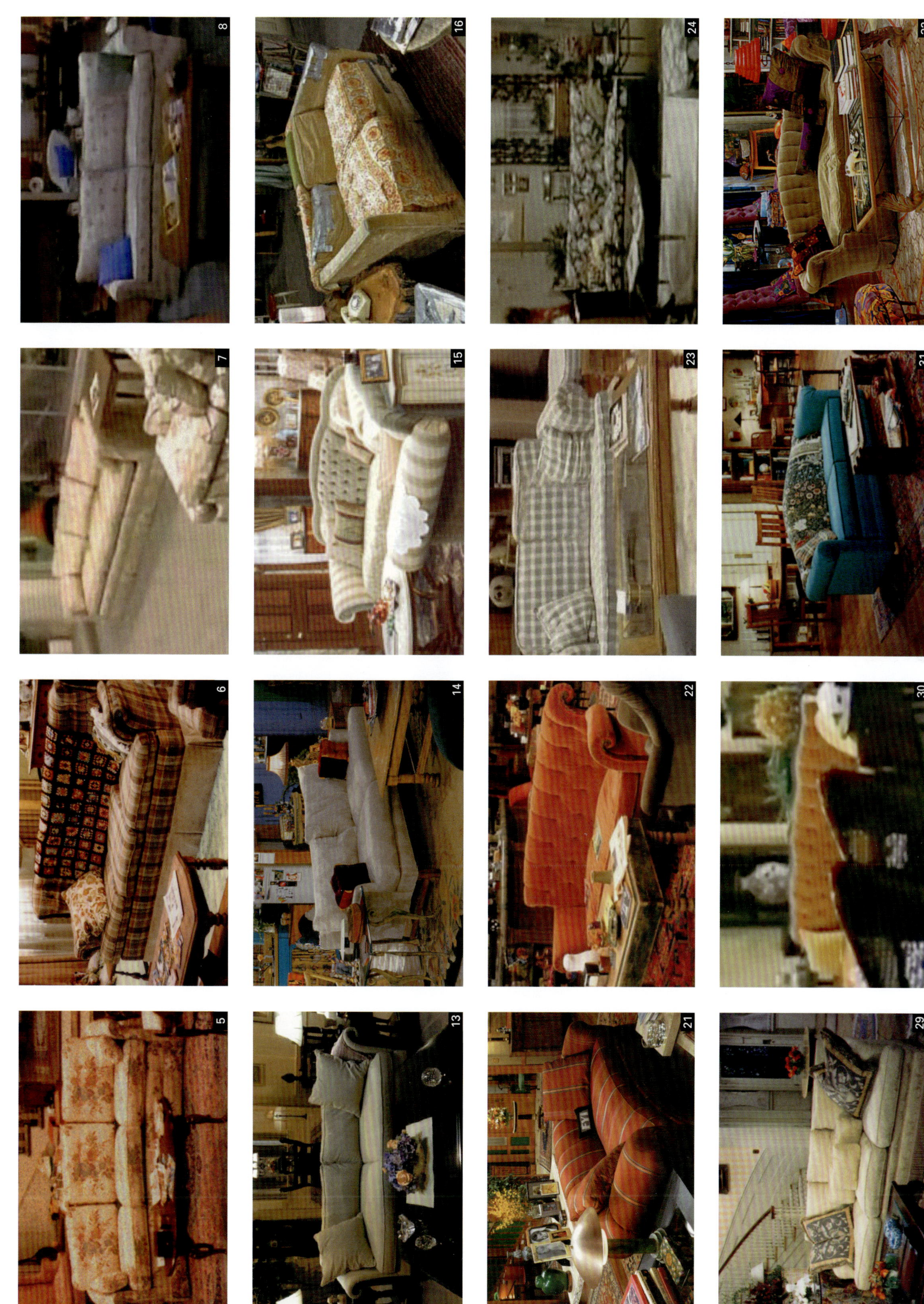

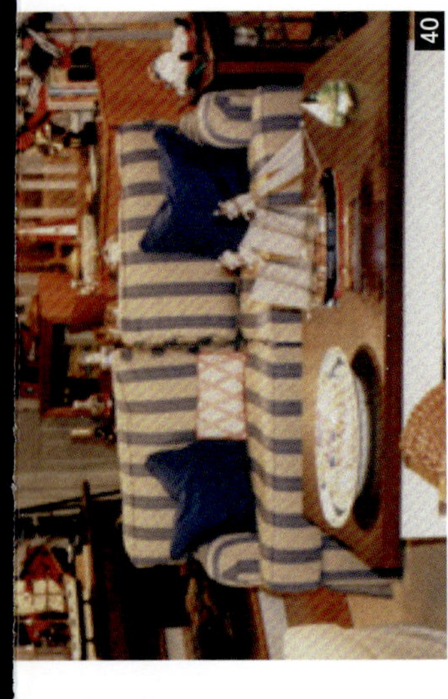
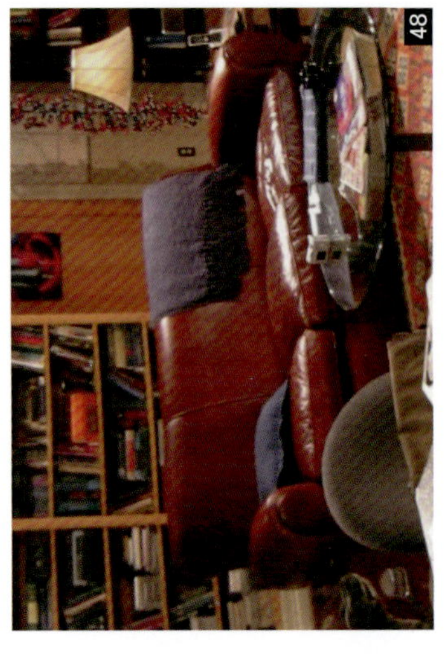
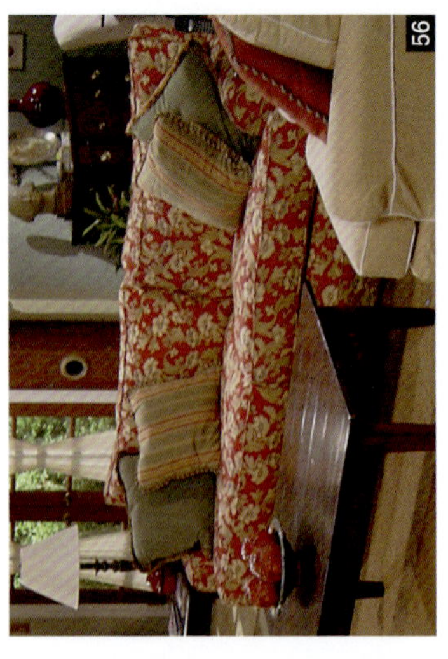
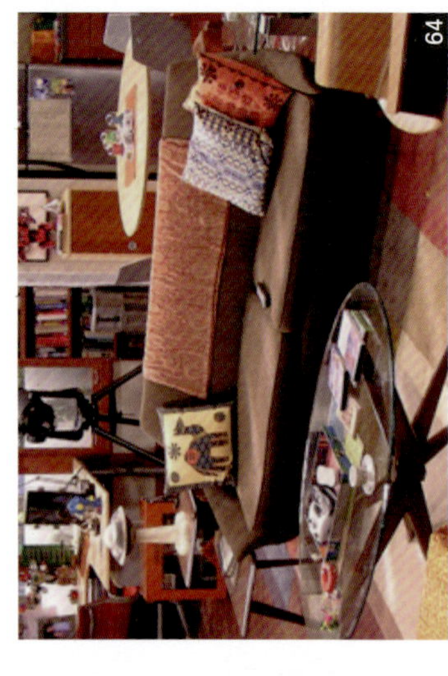
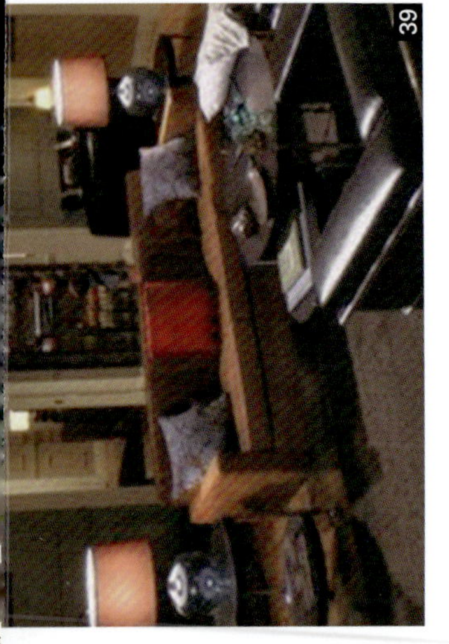
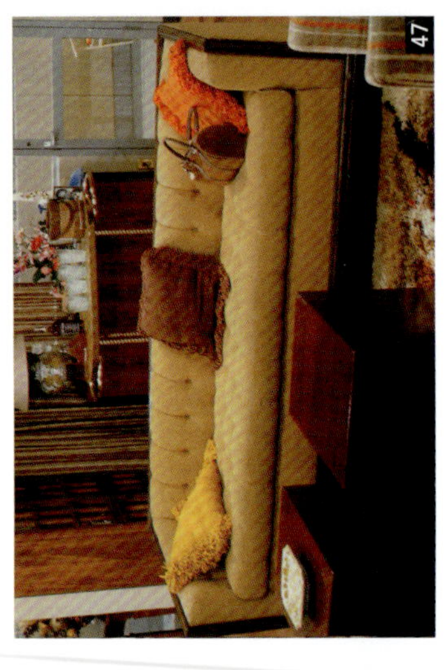
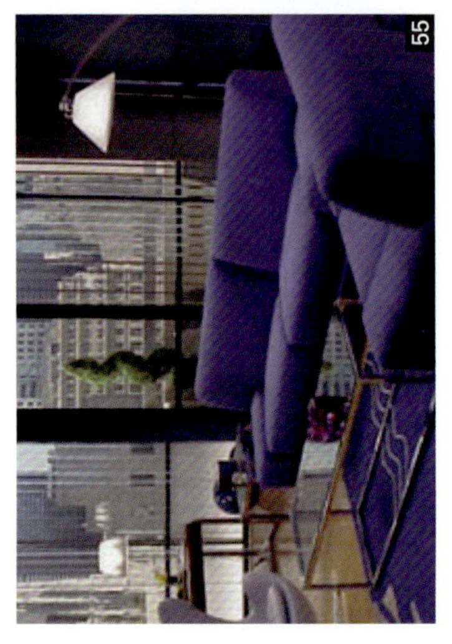
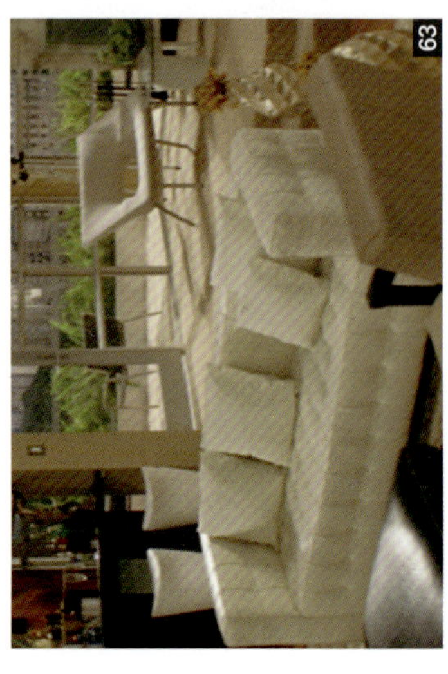
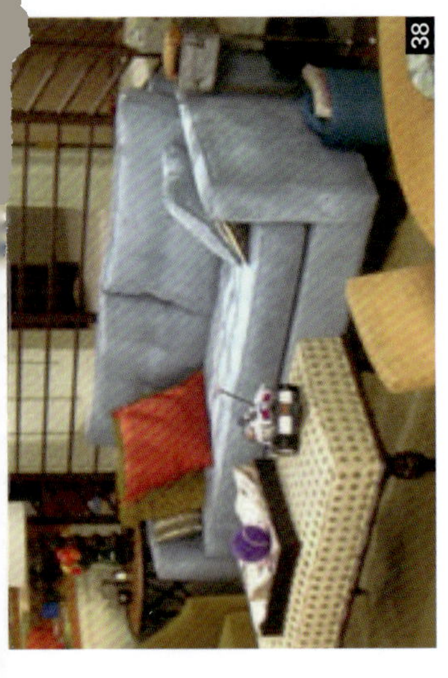
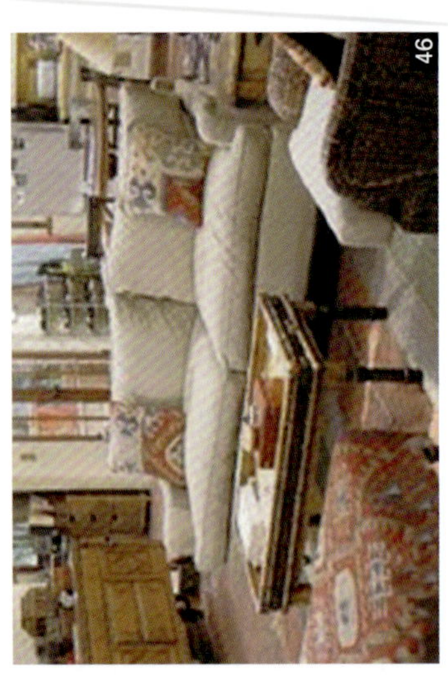
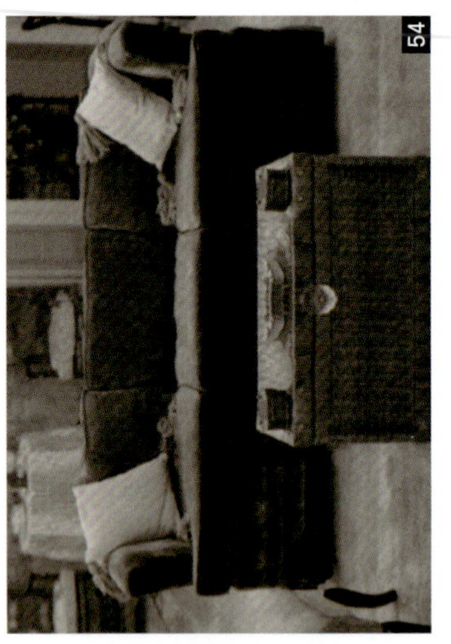
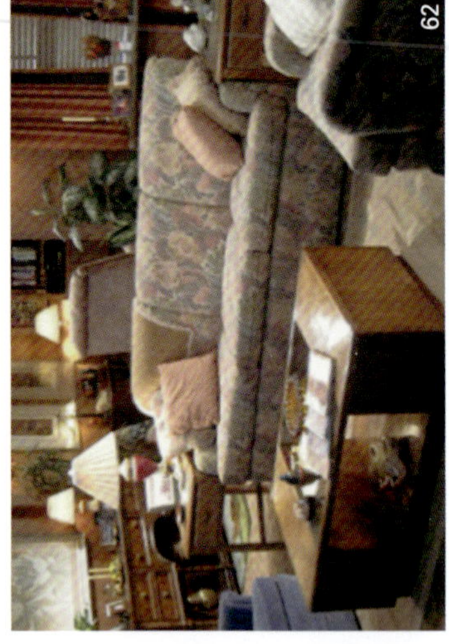
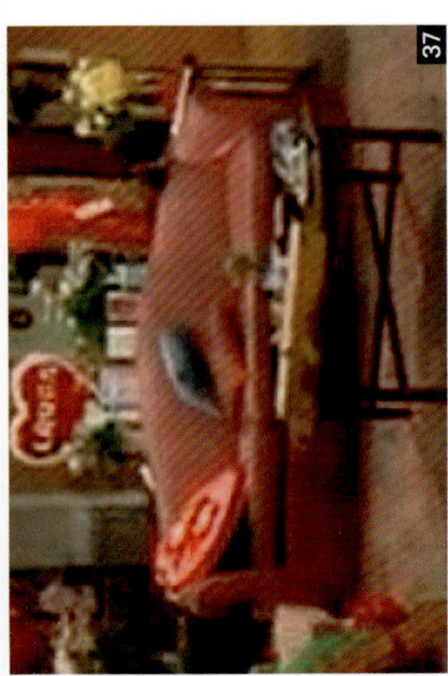
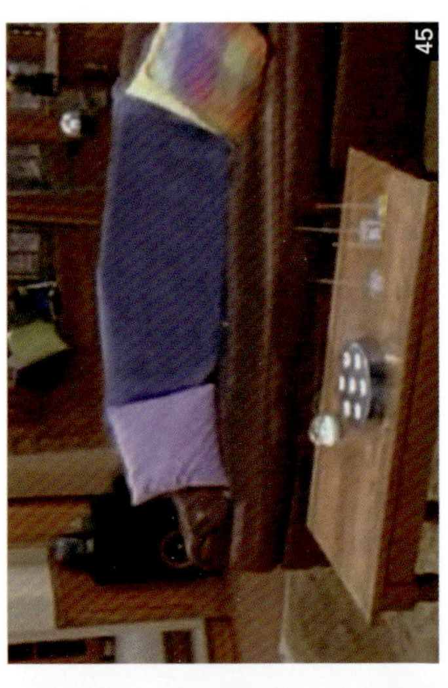
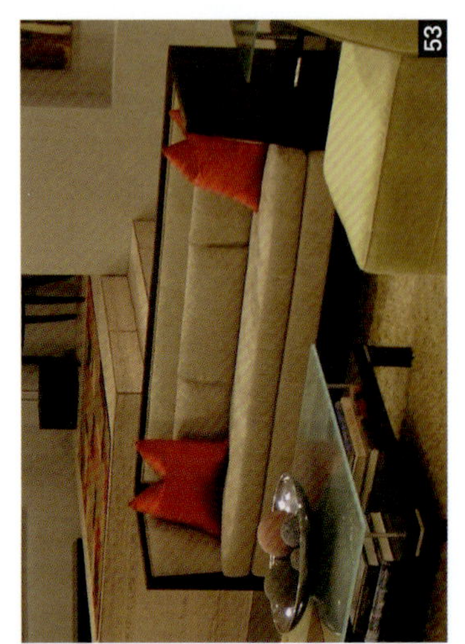
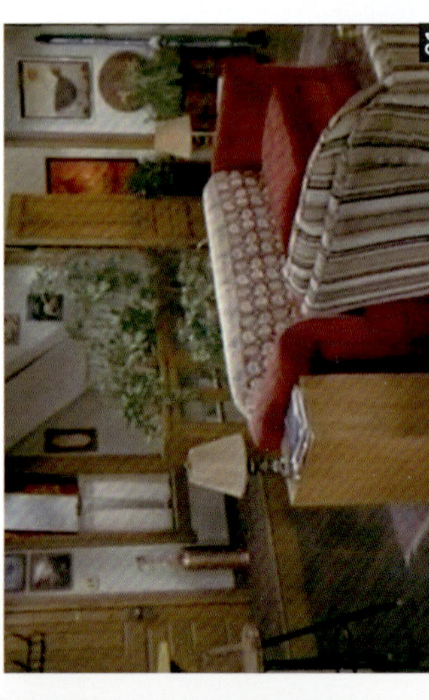

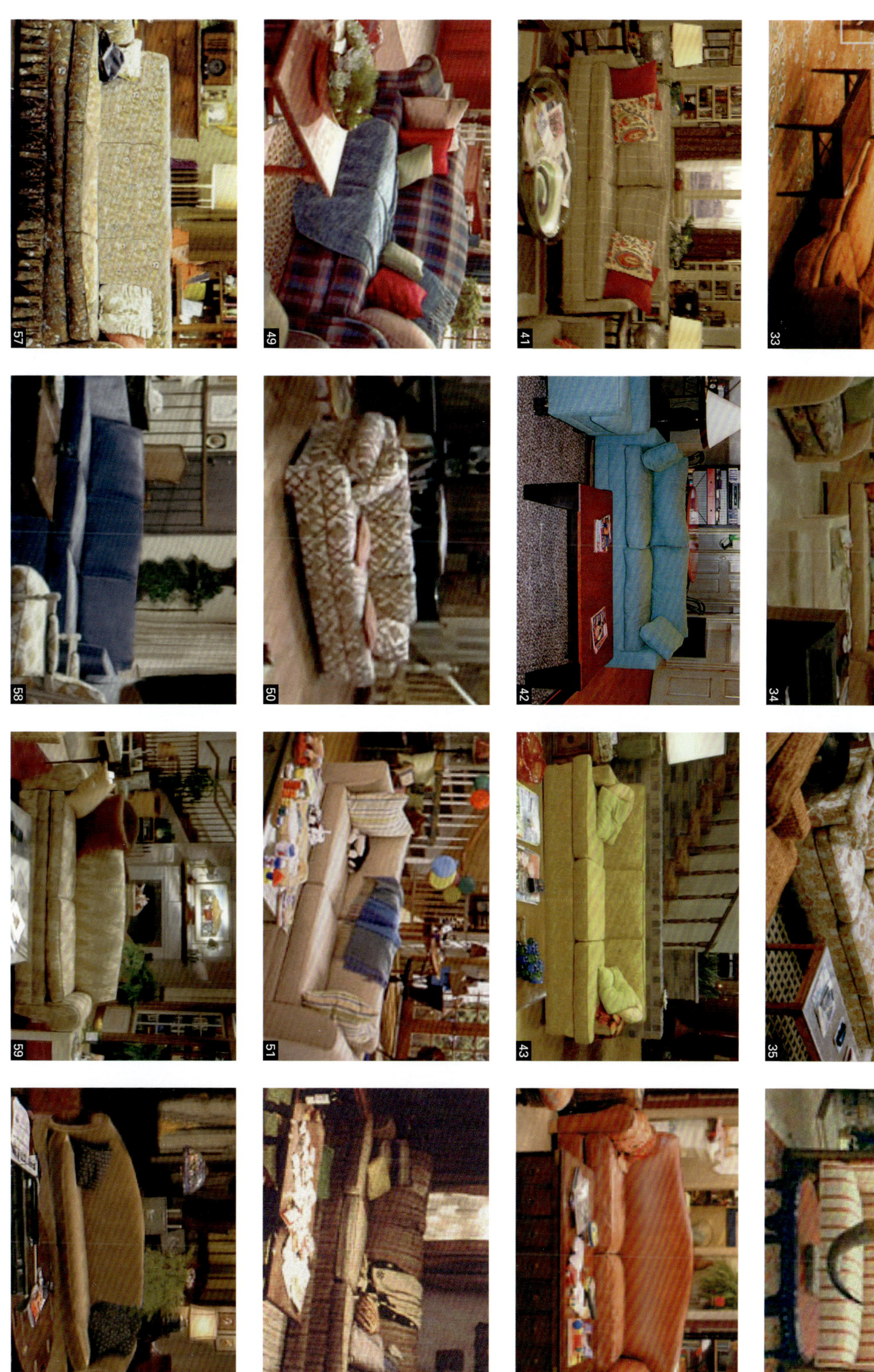

THESE 64 SOFAS ARE FROM THE FOLLOWING TELEVISION SHOWS:

1. _______________________________
2. _______________________________
3. _______________________________
4. _______________________________
5. _______________________________
6. _______________________________
7. _______________________________
8. _______________________________
9. _______________________________
10. _______________________________
11. _______________________________
12. _______________________________
13. _______________________________
14. _______________________________
15. _______________________________
16. _______________________________
17. _______________________________
18. _______________________________
19. _______________________________
20. _______________________________
21. _______________________________
22. _______________________________
23. _______________________________
24. _______________________________
25. _______________________________
26. _______________________________
27. _______________________________
28. _______________________________
29. _______________________________
30. _______________________________
31. _______________________________
32. _______________________________

33. _______________________________
34. _______________________________
35. _______________________________
36. _______________________________
37. _______________________________
38. _______________________________
39. _______________________________
40. _______________________________
41. _______________________________
42. _______________________________
43. _______________________________
44. _______________________________
45. _______________________________
46. _______________________________
47. _______________________________
48. _______________________________
49. _______________________________
50. _______________________________
51. _______________________________
52. _______________________________
53. _______________________________
54. _______________________________
55. _______________________________
56. _______________________________
57. _______________________________
58. _______________________________
59. _______________________________
60. _______________________________
61. _______________________________
62. _______________________________
63. _______________________________
64. _______________________________

GOING TO BLACK

DARA BIRNBAUM

The following 16 pages feature sequential stills from one of five channels of the video-installation work *Tiananmen Square: Break-In Transmission* (© 1990 Dara Birnbaum). These stills reveal the exact seconds when CBS and CNN were forced by the Chinese government to cease transmission at the height of the occupation of Tiananmen Square in 1989. They constitute a historic moment in broadcast television.

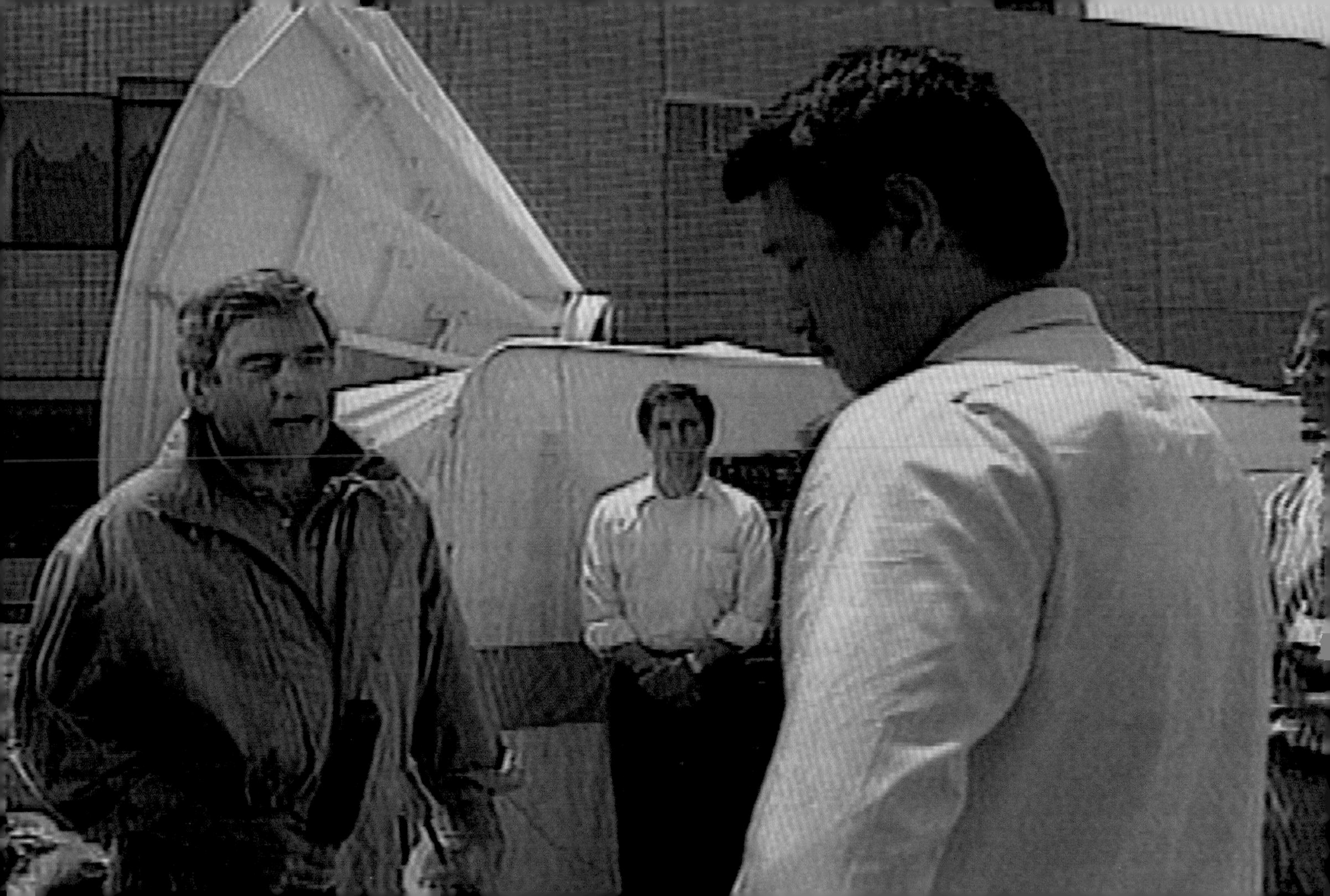

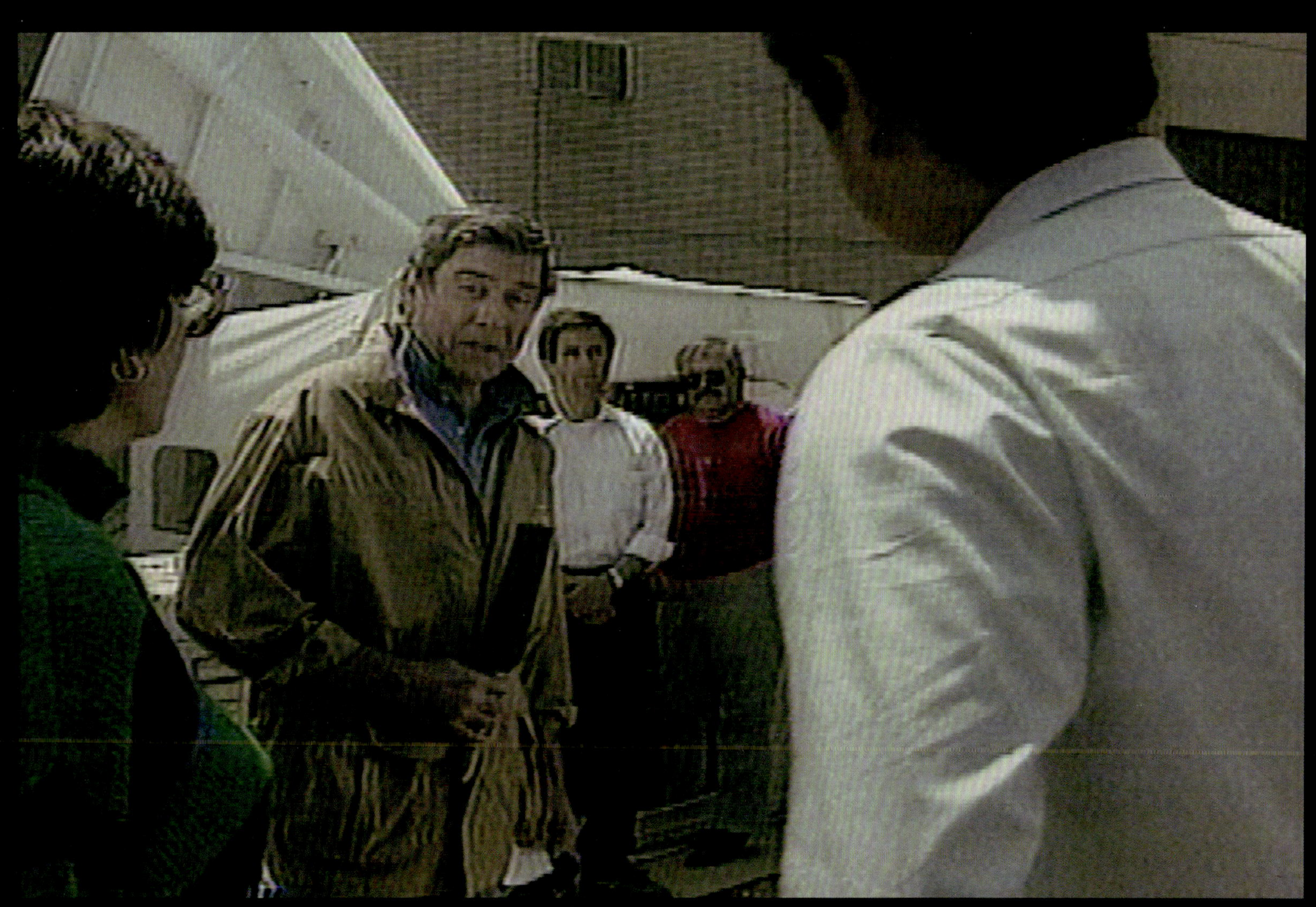

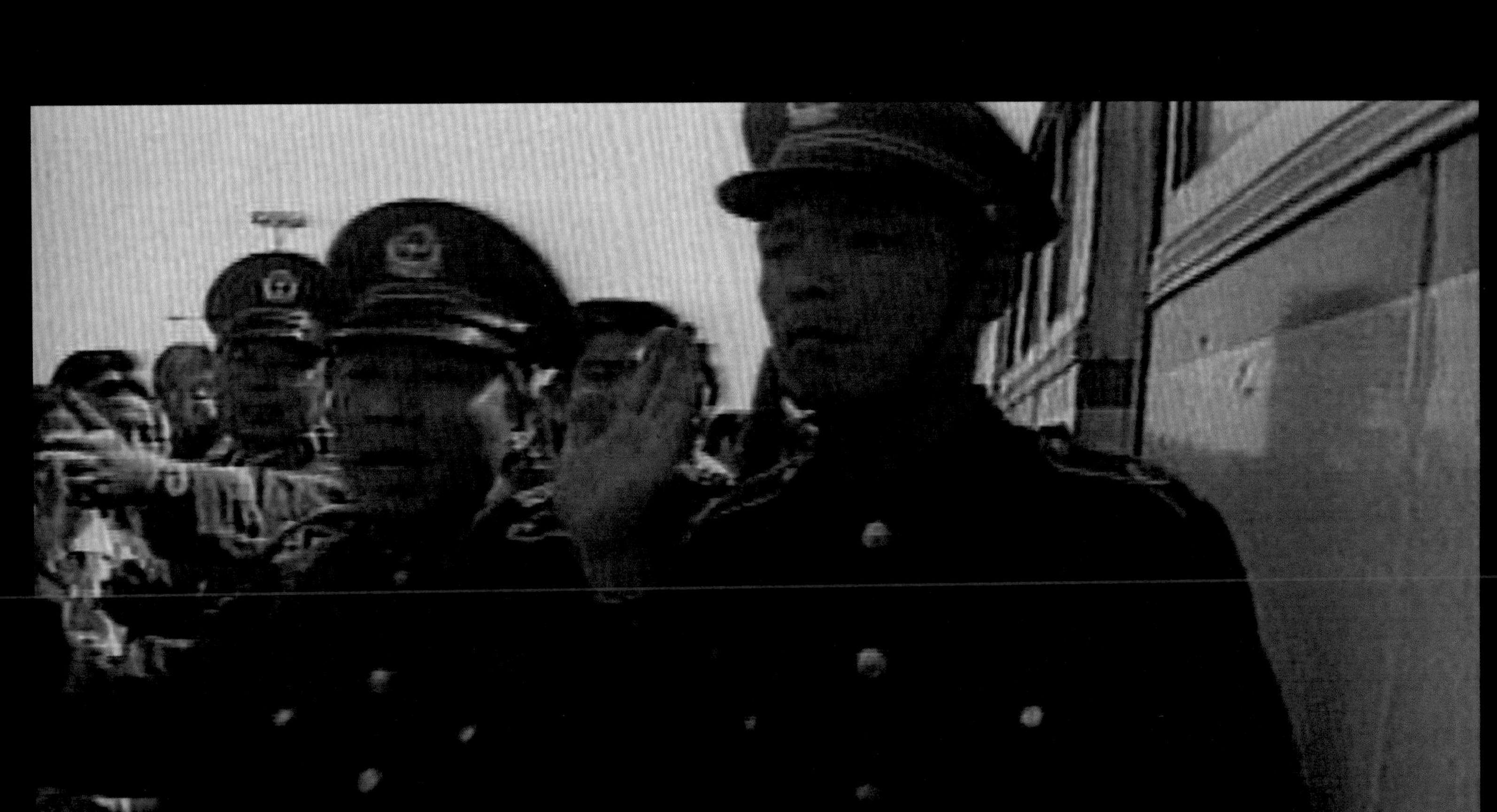

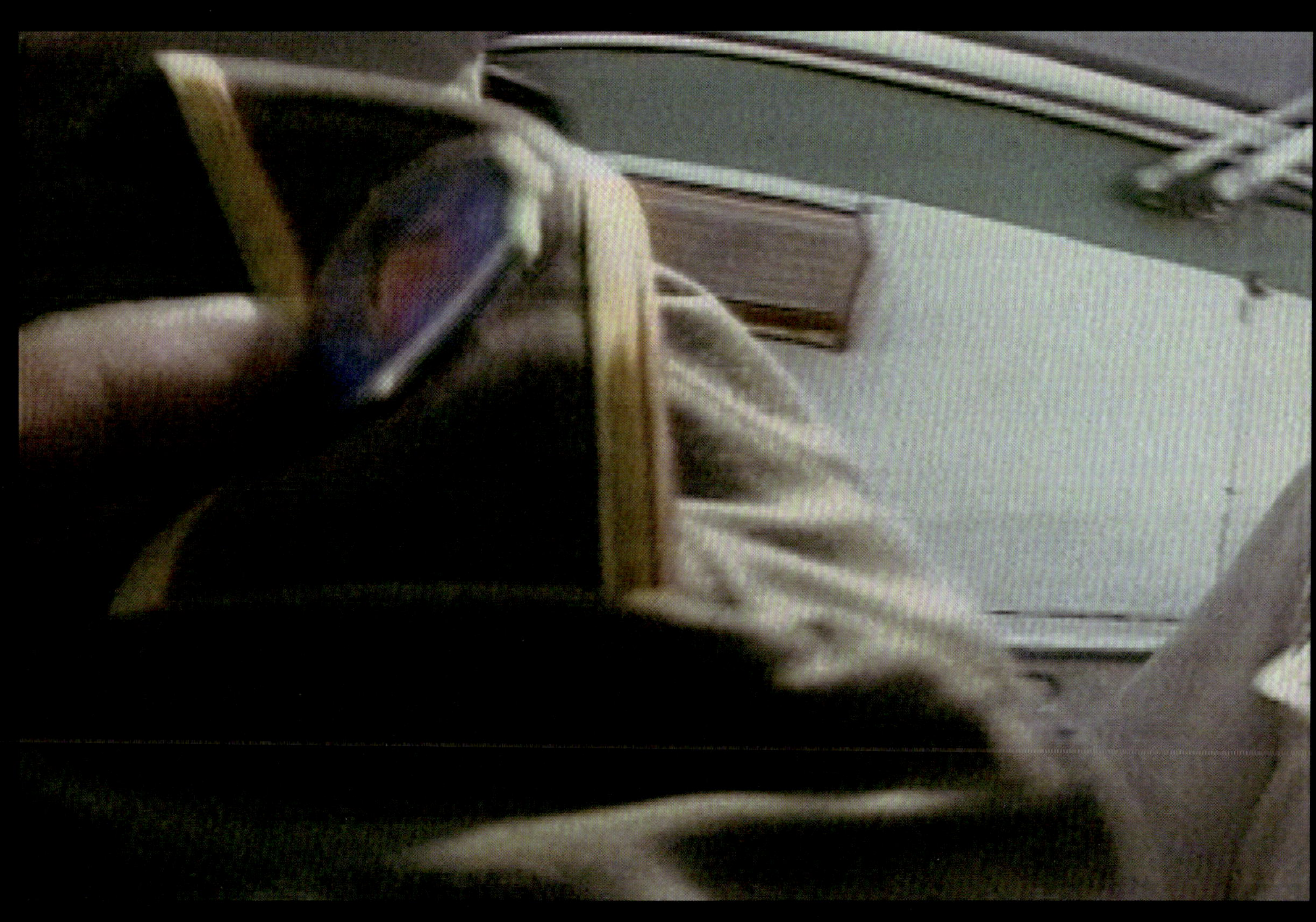

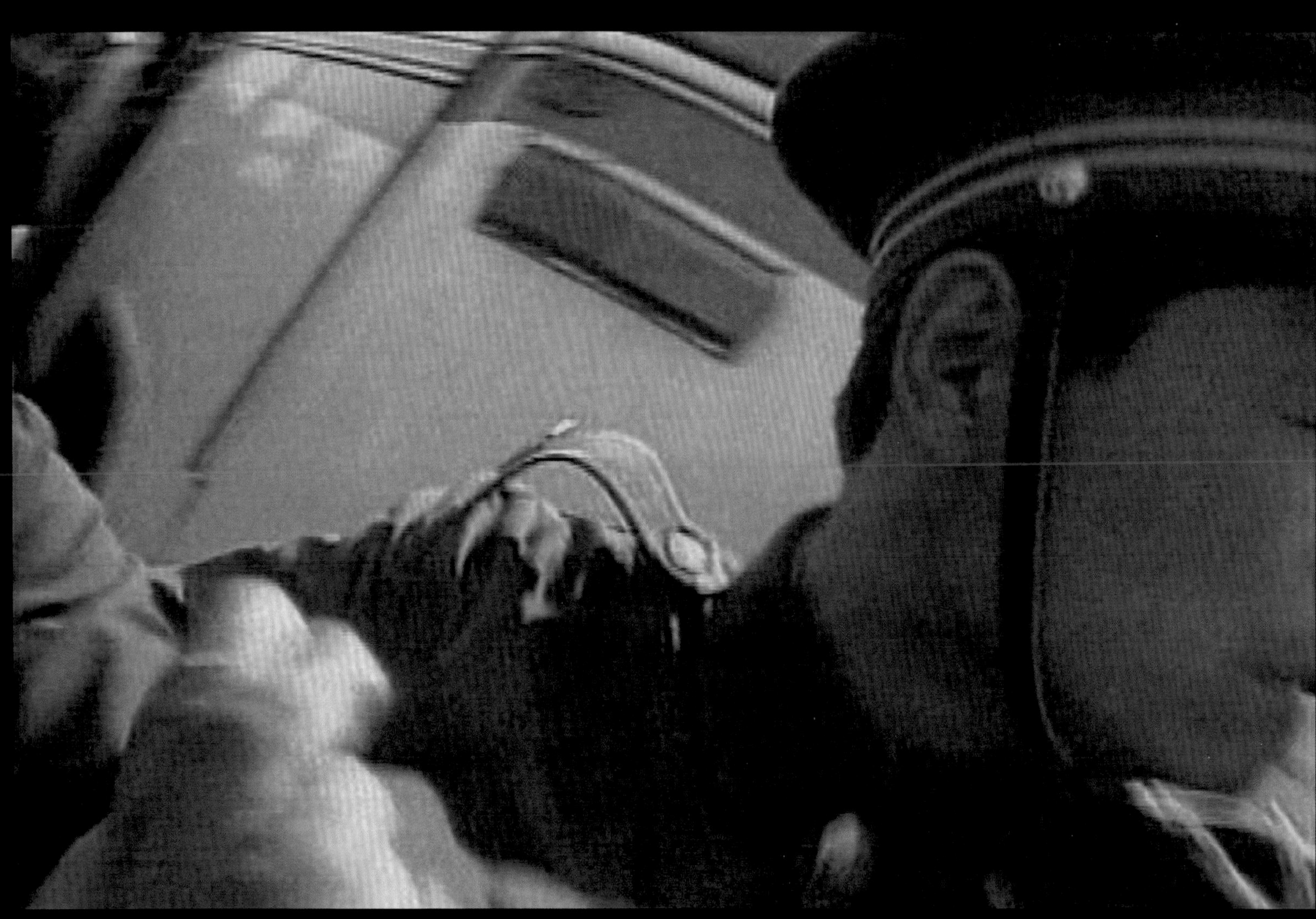

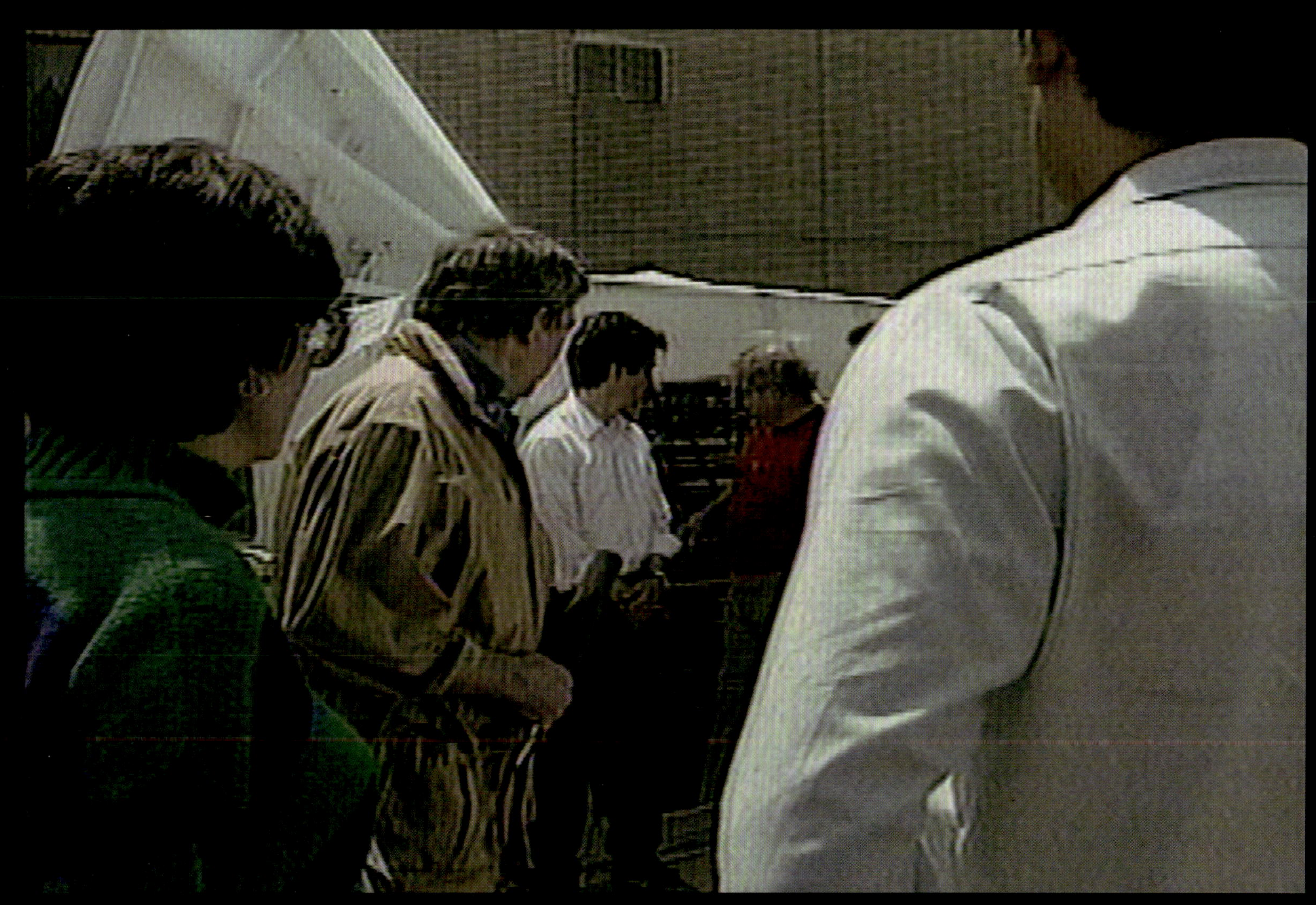

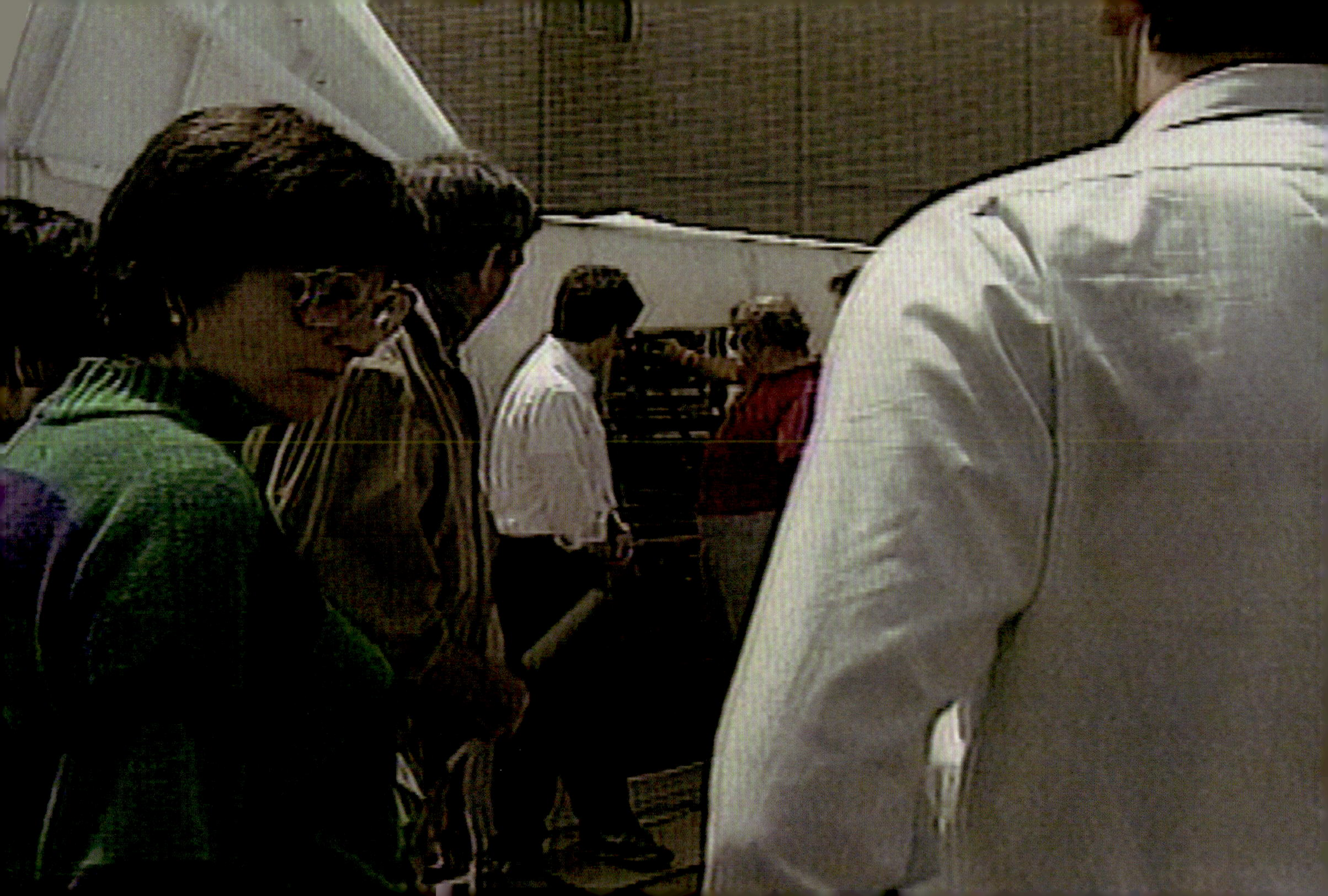

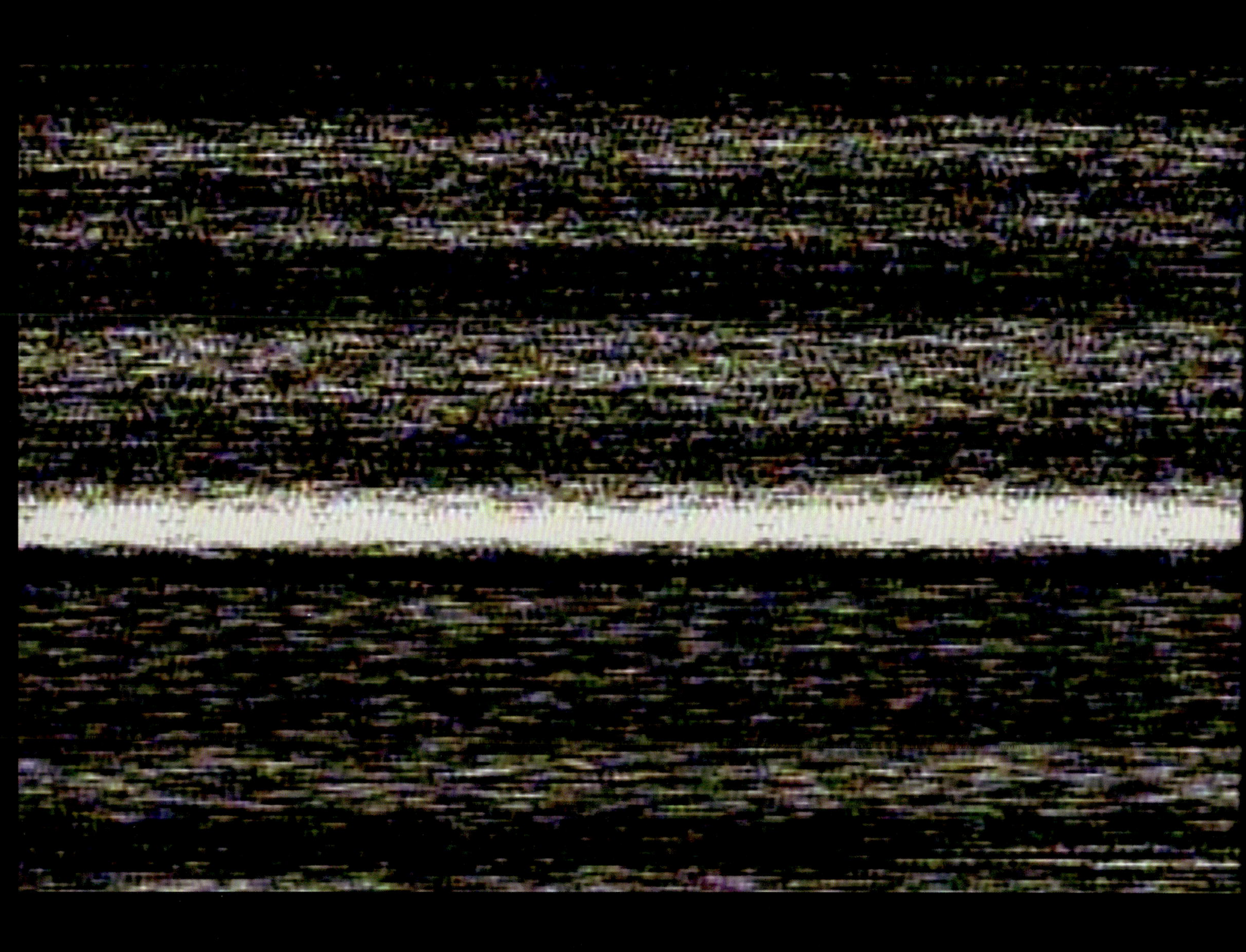

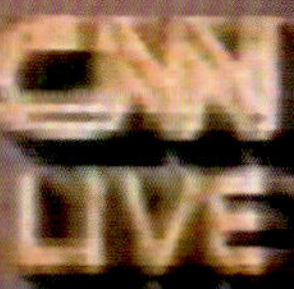

10:16 am
Saturday
Beijing
CNN
LIVE

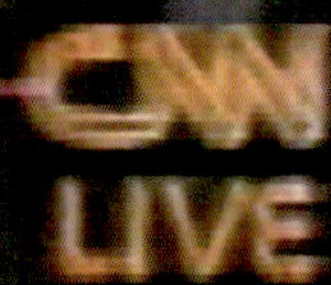

10:16 am
Saturday
Beijing
CNN
LIVE

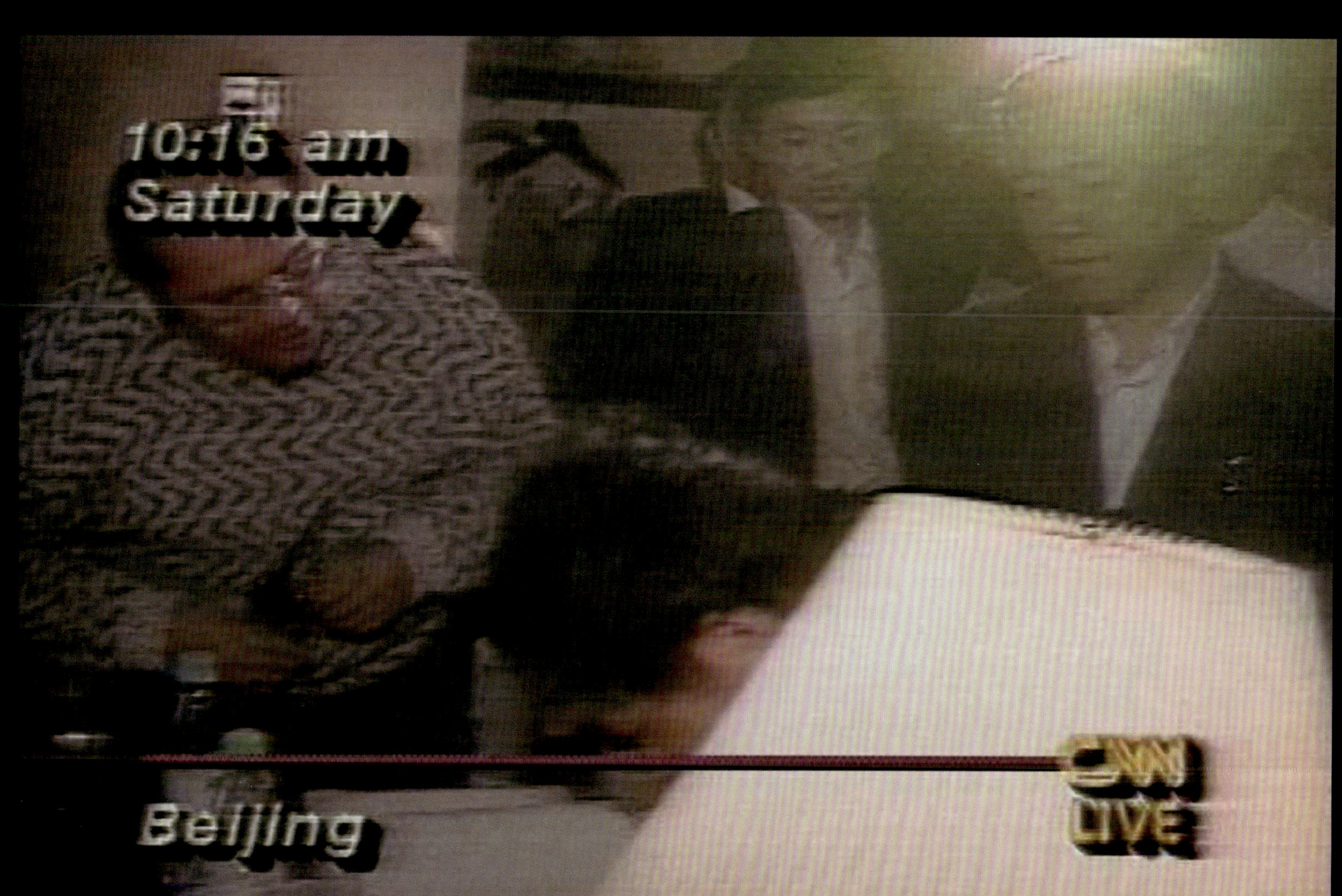
10:16 am
Saturday
Beijing
CNN
LIVE

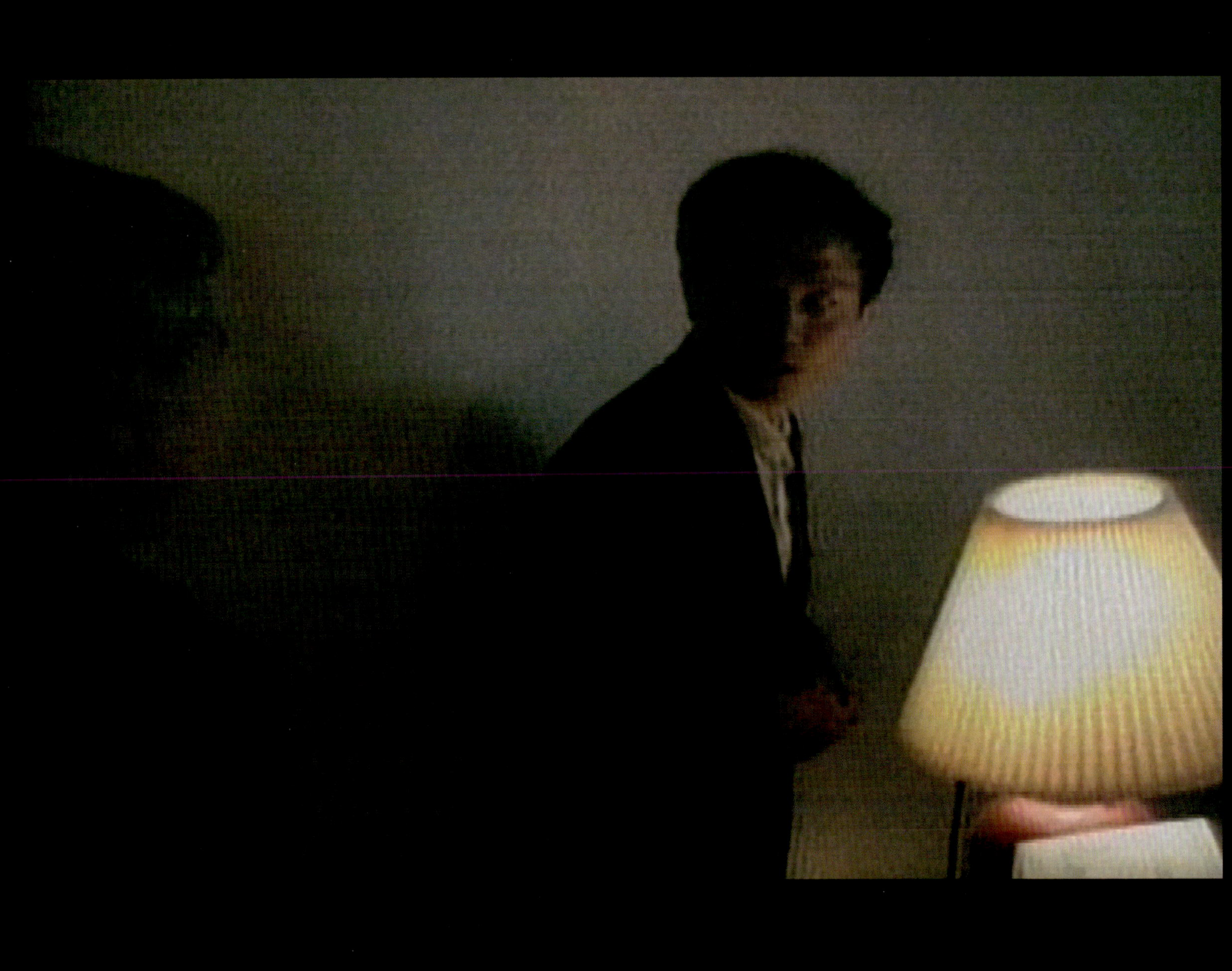

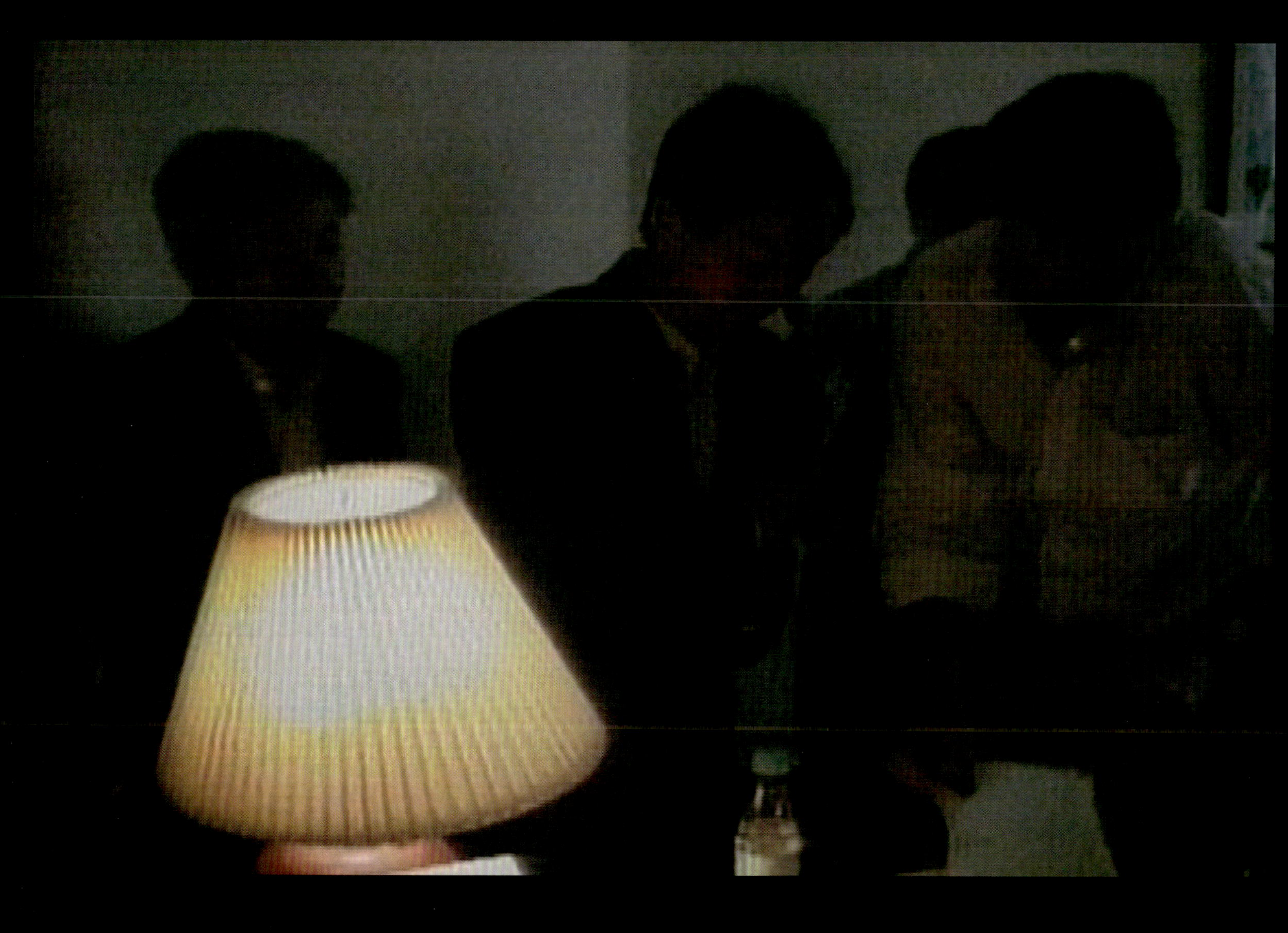

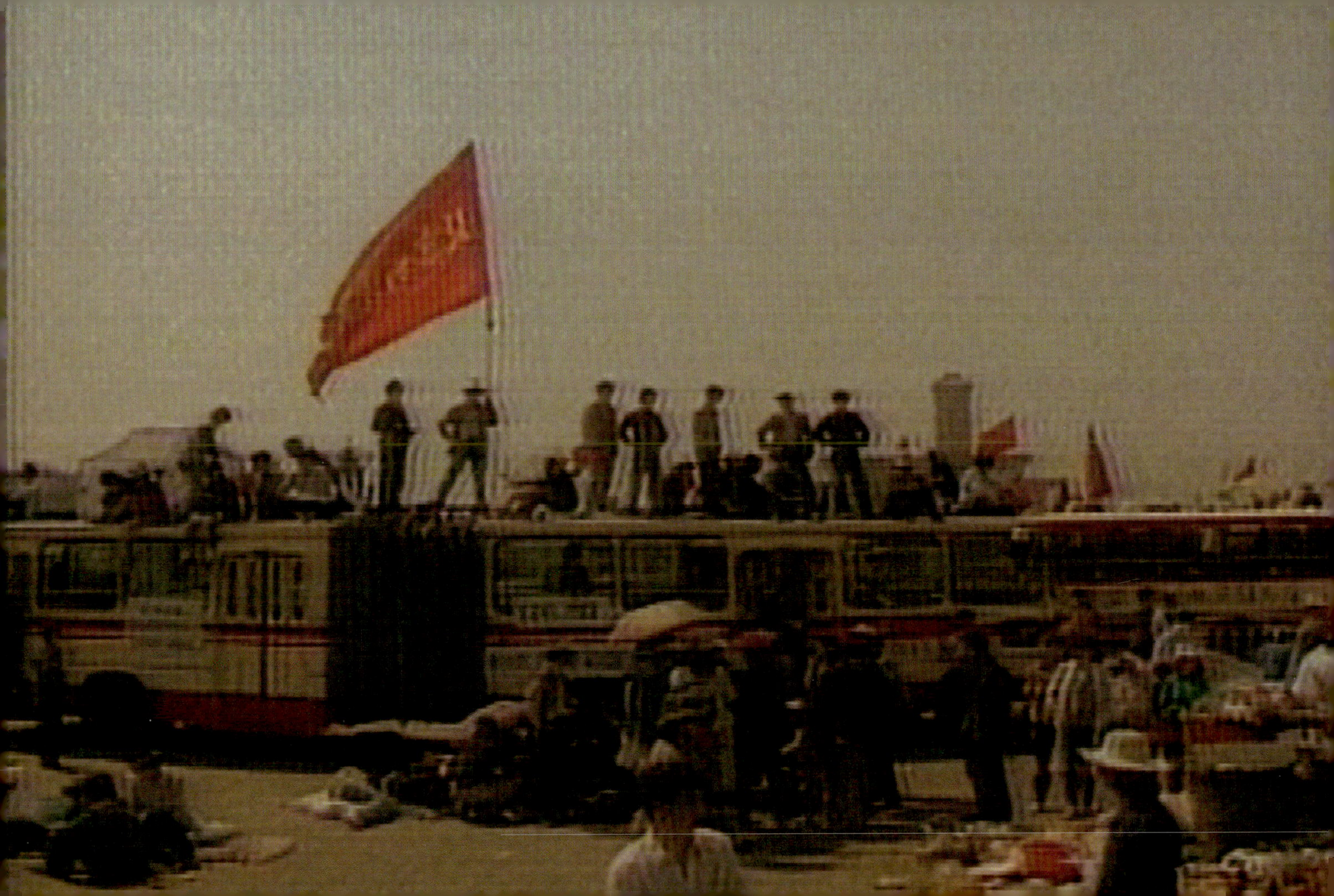

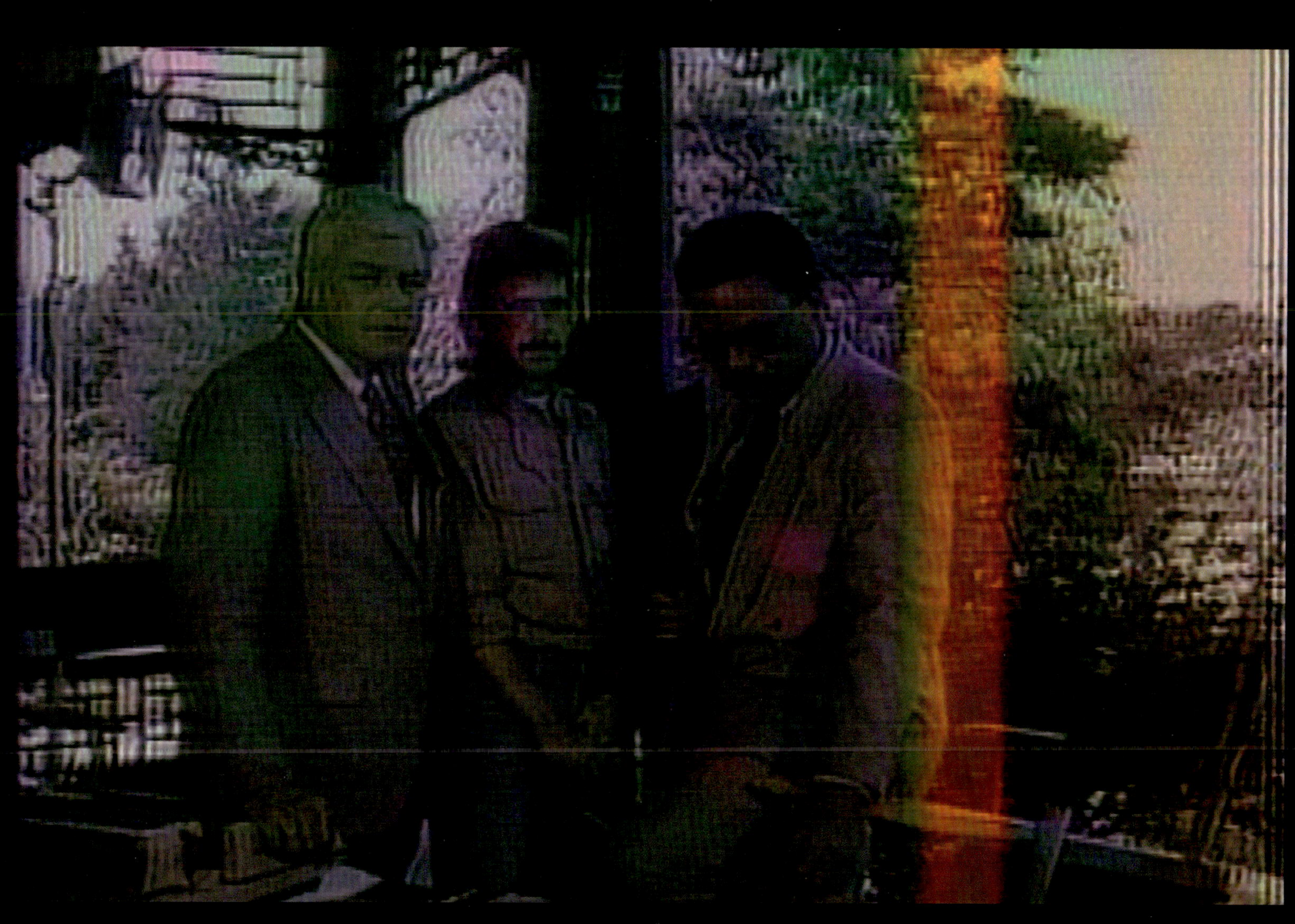

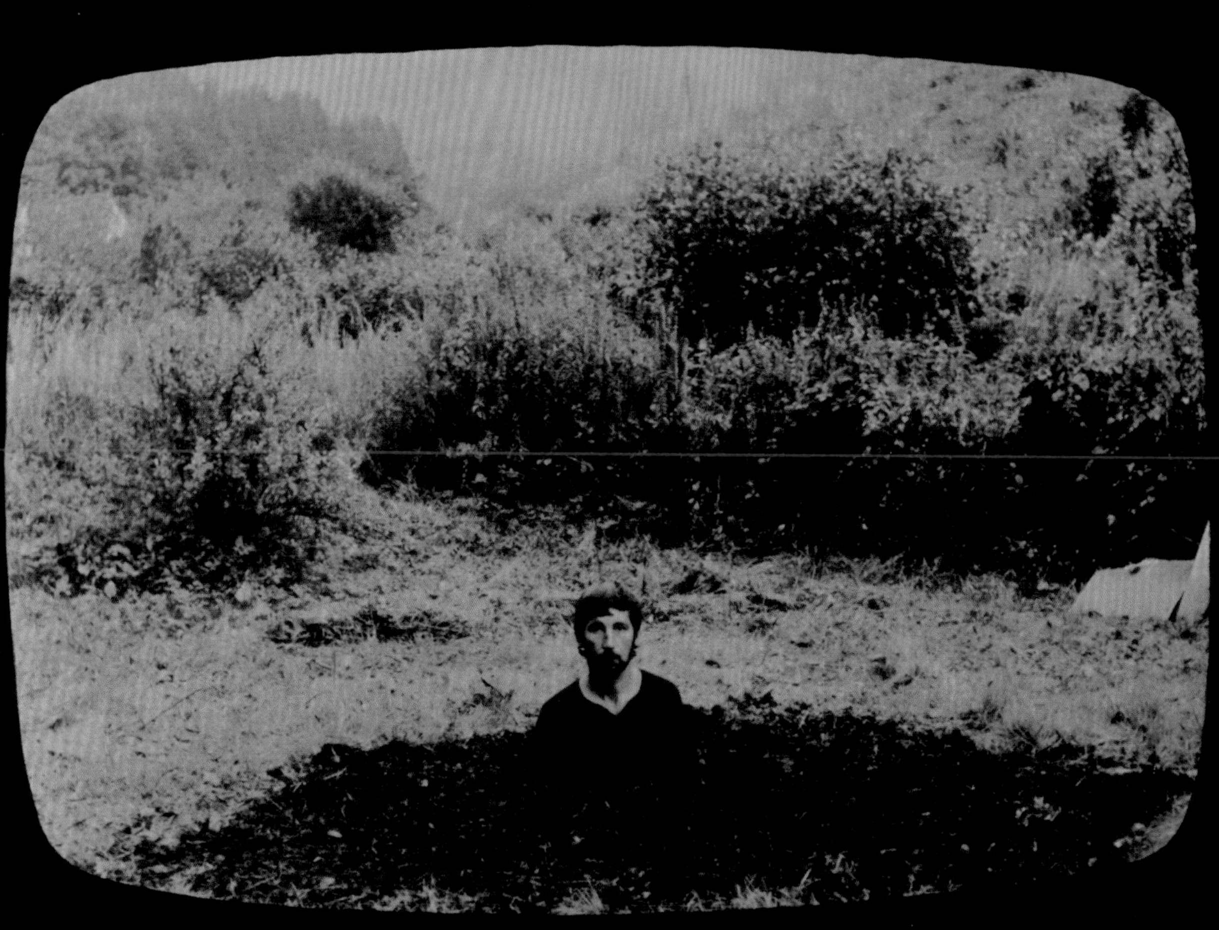

WORLD ON A WIRE

[WELT AM DRAHT, 1973]

A telefilm by Rainer Werner Fassbinder

Introduction by J. Hoberman

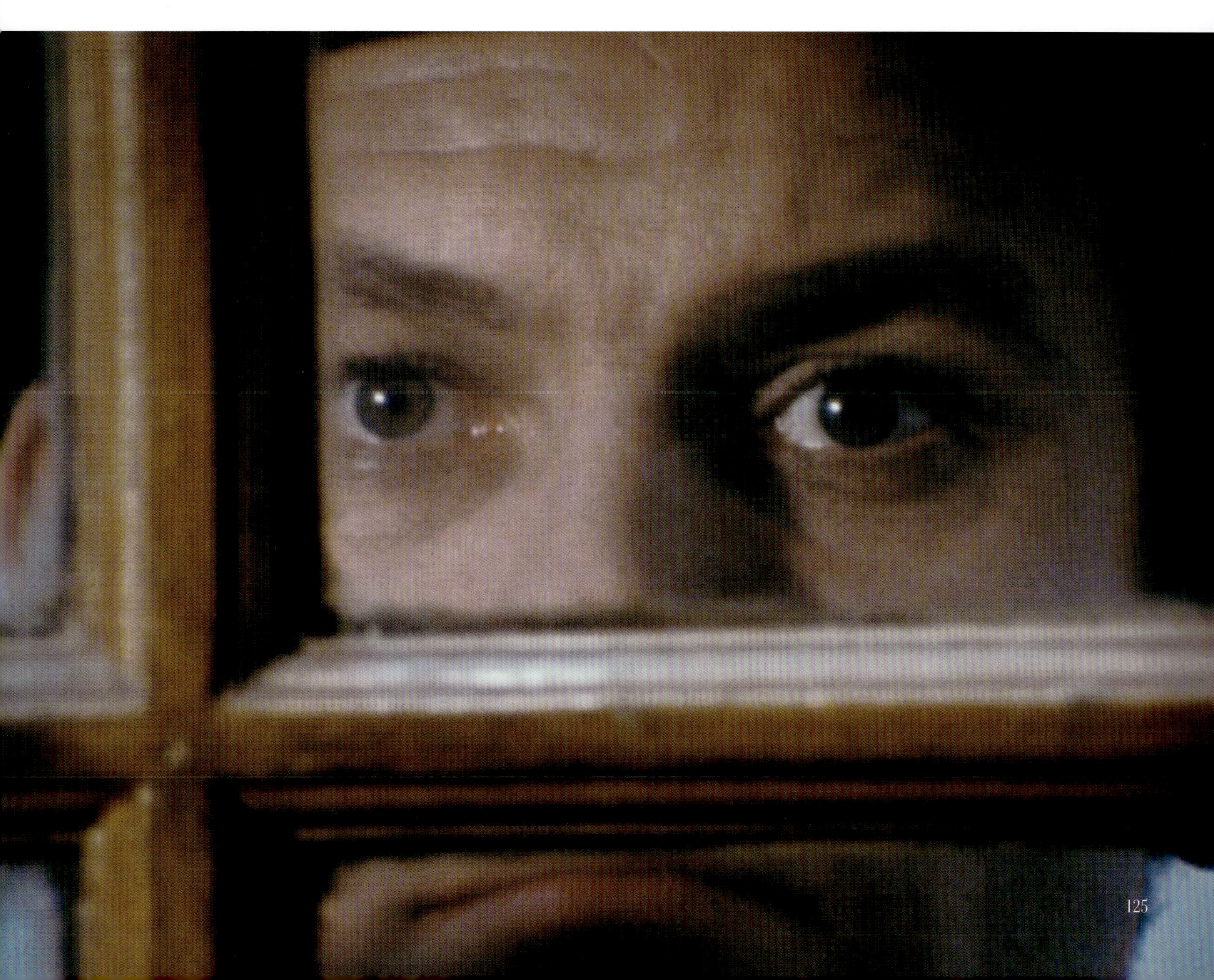

In movies, the simplest special effects can be the most powerful. *World on a Wire [Welt am Draht]* is one sustained example, materializing after decades of obscurity: a virtually unknown, newly restored, two-part telefilm directed and cowritten by long-gone wunderkind R.W. Fassbinder at the height of his powers.

Fassbinder's most sustained genre riff, *World on a Wire* was taken from Daniel F. Galouye's 1964 sci-fi novel *Simulacron-3* (Fassbinder working with Fritz Müller-Scherz) and predicated on the notion of a computer-generated reality populated by "identity units" who believe themselves human; the premise looks back at *The Creation of the Humanoids,* forward to *Blade Runner* and *The Matrix,* and directly at master manipulator Fassbinder's notoriously cultlike power over his acting ensemble. Mind games are a constant, and one scientist jokingly characterizes the identity units as performers: "They're like the people dancing on TV for us."

Fassbinder made *World on a Wire* for German television immediately after his art-film breakthrough, *Effi Briest,* based on the 19th-century classic novel by Theodor Fontane, and, abetted by many of his regular actors, the 27-year-old filmmaker seemed eager to reestablish his punk bona fides. As wildly ambitious as it is cinephilic, *World on a Wire* (shot largely in Paris) mixes the architectural critique and pop-art effrontery of Godard's *Alphaville* with the cyber-phobic metaphysics of Kubrick's *2001* (to name the two movies most bluntly referenced) while remaining wholly Fassbinderian in its insolently lugubrious ironies. Less characteristic, if equally deadpan, are the choreographed action sequences—notably the lurking crane that threatens to dump a load of debris on the movie's angst-ridden protagonist (Klaus Löwitsch).

A power-elite conspiracy yarn played out on two levels of reality—virtual and real, both suffused with free-floating paranoia—*World on a Wire* hardly lacks for narrative. But its meaning is largely delivered via an economical yet stylish mise-en-scène. This is corporate hell—the blandly futuristic, neon-lit look leans heavily on molded-plastic furniture and ubiquitous TV monitors. (That the men are uniformly dressed in power suits and the women as Barbie dolls may remind some of *Mad Men.*) Strategically placed mirrors suggest the characters' illusory or divided nature, while the alienated performances—alternately declamatory and uninflected—as well as Fassbinder's Warholian deployment of actors stolidly hanging out in frame, encourage the thought that the real world, too, is rife with "identity units."

Running a leisurely 205 minutes, *World on a Wire* builds up to a satisfyingly nutty finale—as the identity units grow restless, their virtual world begins to develop certain glitches. One conceit worthy of Philip K. Dick is the shrink whose job is to treat simulation neurosis (although Fassbinder is also an artist who loves a good nervous breakdown, the more baroque the better). With "The Blue Danube" waltz and *Tristan and Isolde* periodically erupting out of Gottfried Hüngsberg's impressively ominous score, *World on a Wire* is almost a literal space opera. There are frequent verbal arias—one character ranting while everyone else goes blank—and the action is further enlivened, or rather rendered provocatively entropic, by intermittent cabaret acts (mainly chanteuse Solange Pradel doing a Dietrich impersonation while people dance in their underwear as if underwater).

It's remarkable how contemporary it all seems. *World on a Wire*'s mod furnishings, already dated in 1973, have been several times revived and are even now currently in vogue. The movie's last 45 minutes have a computer-game logic anticipating Cronenberg's *eXistenZ* and Oshii's *Avalon,* not to mention the level-hopping climax of *Inception.* And the improbably romantic ending is pure 21st century—who would have imagined Fassbinder an avatar of *Avatar?—J. Hoberman*

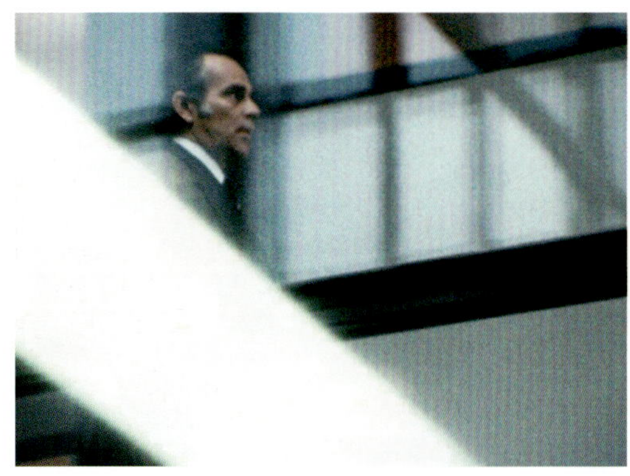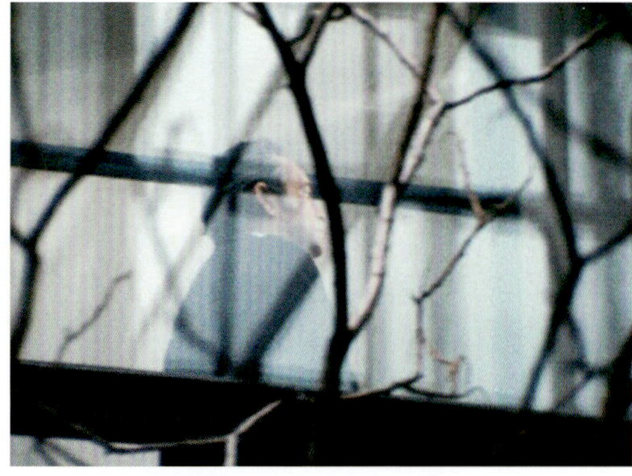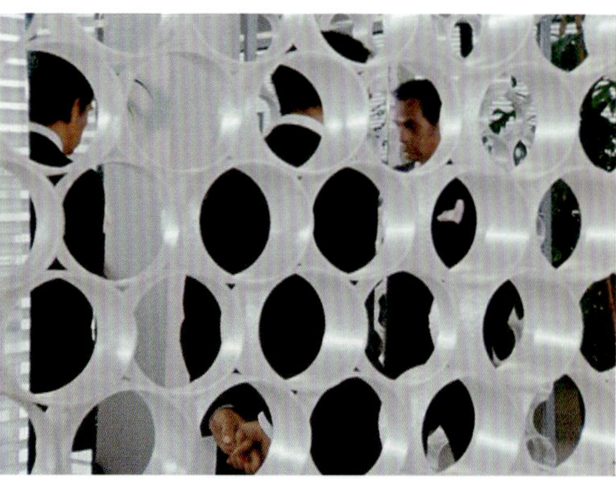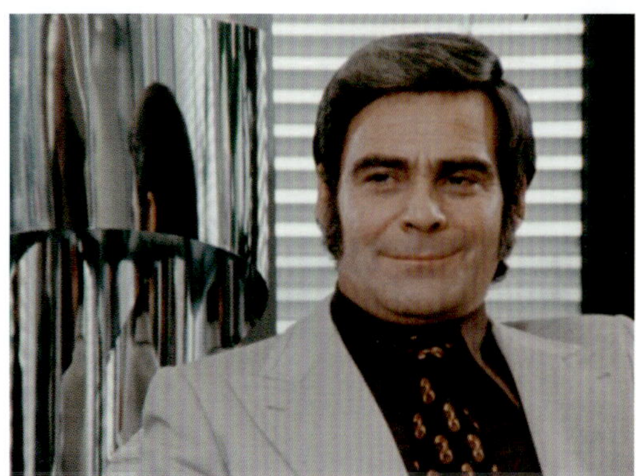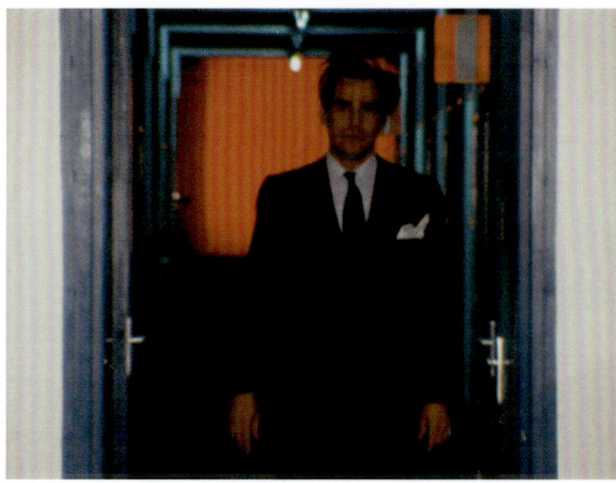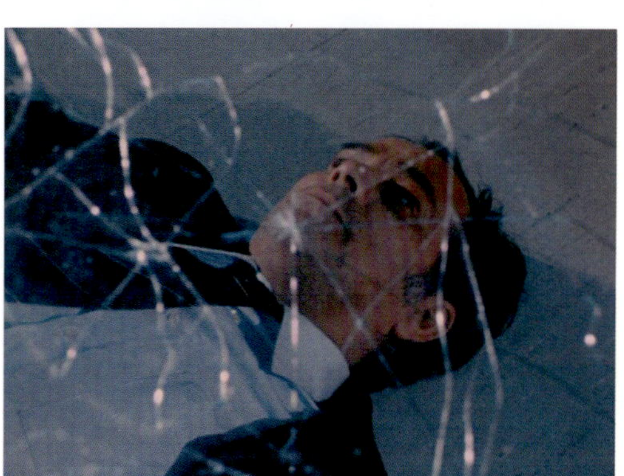

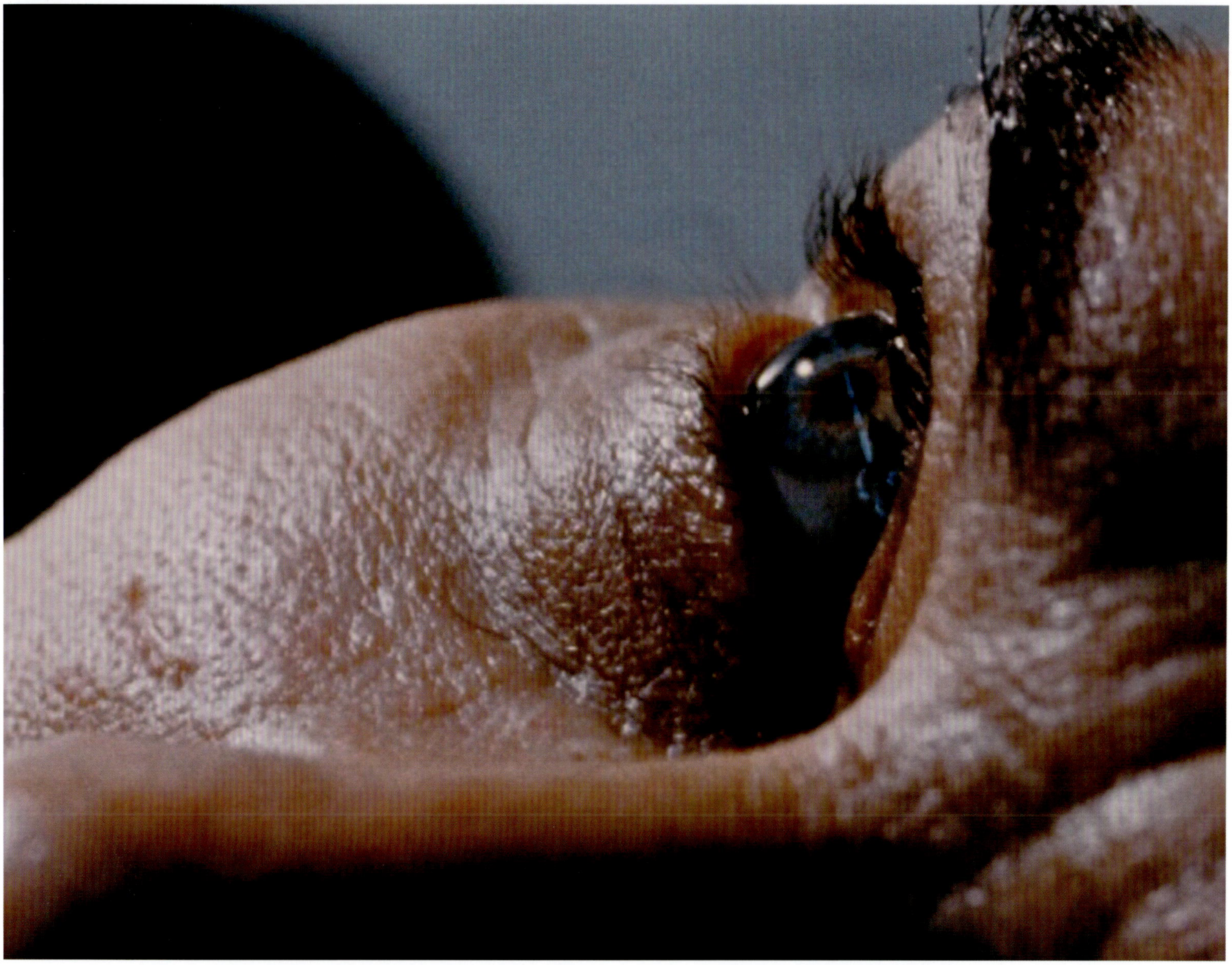

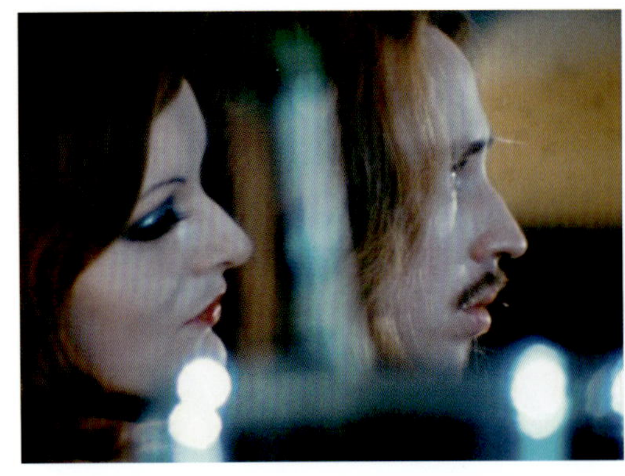
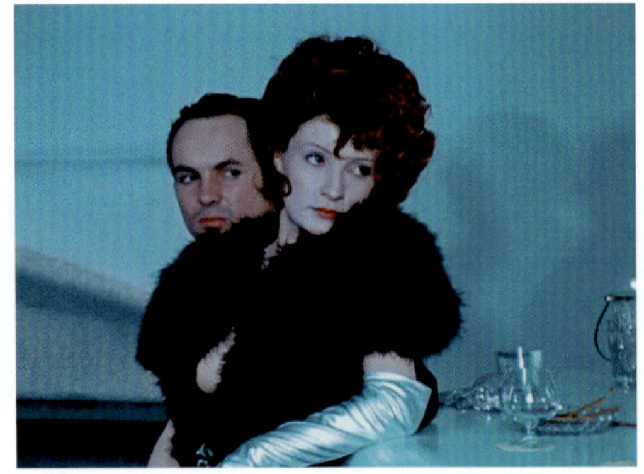
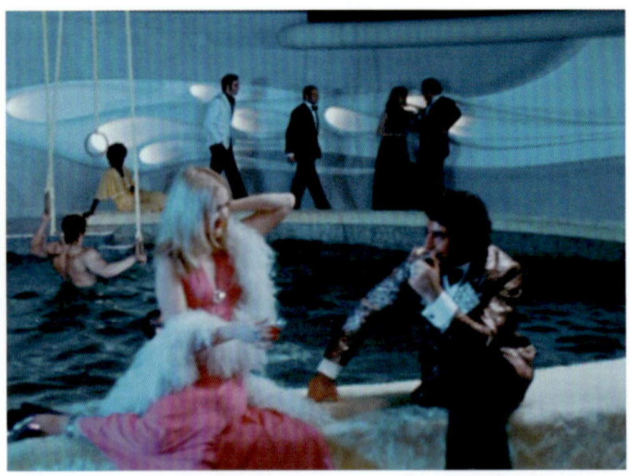
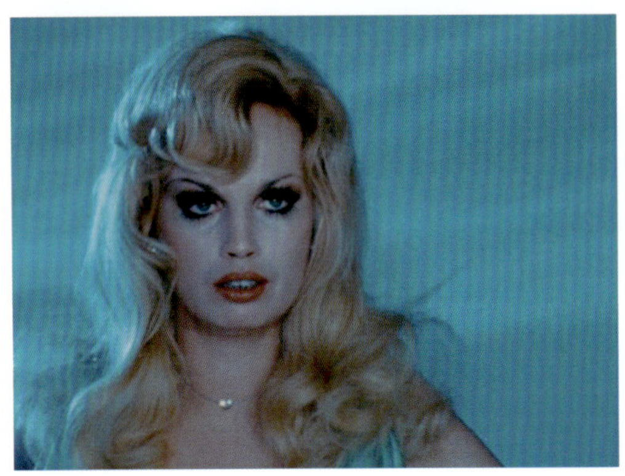
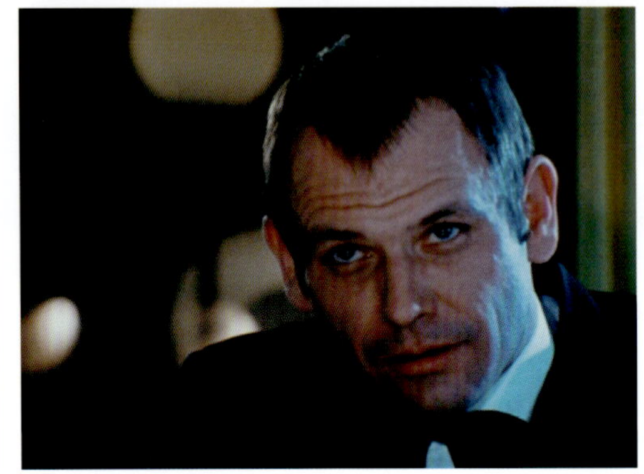
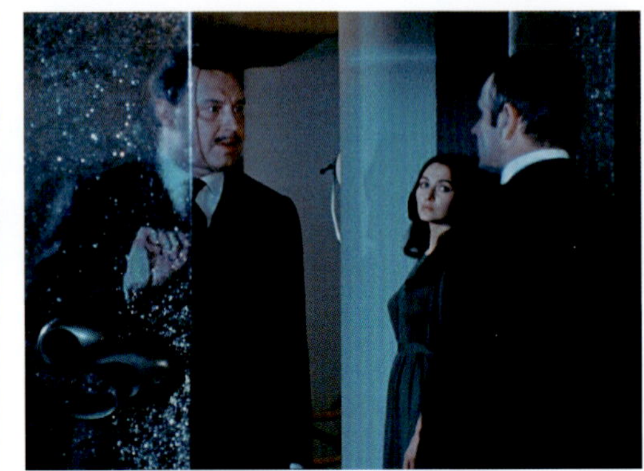
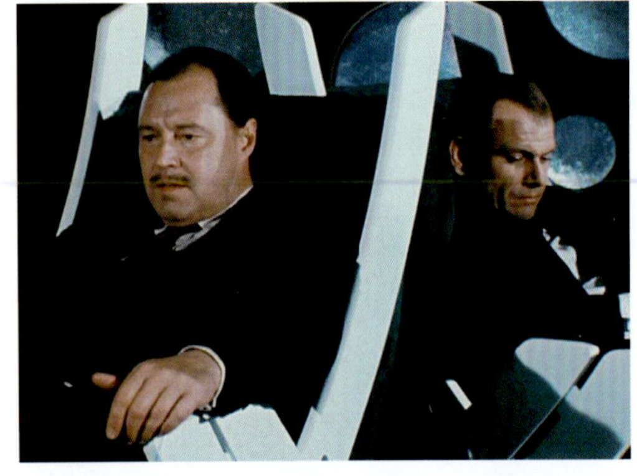
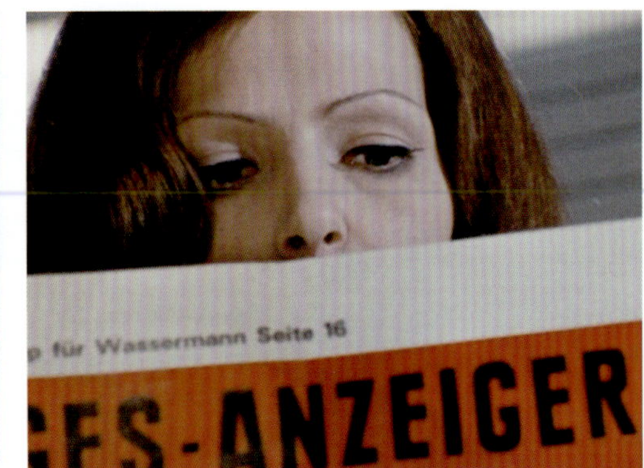
p für Wassermann Seite 16
GES-ANZEIGER
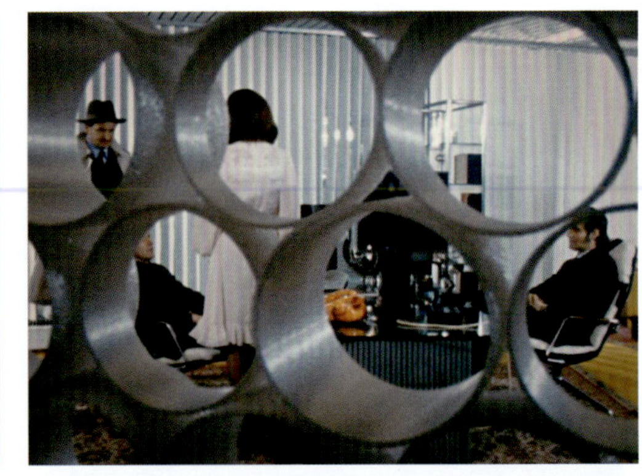
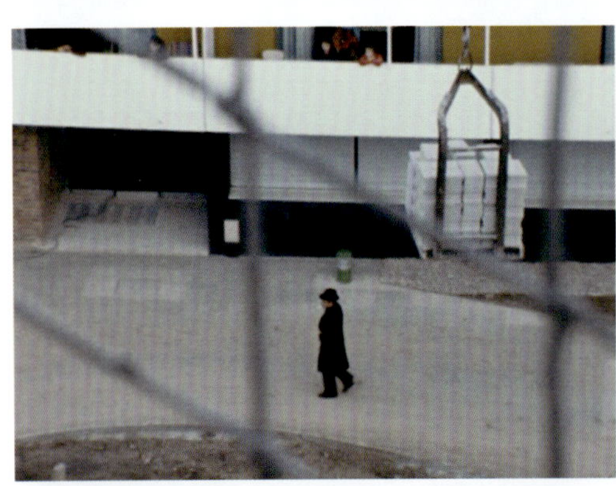
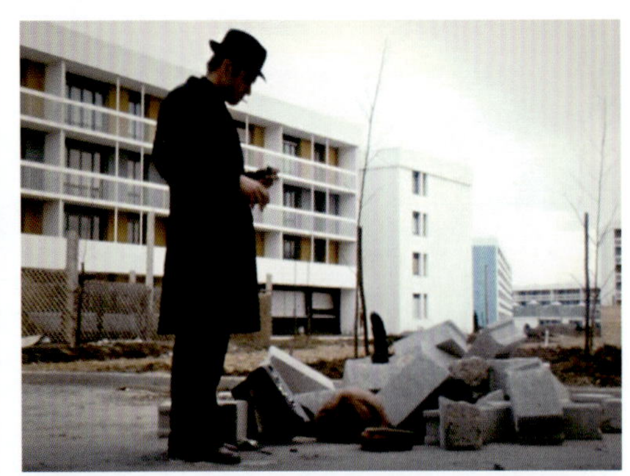
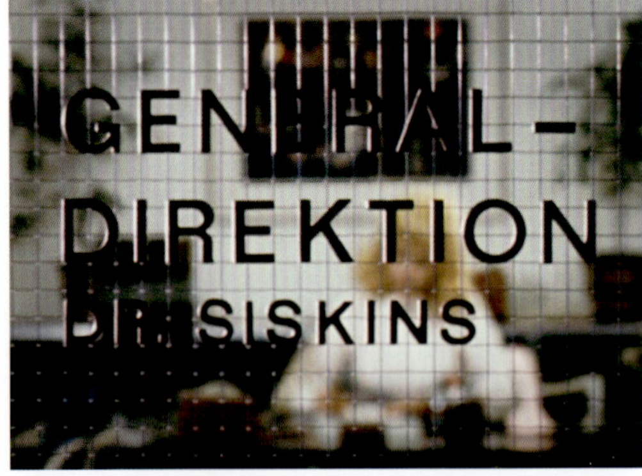
GENERAL-
DIREKTION
DR. SISKINS
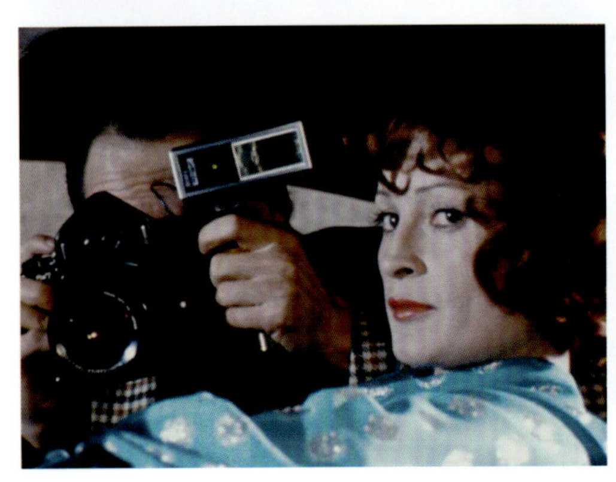
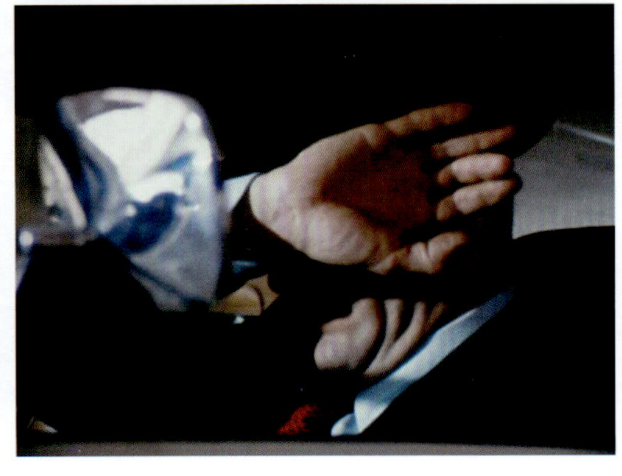
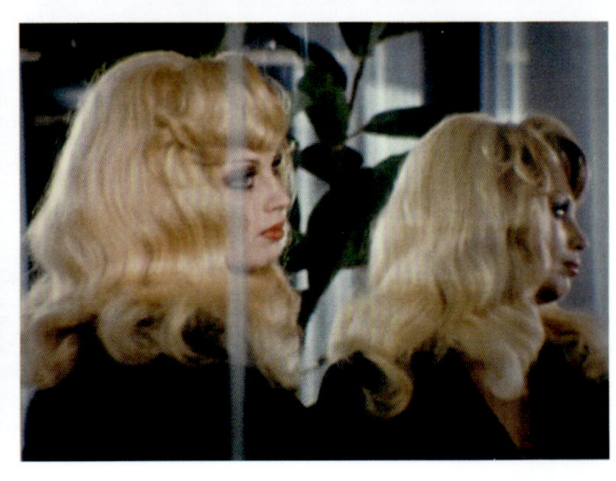

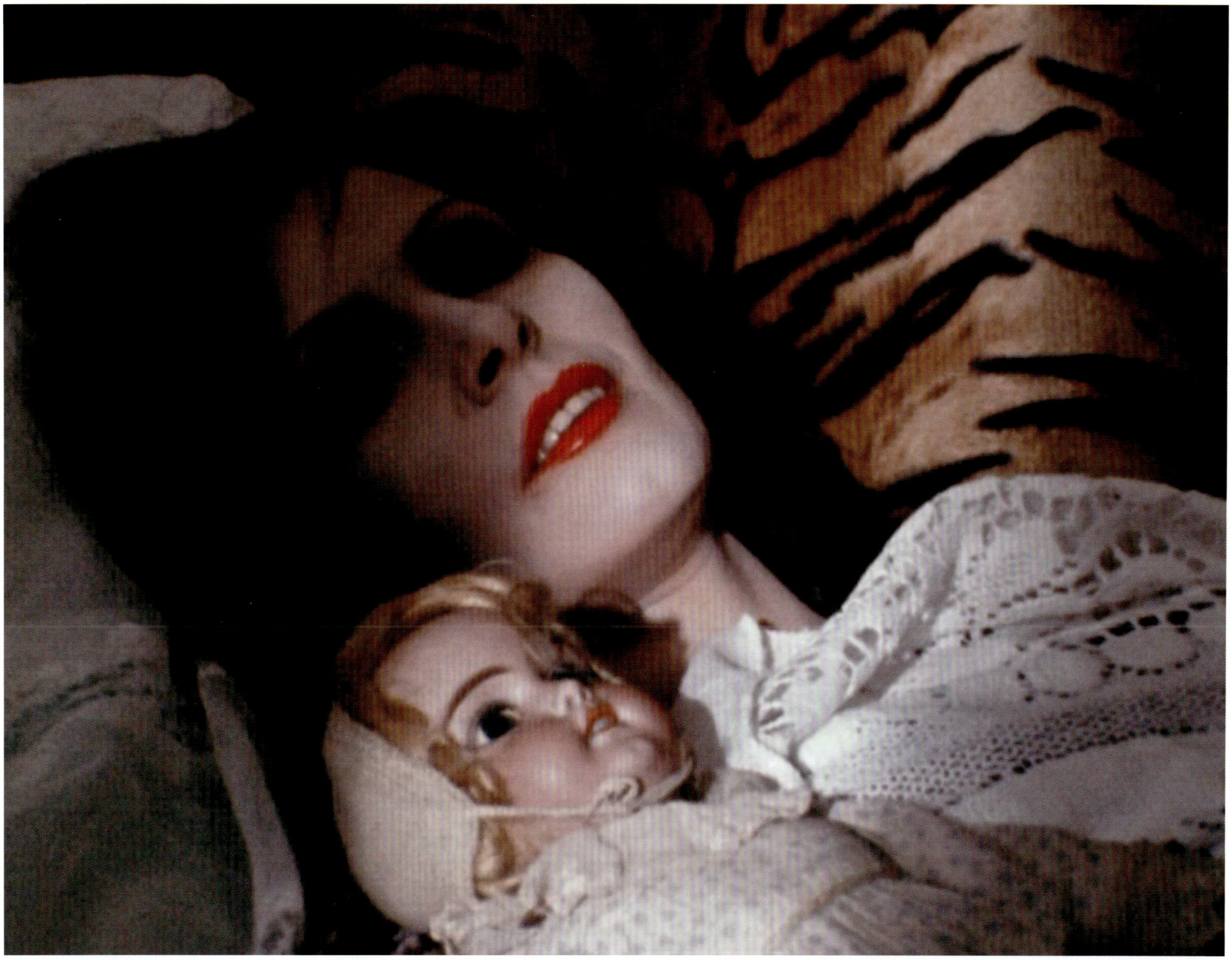

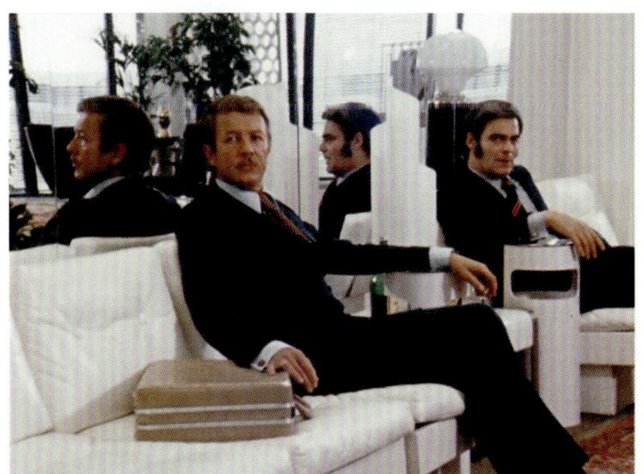
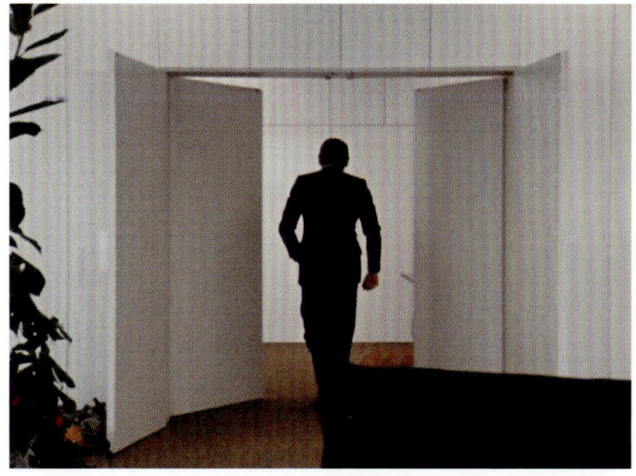
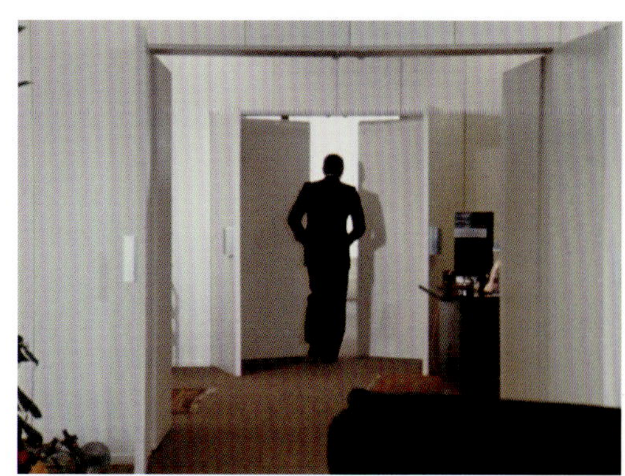
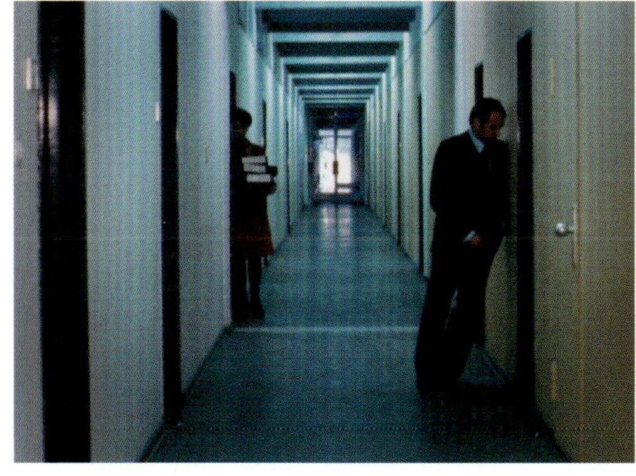
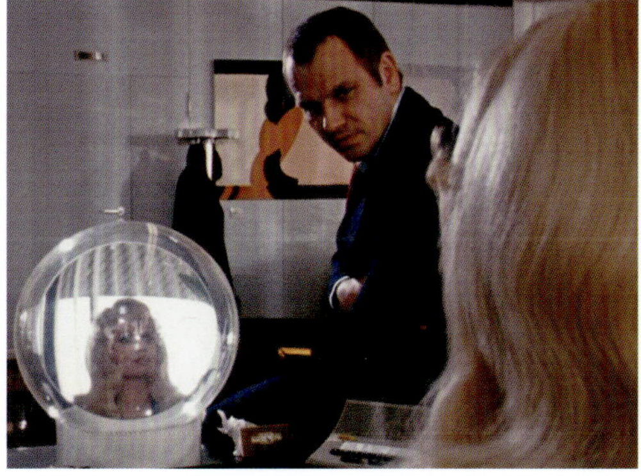
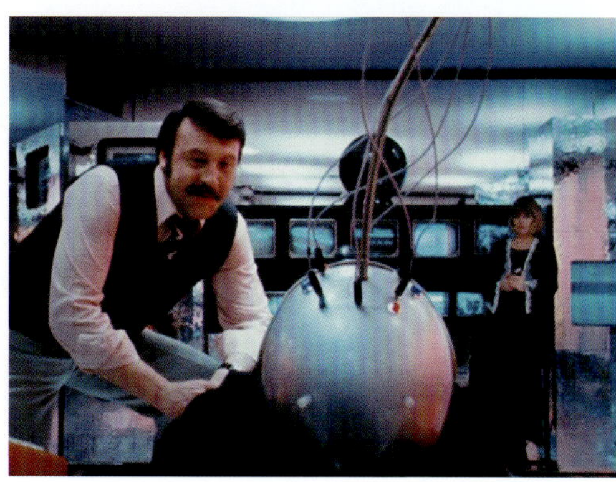

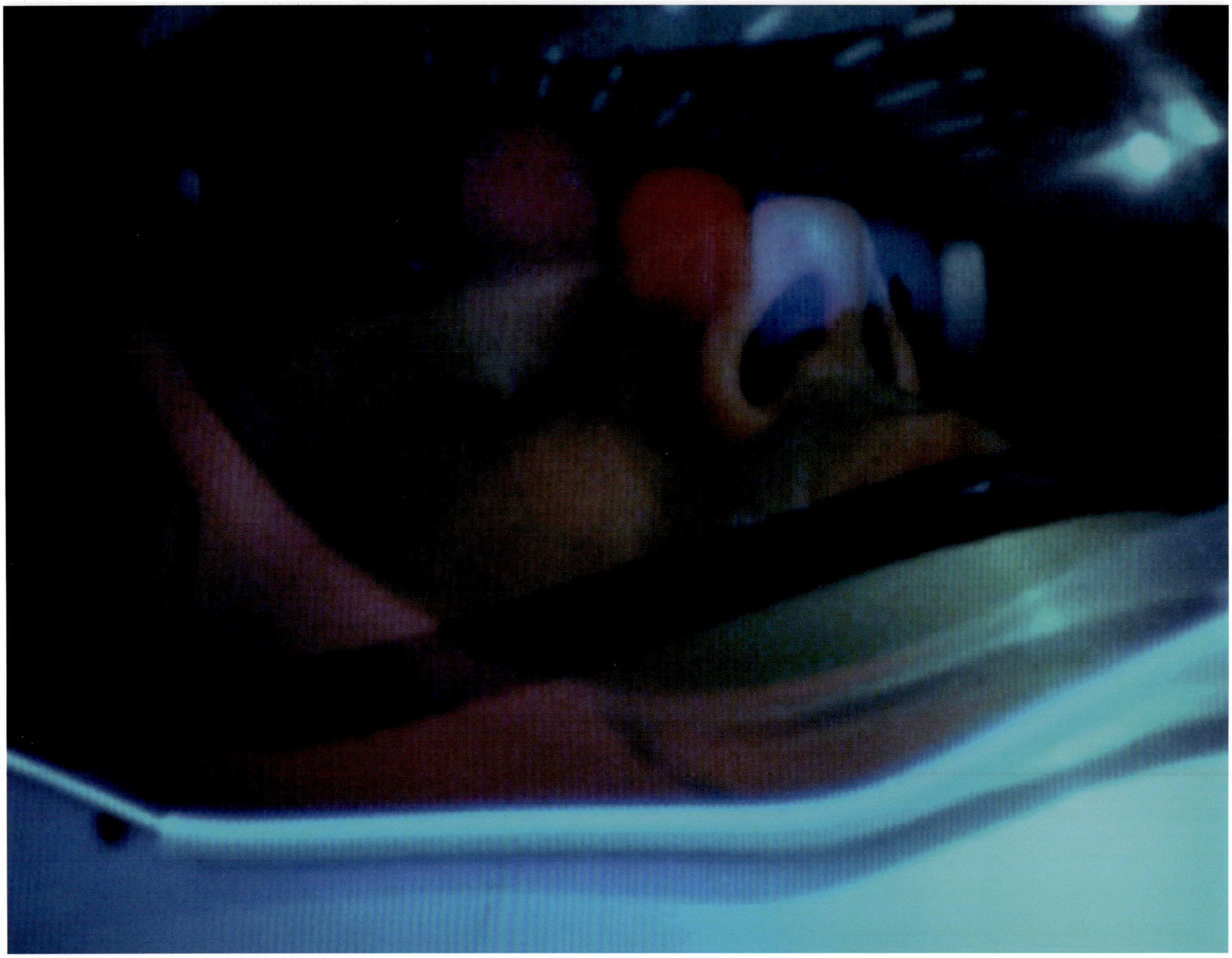

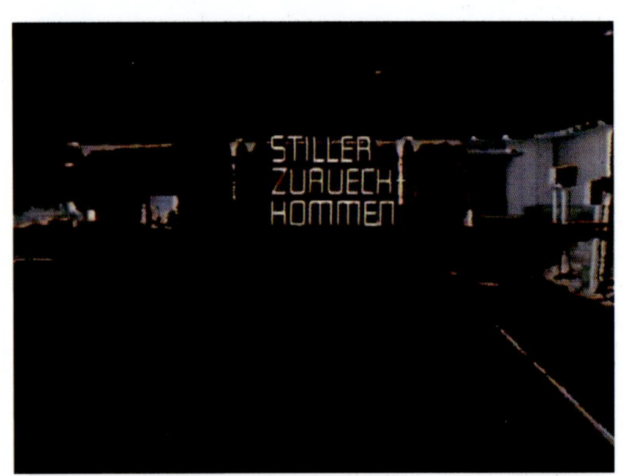
STILLER
ZURUECK-
KOMMEN
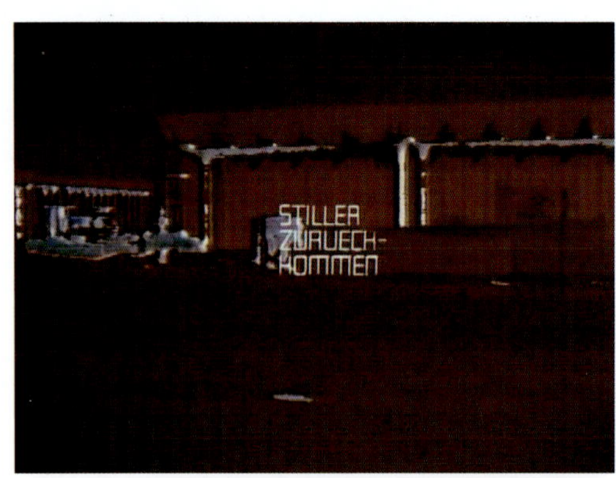
STILLER
ZURUECK-
KOMMEN
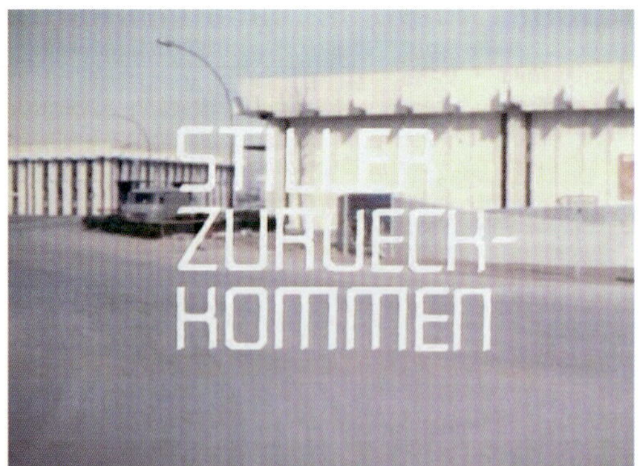
STILLER
ZURUECK-
KOMMEN
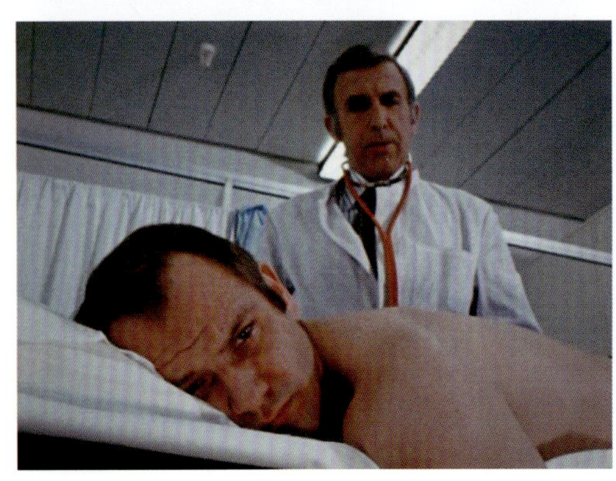
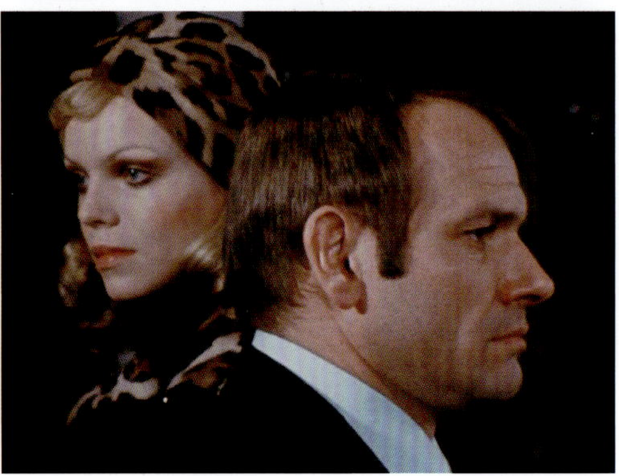
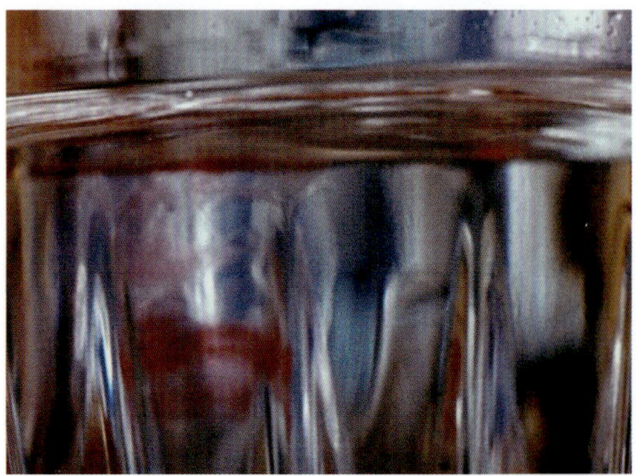

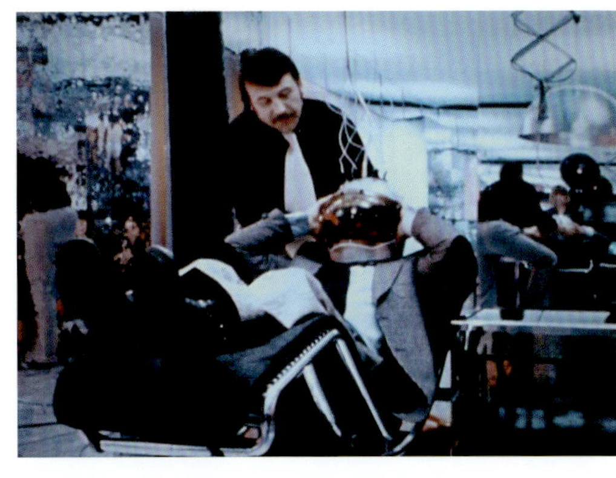
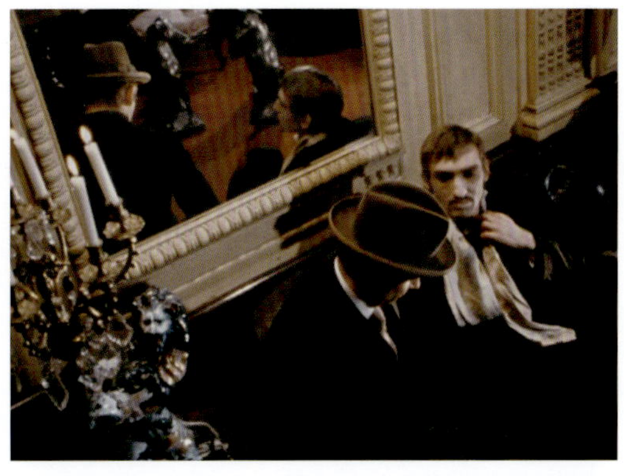
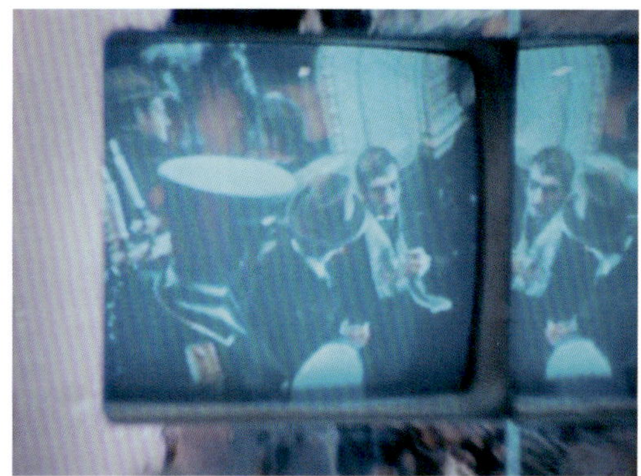
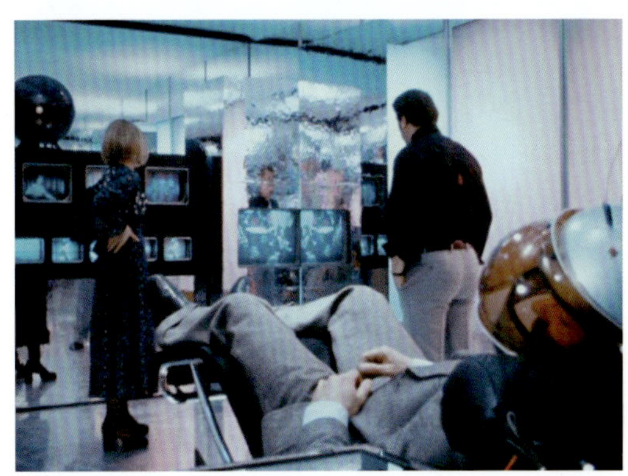
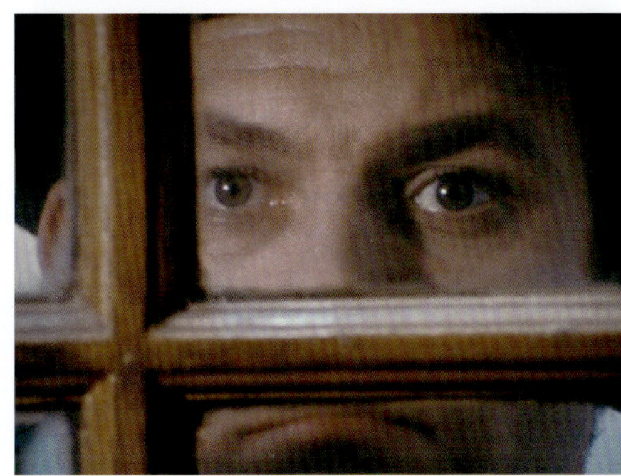
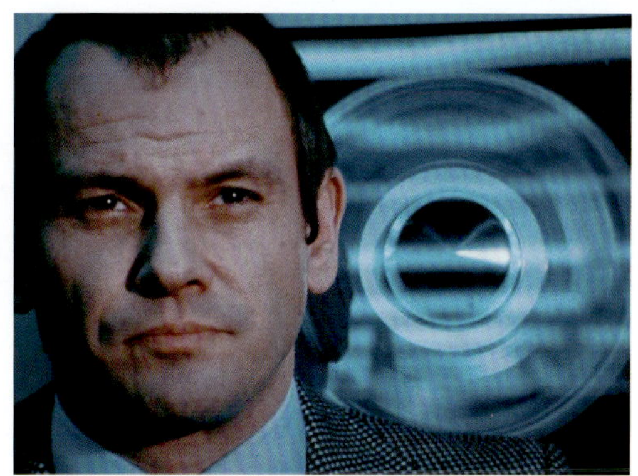

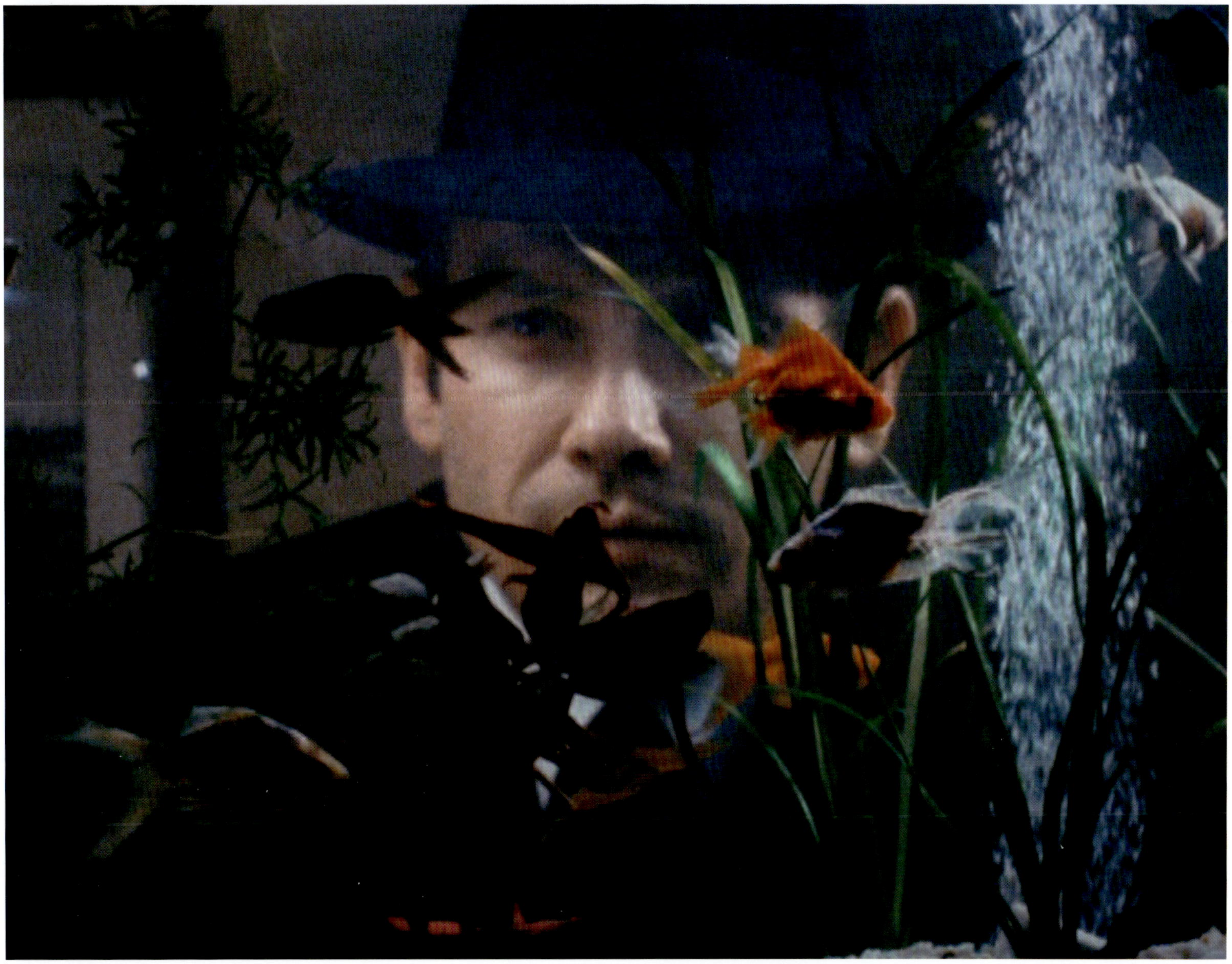

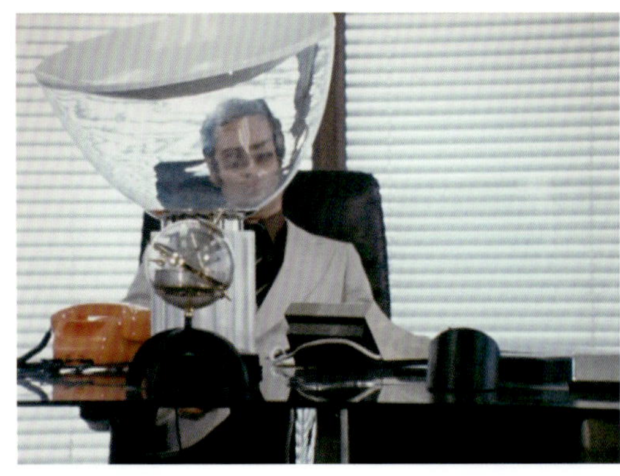
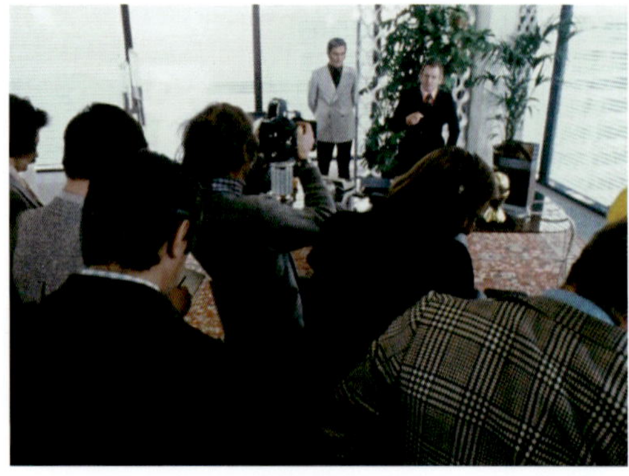
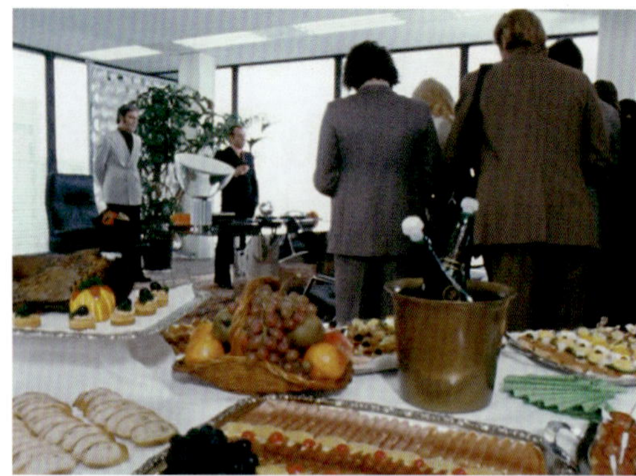
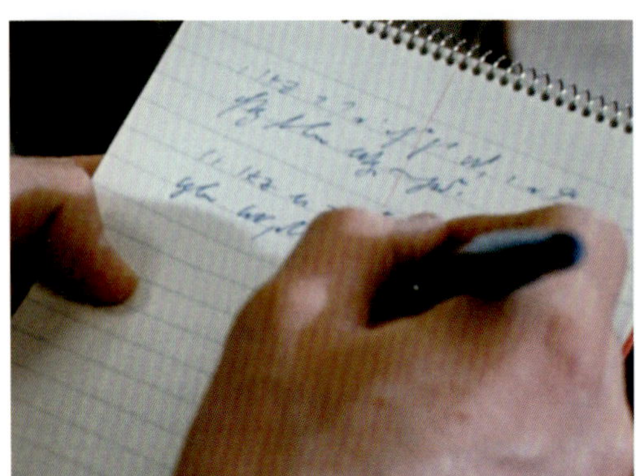
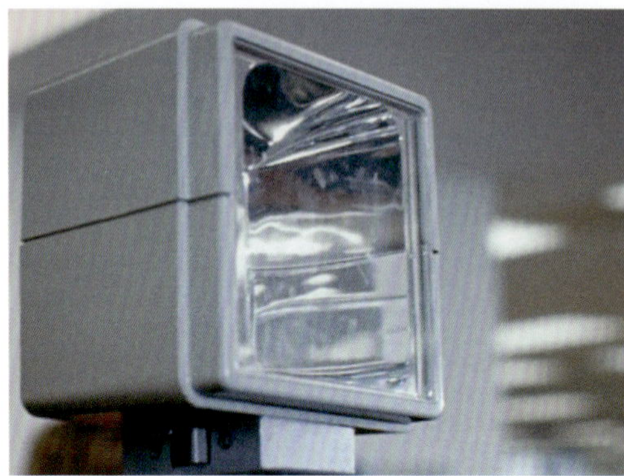

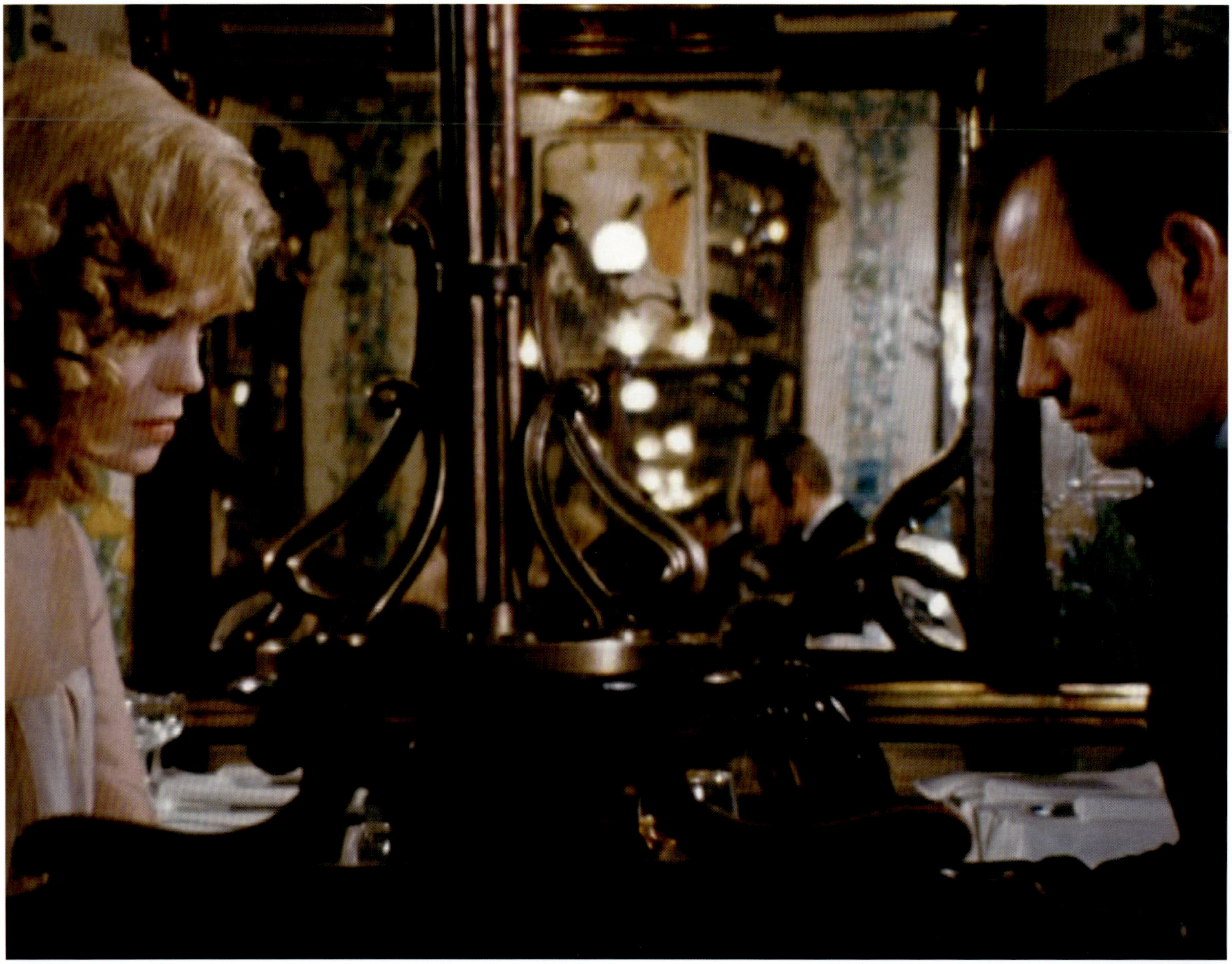

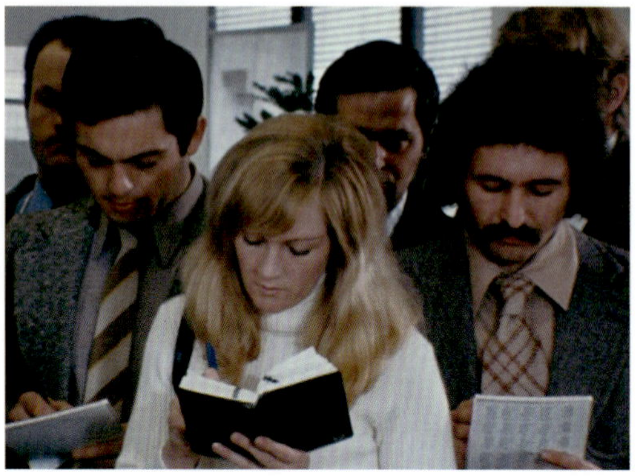

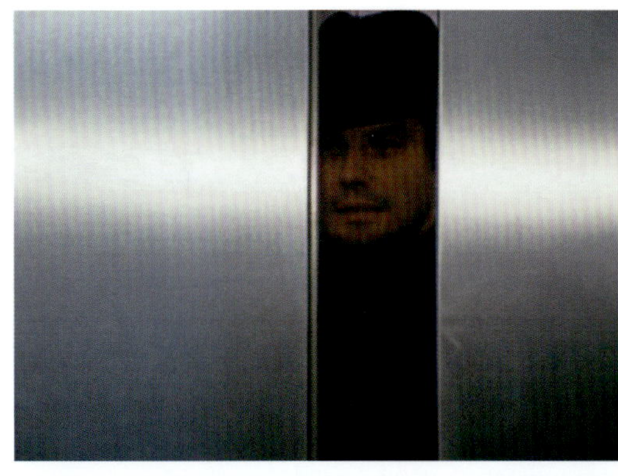 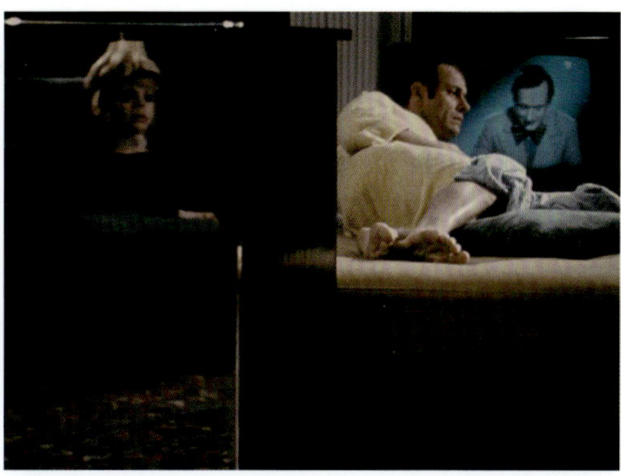 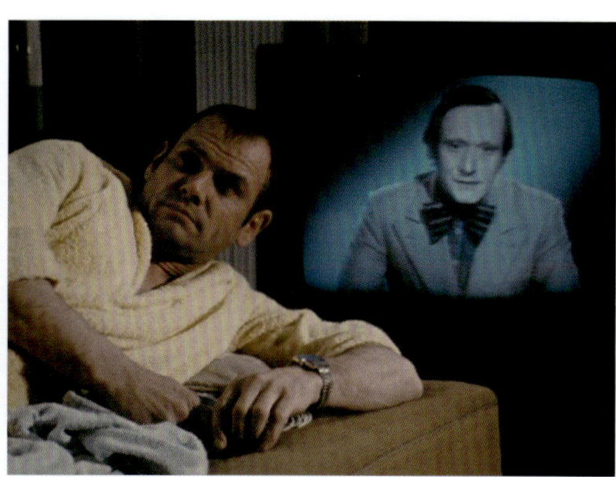

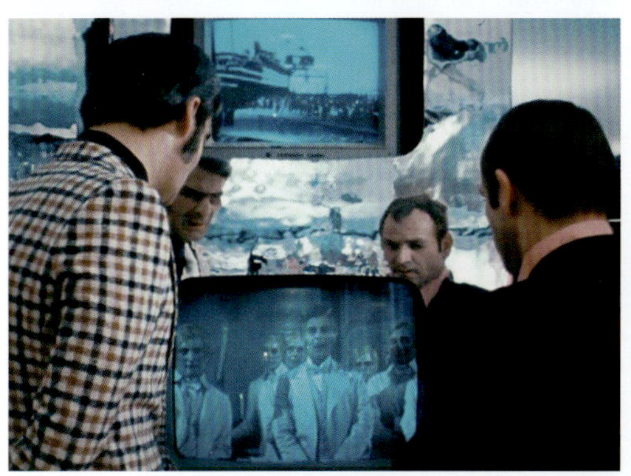 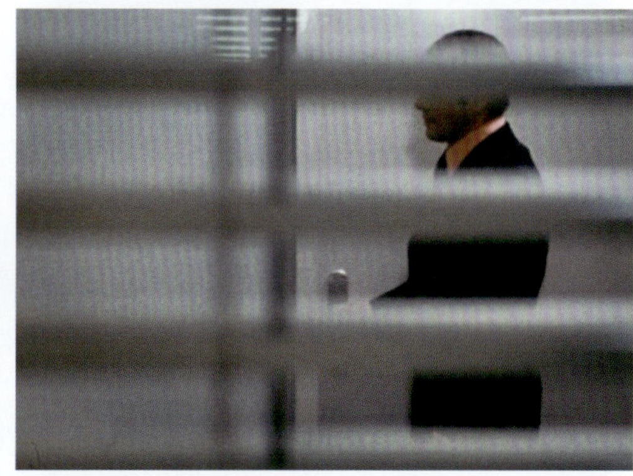 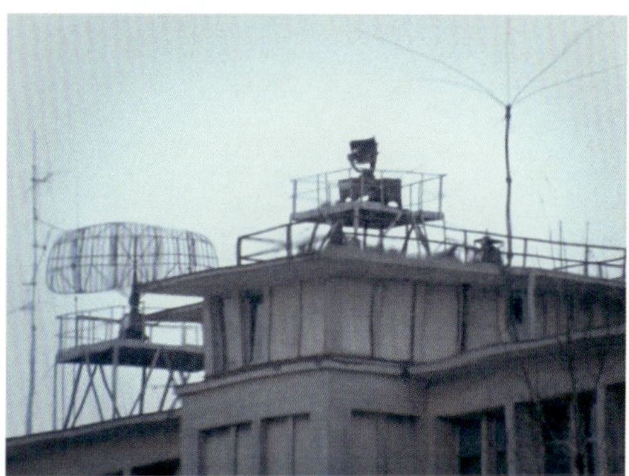

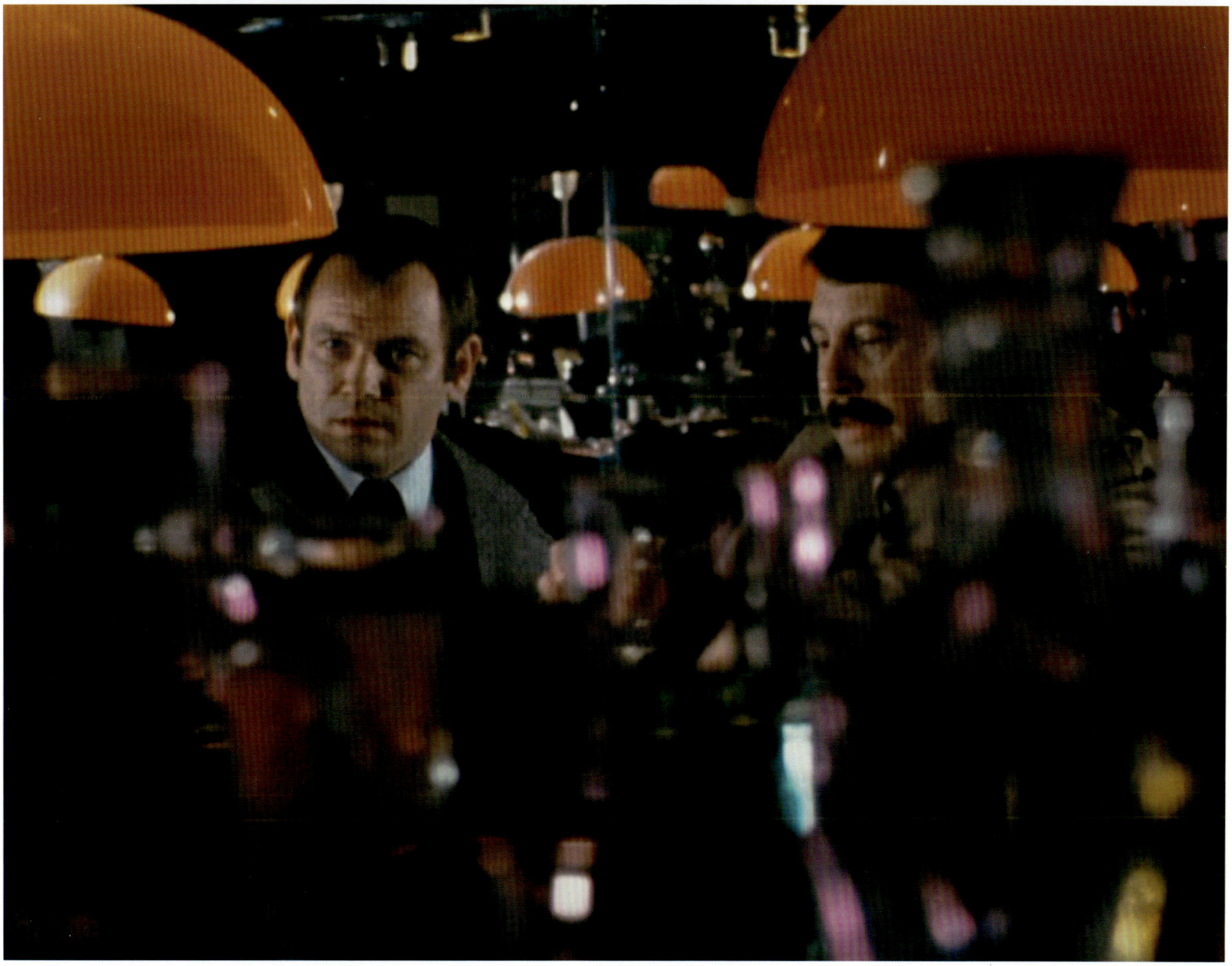

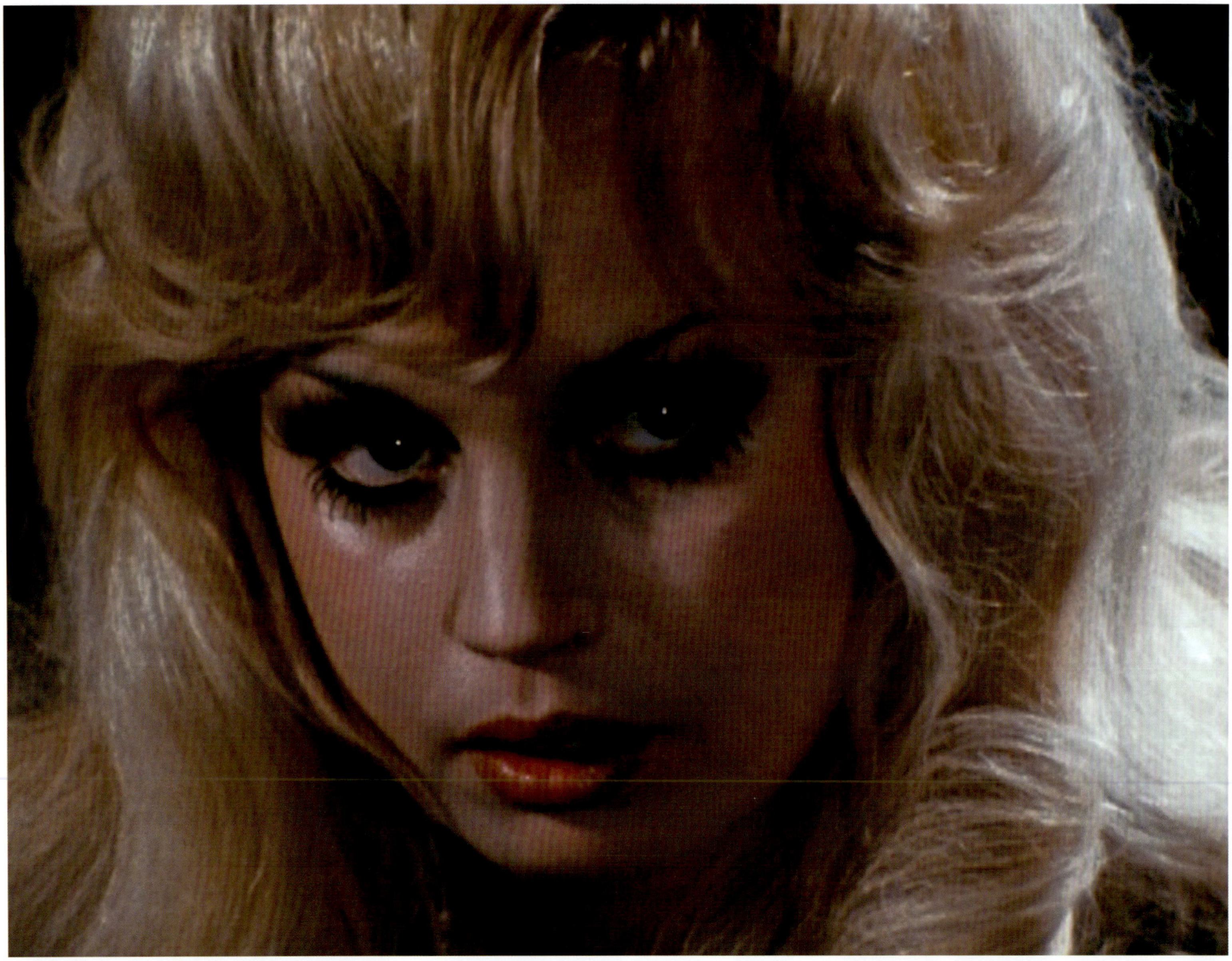

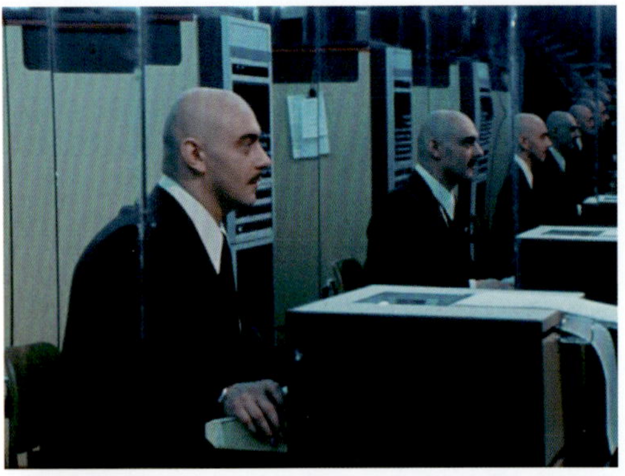
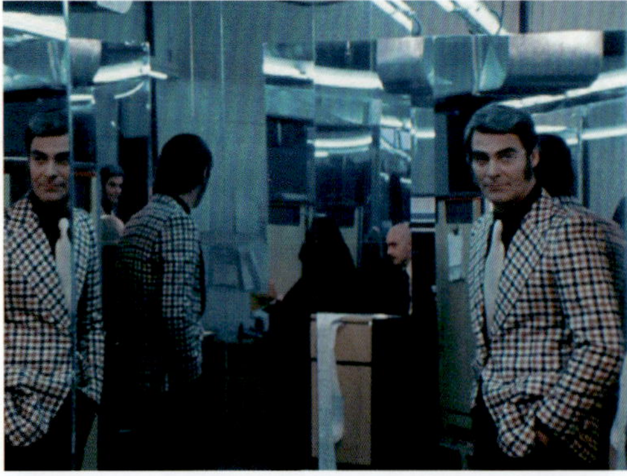
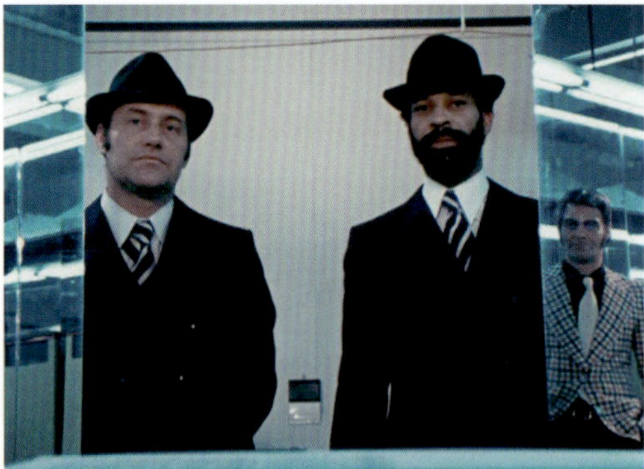
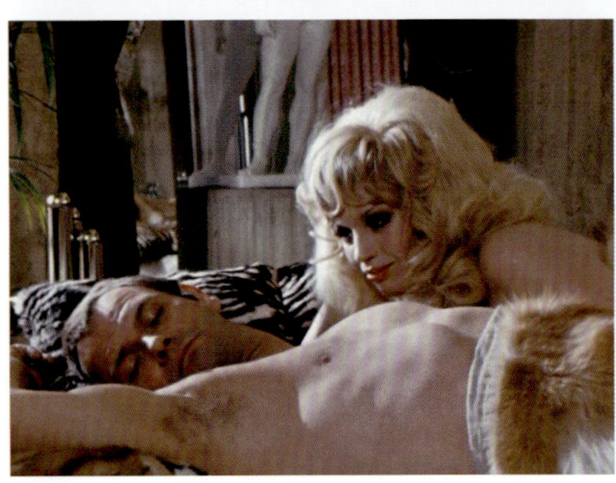
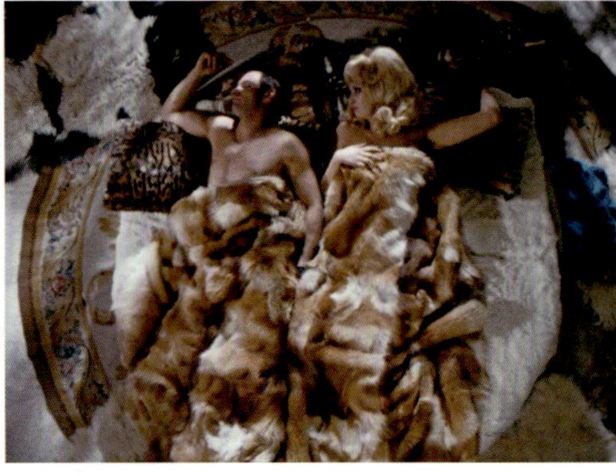
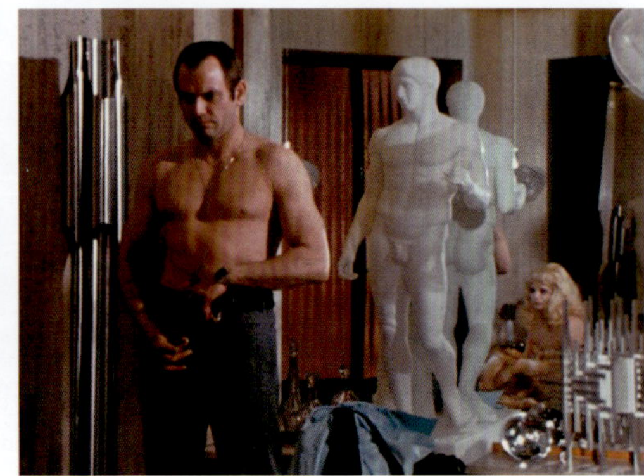

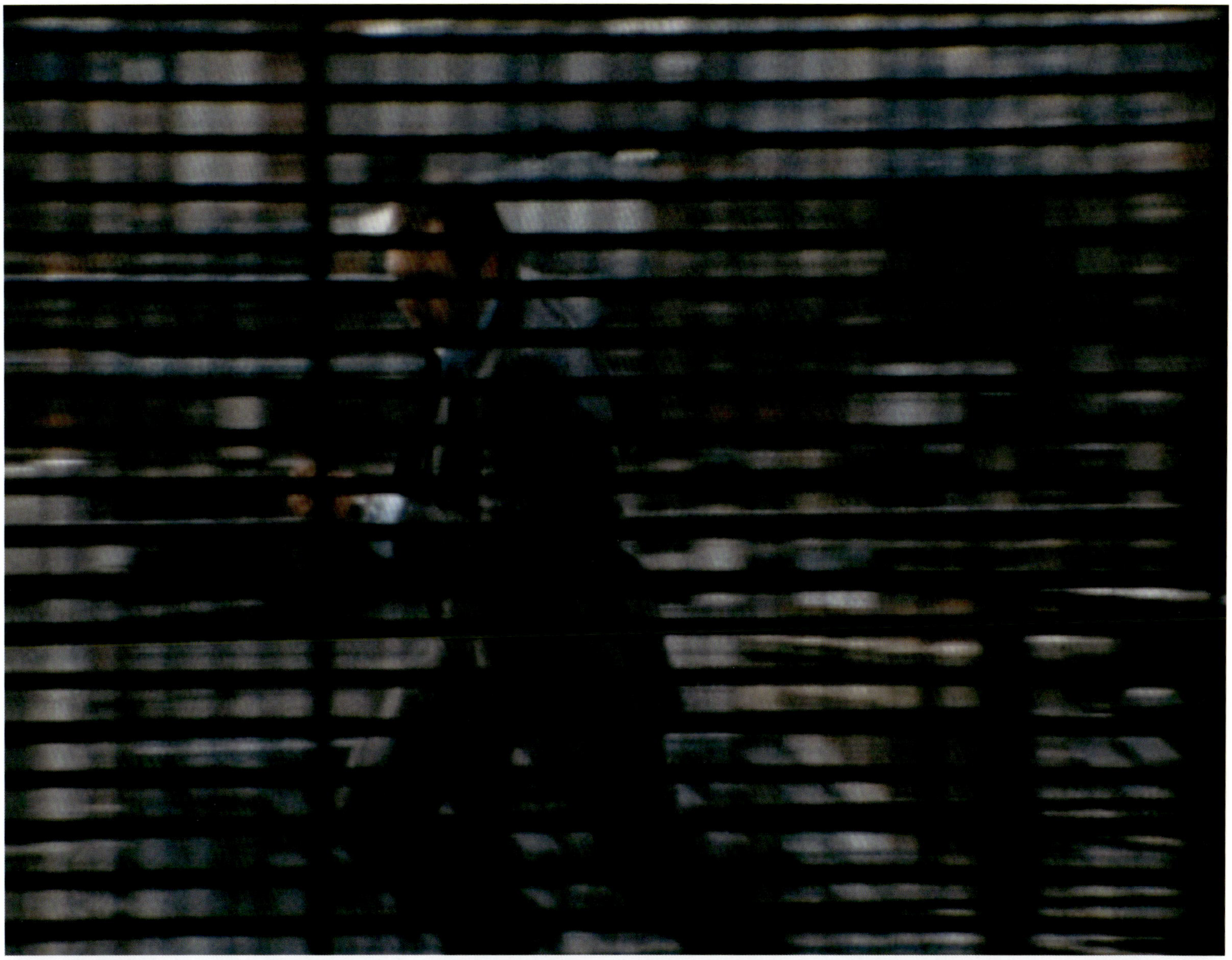

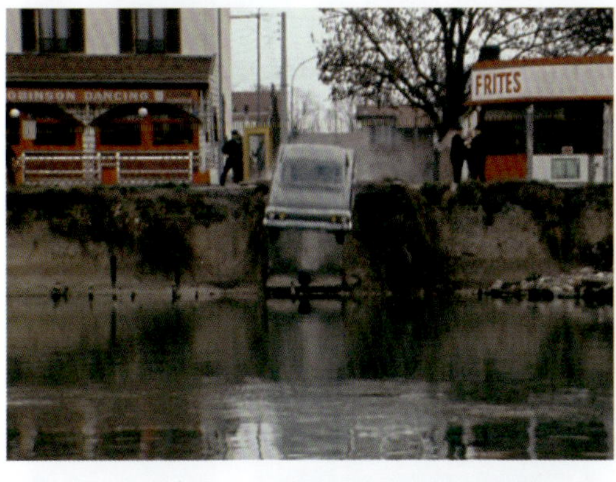
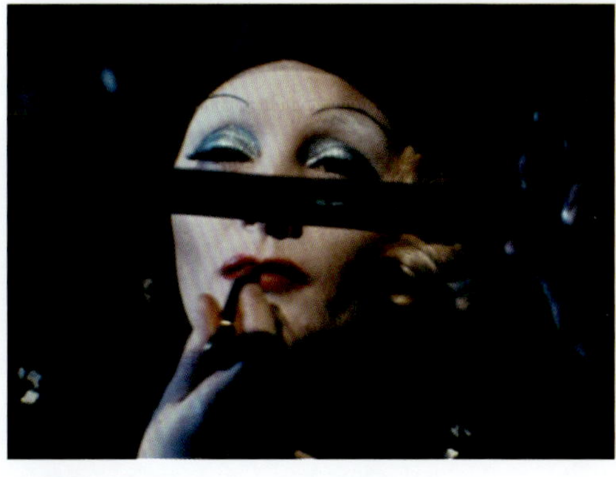
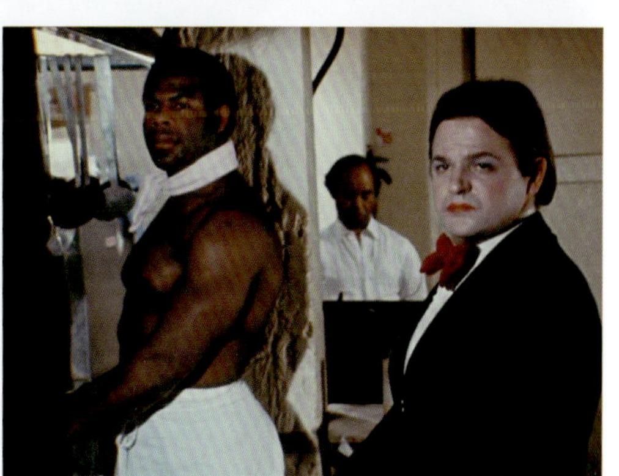
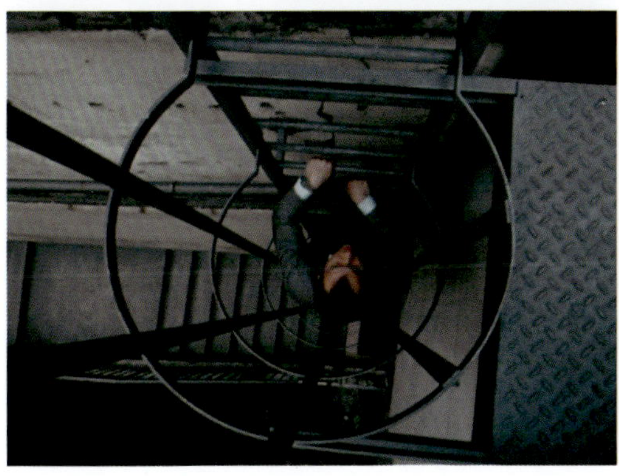
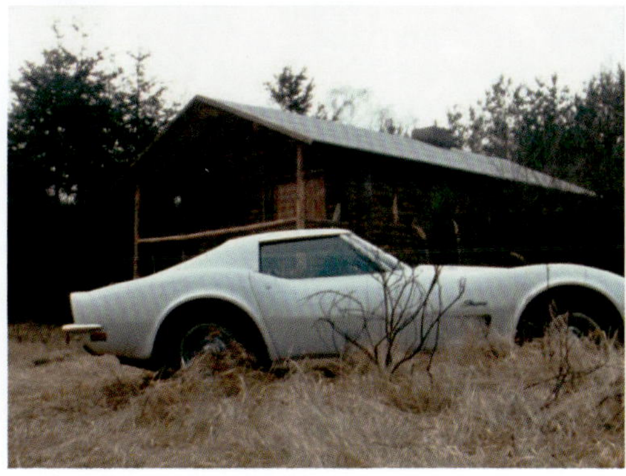
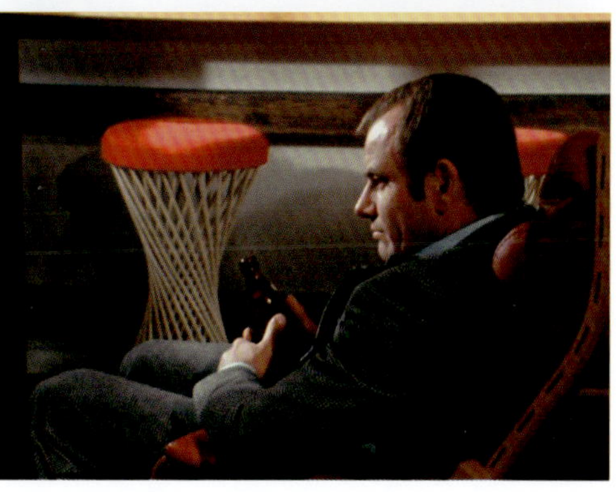

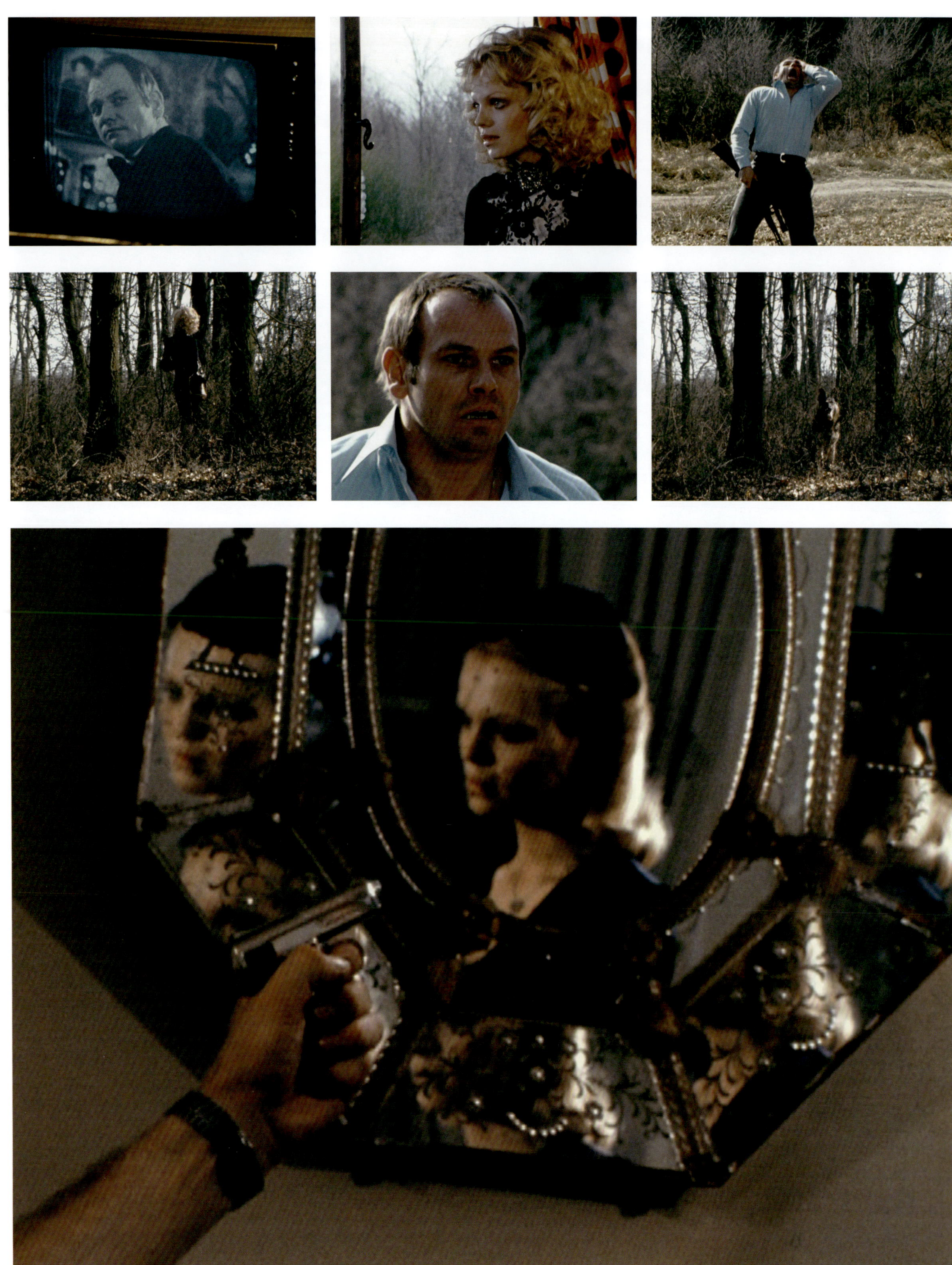

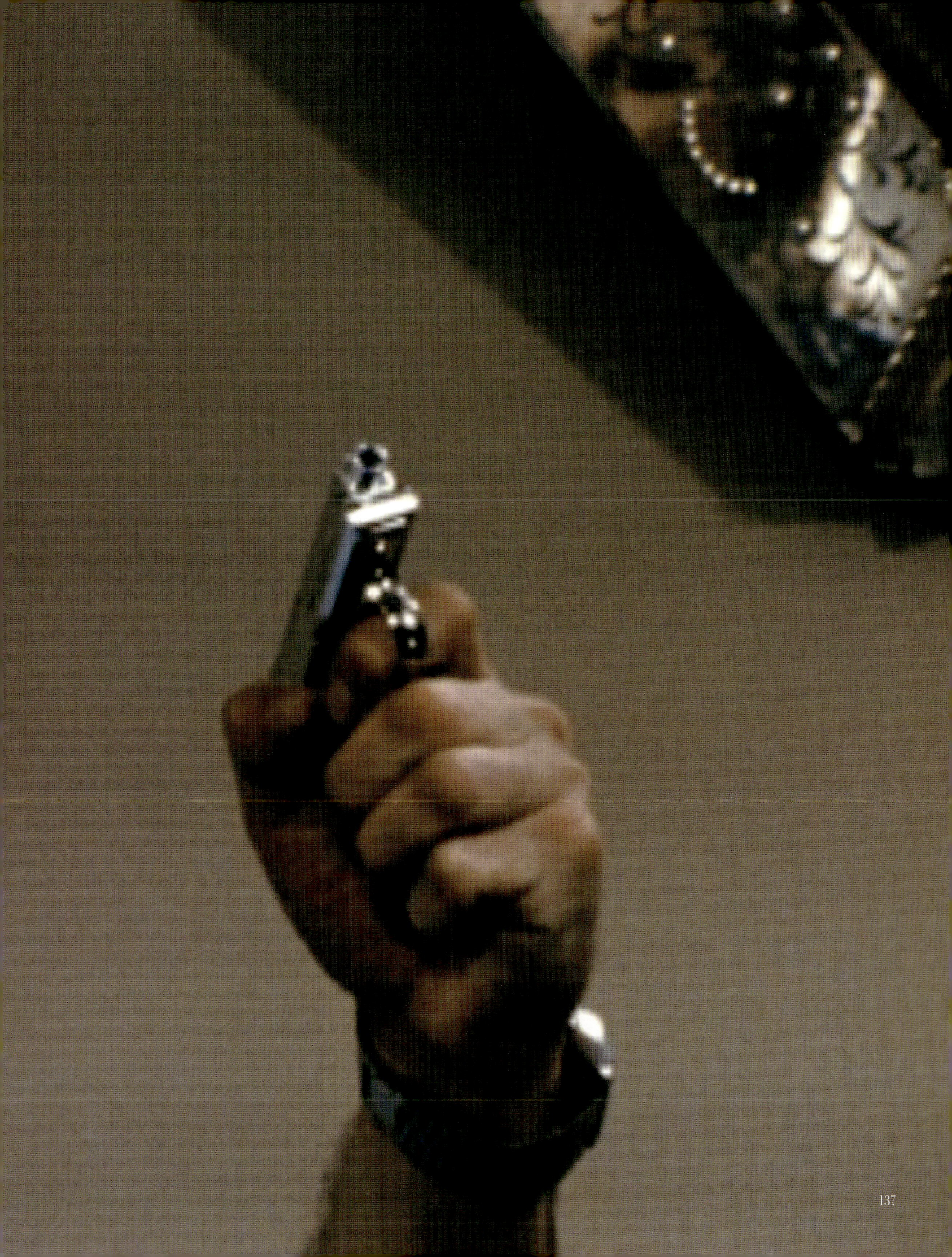

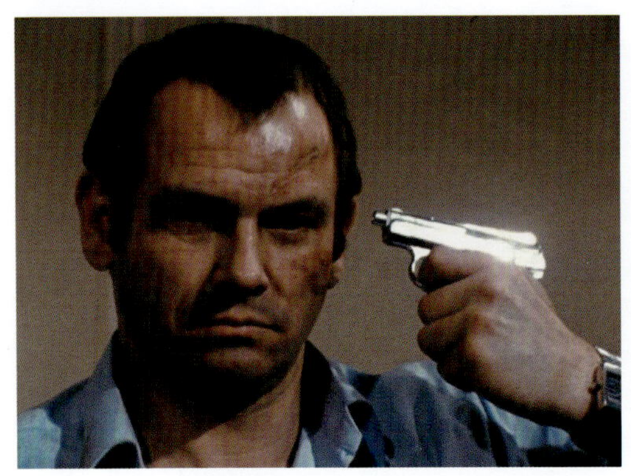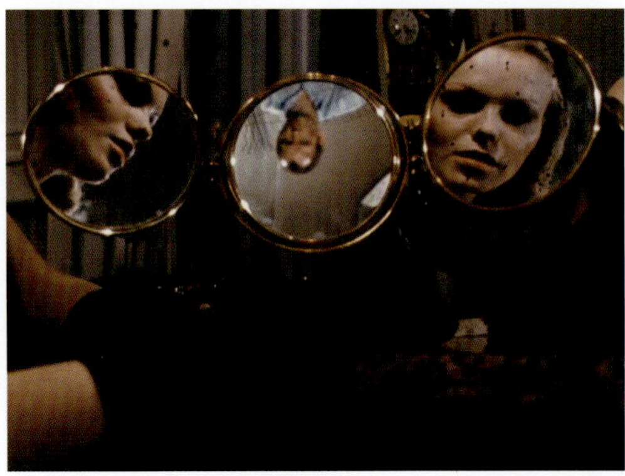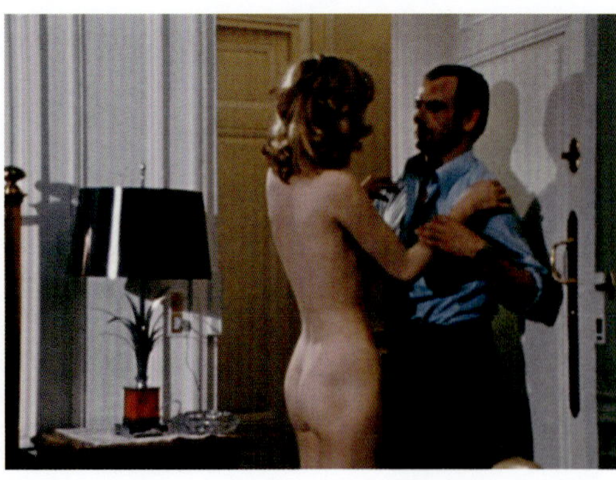

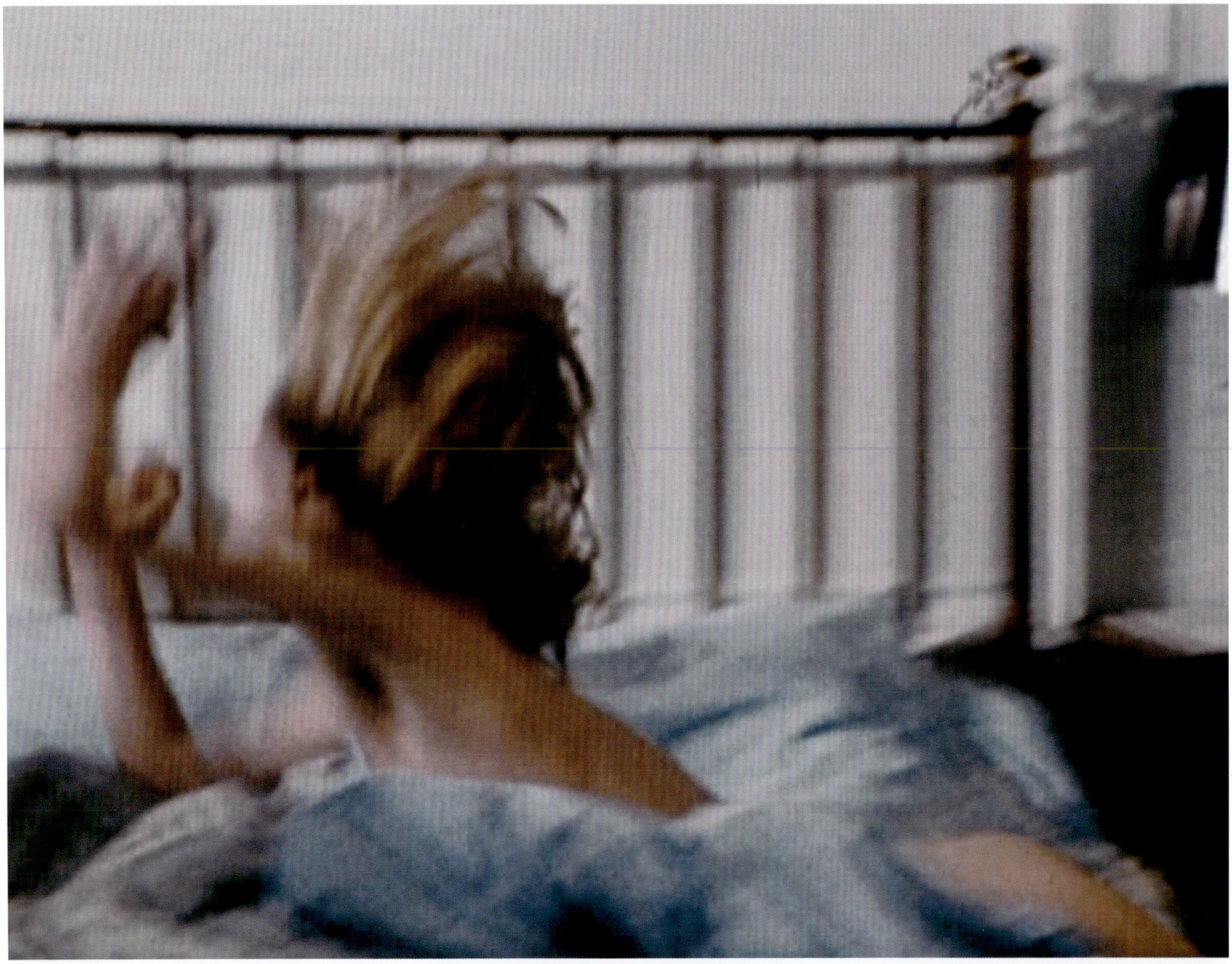

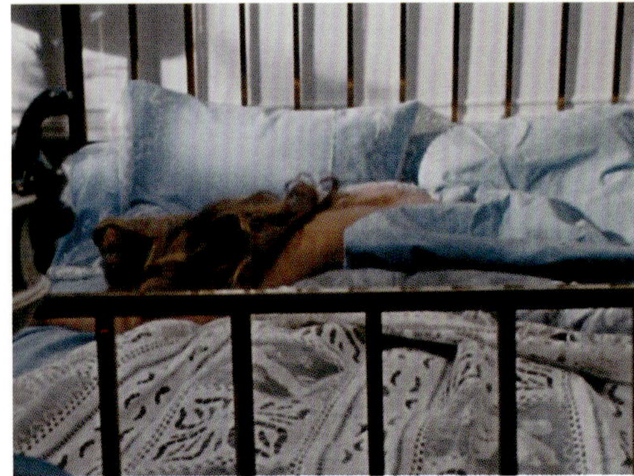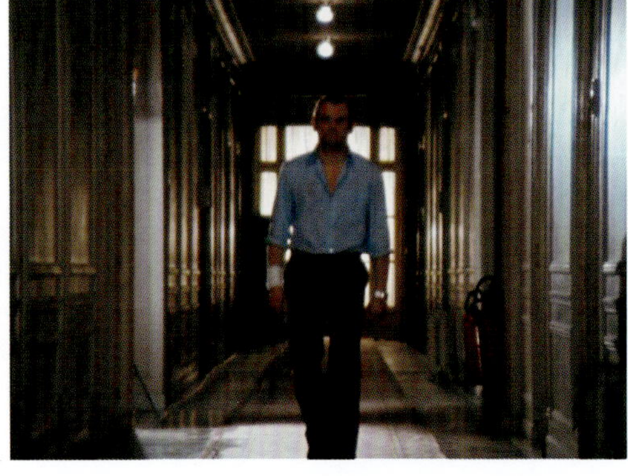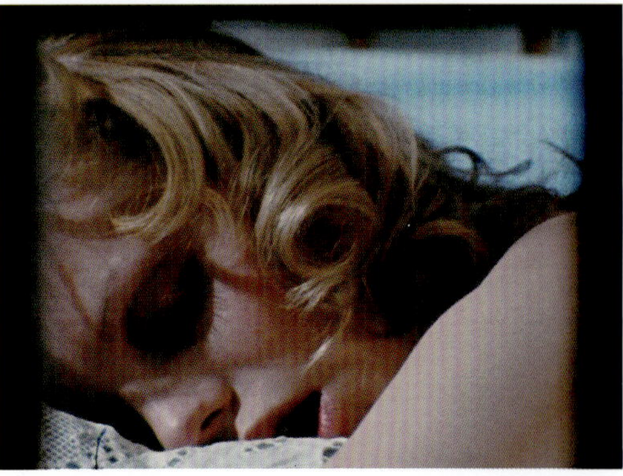

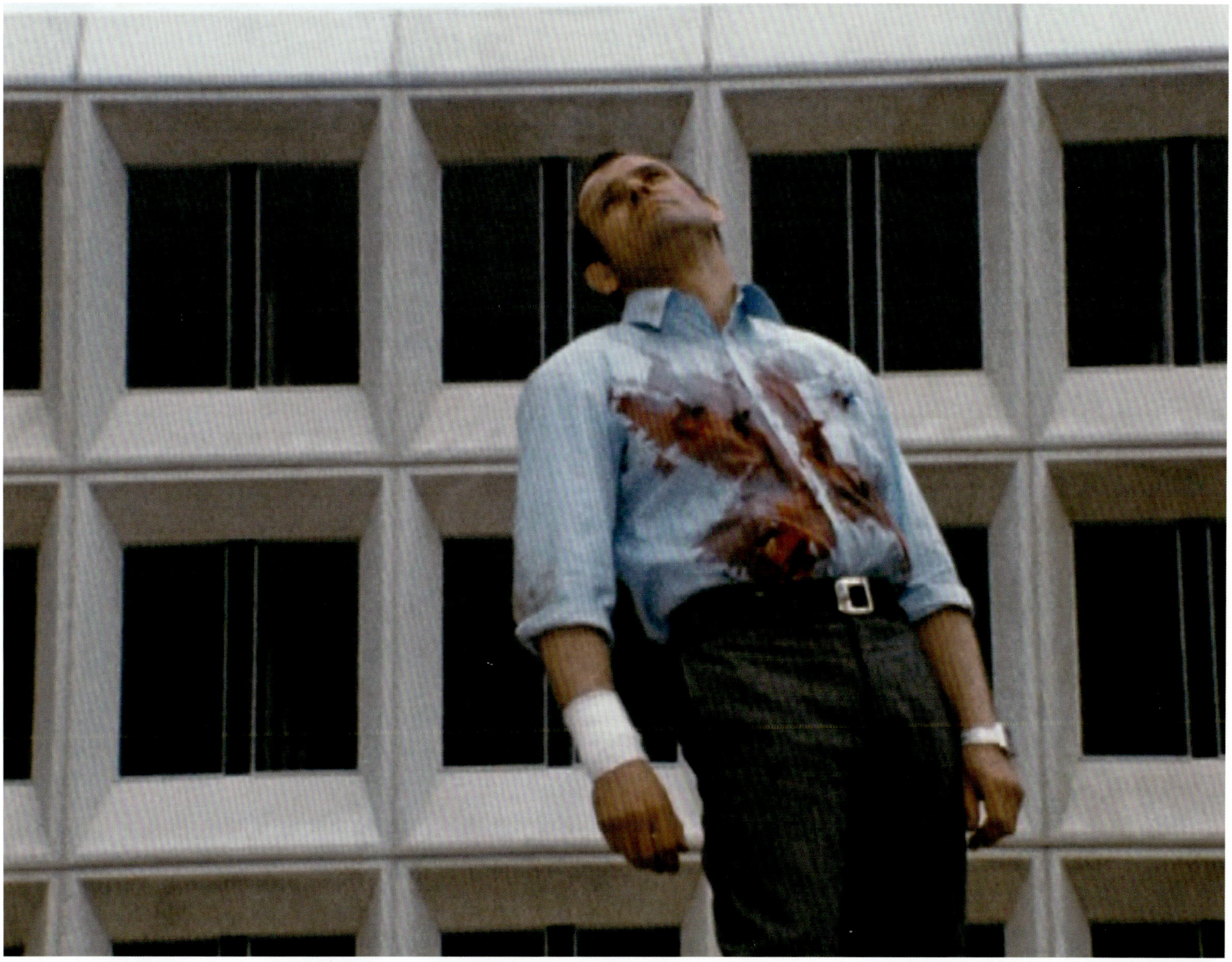

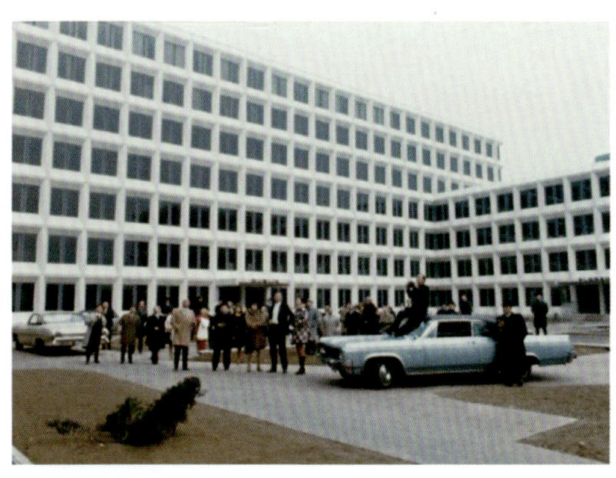
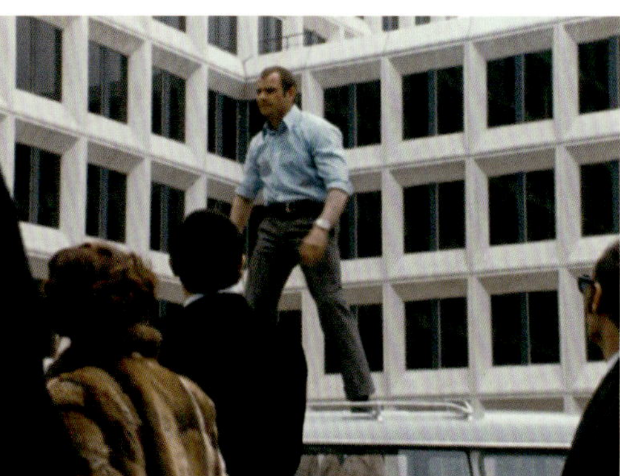
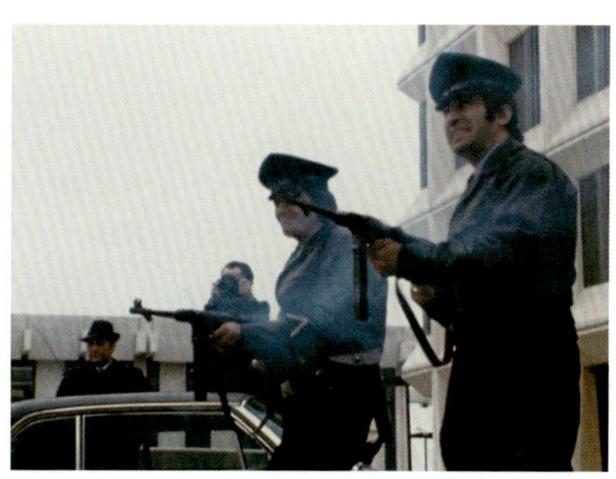
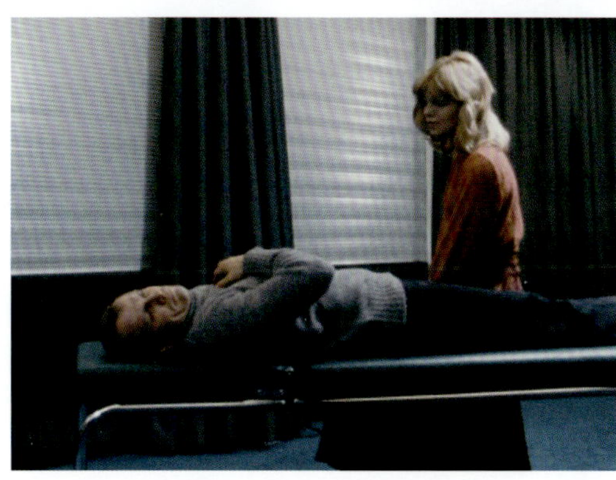
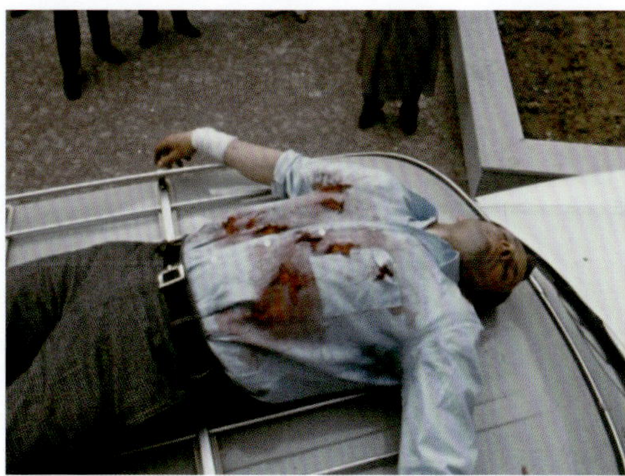
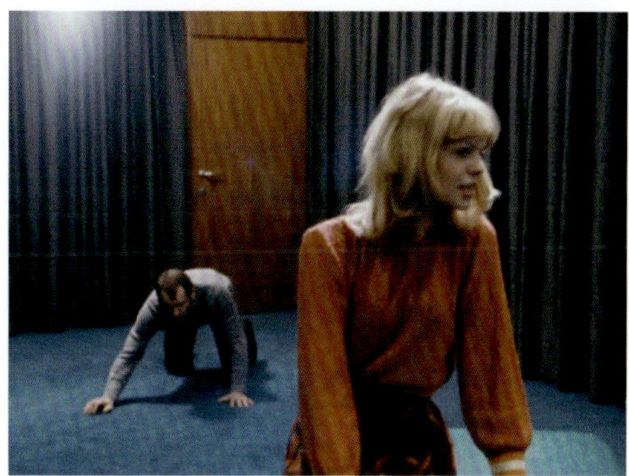

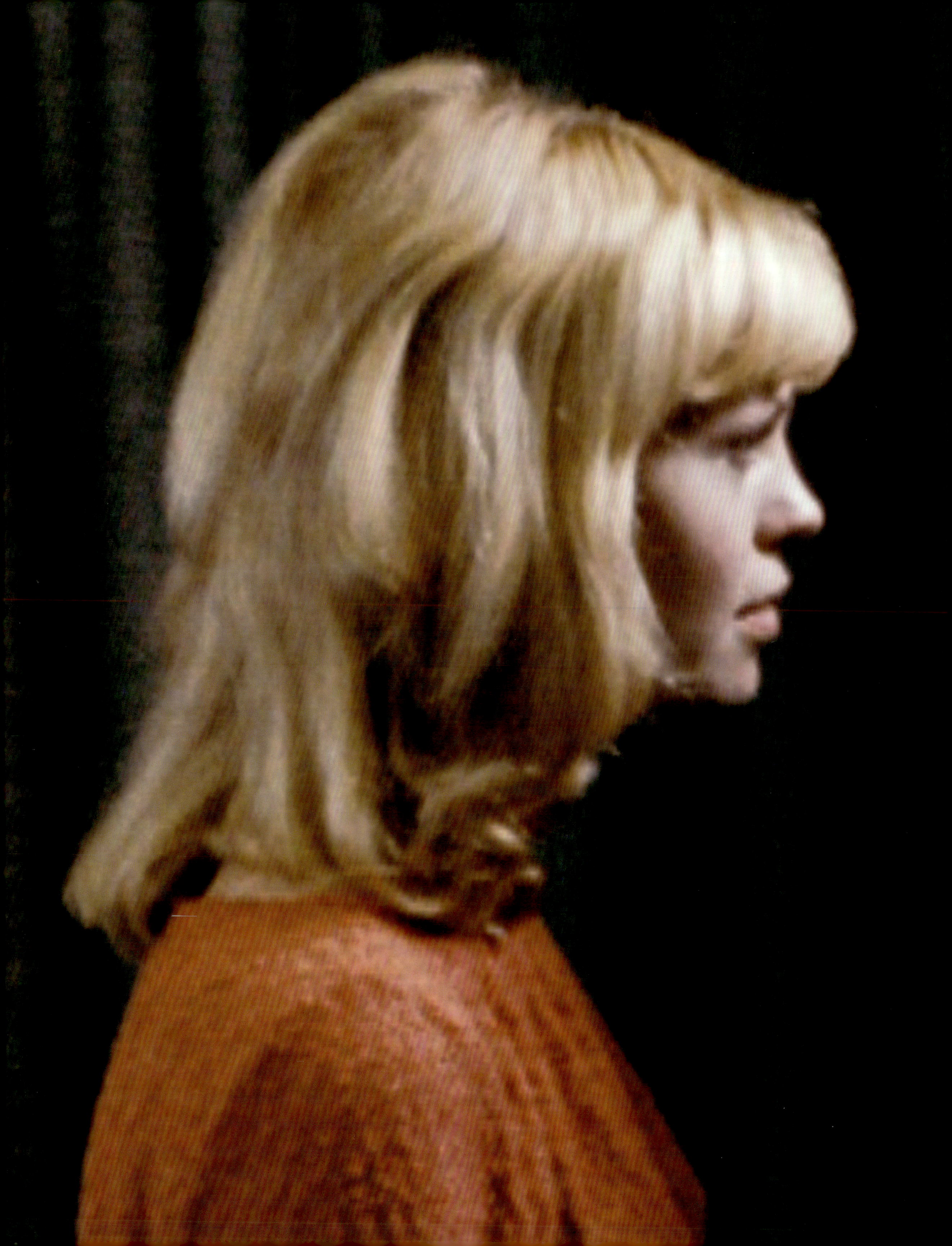

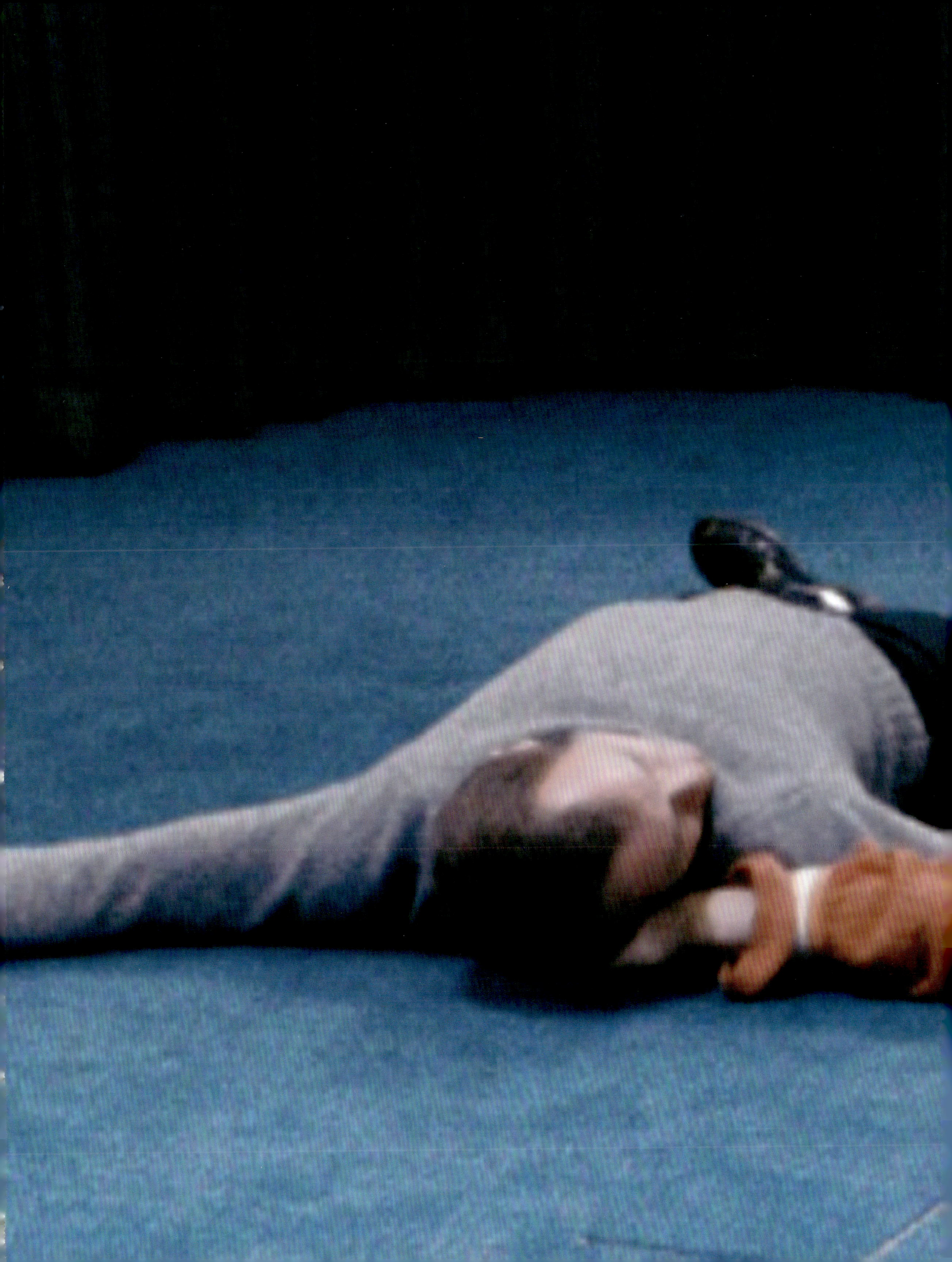

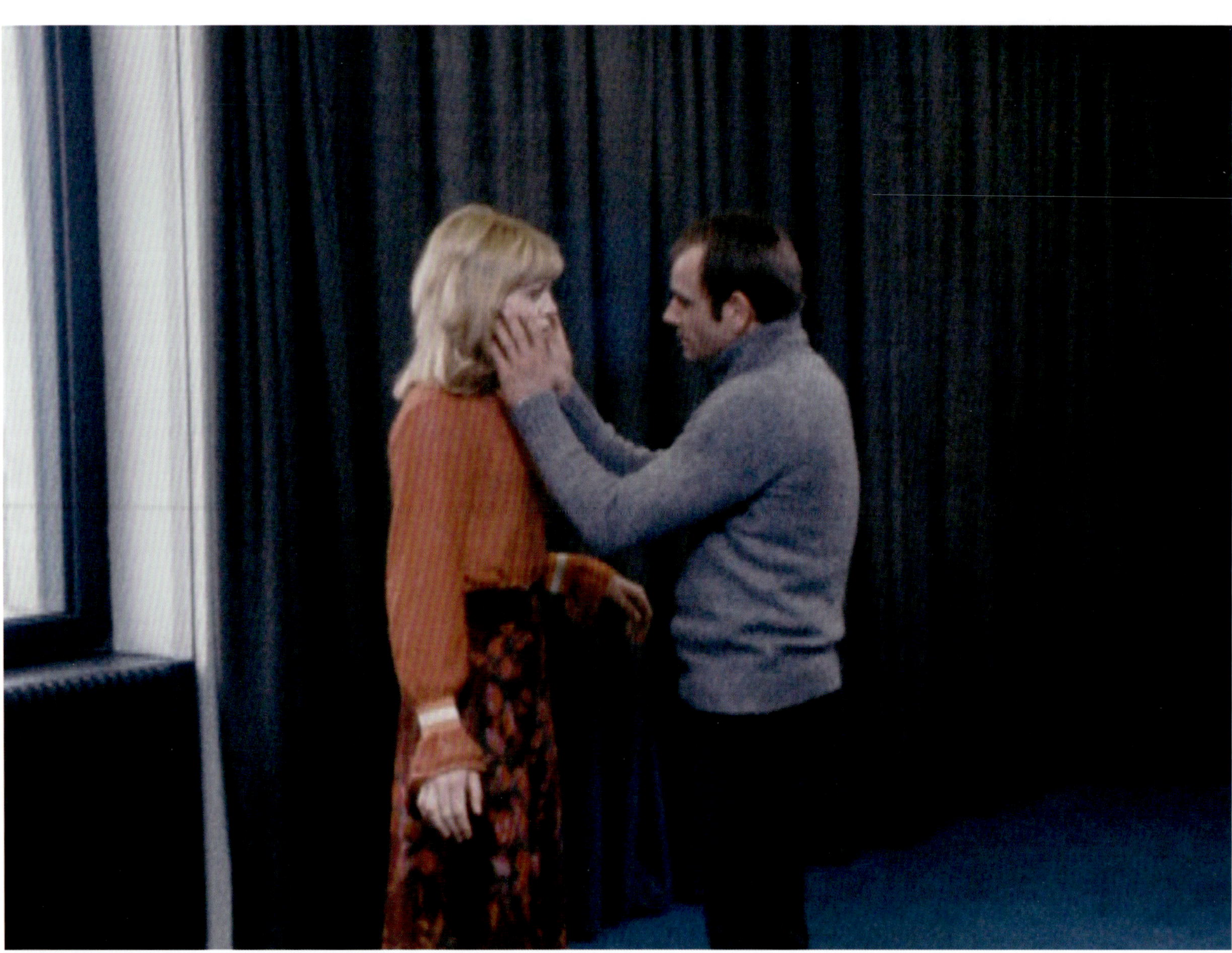

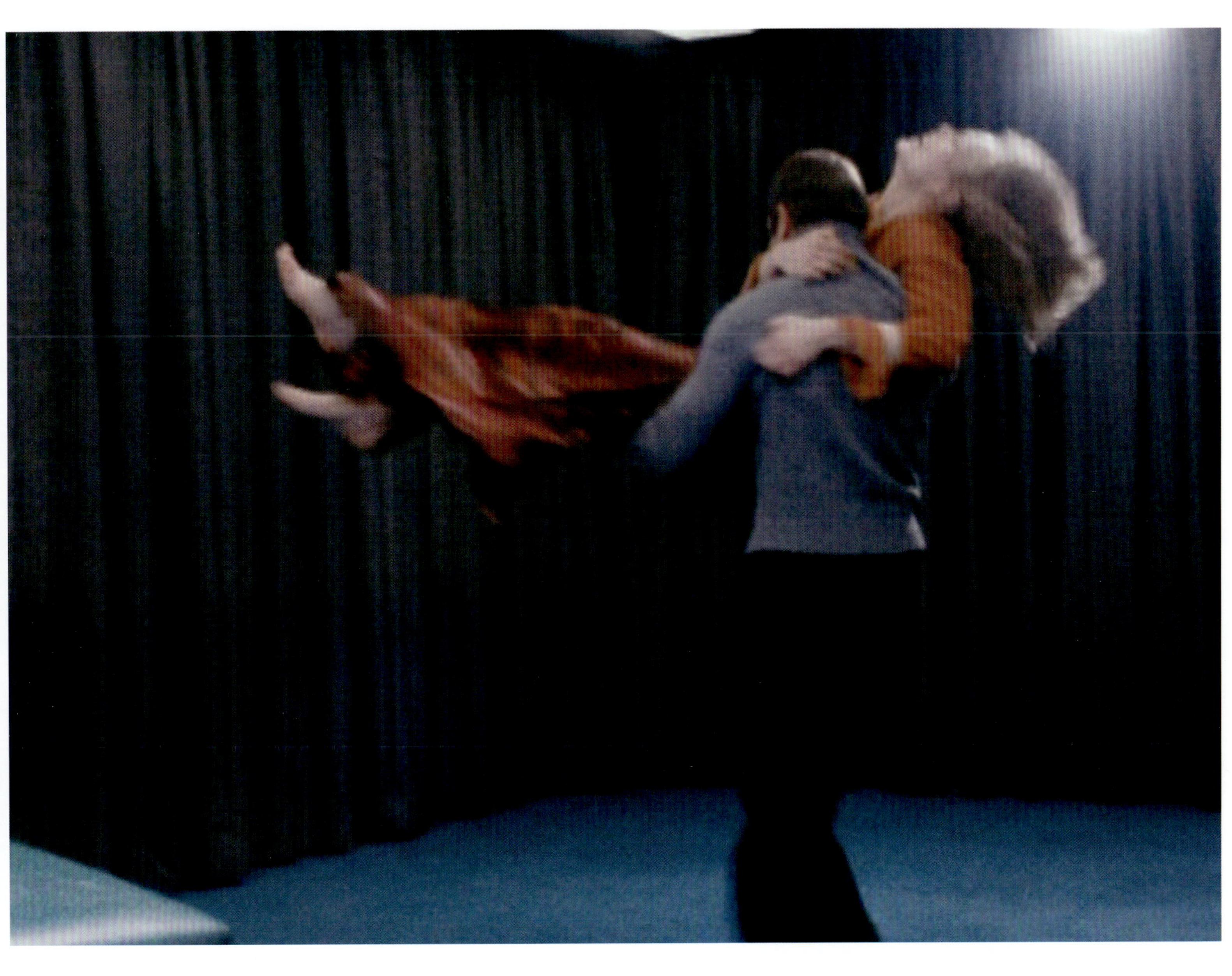

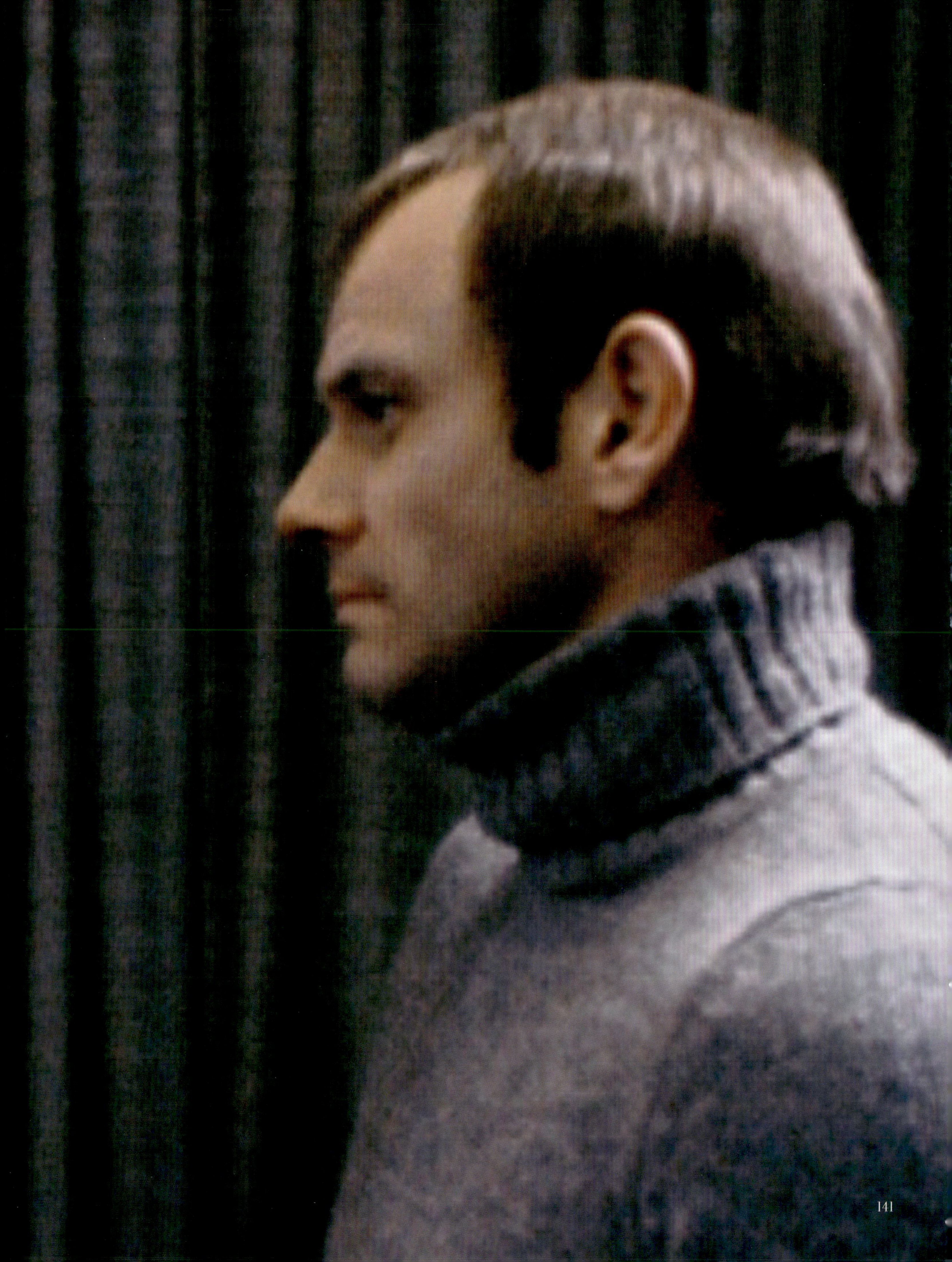

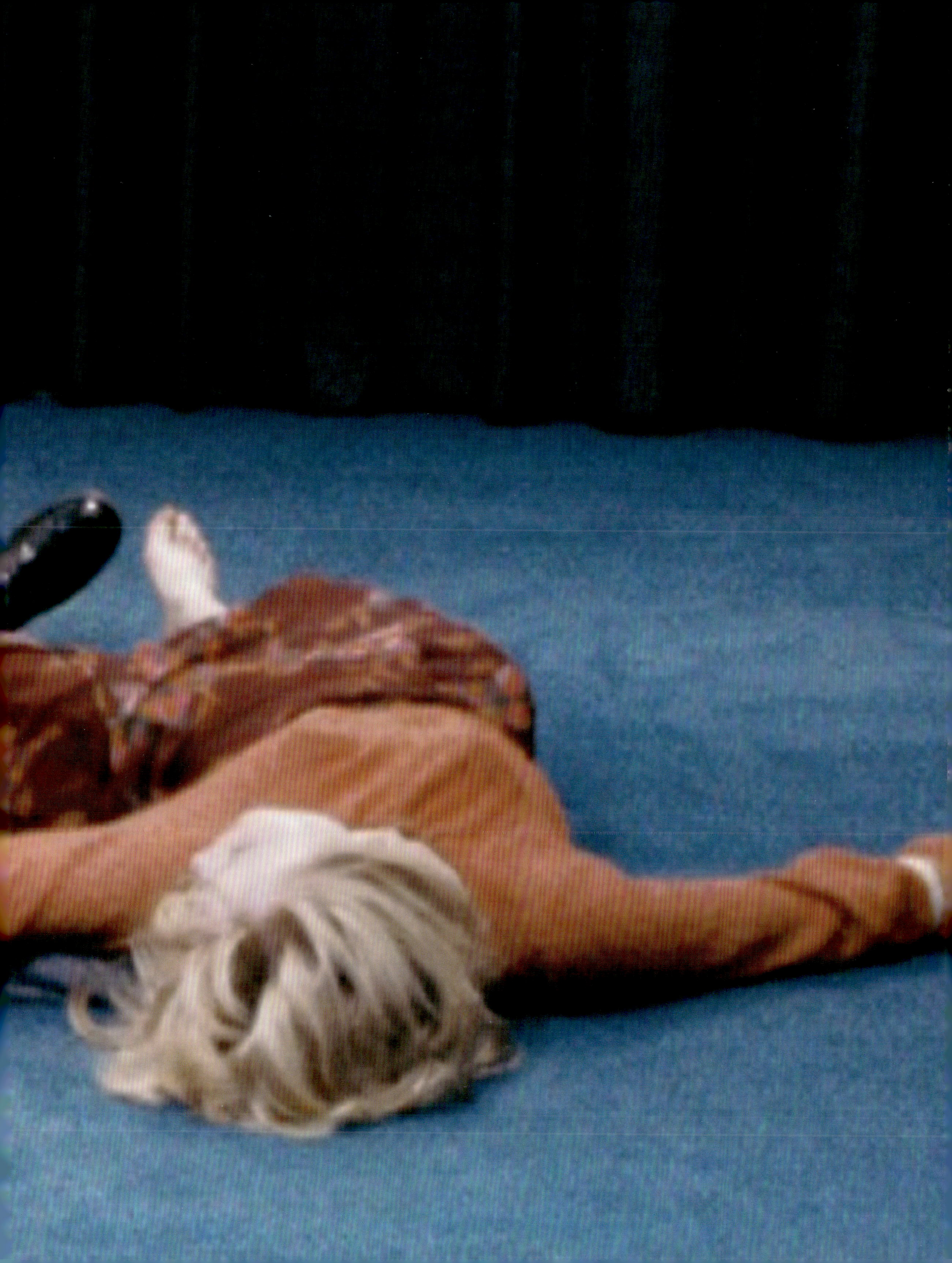

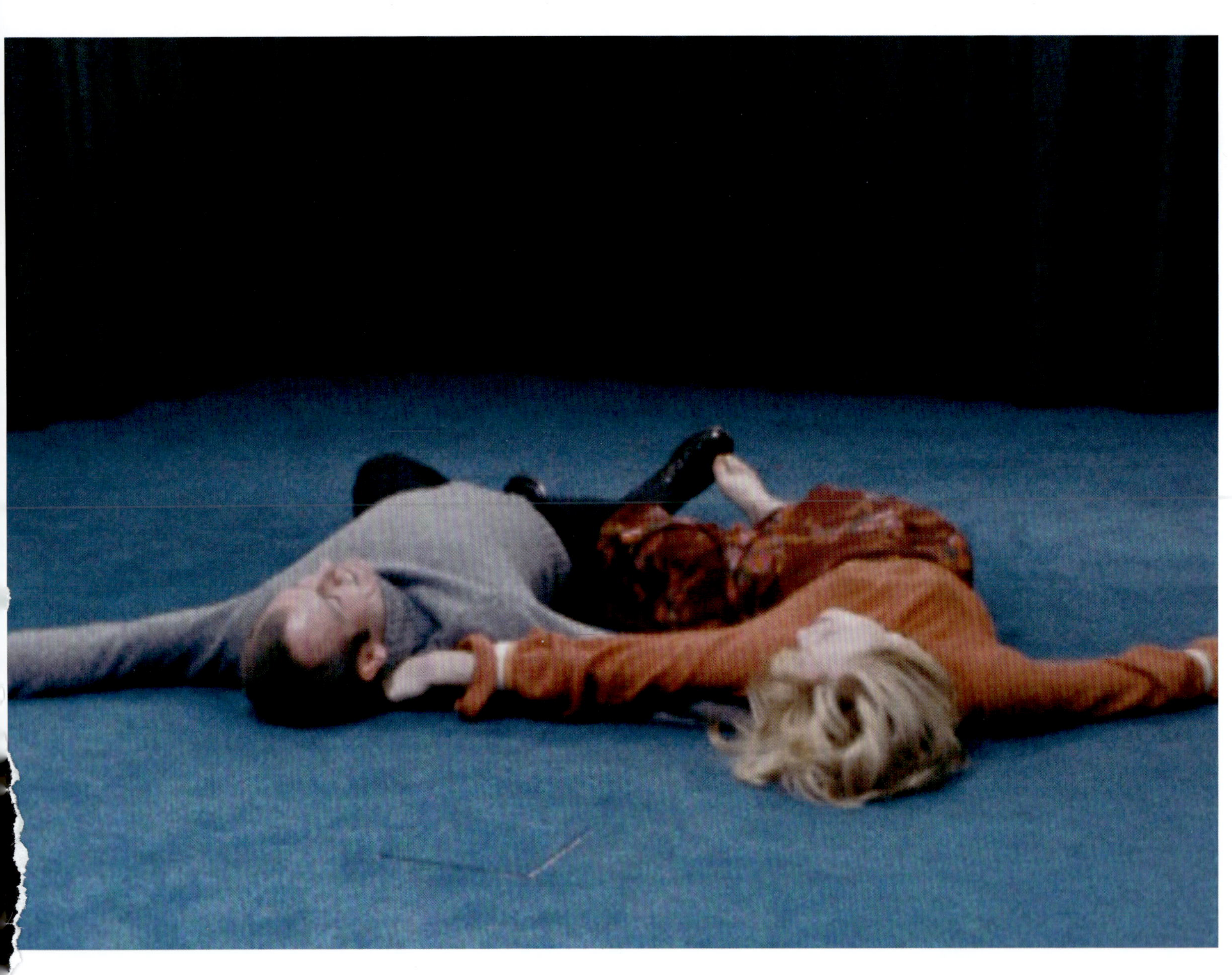

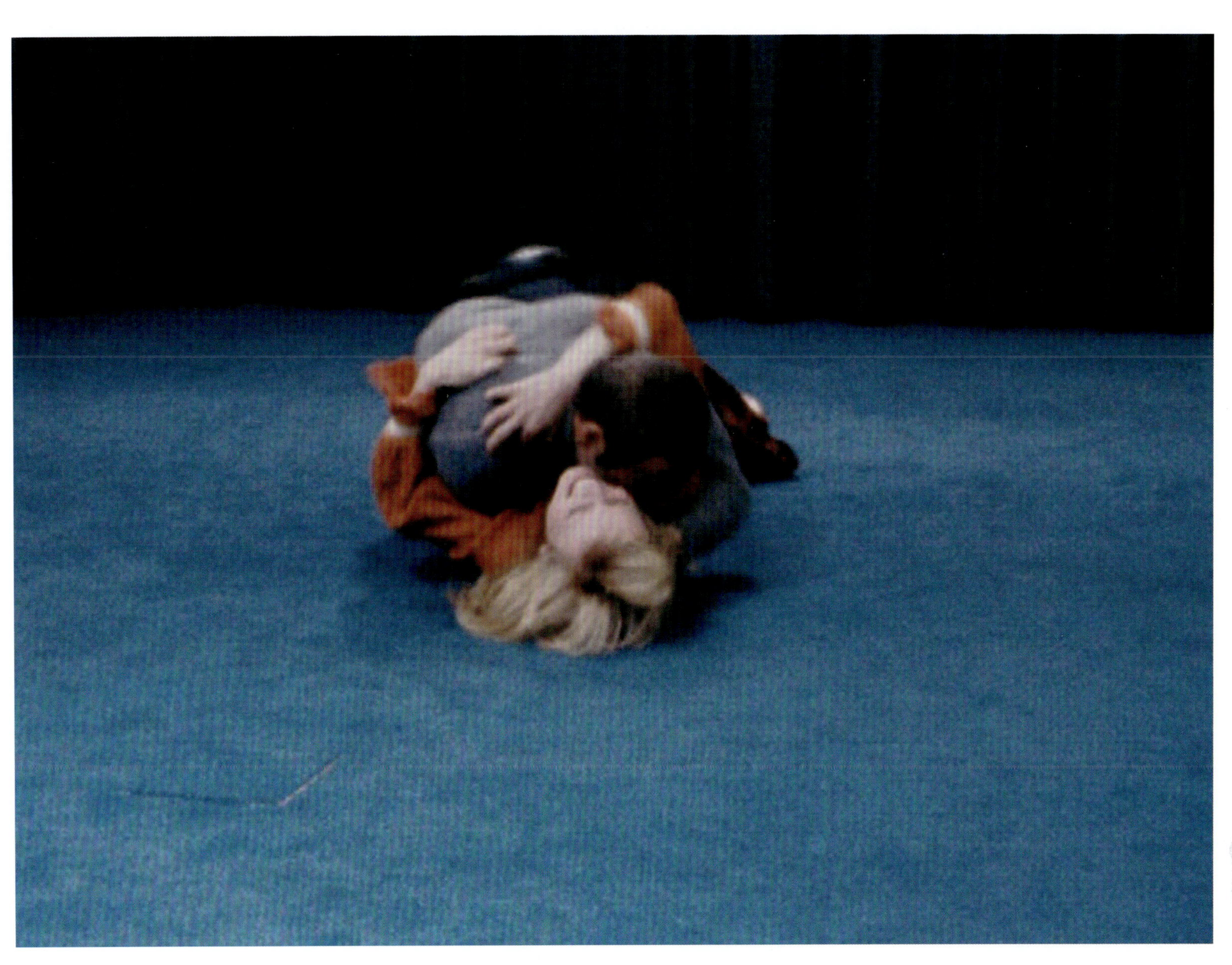

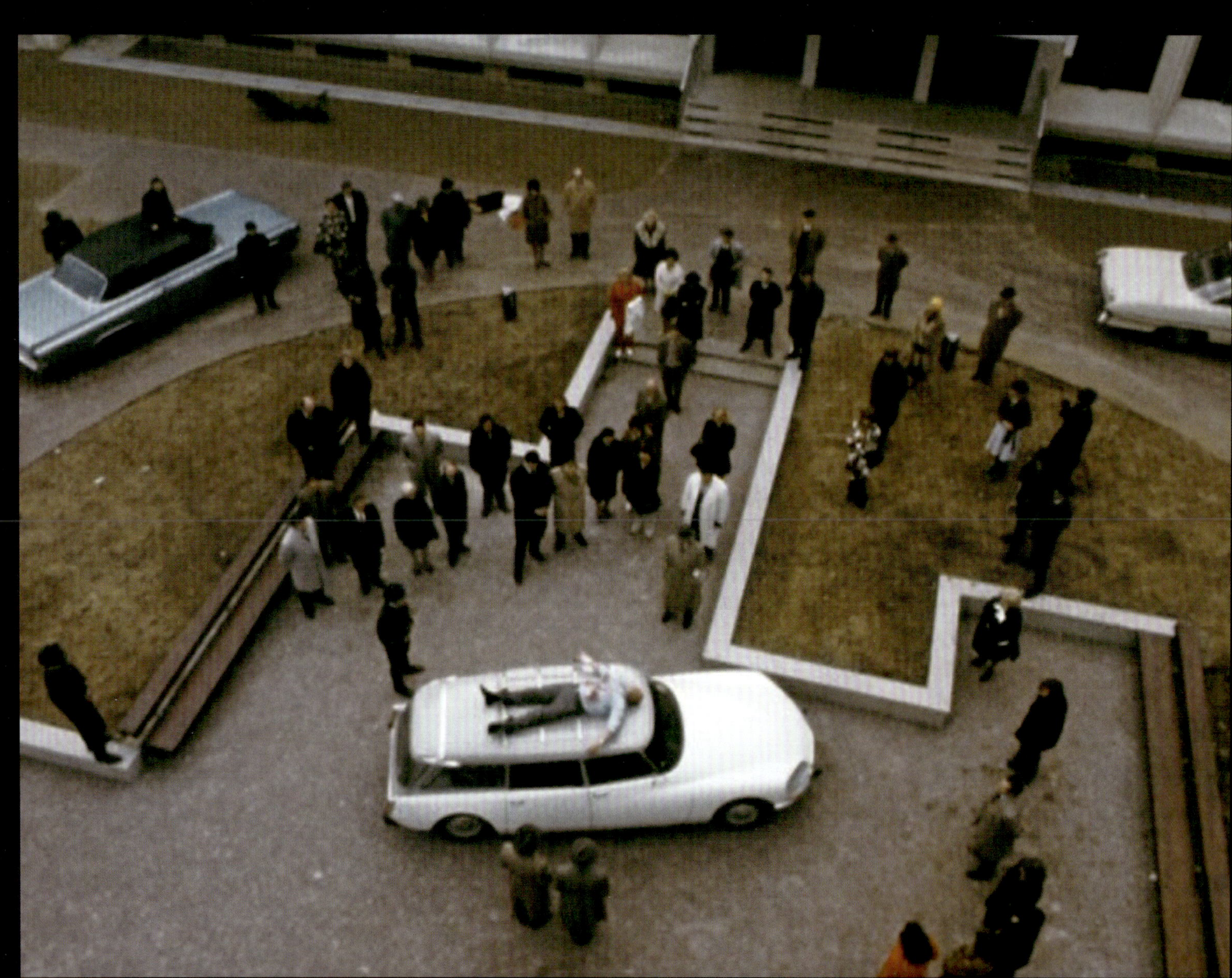

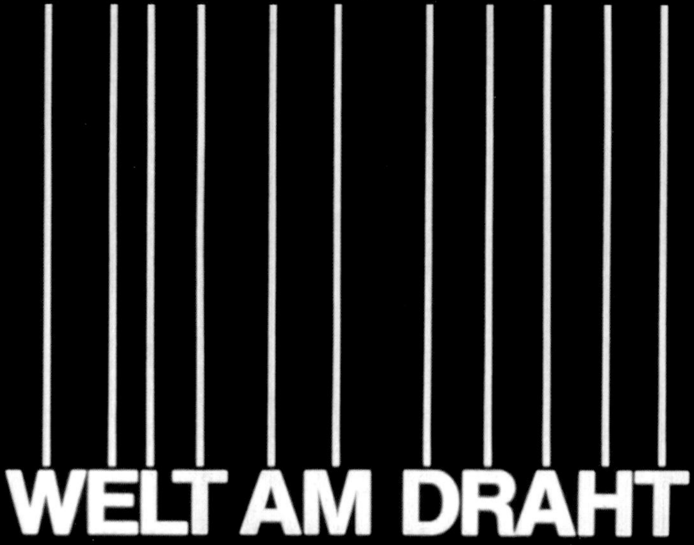

WORLD ON A WIRE
[WELT AM DRAHT]

Directed by Rainer Werner Fassbinder

Produced by Peter Märthesheimer, Alexander Wesemann

Written by Rainer Werner Fassbinder and Fritz Müller-Scherz

Based on the novel *Simulacron-3* by Daniel F. Galouye

Cinematography: Michael Ballhaus

Production designer: Kurt Raab

Costume designer: Gabriele Pillon

Editor: Marie Anne Gerhardt

Cast: Klaus Löwitsch, Barbara Valentin, Mascha Rabben, Karl Heinz Vosgerau,
Wolfgang Schenck, Günter Lamprecht, Ulli Lommel, Adrian Hoven, Ivan Desny,
Joachim Hansen, Kurt Raab, Margit Carstensen, Gottfried John, Werner Schroeter,
Eddie Constantine, Rudolf Waldemar Brem, Peter Kern, Ingrid Caven, El Hedi ben Salem

Commissioned by German television network WDR

Original air date: October 14, 1973

Reproduced with the permission of
The Rainer Werner Fassbinder Foundation
and
The Criterion Collection

©1973 WDR
©2010 The Rainer Werner Fassbinder Foundation

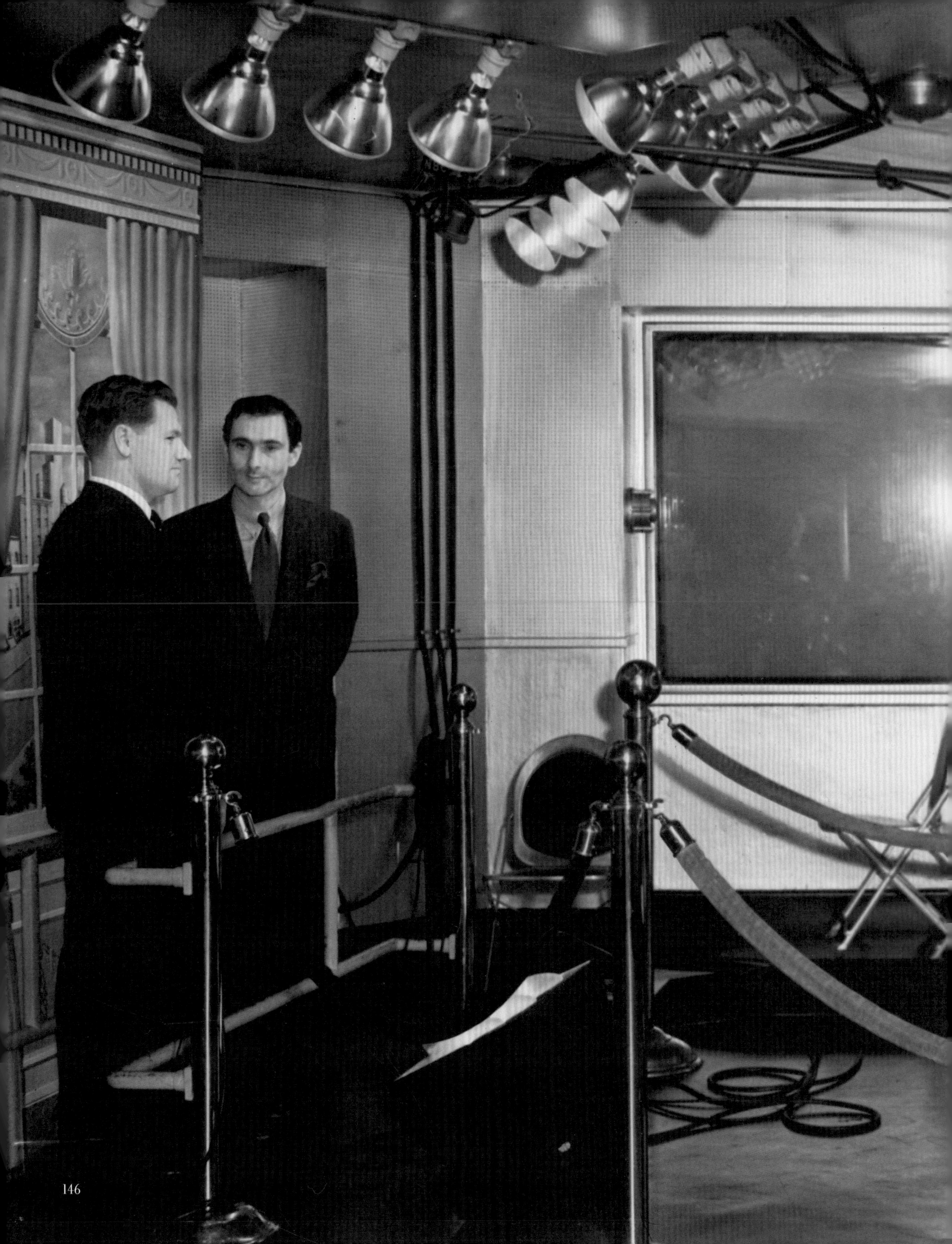

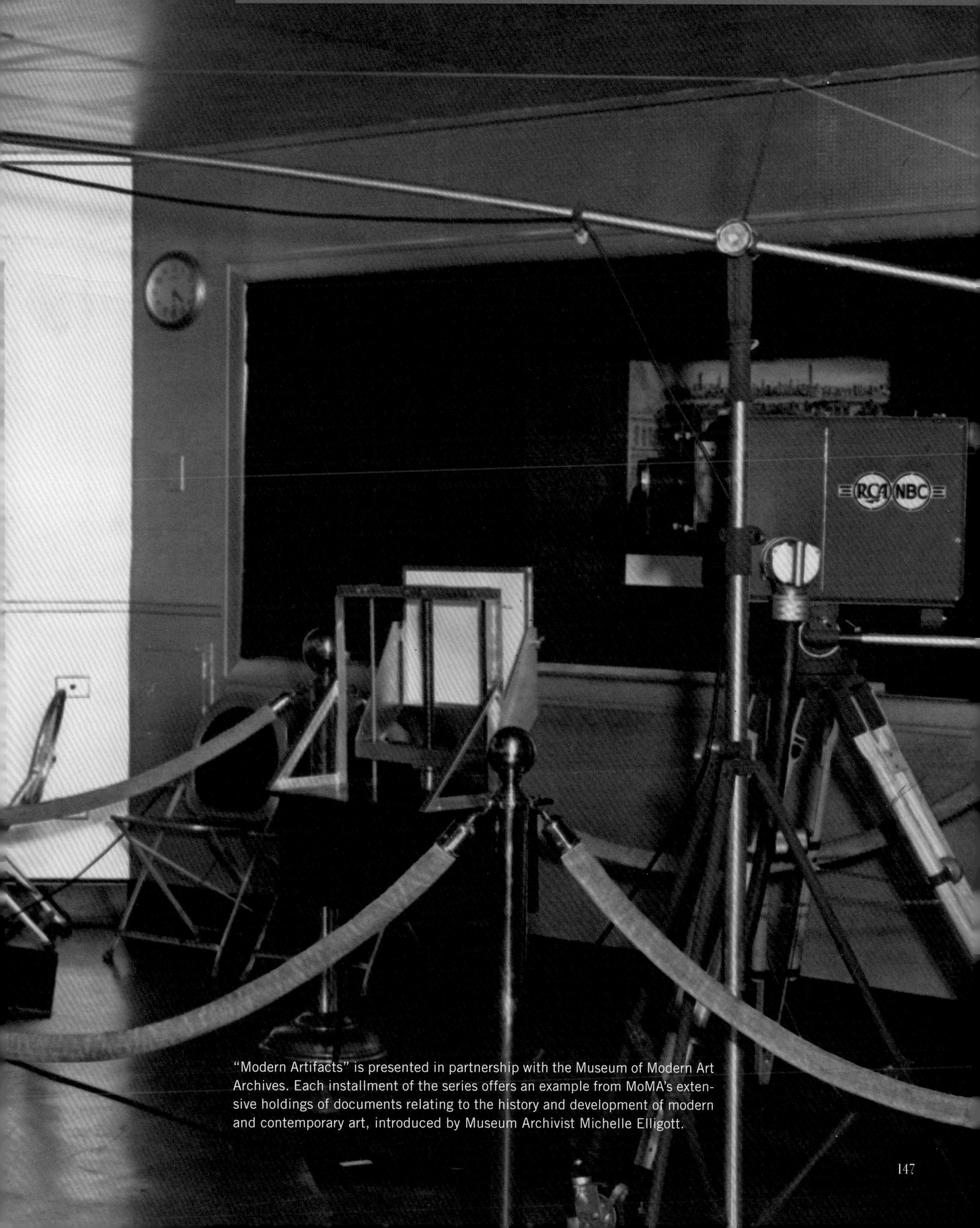

"Modern Artifacts" is presented in partnership with the Museum of Modern Art Archives. Each installment of the series offers an example from MoMA's extensive holdings of documents relating to the history and development of modern and contemporary art, introduced by Museum Archivist Michelle Elligott.

The Museum of Modern Art has had a long and pioneering, yet complex, relationship to television, riddled with ambiguity, multiple agendas, and several false starts. The Museum's eager embrace of this new medium—much like its earlier embrace of radio—in part reflected a long-standing interest in evolving technologies. But it was television's incorporation of the visual—so critical to an understanding of art—that aligned particularly well with the Museum's primary mission of popularizing and democratizing modern art.

As early as 1939, in conjunction with its 10th-anniversary celebration, the Museum gave the first television broadcast ever held by an American museum [pp. 146–147]. By 1950, the Museum was participating in TV shows at least once weekly.

In 1952, under the leadership of its open-minded, programmatically ambitious director, René d'Harnoncourt, the Museum deepened its engagement with the medium by creating the Television Project, funded by a three-year grant from the Rockefeller Brothers Fund. Douglas MacAgy, former director of the California School of Fine Arts (now the San Francisco School of Art), was brought on as consultant to the director of the Museum and director of the Television Project; Sidney Peterson, noted avant-garde filmmaker, led this effort as special consultant to the Television Project. MacAgy handled the organizational aspects of the project while Peterson developed scenarios for actual programs.

These scenarios involved a variety of approaches. There were rather straightforward exhibition tie-ins, for example, such as a series of spots on Margaret Arlen's morning show on CBS in 1954 promoting the Museum's popular exhibition series *Good Design*. The Television Project also sponsored the Museum's series *Through the Enchanted Gate*, which ran for two seasons on NBC in 1952 and 1953. The show mimicked programs at the Museum that involved children in art-making activities with skilled art educators. Rather than providing an imitative model, the program encouraged youngsters to develop artworks expressing their own ideas and feelings. As Victor D'Amico, pioneering art educator and director of the program, wrote in a final report, "The tremendous implication here is that any child within range of a television set is able to receive the best art training available."[1]

Home, a popular morning show on NBC geared largely toward a female viewing audience, offered another opportunity for the Museum to harness the potential of this emerging medium. As documented in the materials from the MoMA Archives reproduced here, the *Home* program on September 29, 1955, invited Museum director Alfred H. Barr, Jr., to familiarize its audience with the ideas underpinning his book *What Is Modern Painting?*, written specifically to dispel the confusion—and often disdain—of the "common man" toward contemporary art. For the program, the Museum transported paintings by Giorgio de Chirico, Arthur B. Dove, and Marc Chagall from its collection to NBC's New York studios. (The correspondence in the Archives indicates that the Museum required a thorough review of the script in advance, in order to ensure an appropriate separation of the works of art from anything commercial or advertised.) Using the same clarity of language that informed his book, Barr endeavored to explain modern art by discussing its similarities to poetry and biblical verse (intentionally sedate comparisons). For example, he discussed the "Song of Solomon" as love poetry and compared it to Chagall's canvas *Birthday*, created in the spirit of "enthusiastic love" [pp. 151–152]. Barr, note cards in hand [p. 159], spoke in front of each painting for the live broadcast, which also happened to be one of the first to utilize color. This fact was noted in the script for the series [p. 154] and was made even more dramatic with the decision by NBC to broadcast the lead-in to the show in black-and-white, only switching to color once Barr and the canvases were introduced—something akin to the moment when Dorothy realizes she is no longer in Kansas in *The Wizard of Oz*. The show generated enthusiastic viewer response, much to the delight of Barr [pp. 160–163].

In addition, the Television Project developed a series of other initiatives, with mostly disappointing results. Another series, *Point of View,* employed "a format which would make possible the sustained use of the city of New York itself as a museum."[2] The pilot, "Architectural Millinery," depicted hats and roofs in New York and elsewhere. It was followed by "Manhole Covers," which showed images of manhole covers around the city, featured in photographs as well as in footage pulled from films by Charlie Chaplin. A 1954 television-progress internal report curtly declared that "the Museum did not see the point"[3] of these programs, and the Museum divorced itself from this project. The final proposal of the Television Project was to create an archive of television programs, modeled on the collection of the Museum's Film Library, founded in 1935. This, however, also went unrealized, and by early 1956, with the completion of the Rockefeller Brothers Fund grant, the Museum terminated its Television Project.

In the ensuing years, the Museum continued to pursue a tentative relationship with TV. In 1963, the Museum presented *Television U.S.A.: 13 Seasons.* The goal of the retrospective series, which ran for 13 weeks with a 90-minute program screened twice daily, was to focus "attention on those areas in which the Museum feels the medium has made significant contributions to the art of our time" and to "…help the public to develop general standards of understanding, enjoyment and evaluation."[4] In 1967, the Museum announced its establishment of a Television Archive of the Arts, a collection of television programs about artists and contemporary art. The program dissipated a few years later, however, when the International Study Center at the Museum was discontinued.

The Museum's *Open Circuits* conference in 1974—the same year the video program at MoMA was founded—presented important works of contemporary video art and invited artists such as Nam June Paik, Shigeko Kubota, Hollis Frampton, Joan Jonas, Allan Kaprow, Richard Serra, and Michael Snow to speak while considering the effect of television on perceptual experience and on the development of art. In a similar vein, the Museum hosted an exhibition in 1989 called *The Arts for Television,* which examined the potential role of TV as a forum for contemporary art. But in these exhibitions, and in curatorial practice at the museum in general, television itself was gradually replaced by the actual medium of video, which eventually morphed into the broader curatorial category now referred to as "media."

The Museum's long-standing, if problematic, relationship with the medium of television reveals its desire to remain at the forefront of new technologies, even those whose rapid evolution proves challenging for their proper comprehension and implementation in an institutional setting. The Museum's current acquisition of Web- and time-based art, as well as its use of blogs, Web-casting and the newest iPhone and iPad applications, suggest that these efforts of experimenting with the newest mediums, whether for art production or for dissemination and communication, will continue in the 21st century.—*Michelle Elligott*

FOOTNOTES

[1] Report by Victor D'Amico, *Through the Enchanted Gate*, Early Museum History Records, III.3
[2] Progress report: Television Project, February 1954. EMH III.17
[3] Undated, unsigned report, *Point of View*, EMH III.16.b.
[4] Letter from René d'Harnoncourt to Leonard Goldenson, president of ABC, April 17, 1961, René d'Harnoncourt Papers, IV.221.

WHAT IS MODERN PAINTING ?

MUSEUM OF MODERN ART, NEW YORK

ALFRED H. BARR, JR., PAPERS
I.221

September 23, 1955

Mr. Robert B. Ruthman
"Home" - N.B.C. - T. V.
Hotel Dauphin
67th and Broadway
New York 23, New York

Dear Bob,

This is to confirm our telephone conversation regarding arrangements in connection with Alfred H. Barr, Jr.'s appearence on the
"Home" show Thursday, September 29th.

Museum custodians will deliver four paintings to the studio at
101 West 67th Street, directed to the attention of George Roberts,
on Wednesday afternoon in time for your rehersal. You will let
me know on Tuesday what your rehersal schedule is.

After the rehersal our men will place the four pictures in a
fireproof storage closet which will be locked until the pictures
are removed for the show Thursday morning. All handling of the
pictures will be done by the Museum custodians. N.B.C. will
have one man standing by to assist when needed.

We understand that N.B.C.'s insurance will cover the paintings.
The insurance evaluations are:

Dove - Grandmother	$ 1,500
Chagall - Birthday	$10,000
Kandinsky - Watercolor No. 13	$ 1,200
de Chirico - Anxious Journey	5,000
(also listed as Disturbing Journey)	

We will also appreciate it if you will send your sceipt outline
for this segment of the show over to us Monday or Tuesday so
that there will be plenty of time to discuss changes and second
thoughts. Incidentally, I believe that on one of the N.B.C.
releases Mr. Barr's first name was given incorrectly. He should
be called Alfred H. Barr, Jr., Director of the Museum's Collection.

The paintings will be delivered and picked up by Hahn Brothers.
The total cost of the trucking and for the custodians' time will
be approximately $30 to $35. I will bill you for this next week.

It is not easy to answer the question: What is modern painting?

I have tried to give some brief answers in the little book which Miss Francis

showed you, but even there it took 10,000 words and 50 pictures. Modern

painting is almost as complex a subject as modern life. There are a great

many kinds of modern painting. There are pictures of not so realistic that

at first glance they look like photographs. There are paintings which are

saturated with emotion and seem to have been painted in a state of high

excitement. There are other pictures which are painted with the help of

rulers and compasses and look like geometrical figures.

One way to approach modern painting is by way of poetry. We all

learned to read when we were children. And when we learned to read we

learned something of the language of poetry. But few of us learned the

language of painting. Perhaps to begin with poetry would be worthwhile.

Poetry is a broad term. We speak of poetry of movement, poetry of life.

We even use the term "poetic justice." I suppose we could speak of the poetry

of line and the poetry of color, but let's instead think of poetry in its

most traditional sense. Poetry has above all to do with images, with figures

of speech. Listen. (Song of Solomon)

Now of course what the poet was saying here from a common sense

point of view is ridiculous. (He says she's beautiful, etc.)

Yet these absurdities are the very essence of poetry when they are

combined with beauty of language, rhythm and form.

CHAGALL

The Song of Solomon is of course love poetry in which the lover is

carried away by his passion so that he has to speak in extravagant
far-fetched images. This painting, called <u>Birthday</u>, by Marc Chagall is
painted in something of the same spirit of enthusiastic love. It is a
love song.

It was painted 40 years ago when Chagall was a young man, very much
in love. In fact, it was painted just two weeks before he was married. It
was his birthday. His fiancée had come to see him with flowers in her hand
wearing some colored shawls. Her name was Bella and years later she wrote
a book of reminincences. Listen to what she says about this picture:

"I took my colored shawls and hung them on the wall. You
hardly paid any attention. Then hurriedly you went over to your canvases
stacked in the corner, grabbed one and put it on your easel. "Dont move,"
you said, "stay right where you are." The flowers are still in my hands but
soon I forget the flowers. You fell upon your canvas which shakes under
your hand. You work with your brushes. You spread color - red, blue, black.
You carry me away with a stream of color. Suddenly you tear me from the
earth. You jump into the air. You float up above the rafters. You turn
you head, twist mine too. I listen as you sing a song in your soft low
voice. Even your eyes sing and both together we rise over the clean little
room and float away. We float over fields with flowers, over little houses,
roofs and harbors.

"How do you like my picture"you ask and move aside from the canvas.
"Is there still much to do," I ask. "You can't leave it that way, can you?"
"Tell me, what I should still do," you ask. You wait and are afraid of what
I may tell you, but I answer, "It's very good." You float away so very
beautifully. "We'll call it The Birthday."

De CHIRICO: Anxious Voyage

All poetry is not gay. Indeed, Much of the greatest poetry has to do with sorrow and mystery. In fact I suppose the most famous poem *verses* written by an American are some very melancholy stanzas called The Raven.

This painting, called Anxious Voyage by the Italian painter, Giorgio de Chirico, is in a sense a poem about anxiety. It's almost a nightmare image, a bad dream which many of us have about being lost in a railroad station (describe the painting). Of course we know from modern psychoanalysis that such dreams do not really concern our worry for fear we are going to miss a train, but refer to some more deep seated state of foreboding or *anxiety* worry. Here the painter has translated this deep feeling into a vivid and haunting pictorial image.

DOVE: Grandmother

Here we are back at the picture which we saw at the beginning. What do you see here? A flat, rectangular shape filled with different surfaces and forms (describe textures and materials). Now this, of course, could stand on its own feet as an abstract composition of shapes and surfaces, but the artist, an American named Arthur Dove, has called it "Grandmother", and by his title he immediately changes one point of view towards the picture. This new point of view is poetic. What he is doing here is like the Song of Solomon, although the subject is very different. Each of the images in the picture, the silvery weather-worn shingle, the petitpoint, the delicate dried pressed fern, the slightly yellowed page from the Concordance of the Bible - all these can easily be associated with the idea of "grandmother". The painter does not, of course, address grandmother as the Hebrew poet addressed his beloved. He doesn't say: "Your hair is as silvery as an old shingle." He simply composes these forms and textures

5-

into something that is good to look at and something that is poetically

touching to think about with poetic sentiment.

In the past few minutes I have compared painting and poetry.

This is an ancient comparison which goes back to ~~Aristotle.~~ *Horace.*

the Roman poet,

UT pictura

-43-

LEAD TO COLOR

SHOW CAMERA OF FLIP

ARLENE: (VO)
Our next feature will be televised
in both color and black and white...
using the RCA Compatible Color
Television System. And owners
of color sets are in for a real
treat, because today's subject
is Modern Art....

154

WHAT IS MODERN PAINTING - PRECIS
(Ruthman)

<u>COLOR SPOT</u>

TITLE: ~~WHAT IS~~ MODERN PAINTING *as Poetry*

TALENT: Arlene; Alfred Barr, Director of Museum's
                Collections at the Museum of Modern Art.

PURPOSE: To encourage people to whom modern art doesn't
                say anything to take another look. *~~One kind of modern~~*

PROCEDURE: Alfred Barr, Director of Museum's collections,
                Museum of Modern Art, will do a spot after a
                brief intro by Arlene.

                Arlene's intro in black-and-white raises the
                question, "Is it art?" - as we see a poetic
                treatment of color with no recognizable form.

                We see this picture again, this time with
                Barr explaining what the "poet painter" had in
                mind.

                Our guest then quotes some of the images from
                the "Song of Solomon"; points out that the
                conception of imagery is not exclusively a
                modern idea. He then explains in detail what
                three painters are trying to convey in the
                following modern paintings:

                    ~~"Improvisation", by Kandinsky~~
                    "Birthday", Chagall
                    "Grandmother", Dove

2 de Chirico: Anxious Voyage

                At the close of the spot, Barr mentions the
                bible passage again, and stresses that modern
                art is only possible in a cultural climate
                where the spirit of the painter is unfettered
                with political ties.

WHAT IS MODERN PAINTING?
(Ruthman)

(CU OF ~~IMPROVISATION~~ BY KANDINSKY: B&W)

Dove

ARLENE: (VO)
Is this a masterpiece? A ~~mess~~?
Or a poetic interpretation...?

⑦ TELOP: MODERN PAINTING - IS IT ART?

...perhaps you've heard or used such
words yourself..as...puzzling, ~~baffling~~
or -- crazy, when referring to modern
paintings?

(CUT TO ARLENE)

If you have, I would like you to
meet the author of this booklet.
(HOLDS BOOKLET)

CU OF BOOKLET

...It's..."What is Modern Painting?"
and the excellent explanations of
the pictures in it have helped
thousands to answer the question,
"What is Modern Painting?" Here is
the author, and also, director of
the museum collections of the Museum
of Modern Art...Mr. Alfred H. Barr.

COLOR
(CUT TO BARR STANDING NEXT TO THE
KANDINSKY)

MR. BARR:
It's not easy to answer the question,
what is modern painting?... If you
feel you don't like modern painting,
words may help you to change your
mind. But in the end, you must look
at these works of art with your own
eyes and heart and head.

Let's take another look at this
painting by Kandinsky which you saw a
minute ago.

(CUT TO CU OF KANDINSKY: IN COLOR)

BARR: (VO)
(AD LIBS...importance of color;
painting, should it be pure?
important not to fool yourself)

(CUT TO LS OF BARR AS HE MOVES
INTO AREA WHERE 3 MODERN PAINTINGS
ARE HUNG)

BARR:
(AD LIBS..modern paintings are not
paintings you can understand at a
glance; look at paintings and read
poetry with spirit of adventure..
(LEAD TO BIBLE QUOTE) I'd like you
to listen to some written images,
before we consider the detail of
the painted images here...(PICKS
UP BIBLE) ..these images are from
the Song of Solomon...READS...

Behold you are beautiful my love...

Your eyes are doves behind your veil...
Your teeth are like a flock of shorn ewes,
that have come up from the washing, all
of which bear twins.
Your lips are like a scarlet thread...
Your neck is like the tower of David,
built for an Arsenal...

BARR:
(AD LIB COMMENT ON THE IMAGERY)
...appreciating paintings,is like
learning a language, but its worth
the effort because they can lift
us out of humdrum ruts...

CUE: Look at this picture for a few
seconds!

(CUT TO CHAGALL'S "BIRTHDAY")

BARR: (VO & POINTING WITH FINGER)
(COMMENTS ON THE STORY OF EXHUBERENT
LOVE OF CHAGALL & HIS FIANCEE...)

(PULL BACK)

BARR:
(AD LIBS...what modern paintings
have to do with our everyday life,
joy, sadness, sentiment..(MOVE
CLOSE TO DOVE'S WORK)

Handwritten annotations:

left margin: de Chirico

top right: — preview statement

right column (pencil draft):
There are many kinds of modern painting
[crossed out] many ways to approach it.
One [crossed out] approach is by way of poetry —
Now poetry's a broad term — poetry [crossed out] of movement,
poetry of life, even poetic justice. I
suppose we could speak of the poetry of
line and above all the poetry of color
when we look at this Kandinsky — [crossed out]
Kandinsky would have preferred you
to think [crossed out] of music not of
poetry when he framed this glowing
gem-like little abstraction; and he
was right. For poetry is not abstract or pure
it has color with images, with figures
such. Listen: (Song of Solomon

(CUT TO CU OF DOVE'S GRANDMOTHER)

BARR:
Study this painting for a few
seconds...(Comments on arrangement
& textures & the message of the
arrangement that tells what sort
of person his grandmother was.)

(PULL BACK)

BARR:
(AD LIBS...how the modern painter
uses the elements usually found in
or associated with poetry) and
leads to 'poetic meloncholy.')

(MOVE IN TIGHT FOR CU OF DE
CHIRICO'S DELIGHTS OF THE POET).

Before we take up the details
in this painting, what do you
see in it?

(POINTING WITH FINGER, describes
how the poet-painter expressed
his feelings)

(PULL BACK)

BARR:
AD LIBS SUMMARY...tying in with
the Song of Solomon Images; and,
the liberation of the spirit.

The artist is a human, like the
rest of us. Through his art, he
can see and understand our problems,
for artists are the sensitive antennae
of society. Art is a symbol of the
human spirit in search of truth. A
modern artist needs freedom to think
and work and therefore modern painting
is not popular anywhere but in a
democracy..

(CUT BACK TO ARLENE)

ARLENE:
Our program is a series of pictures too.
But you can't hang them on the wall. The
modern paintings you saw can be seen for
longer periods if you would like to...
because they are hanging on the walls
of the Museum of Modern Art here on
53rd Street, in New York. It's a fine
place to use your eyes, your heart and
your head.

(INTO CLOSING COPY)

NBC TELEVISION 11-12 NOON EST, 10-11 CST

October 10, 1955

Mr. Alfred Barr
Museum of Modern Art
11 West 53rd Street
New York, New York

Dear Mr. Barr:

Thank you so much for your appearance on HOME. Unfortunately, I was
out of town and did not see the show, but all the comments I've heard
have been extremely favorable. We here at HOME enjoyed having you
with us, and I sincerely hope the experience was a happy one for you,
too.

Cordially,

Richard L. Linkroum
Executive Producer

RLL:dh

cc: Dorothy Miller
Liz Shaw

NBC

October 12, 1955

Dear Mr. Linkroum:

	Thank you for your kind letter about my
appearance on the HOME show. I am glad to know
that you had some favorable comments, but I am extremely eager to have some knowledge and, if possible,
some record of the written responses from the public,
if any. Would this be possible?

				Sincerely,

				Alfred H. Barr, Jr.
				Director of the Museum Collections

Mr. Richard L. Linkroum
Executive Producer
HOME
National Broadcasting Company, Inc.
30 Rockefeller Plaza
New York 20, New York

AHB:lh

cc: Mrs Shaw   N BC TV

28 October 1955

Dear Miss Parkhurst:

Mr. Richard Linkroum of the N.B.C. Home television Program has sent me a copy of your letter.

I cannot give you an extended reading list on the relation between poetry and painting, but I think you might find interesting the article by Rensselaer Lee called Ut Pictura Poesis: The Humanistic Theory of Painting which appeared in the ART BULLETIN, Volume XXII, pp. 197-269.

As a matter of fact, I had planned to close my talk with a reference to these words of Horace which Mr. Lee discusses at length with particular reference to 17th century French and Italian painting, but through a miscue for which I had not been prepared, I stopped short before finishing my last sentence.

Sincerely,

Alfred H. Barr, Jr.

Miss Eleanor Parkhurst
51 Acton Road
Chelmsford, Massachusetts

AHB:ma

PV BC

ELEANOR PARKHURST
51 Acton Rd.
Chelmsford, Mass.

25 November 1955

Mr. Alfred H. Barr, Jr.,
The Museum of Modern Art,
New York, New York.

Dear Mr. Barr:

      Thank you ever so much for your courteous and prompt reply to my request for further information on the relationship between Poetry and Painting occasioned by your appearance on the HOME show recently.

      When I was at Wellesley many years ago, I concentrated on the first half of this interesting combination to my increasingly great regret and entirely omitted the other half which now seems important and exciting. I shall probably never be able to make up for missing Miss Avery's course (and others') but I am making an attempt through my own study and the taking of painting lessons. I well remember you in those days, too, and as a graduate student I later came to know Miss Hamilton, Miss Abbott, and Miss Surré of the Art Department.

      Your reading suggestion has been a real help to me. I shall hope to find you at HOME again sometime.

                  Sincerely yours,

                  Eleanor Parkhurst

                  Wellesley 1931

ALL ITEMS FROM THE MUSEUM OF MODERN ART ARCHIVES, NY

pp. 146–147: Photo of Nelson A. Rockefeller (left) and Alfred H. Barr, Jr., at NBC telecast in 1939 on the occasion of the opening of the Museum's new building. Photographic Archive.

p. 149: Alfred H. Barr, Jr., *What Is Modern Painting?*, New York: The Museum of Modern Art, 1943.

pp. 150–163: Letters, script, notes all from Alfred H. Barr, Jr., Papers, I.221.

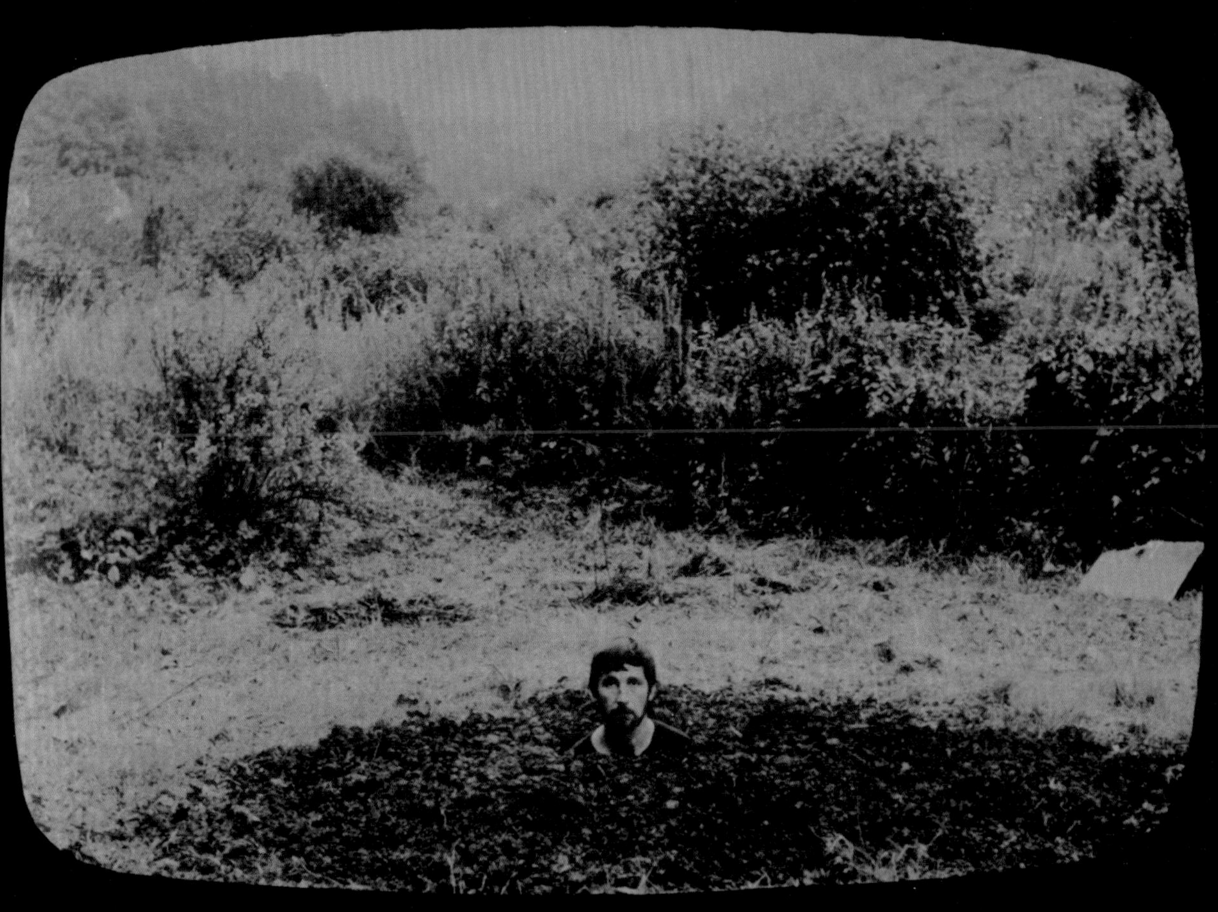

Devendra Banhart

Judith Barry

David Carr

Liam Gillick

Ulu Grosbard

Trenton Doyle Hancock

Buck Henry

Paul Hoffman

John Kelly

Richard Kostelanetz

Louis Menand

Laura Mulvey

Jayne Anne Phillips

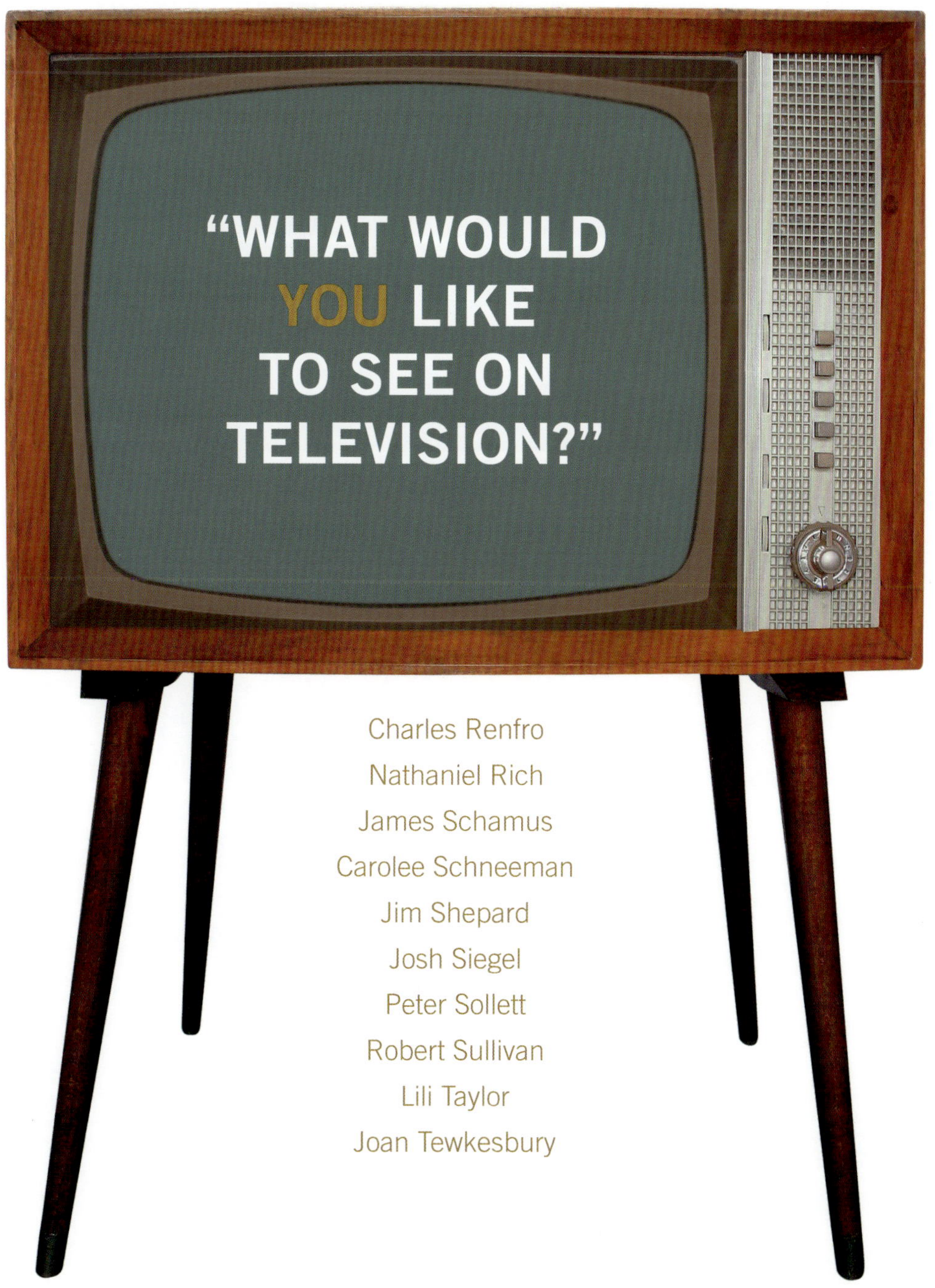

Charles Renfro

Nathaniel Rich

James Schamus

Carolee Schneeman

Jim Shepard

Josh Siegel

Peter Sollett

Robert Sullivan

Lili Taylor

Joan Tewkesbury

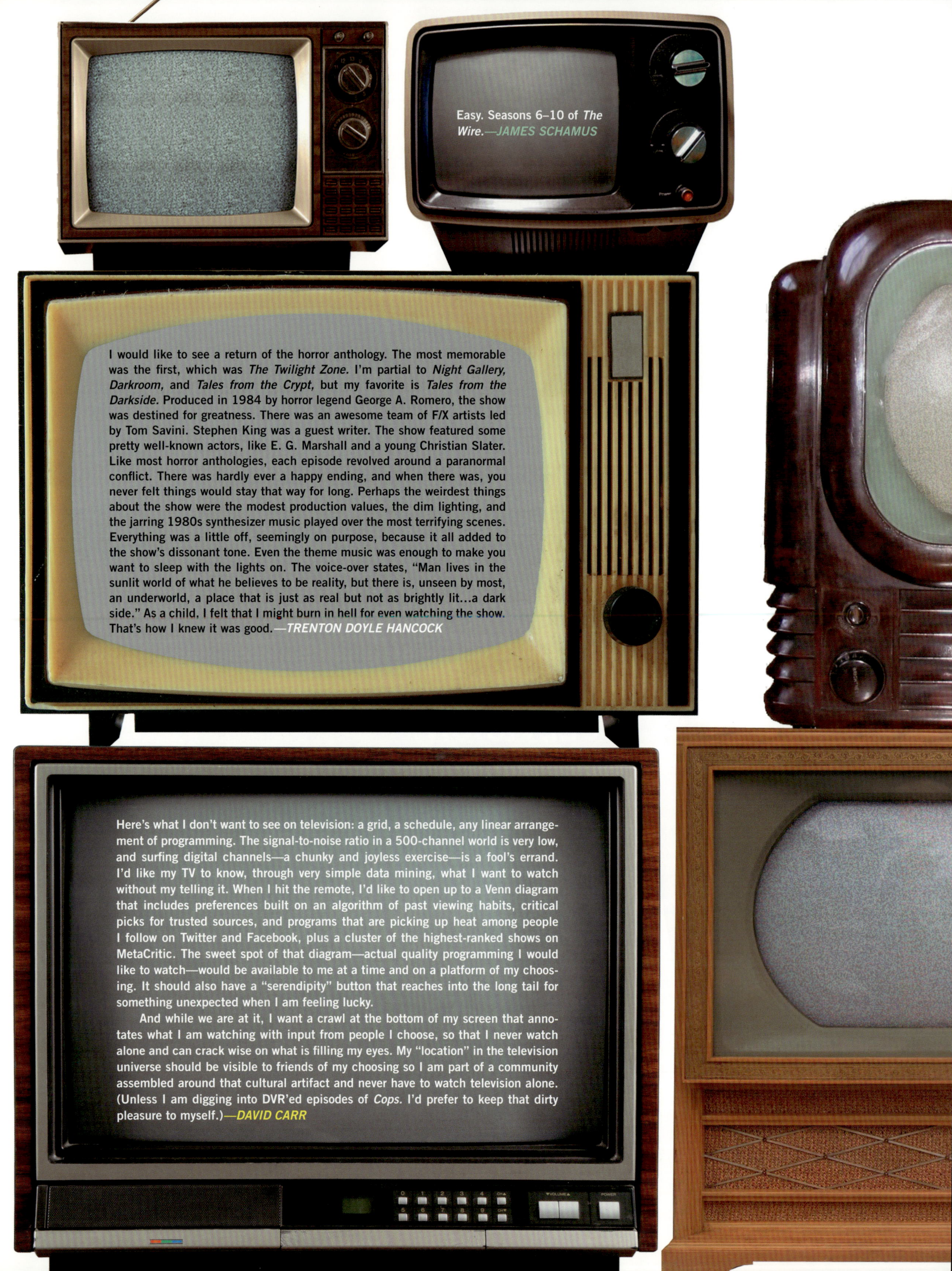

Easy. Seasons 6–10 of *The Wire.*—JAMES SCHAMUS

I would like to see a return of the horror anthology. The most memorable was the first, which was *The Twilight Zone.* I'm partial to *Night Gallery, Darkroom,* and *Tales from the Crypt,* but my favorite is *Tales from the Darkside.* Produced in 1984 by horror legend George A. Romero, the show was destined for greatness. There was an awesome team of F/X artists led by Tom Savini. Stephen King was a guest writer. The show featured some pretty well-known actors, like E. G. Marshall and a young Christian Slater. Like most horror anthologies, each episode revolved around a paranormal conflict. There was hardly ever a happy ending, and when there was, you never felt things would stay that way for long. Perhaps the weirdest things about the show were the modest production values, the dim lighting, and the jarring 1980s synthesizer music played over the most terrifying scenes. Everything was a little off, seemingly on purpose, because it all added to the show's dissonant tone. Even the theme music was enough to make you want to sleep with the lights on. The voice-over states, "Man lives in the sunlit world of what he believes to be reality, but there is, unseen by most, an underworld, a place that is just as real but not as brightly lit…a dark side." As a child, I felt that I might burn in hell for even watching the show. That's how I knew it was good.—TRENTON DOYLE HANCOCK

Here's what I don't want to see on television: a grid, a schedule, any linear arrangement of programming. The signal-to-noise ratio in a 500-channel world is very low, and surfing digital channels—a chunky and joyless exercise—is a fool's errand. I'd like my TV to know, through very simple data mining, what I want to watch without my telling it. When I hit the remote, I'd like to open up to a Venn diagram that includes preferences built on an algorithm of past viewing habits, critical picks for trusted sources, and programs that are picking up heat among people I follow on Twitter and Facebook, plus a cluster of the highest-ranked shows on MetaCritic. The sweet spot of that diagram—actual quality programming I would like to watch—would be available to me at a time and on a platform of my choosing. It should also have a "serendipity" button that reaches into the long tail for something unexpected when I am feeling lucky.

And while we are at it, I want a crawl at the bottom of my screen that annotates what I am watching with input from people I choose, so that I never watch alone and can crack wise on what is filling my eyes. My "location" in the television universe should be visible to friends of my choosing so I am part of a community assembled around that cultural artifact and never have to watch television alone. (Unless I am digging into DVR'ed episodes of *Cops.* I'd prefer to keep that dirty pleasure to myself.)—DAVID CARR

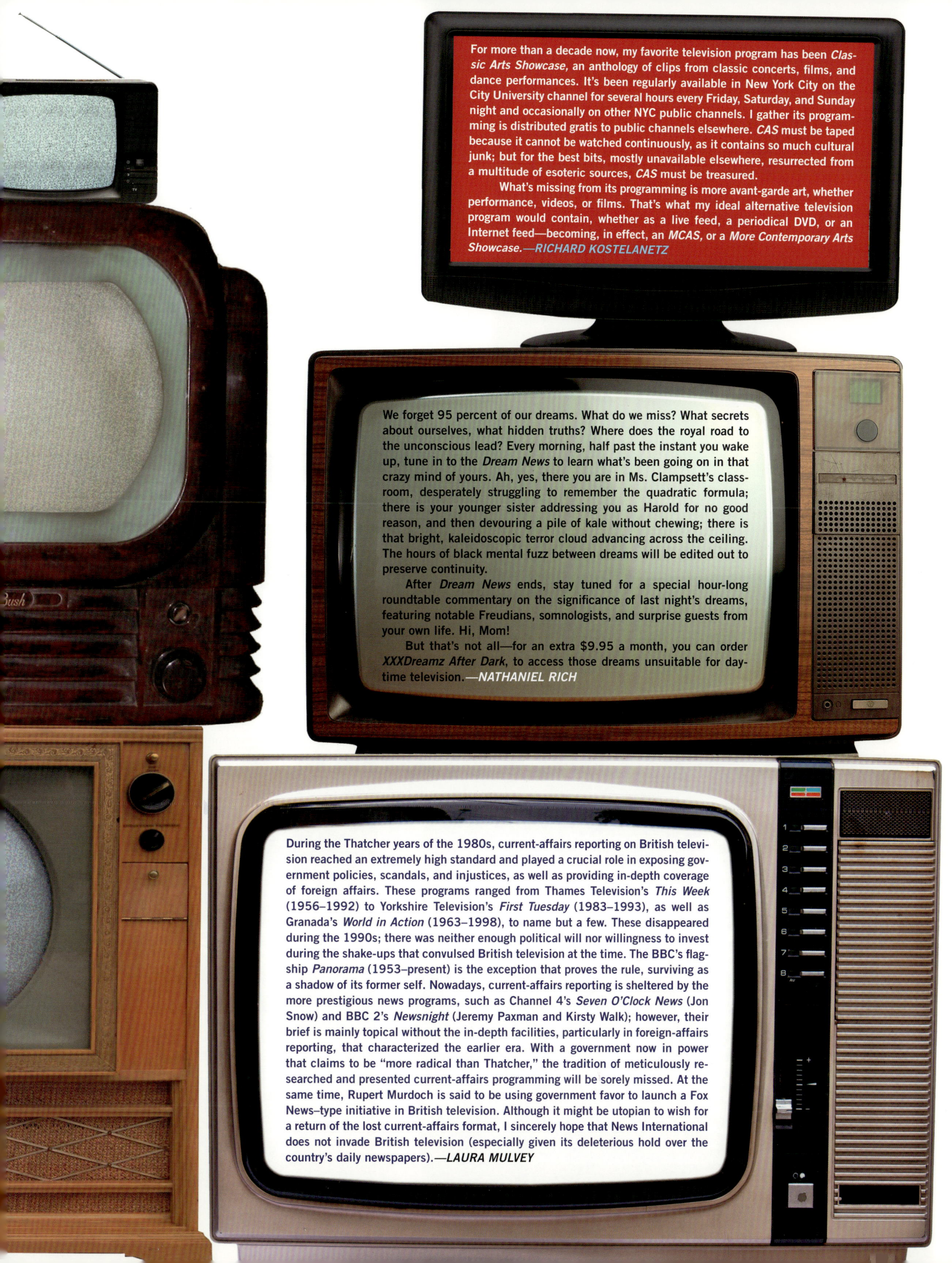

For more than a decade now, my favorite television program has been *Classic Arts Showcase,* an anthology of clips from classic concerts, films, and dance performances. It's been regularly available in New York City on the City University channel for several hours every Friday, Saturday, and Sunday night and occasionally on other NYC public channels. I gather its programming is distributed gratis to public channels elsewhere. *CAS* must be taped because it cannot be watched continuously, as it contains so much cultural junk; but for the best bits, mostly unavailable elsewhere, resurrected from a multitude of esoteric sources, *CAS* must be treasured.

What's missing from its programming is more avant-garde art, whether performance, videos, or films. That's what my ideal alternative television program would contain, whether as a live feed, a periodical DVD, or an Internet feed—becoming, in effect, an *MCAS,* or a *More Contemporary Arts Showcase.*—RICHARD KOSTELANETZ

We forget 95 percent of our dreams. What do we miss? What secrets about ourselves, what hidden truths? Where does the royal road to the unconscious lead? Every morning, half past the instant you wake up, tune in to the *Dream News* to learn what's been going on in that crazy mind of yours. Ah, yes, there you are in Ms. Clampsett's classroom, desperately struggling to remember the quadratic formula; there is your younger sister addressing you as Harold for no good reason, and then devouring a pile of kale without chewing; there is that bright, kaleidoscopic terror cloud advancing across the ceiling. The hours of black mental fuzz between dreams will be edited out to preserve continuity.

After *Dream News* ends, stay tuned for a special hour-long roundtable commentary on the significance of last night's dreams, featuring notable Freudians, somnologists, and surprise guests from your own life. Hi, Mom!

But that's not all—for an extra $9.95 a month, you can order *XXXDreamz After Dark,* to access those dreams unsuitable for daytime television.—NATHANIEL RICH

During the Thatcher years of the 1980s, current-affairs reporting on British television reached an extremely high standard and played a crucial role in exposing government policies, scandals, and injustices, as well as providing in-depth coverage of foreign affairs. These programs ranged from Thames Television's *This Week* (1956–1992) to Yorkshire Television's *First Tuesday* (1983–1993), as well as Granada's *World in Action* (1963–1998), to name but a few. These disappeared during the 1990s; there was neither enough political will nor willingness to invest during the shake-ups that convulsed British television at the time. The BBC's flagship *Panorama* (1953–present) is the exception that proves the rule, surviving as a shadow of its former self. Nowadays, current-affairs reporting is sheltered by the more prestigious news programs, such as Channel 4's *Seven O'Clock News* (Jon Snow) and BBC 2's *Newsnight* (Jeremy Paxman and Kirsty Walk); however, their brief is mainly topical without the in-depth facilities, particularly in foreign-affairs reporting, that characterized the earlier era. With a government now in power that claims to be "more radical than Thatcher," the tradition of meticulously researched and presented current-affairs programming will be sorely missed. At the same time, Rupert Murdoch is said to be using government favor to launch a Fox News–type initiative in British television. Although it might be utopian to wish for a return of the lost current-affairs format, I sincerely hope that News International does not invade British television (especially given its deleterious hold over the country's daily newspapers).—LAURA MULVEY

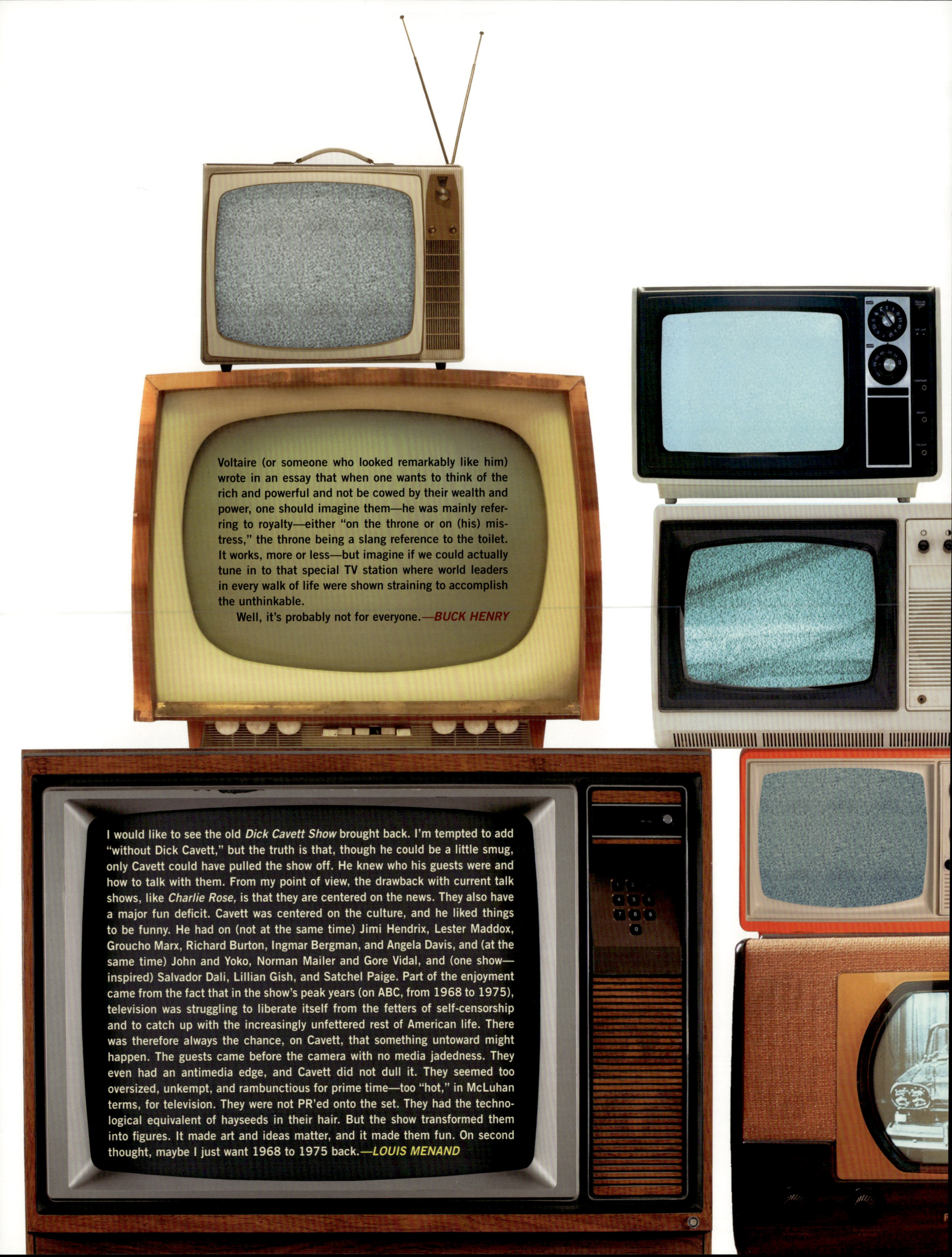

Voltaire (or someone who looked remarkably like him) wrote in an essay that when one wants to think of the rich and powerful and not be cowed by their wealth and power, one should imagine them—he was mainly referring to royalty—either "on the throne or on (his) mistress," the throne being a slang reference to the toilet. It works, more or less—but imagine if we could actually tune in to that special TV station where world leaders in every walk of life were shown straining to accomplish the unthinkable.

Well, it's probably not for everyone.—BUCK HENRY

I would like to see the old Dick Cavett Show brought back. I'm tempted to add "without Dick Cavett," but the truth is that, though he could be a little smug, only Cavett could have pulled the show off. He knew who his guests were and how to talk with them. From my point of view, the drawback with current talk shows, like Charlie Rose, is that they are centered on the news. They also have a major fun deficit. Cavett was centered on the culture, and he liked things to be funny. He had on (not at the same time) Jimi Hendrix, Lester Maddox, Groucho Marx, Richard Burton, Ingmar Bergman, and Angela Davis, and (at the same time) John and Yoko, Norman Mailer and Gore Vidal, and (one show—inspired) Salvador Dali, Lillian Gish, and Satchel Paige. Part of the enjoyment came from the fact that in the show's peak years (on ABC, from 1968 to 1975), television was struggling to liberate itself from the fetters of self-censorship and to catch up with the increasingly unfettered rest of American life. There was therefore always the chance, on Cavett, that something untoward might happen. The guests came before the camera with no media jadedness. They even had an antimedia edge, and Cavett did not dull it. They seemed too oversized, unkempt, and rambunctious for prime time—too "hot," in McLuhan terms, for television. They were not PR'ed onto the set. They had the technological equivalent of hayseeds in their hair. But the show transformed them into figures. It made art and ideas matter, and it made them fun. On second thought, maybe I just want 1968 to 1975 back.—LOUIS MENAND

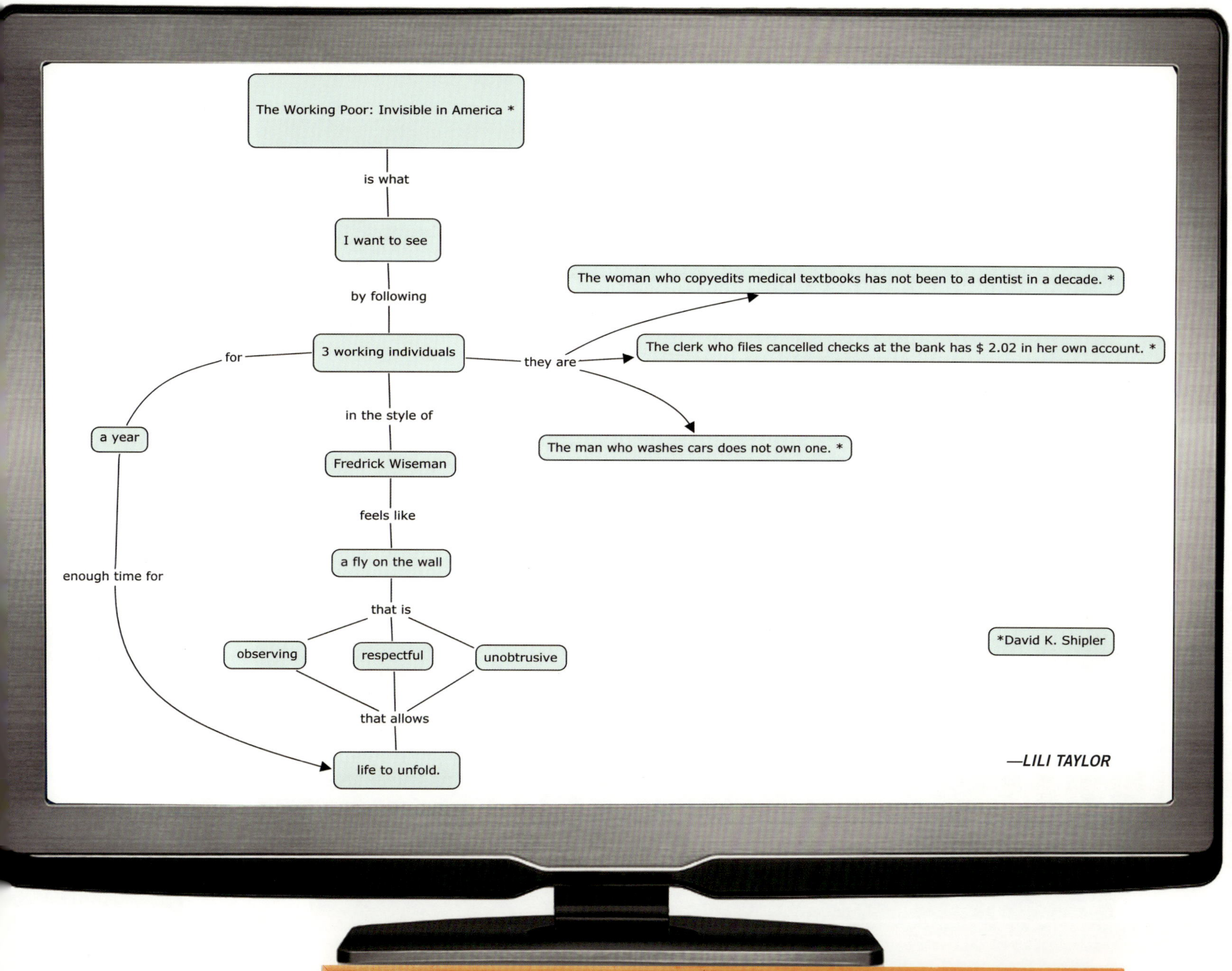

The Working Poor: Invisible in America *

is what

I want to see

by following

3 working individuals — they are →

The woman who copyedits medical textbooks has not been to a dentist in a decade. *

The clerk who files cancelled checks at the bank has $ 2.02 in her own account. *

The man who washes cars does not own one. *

for — a year

in the style of

Fredrick Wiseman

feels like

a fly on the wall

that is

observing — respectful — unobtrusive

that allows

enough time for

life to unfold.

*David K. Shipler

—LILI TAYLOR

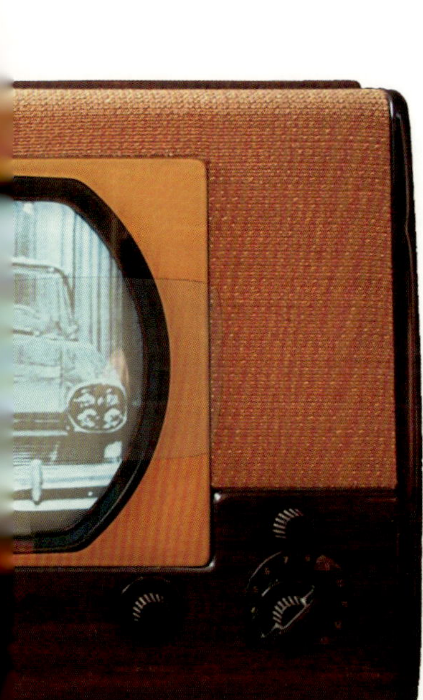

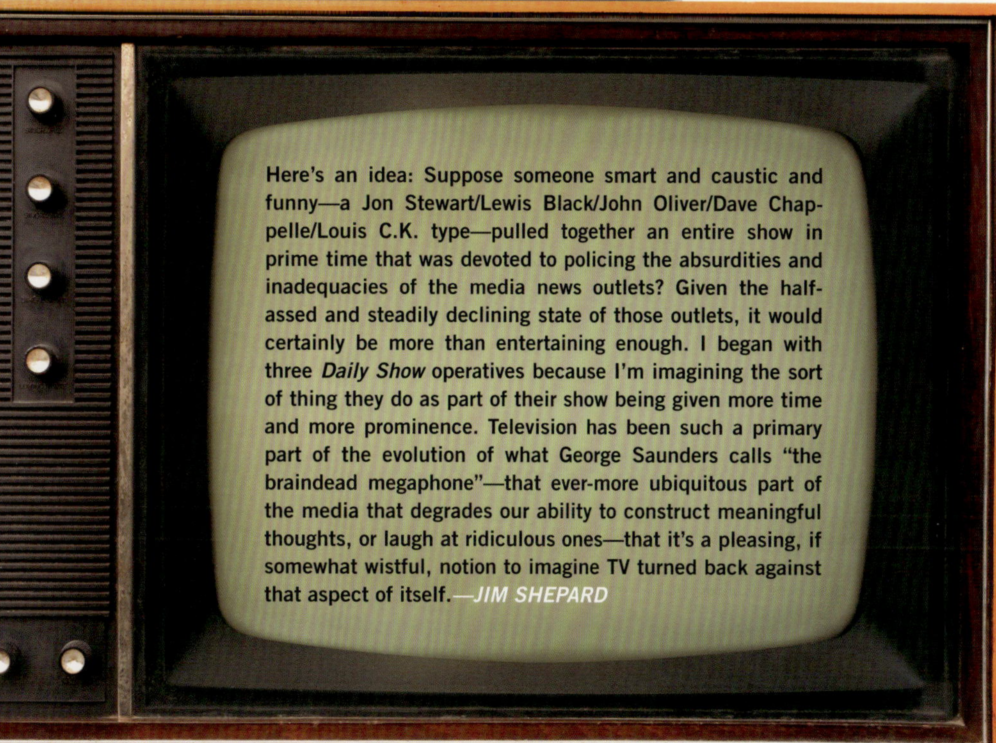
Here's an idea: Suppose someone smart and caustic and funny—a Jon Stewart/Lewis Black/John Oliver/Dave Chappelle/Louis C.K. type—pulled together an entire show in prime time that was devoted to policing the absurdities and inadequacies of the media news outlets? Given the half-assed and steadily declining state of those outlets, it would certainly be more than entertaining enough. I began with three *Daily Show* operatives because I'm imagining the sort of thing they do as part of their show being given more time and more prominence. Television has been such a primary part of the evolution of what George Saunders calls "the braindead megaphone"—that ever-more ubiquitous part of the media that degrades our ability to construct meaningful thoughts, or laugh at ridiculous ones—that it's a pleasing, if somewhat wistful, notion to imagine TV turned back against that aspect of itself.—*JIM SHEPARD*

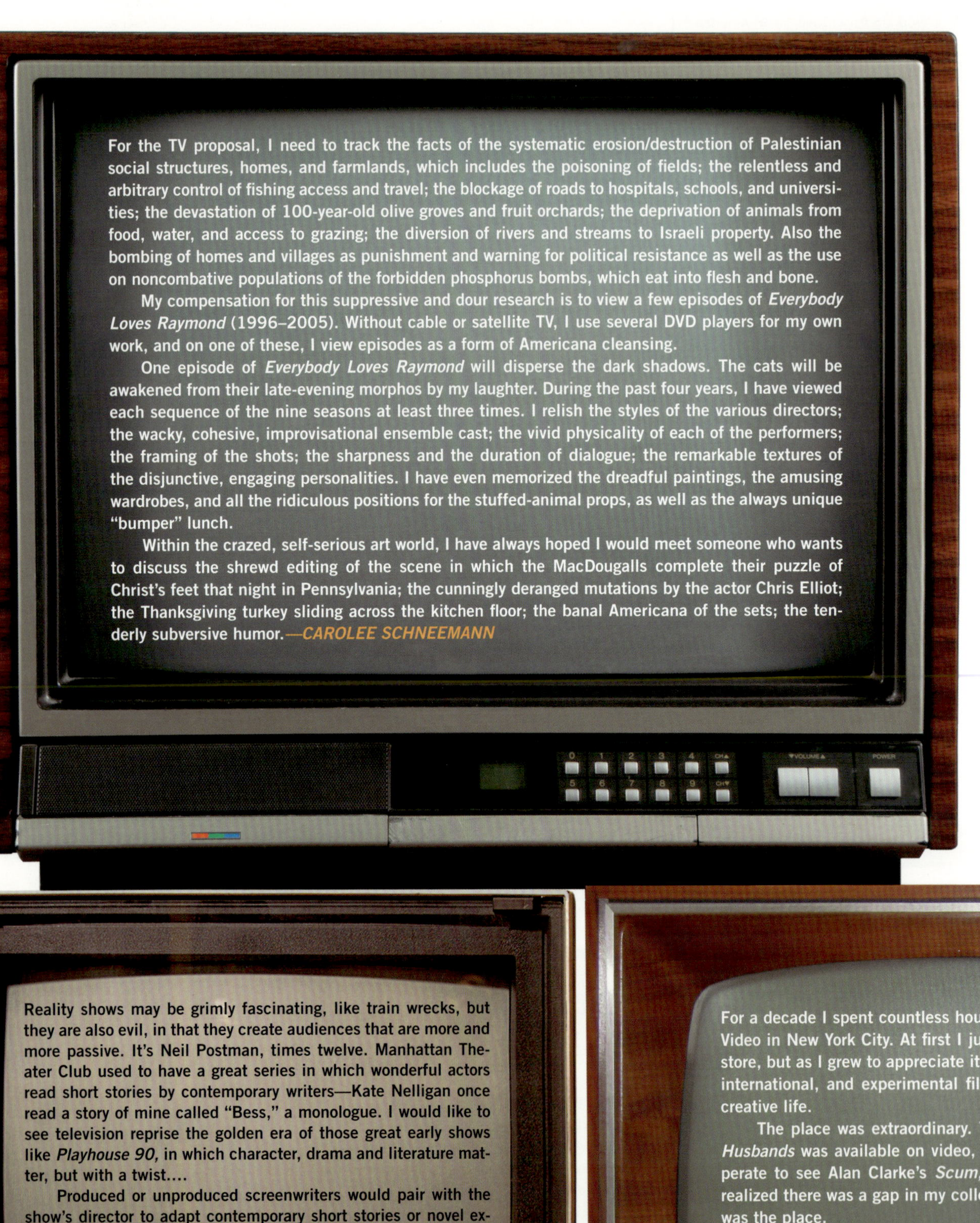

For the TV proposal, I need to track the facts of the systematic erosion/destruction of Palestinian social structures, homes, and farmlands, which includes the poisoning of fields; the relentless and arbitrary control of fishing access and travel; the blockage of roads to hospitals, schools, and universities; the devastation of 100-year-old olive groves and fruit orchards; the deprivation of animals from food, water, and access to grazing; the diversion of rivers and streams to Israeli property. Also the bombing of homes and villages as punishment and warning for political resistance as well as the use on noncombative populations of the forbidden phosphorus bombs, which eat into flesh and bone.

My compensation for this suppressive and dour research is to view a few episodes of *Everybody Loves Raymond* (1996–2005). Without cable or satellite TV, I use several DVD players for my own work, and on one of these, I view episodes as a form of Americana cleansing.

One episode of *Everybody Loves Raymond* will disperse the dark shadows. The cats will be awakened from their late-evening morphos by my laughter. During the past four years, I have viewed each sequence of the nine seasons at least three times. I relish the styles of the various directors; the wacky, cohesive, improvisational ensemble cast; the vivid physicality of each of the performers; the framing of the shots; the sharpness and the duration of dialogue; the remarkable textures of the disjunctive, engaging personalities. I have even memorized the dreadful paintings, the amusing wardrobes, and all the ridiculous positions for the stuffed-animal props, as well as the always unique "bumper" lunch.

Within the crazed, self-serious art world, I have always hoped I would meet someone who wants to discuss the shrewd editing of the scene in which the MacDougalls complete their puzzle of Christ's feet that night in Pennsylvania; the cunningly deranged mutations by the actor Chris Elliot; the Thanksgiving turkey sliding across the kitchen floor; the banal Americana of the sets; the tenderly subversive humor.—*CAROLEE SCHNEEMANN*

Reality shows may be grimly fascinating, like train wrecks, but they are also evil, in that they create audiences that are more and more passive. It's Neil Postman, times twelve. Manhattan Theater Club used to have a great series in which wonderful actors read short stories by contemporary writers—Kate Nelligan once read a story of mine called "Bess," a monologue. I would like to see television reprise the golden era of those great early shows like *Playhouse 90,* in which character, drama and literature matter, but with a twist….

Produced or unproduced screenwriters would pair with the show's director to adapt contemporary short stories or novel excerpts to a half-hour or one-hour format. The shows would be cast with wonderful actors, including actors not well known, and also have a big budget, pay the talent well, and engage audiences in—gasp—thinking, and then reading, pages, in books.

Alternate idea: a show called *Chekhov,* which dramatizes Chekhov's stories, one by one, starting with "Three Years," which would require one season of episodes….—*JAYNE ANNE PHILLIPS*

For a decade I spent countless hours exploring the aisles of Kim's Video in New York City. At first I just considered it my local video store, but as I grew to appreciate its exceptional collection of rare, international, and experimental films, it became a center of my creative life.

The place was extraordinary. Years before John Cassavetes's *Husbands* was available on video, Kim's had it. When I was desperate to see Alan Clarke's *Scum,* Kim's had a bootleg. When I realized there was a gap in my collection of Tarkovsky films, Kim's was the place.

It wasn't unusual to see Jim Jarmusch browsing the anime section…or Joey Ramone flipping through Satyajit Ray.

The place took on great emotional importance to me, and when I began making films of my own, I desperately hoped they'd stock them. The first time I saw my name on the spine of a DVD there, I felt like I had arrived.

Kim's closed in December 2008, and I don't think it can ever be replaced as a personal landmark.

What I'd like to see on television are films as daring and diverse as what I found there.—*PETER SOLLETT*

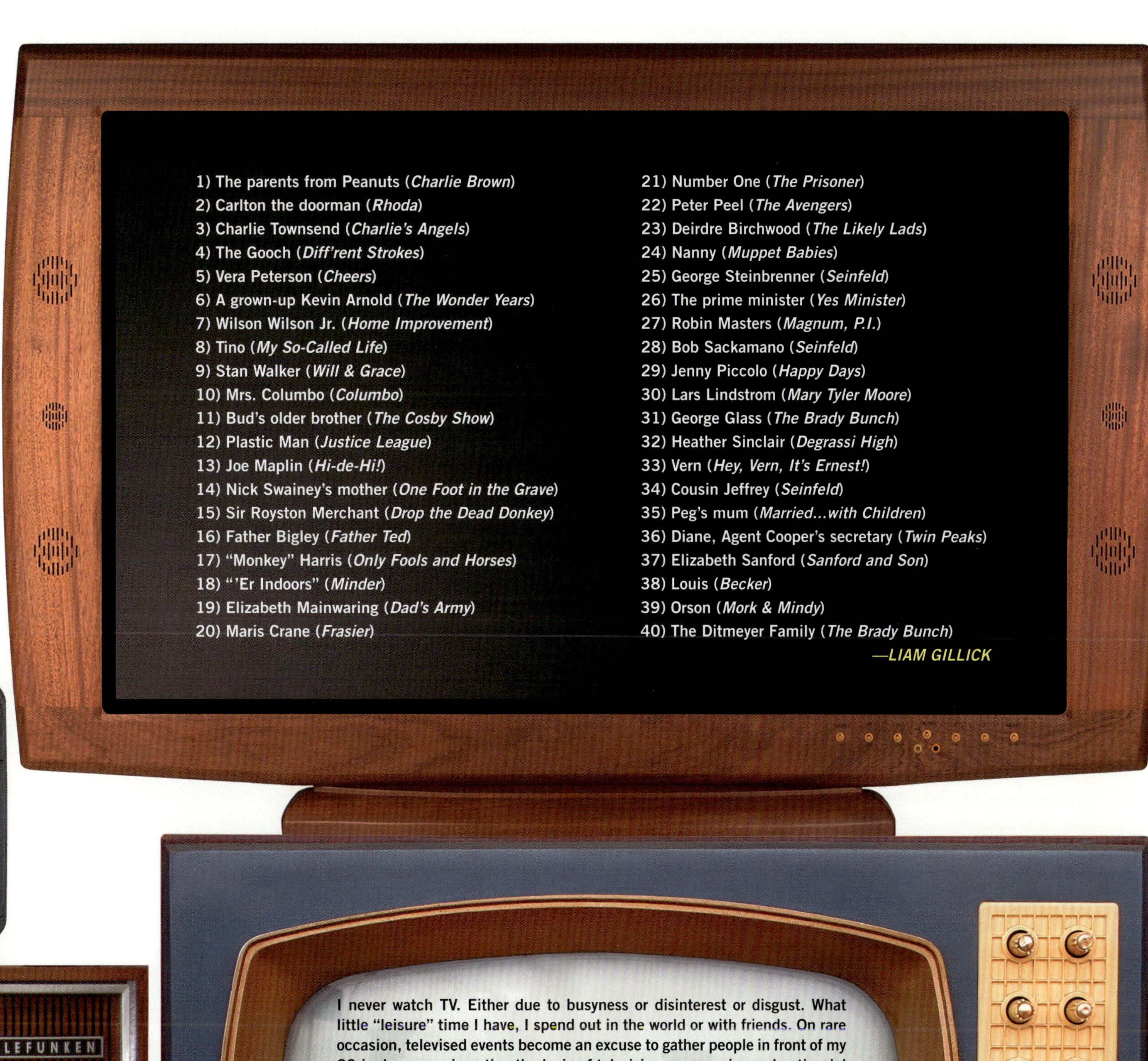

I never watch TV. Either due to busyness or disinterest or disgust. What little "leisure" time I have, I spend out in the world or with friends. On rare occasion, televised events become an excuse to gather people in front of my 20-inch screen, inverting the logic of television as a passive and antisocial agent. The Academy Awards, the season premiere of *Glee,* Sunday-night broadcasts of *The X-Files* have all been silly opportunities for partying.

We lament the demise of TV and consider it victim of the much more supple Internet. Yes, the Internet has lubricated the process and precision of social interaction, but it has eviscerated many aspects of spontaneous behavior that make living in a city exciting. This is an opportunity in disguise. TV is not ambitious enough. It should be the Internet antidote. It should inspire a new form of collective, time-based experience that reinvigorates our social life.

Why couldn't TV make itself more event oriented and urban at the same time? It could use TJs (television jockeys) or encourage viewer override (hacking) or throw parties while it concurrently reestablishes street cruising or brings back independent bookstores. A tall order, you might say, but TV should rise to the challenge to get everyone off their asses and out of the house.—*CHARLES RENFRO*

What television needs is a good curator. Better yet, a network devoted entirely to curated programming. Last year my friend, the artist John Pilson, sent me a series of YouTube clips all centered on the theme of cock swinging, from Rip Torn going after Norman Mailer with a hammer during the filming of *Maidstone* to Noam Chomsky calmly eviscerating William F. Buckley Jr. in a debate on the origins of the Vietnam War (how quaint it is to imagine a show like *Firing Line* thriving on prime time today). Our network would similarly aspire to keep faith with the utopian ideal of a civic forum for the spirited and polemical exchange of ideas. Expanding on Pilson's clever conceit, we would invite the leading thinkers and visionaries of our time to delve into the history of moving images for a show-and-tell of the things that fascinate them. We would commission new work in the tradition of legendary enterprises like *The Medium Is the Medium* on WGBH Boston, the Experimental Television Center in upstate New York, and Gerry Schum's Television Gallery in Berlin, which nurtured experimental video art by Nam June Paik, Shigeko Kubota, Steina and Woody Vasulka, Allan Kaprow, Ken Jacobs, Shirley Clarke, Bill Viola, Twyla Tharp, and many others. We would broadcast Christopher Williams's insane, hilarious, interminable, and conceptually brilliant cooking show, created in 2003 for an annual report, in which he subjected a Swiss television studio audience to a meal being prepared in real time (picture a watched pot simmering for five-and-a-half hours). And for those with a shorter attention span, we would recall the absurdist and suspenseful postwar films of Britain's forgotten comic genius Richard Massingham, who taught civilians on the home front how to cross roads, bathe in five inches of water, avoid "jet-propelled germs," and post early for Christmas—a series of pithy "dos and don'ts" for the shell-shocked everyman that still seems far more unnerving and persuasive than our present-day "If You See Something, Say Something" campaign.—*JOSH SIEGEL*

1) More moon landings.

2) The end of "gotcha" reporting.

3) David Strathairn as Edward R. Murrow delivering all newscasts all the time, and he can smoke if he wants to.

4) Political-campaign commercials banned unless created by the authors and director of *Wag the Dog.*

5) Bring back Elsa Klensch.

6) Images and rants of Coulter, Limbaugh, Palin, and O'Reilly would instantly pixelate and vanish.

7) All breaking news regarding Obama's shortcomings, as well as laundry lists of tragedies, would suffer the same fate as #6. See above.

8) Sound monitoring. All sound reaching a certain decibel level would suffer the same fate as #6. See above.

9) A ban on the everyman self-expression known as reality TV.

10) A ban on any drug commercial discussing life-threatening side effects.

11) A ban on bottom-of-the-screen scrolling, and on coming attractions flashing on and off in the lower right- or left-hand corner.

12) Commercials created by philosophy majors fluent in Chinese, Japanese, or Spanish with a minor in fine art.

13) One channel devoted to the entire *Law and Order* franchise.

14) Political debates shown back-to-back with scorned ex-spouses reading excerpts from their tell-all books.

15) On separate channels, playing 24 hours a day, reruns of Rod Serling's *The Twilight Zone,* Norman Lear's *All in the Family* and everything Monty Python has ever done or dreamed of doing.

16) At one a.m., every channel would be required to play the national anthem and go off the air.—*JOAN TEWKESBURY*

I would like to see *Charlie Rose* moved up to the 9 to 10 p.m. slot.—*ULU GROSBARD*

I want to extract chocolate bars from my TV and free my life of all obligations and distractions so that I can watch television 24/7. As a child growing up in the only dilapidated house in the Cheever-esque bedroom suburb of Westport, Connecticut, I was forbidden by my Trotskyite parents from watching more than 30 minutes of television a week, and so I always faced a difficult choice: Did I want to see Samantha twitch her nose that week or Colonel Klink get doused in the face? By the age of 10 I discovered channel surfing, and I contentedly spent that restricted half-hour rapidly flipping back and forth between *Bewitched* and *Hogan's Heroes*—and unintentionally developing the fine finger movements that later would make me victorious in Rubik's Cube competitions. I also developed undiagnosed attention deficit disorder, as well as myopia from sitting so close to the TV (no remote controls back then), precancerous fibroblasts from the UHF radiation, and itchy bites from no-see-ums that were attracted to our glowing black-and-white television and got into our home through unrepaired tears in the window screens. I owe my lifelong interest in entomology—and my appreciation of calamine lotion—to that TV set. And they say TV rots the mind.—*PAUL HOFFMAN*

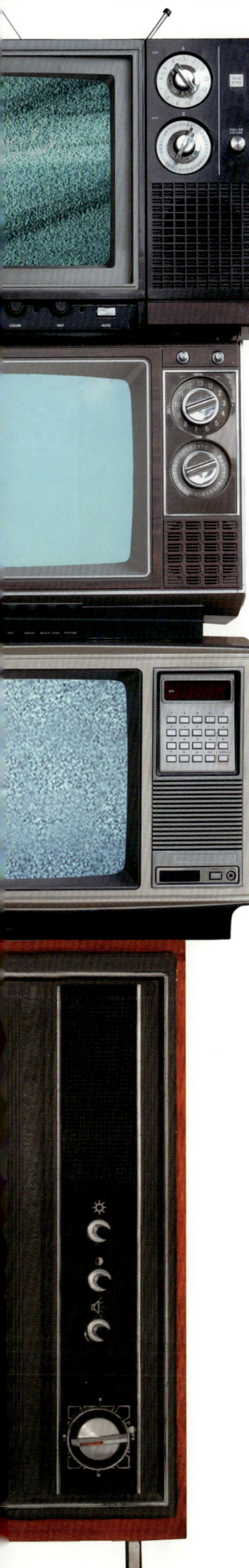

Over the past 10 years or so, I have noticed in many American cities more and more cable channels that broadcast live footage of major traffic arteries. These channels are designed with traffic awareness in mind, but I find them more generally captivating: one channel switching between six or seven views of road and cars and barely perceptible vistas, like an accidental industrial landscape painting where people are not so much part of the view. I know of a few non-car-centered video corollaries—for instance, a Web-based camera in Massachusetts that shows the canopy of a forest, which I check from time to time to see the effects of a new snow, or the appearance of a full moon, in the pixelated frame. And then, of course, there are cameras that will show you downtowns in world capitals. But what if we put them all together on one channel? There would be highway views and rural vistas and a camera that just spun around a city's tallest tower, like the Frank Lloyd Wright skyscraper in Bartlesville, Oklahoma, with its gorgeous view of that state's bowl-like panorama and Robert Indiana's giant 66. What if an Iowa farmer volunteered his cornfield, or a vineyard in California let us watch its grapes? The sound of local chamber music ensembles might play as cars take off-ramps, as hawks circle canyons you've never heard of, as crowds mill in downtowns you may never really see.—*ROBERT SULLIVAN*

News, news, and more news: many more channels devoted to actual news coverage, based on facts and analysis, not opinions, running on separate stations with different points of view, from different countries, and from all over the world. While information overload and continuous partial attention are increasingly part of daily life, in-depth news coverage is much less so.

Television, over the last 20+ years of "narrowcasting" (identifying specific market demographics, something that television does better than any other form of current media), has shown that it has the technological and intellectual capabilities to provide in-depth reporting and analysis. Yet, increasingly, our television news programs are opinion biased and often only reactions to other newscasters' POVs as evidenced by programming on MSNBC, Fox, and now, even CNN, which has just announced that it will be replacing some of its evening anchors with nonjournalists. Not news.

Why? Ratings = advertising dollars = profits.

Now is the moment when multinational TV corporations could be partnering with newspapers such as *The New York Times, Washington Post,* et al., to keep their foreign bureaus open and their resident correspondents working. Rather than resorting to "parachute journalism"—dispatching journalists to countries as news breaks—newspapers, who so far have failed to realize that they are in the news business and not the paper business, are still closing their foreign desks at an alarming rate and at a moment when the world needs their collective expertise now more than ever.

And there is something else…as I write this, sitting in a field, with no television and only late-night NPR, Mexico City's Televisa has just gone dark in protest of the four journalists kidnapped by one of the many narco coalitions vying with the Mexican government for control of the country. Last year, 2009, 77 journalists were murdered, many of them local newspaper journalists. While publicity may be no guarantee of safety, as the still unsolved 2006 murder in broad daylight of the Russian journalist Anna Politkovskaya shows, I think in-depth television news coverage, broadcast worldwide, with substantive reporting and news analysis, would begin to make a difference in these statistics, too.—*JUDITH BARRY*

• A 25-part miniseries that reinjects the sociopolitical issues of our current state of world affairs into the *Planet of the Apes* series. It's about time a new generation discovered the magic of *Planet of the Apes*, and it's an opportunity to rectify the flimsy and incredulous plots of the films that followed the original.

• *The Ex Conference,* a show where one man or woman calls their last five exes in a conference-call format, but none of the exes knows they are on conference call. The objective of the player is to keep the conversation as vague as possible to win one, two, three, four, or all of the exes back. Points are scored depending on how many exes he or she manages to win back and how long they avoid letting the five exes figure out that anything suspicious is happening.

• *The Amateur Hour,* where experts and professionals in their respective fields are placed in disciplines/dialogues/environments that are the complete antithesis of their own.

• Hosted by someone in Aerosmith or by John Popper, a show wherein the physicists at CERN take time out from smashing particles together, creating black holes, collecting dark matter, finding the Higgs Boson, and dealing with time travelers sent to stop them from their various quantum exploits to start a band, record a song, and film an accompanying music video.

• The cast of *Jersey Shore* has to write a science-fiction novella.

• *Children of Porn Stars:* A docudrama that interviews the children of porn stars and examines the effects that such a difficult subject has had on their life. The show focuses on the moment they found out their parents earn their living by sleeping with various people to assuage the concupiscent and onanistic desires of the public. How has it affected their outlook on sexuality? What is their relationship with their parents? On the season finale, children who had no idea what their parents do are told, for the first time, in front of a camera.

• *Ingredients:* Ever wondered what phosphoric acid, ferrous sulfate, riboflavin, disodium phosphate, thiamin monoitrate, and a host of other ingredients are? This in-your-face series sheds light on the origin, meaning, means of acquisition, chemical construction, health perils and benefits, and a slew of other enlightening facts that the FDA doesn't want you to know!

• *Neighborhood Watch,* a reality-TV series shot in the *Cops* format that follows a group of zealous Samaritans as they troll the streets lookin' to bust crooked cops!—*DEVENDRA BANHART*

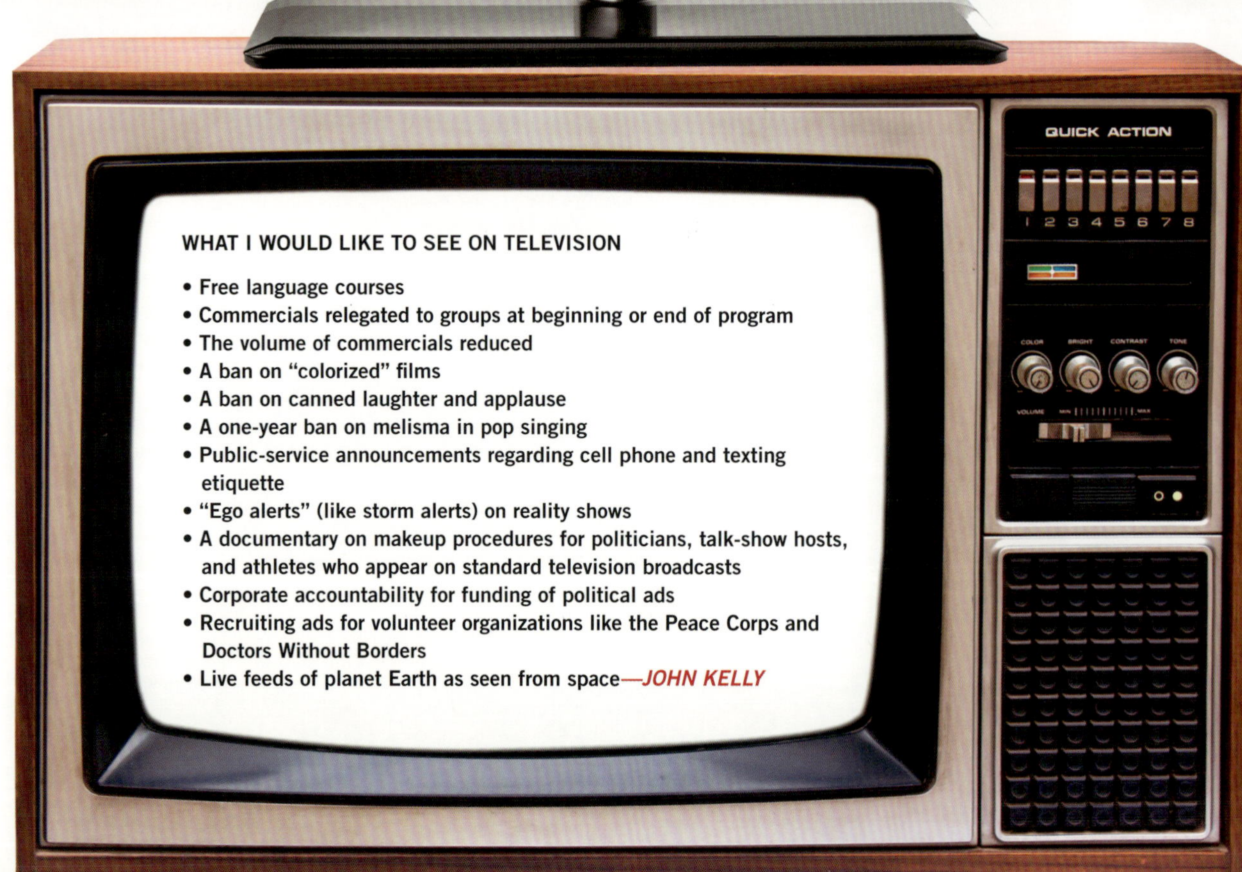

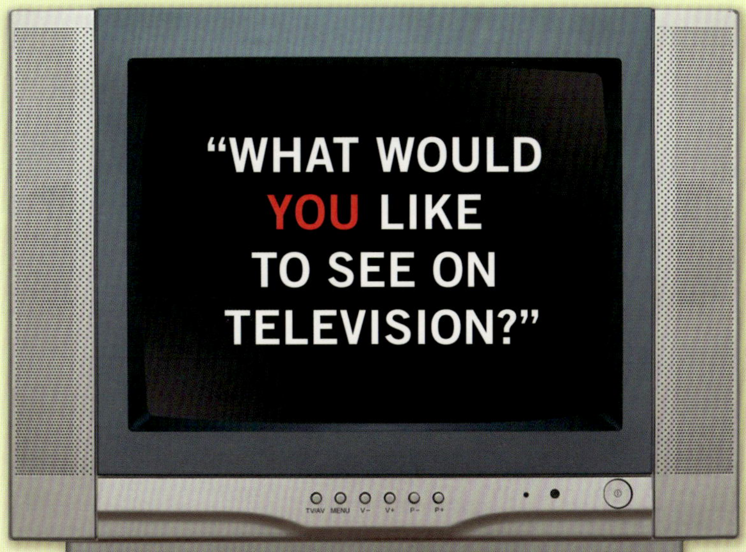

Singer-songwriter **Devendra Banhart**'s albums include *Oh Me Oh My...*, *Cripple Crow,* and *What Will We Be.* He co-founded the record label Gnomonsong with Andy Cabic in 2005.

Artist **Judith Barry**'s work incorporates performance, installation, film and video, sculpture, and new media, and has been exhibited at the Venice Biennale and the Carnegie International, among many other venues.

David Carr is a media and culture columnist for *The New York Times.* His memoir, *The Night of the Gun,* was published in 2008.

Artist **Liam Gillick** was nominated for the Turner Prize in 2002 and was selected to represent Germany in the 2009 Venice Biennale.

Director **Ulu Grosbard**'s films include *Straight Time, True Confessions*, and *Georgia*; his extensive work in theater includes *American Buffalo,* which earned him a Tony nomination for best director.

Houston-based artist **Trenton Doyle Hancock** participated in the 2000 and 2002 Whitney Biennials and was the subject of an exhibition at the Fruitmarket Gallery in Edinburgh, Scotland, in 2007.

Buck Henry is a writer, actor, director, and the cocreator of the television series *Get Smart.* His screenplays include *The Graduate; What's Up, Doc?;* and *To Die For.*

Paul Hoffman wrote *The Man Who Loved Only Numbers* and a memoir, *King's Gambit: A Son, a Father and the World's Most Dangerous Game.* He is a former editor-in-chief of *Discover* Magazine.

Performance and visual artist **John Kelly** has performed and/or exhibited at Tate Modern, The Kitchen, the Brooklyn Academy of Music's Next Wave Festival, and countless other venues.

Richard Kostelanetz is a writer, poet, artist, and critic who has received a Guggenheim Fellowship, a Pollock-Krasner Award, and numerous grants from the National Endowment for the Arts.

Louis Menand won the Pulitzer Prize in history for his 2001 book *The Metaphysical Club.* He is currently professor of English and American literature and language at Harvard University.

Laura Mulvey, author of the influential 1976 critical essay "Visual Pleasure and Narrative Cinema," is a professor of film and media studies at Birkbeck, University of London.

West Virginia–born writer **Jayne Anne Phillips**' novels include *Machine Dreams, Fast Lanes,* and *Lark and Termite.* She currently heads the M.F.A. writing program at Rutgers University.

Charles Renfro is a principal of the New York City architectural firm Diller Scofidio + Renfro as well as a visiting professor at Columbia University and Rice University.

Nathaniel Rich's books include his novel *The Mayor's Tongue* and *San Francisco Noir: The City in Film Noir from 1940 to the Present.*

James Schamus is the president of Focus Features and frequently collaborates with director Ang Lee. His screenplays include *The Ice Storm* and *Brokeback Mountain.*

The work of artist **Carolee Schneemann** has been exhibited at the Whitney Museum of American Art and the Museum of Modern Art, among many other institutions, and she has served on the faculty of New York University, Bard College, and the School of the Art Institute of Chicago.

Jim Shepard's novels include *Flights, Nosferatu,* and *Project X.* His 2008 short-story collection, *Like You'd Understand, Anyway,* was a National Book Award finalist. He teaches writing at Williams College.

Josh Siegel is a film and media curator at the Museum of Modern Art, where he has organized or co-organized more than 90 exhibitions, including *India Now* in 2007.

Director **Peter Sollett**'s films include *Five Feet High and Rising, Raising Victor Vargas,* and *Nick and Norah's Infinite Playlist.*

Robert Sullivan is the author of the books *Cross Country, Rats,* and *The Thoreau You Don't Know.* He is a contributing editor at *Vogue* magazine.

Lili Taylor has acted in dozens of films, including *Short Cuts, Dogfight,* and *I Shot Andy Warhol.* She received Emmy-Award nominations for her work in the TV series *The X-Files* and *Six Feet Under.*

Joan Tewkesbury wrote the screenplays for the Robert Altman films *Nashville* and *Thieves Like Us* and has directed episodes for TV shows such as *The Guardian, Felicity,* and *Northern Exposure.*

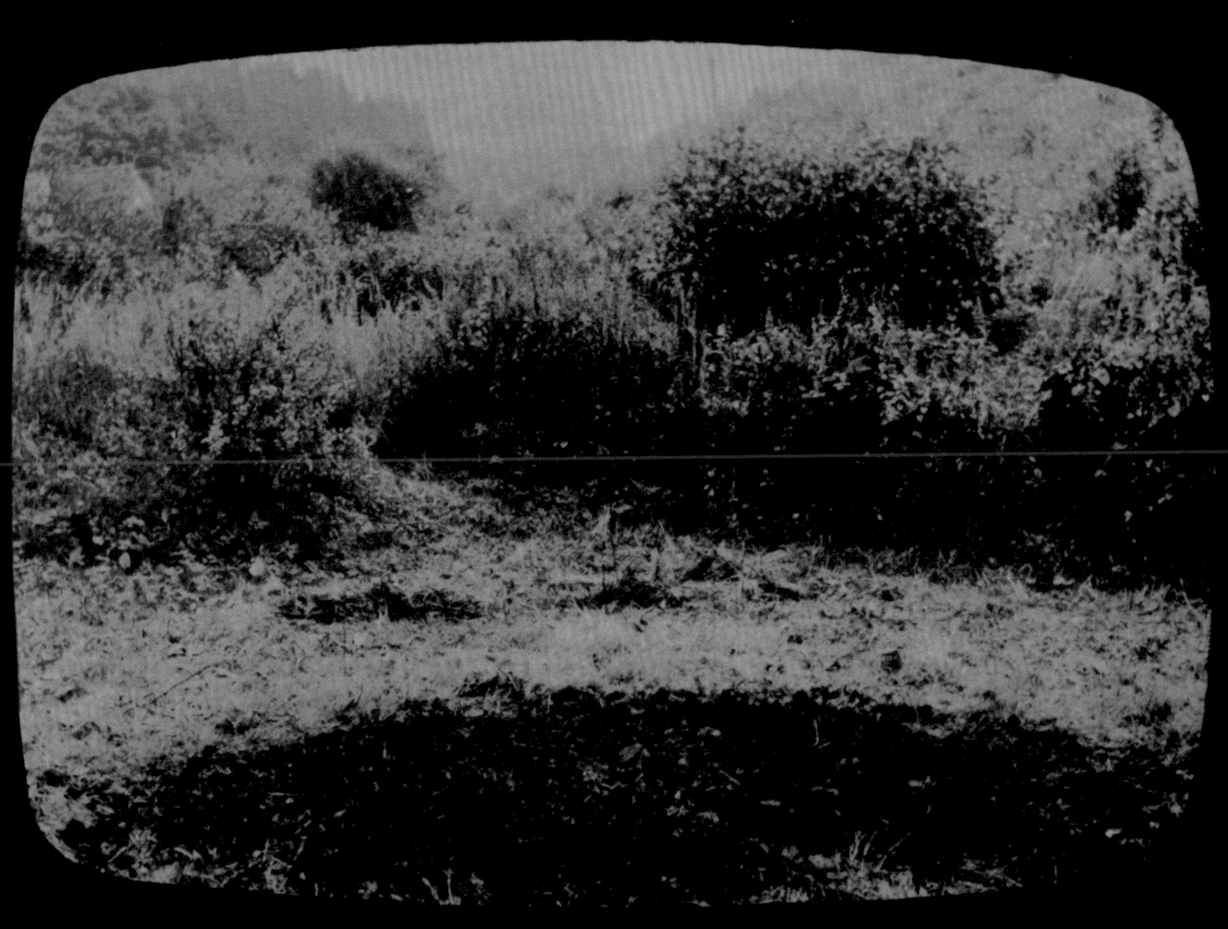

Keith Arnatt, *Self-Burial (Television Interference Project)*, 1969

With no announcement or further commentary, WDR 3 television in Germany inserted into the programmes showing between 11 and 18 October 1969 a series of nine photographs depicting Arnatt gradually sinking into the ground. Two consecutive photos were shown each evening, the first one at 8.15 p.m., directly after the main news broadcast, the second one in the middle of whatever programme was running at 9:15 p.m. The enigma was solved at the end of the one-week series by an interview with the artist. As Arnatt explained, the series was not created specifically for TV transmission: "It was originally made as a comment upon the notion of the 'disappearance of the art object.' It seemed a logical corollary that the artist should also disappear."—*Media Art Net*

Self-Burial (Television Interference Project), 1969, is reproduced here from my father's personal documentation (the actual work is in the Tate Collection). Keith talked to me about this piece shortly before he died in 2008. He reiterated that he had thought of the *Self-Burial*, like other works by him, as being almost meaningless outside of the context for which the work was originally conceived and on which the work commented. Nevertheless, he'd kept eight transparencies (the work had been graphically represented in print in at least three versions: eight individual images following the logical sequence; eight sequenced images plus one "image" of interference-like fuzz; and, as in the Tate work, nine sequenced images mounted in a square grid). It's an open question (that's the type of phrase he liked) whether the eight slides reproduced here, superimposed by his rough approximation of a television-screen border, represent a distaste for reification linked with an acknowledgement of the fact that the work had been reproduced in varying formats already, or just a disinterest in material that he was still required to talk about. In talking about, as well as seeing, his work, those issues connected to reification, the status of art objects, and objects/events linked with and suited to contexts, become a live matter once again.—*Matthew Arnatt*

Images courtesy the Estate of Keith Arnatt and Maureen Paley, London

On *Gilligan's Island* (CBS, April 21), it was learned via shortwave radio that the reverend who married Thurston B. Howell III (Jim Backus) and Lovey (Natalie Schafer) was fake. Therefore the Howells had never been properly married. Inter alia this had serious financial implications for Lovey in respect to Mr. Howell's portfolio of assets, including the hut, the furniture, the diamond mine, the coconut plantation, the railroad, the 40,000 acres of Colorado including the whole of downtown Denver, and the Hatchet–Cuckoo Oil Company in Dust Bowl, Oklahoma. Assisted by Gilligan (Bob Denver), the Skipper (Alan Hale, Jr.) attempted to perform a remedial wedding ceremony in the middle of the lagoon, in other words, "at sea," but this went wrong, and the Howells were temporarily estranged. Mr. Howell then asked Ginger (Tina Louise) on a date, and "Miss Wentworth" counter-dated the Professor (Russell Johnson). Resolution was attained before the final commercial break. There was a coup d'état in Upper Volta.

On *F Troop* (ABC), at Fort Courage, Kansas, Sergeant O'Rourke (Forrest Tucker) and Corporal Agarn (Larry Storch) continued to expand their illegal mixed business in 50/50 partnership with Chief Wild Eagle (Frank DeKova) of the Hekawi Tribe, formerly of Massachusetts ("paleface spoil neighborhood"), the Chief's heir apparent Crazy Cat (Don Diamond) and the medicine man Roaring Chicken (Edward Everett Horton). O'Rourke Enterprises' burgeoning sales of cheap souvenirs and bootleg whiskey for the local saloon were still deftly concealed from Captain Wilton Parmenter (Ken Berry) and his amanuensis, the incompetent blond bugler Private Dobbs (James Hampton). On the basis of the "domino theory," President Lyndon B. Johnson firmly declined to discontinue hostilities against the Vietcong and North Vietnam.

On *Hogan's Heroes* (CBS, April 15), at Stalag 13, Colonel Klink (Werner Klemperer) was distracted from potentially disruptive thoughts of promotion and transfer to a different prisoner-of-war camp by an ingenious scheme devised by Hogan (Bob Crane) to cement an inescapable liaison between Klink and Frau Linkmeyer (Kathleen Freeman), the grotesque widowed sister of General Burkhalter (Leon Askin). As usual, Sergeant Schultz (John Banner) knew nothing. The president of France, General Charles de Gaulle, visited Moscow.

On *The Addams Family* (ABC, January 14), Morticia (Carolyn Jones) and Gomez (John Astin) became anxious when, most uncharacteristically, Uncle Fester (Jackie Coogan) began doing physical exercises prescribed by a television fitness guru. It emerged that Fester wished to lose weight because his ungainly pen pal, Fifi (Peggy Mondo), was planning to come visit. In a curious twist, however, Fester accidentally hypnotized himself, thus revealing a strong desire to become an astronaut. Lurch (Ted Cassidy) viewed this with scorn, as did Thing (also Ted Cassidy), Cousin Itt (Felix Silla, with voice-over engineered by Tony Magro) and Pugsley (Ken Weatherwax). The prime minister of India, Mrs. Indira Gandhi, visited Moscow.

On *Gomer Pyle, U.S.M.C.* (CBS, October 26), at Camp Henderson near Los Angeles, Sergeant Carter (Frank Sutton) ordered Gomer (Jim Nabors) to consult a psychiatrist (Richard Bull) at the double, after he claimed to have seen little men from outer space. These turned out to be genuine (Frank Carpenter and Johnny Silver). United Artists' *The Russians Are Coming, the Russians Are Coming!*, starring Alan Arkin and Eva Marie Saint, grossed $10,164,000, ranking sixth after *Hawaii* (UA), *The Bible* (Fox), *Who's Afraid of Virginia Woolf?* (Warner), *The Sand Pebbles* (Fox), and *A Man For All Seasons* (Columbia). Caesars Palace opened in Las Vegas, Nevada.

On *Get Smart* (NBC, October 15), Maxwell Smart, Agent 86 (Don Adams), infiltrated KAOS by impersonating a professional safe-cracker called Jimmy Ballantine. The Chief (Edward Platt) obtained reliable intelligence to the effect that KAOS was using a barbershop as their rendezvous point. Agent 99 (Barbara Feldon) duly posed as an undercover manicurist, and Agent 13 (Dave Ketchum) was in the towel steamer. KAOS then hired Ballantine/Max to break into the Federal Reserve, but CONTROL caught KAOS red-handed, and, while taking them into custody, Max accidentally locked the Chief inside a vault. President Lyndon B. Johnson signed the Freedom of Information Act.

On *The Lucy Show* (CBS, November 7), Lucy (Lucille Ball) told Mr. Mooney (Gale Gordon) she was sick so she could go in secret to Palm Springs, California, and play in a golfing tournament with her roommate Carol (Carol Burnett), not realizing that Mr. Mooney had arranged to play in it also. Lucy then scrounged a blind dinner date with a distinguished actor, Colin Grant (Dan Rowan), who turned out to be Mr. Mooney's golfing crony. Resolution was partly attained before the final commercial break. The prime minister of Great Britain, the Right Hon. Harold Wilson, O.B.E., M.P., visited Moscow.

On *I Dream of Jeannie* (NBC, October 24), at NASA, whilst immersing himself in an old western on TV, "Master" (Larry Hagman) mentioned to Jeannie (Barbara Eden) that he hankered after those days when men were men, and a man had to be strong, strong, to survive. Jeannie obliged by turning him into the sheriff of Gopher Junction, a lawless frontier settlement somewhere in the vicinity of the Sangre de Cristo mountains. Master learned his lesson, and resolution was attained prior to the final commercial break. King Hussein of Jordan and his English-born second wife, Princess Muna al-Hussein, paid a state visit to Britain. So did the president of Pakistan, General Muhammad Ayub Khan. Helena Bonham Carter was born. Walt Disney died.

For *Scent-imental Reasons*, Charles M. Jones's animated short feature for *Merrie Melodies* (Warner Brothers), continued to enjoy enormous popularity in cinemas and on television, allowing its central protagonist, Pepe Le Pew (voice-over by Mel Blanc), a skunk, to horrify the cycling, top-hatted bourgeois *gentilhomme* proprietor of a Breton parfumerie (voice-over by Mel Blanc) and a mustachioed gendarme (voice-over by Mel Blanc), then deliver these immortal lines to his kitten love interest: *"Ah, la belle femme skunk fatale"* and *"I am ze locksmith of love, no?"* Most audiences disregarded the use here of aggravated sexual assault as a convenient vehicle for slapstick comedy. Angela Lansbury created the title role of *Mame*, Jerry Herman's smash hit on Broadway, and won the Tony Award for best actress in a musical.

On *McHale's Navy* (ABC, April 12), a political big shot from Washington, D.C., who had a reputation for successfully propelling war heroes into public office, visited Taratupa, the PT boat-73 base in the South Pacific. Assisted by Lieutenant Commander Quinton McHale (Ernest Borgnine) and "Chuck," in other words, Ensign Charles Parker (Tim Conway), Captain Binghamton ("Old Leadbottom") (Joe Flynn) set about ditching his "desk jockey" image, the better deliberately to misrepresent himself as a fearless fighting man and plausible congressional aspirant. Chairman Mao launched his so-called Cultural Revolution in what was then universally known as Peking.

On *The Patty Duke Show* (ABC, February 23), in connection with a school project, Patty (Duke) wrote a friendly letter to a Soviet politician and not only received a reply, but also discovered that she had unwittingly chosen the next general secretary of the Soviet presidium. Not surprisingly, the State Department soon wanted to know how Patty ever managed to exercise this sort of leverage. The Metropolitan Opera House opened at Lincoln Center in Manhattan. The secretary-general of the United Nations, U Thant, visited Moscow.

On *Mister Ed* (CBS, January 9), Ed (played by Bamboo Harvester; voice-over by Allan "Rocky" Lane) discovered that he was of Cherokee descent, and on principle therefore absolutely refused to participate in that year's Pioneer Parade. Unfortunately, Wilbur (Alan Young) had already promised Carol (Connie Hines) and Mr. Higgins (Barry Kelly) that Ed would join the parade, as a special favor just for his father-in-law. At this date few audiences found implausible the notion of a suburb-dwelling architect keeping a talking horse in the suburbs. John Lennon met Yoko Ono for the first time in London; Pope Paul VI met the Archbishop of Canterbury, Michael Ramsay, in Rome, and with some skepticism the Emperor of Ethiopia, Haile Selassie I, King of Kings, Lord of Lords, Conquering Lion of the Tribe of Judah, and Elect of God, met some Rastafarians in Jamaica.

On *Batman* (ABC, September 15), posing as the wealthy recluse Minerva Matthews, Catwoman (Julie Newmar) made a deal to buy from a certain Zubin Zucchini (David Fresco) two Stradivarius violins for $250,000. Once she took possession of these purr-ecious mew-sical instruments, Catwoman demanded her money back. But Zucchini evaded this despicable double-cross and, supported by Commissioner Gordon (Neil Hamilton) and Alfred the Butler (Alan Napier), the Caped Crusader (Adam West) and the Boy Wonder (Burt Ward) swooped on Catwoman's hideout, the Pink Sandbox, and conducted mopping-up operations—"Pow! Biff! Wham! Splat!" "And how could a feline feloness like Catwoman also be a fashion model?" asked Robin. "Give credit where credit is due, Robin. She may be evil, but she is attractive. You'll know more about that in a couple of years," explained Batman. Relatively few American audiences fully appreciated this charmingly fetishistic fable of cross-generational male homosexual desire. The Jimi Hendrix Experience took shape in London; the Ronettes disintegrated. Columbia Records released Bob Dylan's *Blonde on Blonde*.

On *Bewitched* (ABC, May 5), Samantha (Elizabeth Montgomery) wanted to go to Miami, but Darrin (Dick York) was far too busy at work. Endora (Agnes Moorhead) decided to split Darrin in two so that Samantha could take her vacation with his fun half, while his industrious, responsible half stayed at the advertising agency. This stratagem backfired, though, when Samantha got sick of Darrin's increasingly wacky and irritating "fun" side, while Larry (David White) and their important client (Frank Maxwell) became exasperated by the lugubrious officiousness of Darrin's hard-working side. The two halves of Darrin were successfully reintegrated before the final commercial break. There were coups d'état in Nigeria, Ghana, and Syria. At the 23rd plenary conference of the Soviet Communist Party in Moscow, General Secretary Leonid Brezhnev announced that Sino–Soviet relations were "not satisfying."

On *My Favorite Martian* (CBS, February 6), in a department store, some chemical constituent of a cologne called Homme Fatale reacted with his molecular structure and turned Uncle Martin (Ray Walston) into a mannequin. The only way to reverse the damage was to receive a blast from his revitalizing Martian ray gun. Unfortunately, Mrs. Lorelei Brown (Pamela Britton) got zapped instead, so then there were two

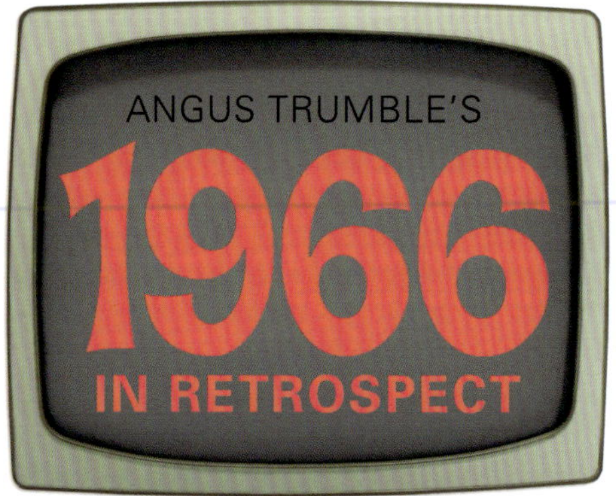

mannequins. The antidote for humans turned out to be a whiff of Homme Fatale, but naturally the store had by then sold their last bottle. Following torrential autumn rains in the Appenines, the River Arno broke its banks and inundated much of Florence. There were two immensely destructive earthquakes in Turkey. Albert Speer was released from Spandau Prison in West Berlin.

On *Lost in Space* (CBS, April 20), Will Robinson (Billy Mumy) and Dr. Zachary Smith (Jonathan Harris) found an alien spaceship, which "Robot"—the series' Class M–3 Model B–9, General Utility Non-Theorizing Environmental Control Robot (voice-over by Dick Tufeld)—claimed was capable of traveling anywhere in the universe. Whilst exploring the interior of the craft, the hatch suddenly closed, and Will was taken on a wild ride into the sixth dimension. Thus exposed to awesomely psychedelic cosmic forces, at length Will returned with superhuman intelligence. Much excited by the idea that taking a ride in the same ship might endow him with comparable mental powers—powers, moreover, that he craved with characteristic wantonness—Dr. Smith took off next, but returned a fragile, dessicated old man, which parlous state he blamed on Will with much bitterness and excoriation. Most American audiences overlooked this daring fable of twisted cross-generational male homosexual desire, as indeed they took in their stride the unusual intimacy enjoyed by Dr. Robinson (Guy Williams) and the handsome unmarried Major Don West (Mark Goddard). There were race riots in Lansing, Michigan. The president of Pakistan, General Muhammad Ayub Khan, visited Tashkent in the Soviet Union.

On *The Beverly Hillbillies* (CBS, October 19), Elly May Clampett (Donna Douglas) and Jethro Bodine (Max Baer, Jr.) decided to hire a gorilla to help Granny (Irene Ryan) with the housework, and asked their banker and next-door neighbor Mr. Drysdale (Raymond Bailey) to make the necessary arrangements. Outraged by this idea, Mr. Drysdale hired a man in a gorilla costume, Mr. Kelly (George Barrows), to make sure the Clampetts ended up hating the new help. However, the new gorilla ("Herby") soon tired of doing the chores, and wanted out. Mr. Drysdale had no option but to put on the discarded gorilla suit and stage an escape, but the Clampetts got a real gorilla from the zoo to replace the fake one. At the Plaza in New York, Truman Capote held his "Black and White" Ball in honor of Mrs. Philip Graham, proprietor of the Washington Post Company. The principal architect of apartheid, Prime Minister Hendrik Frensch Verwoerd, was assassinated in Cape Town.

On *The Flintstones* (ABC, March 25), Fred (voice-over by Alan Reed) and Wilma (voice-over by Jean Vander Pyl) got accepted into a country club largely populated by wealthy socialites. This occurred after wires were crossed during a conversation in which Wilma discussed with another Stone Age housewife the Flintstones' pink prosauropod pet Dino (voice-over by Mel Blanc). Fred then tried to learn some decent manners so they could fit in with the other members, but eventually Fred and Wilma decided just to be themselves, and everyone liked them far better that way. Barbados, Botswana, Lesotho, and Guyana all gained their independence.

An Evening with Carol Channing (February 18) and *Color Me Barbra* (March 30) both aired as specials on CBS. The Miss Universe Pageant went color (July 16). The Miss America Pageant followed suit in September and aired for the first time on NBC. *Charlie Brown* aired for the first time on CBS. The first episode of *Star Trek* aired on NBC. In Britain, Patrick Troughton made his first appearance as the second, eponymous, recorder-playing Time Lord on *Doctor Who* (BBC). Jean Arp died. So did Hedda Hopper, Alberto Giacometti, Buster Keaton, Gino Severini, Montgomery Clift, and Sophie Tucker, "the Last of the Red-Hot Mamas." Pope Paul VI abolished the *Index Librorum Prohibitorum*, thus permitting Roman Catholics to consult the published works of Descartes, Voltaire, Ranke, Flaubert, and Zola without fear of excommunication. There was a failed coup d'état in Togo. A severe tornado devastated Topeka, Kansas. *The Dick Van Dyke Show* (CBS) folded, but *The Flying Nun* (ABC) was in development and almost ready for casting. Approximately 4,380 hours of canned laughter aired on the three American television networks; Ronald Reagan was elected governor of California.

ESOPUS CD #15: **TELEVISION**

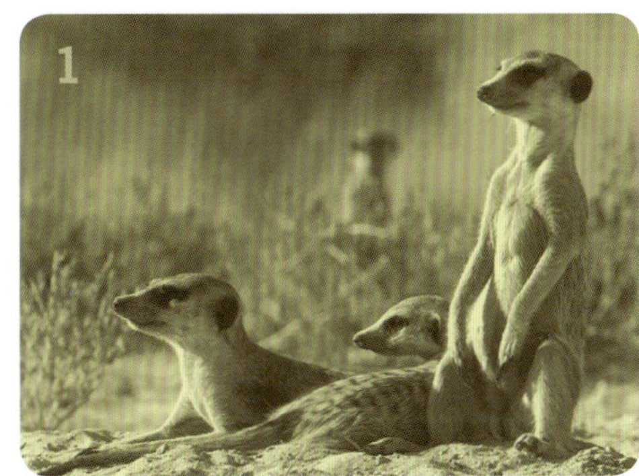

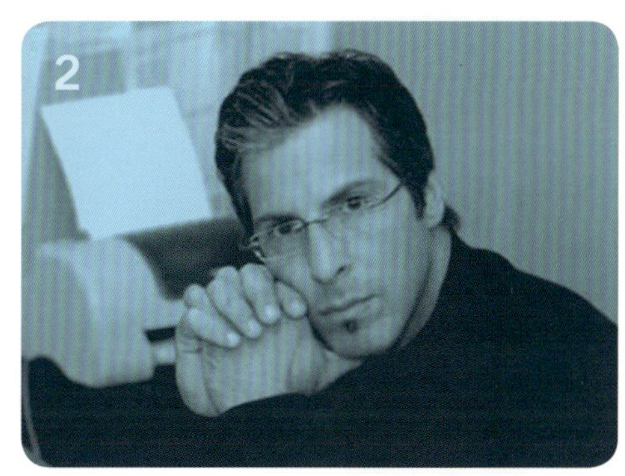

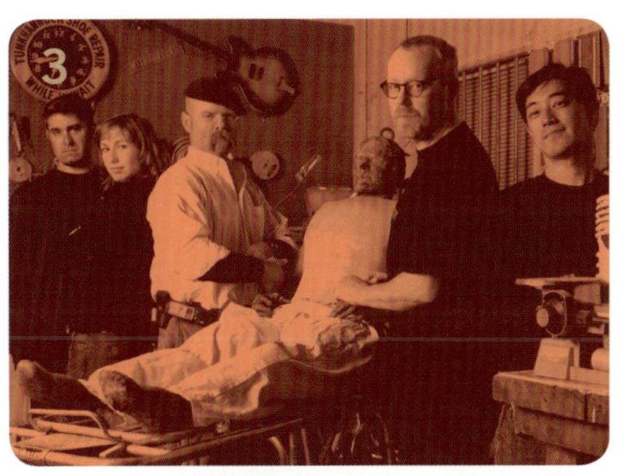

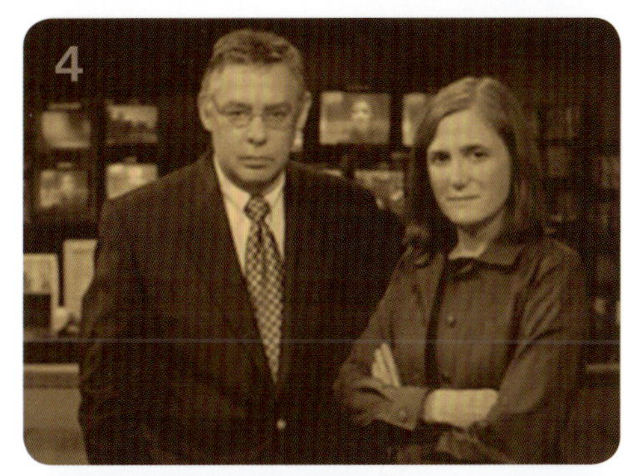

For our 15th CD, *Esopus* asked 10 musicians to create songs from scratch based on the television shows of their choice. Their selections, ranging from *Democracy Now!* to *Cheaters*, are a reminder of how one can run across just about anything on the tube—from the high to the low, the sublime to the ridiculous. The resulting songs offer proof that TV, whatever the cynics may say, can also serve as an excellent source of creative inspiration.

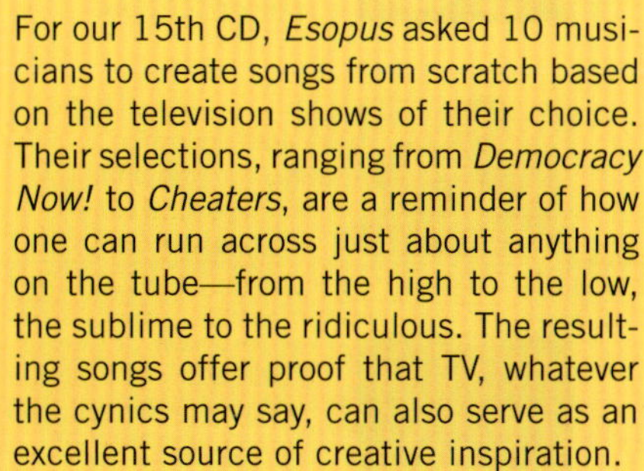

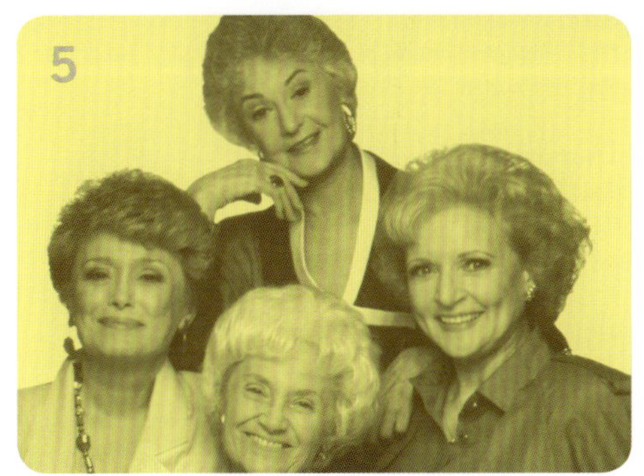

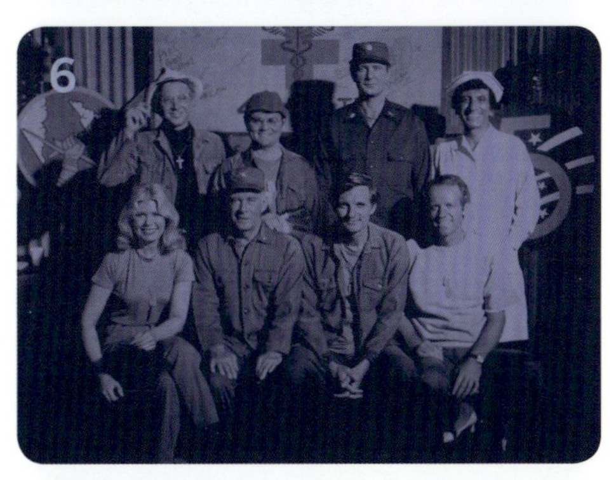

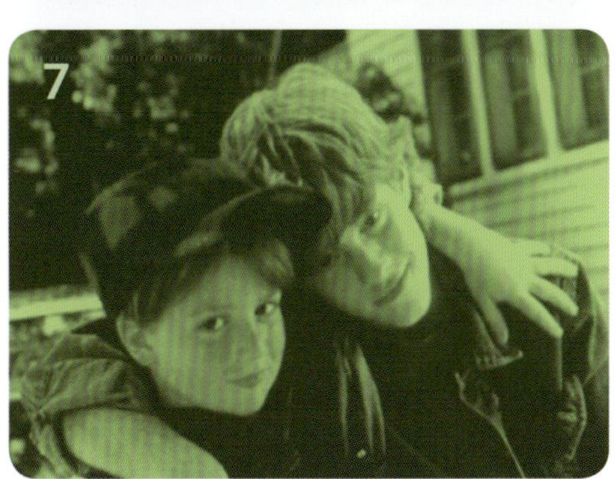

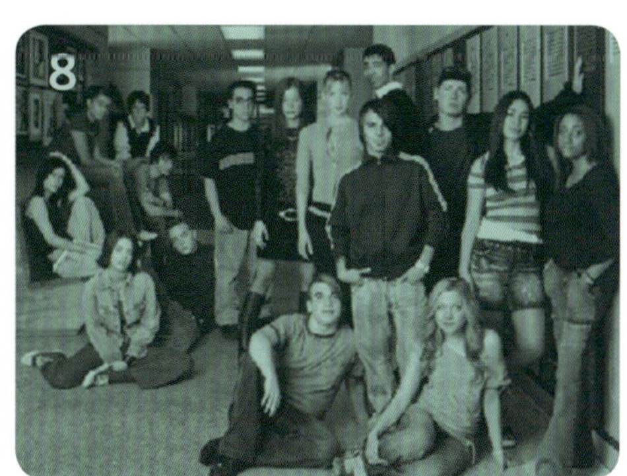

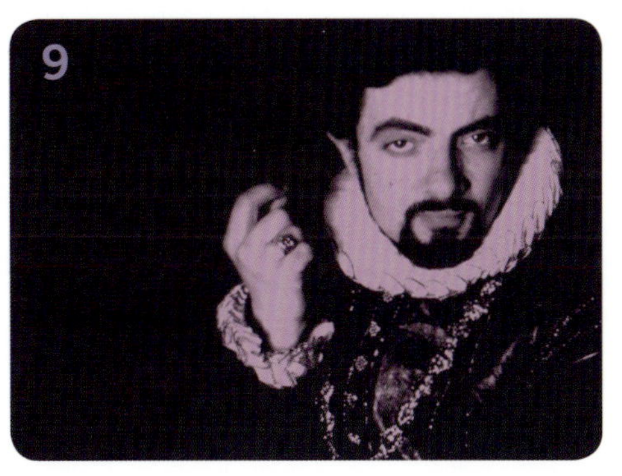

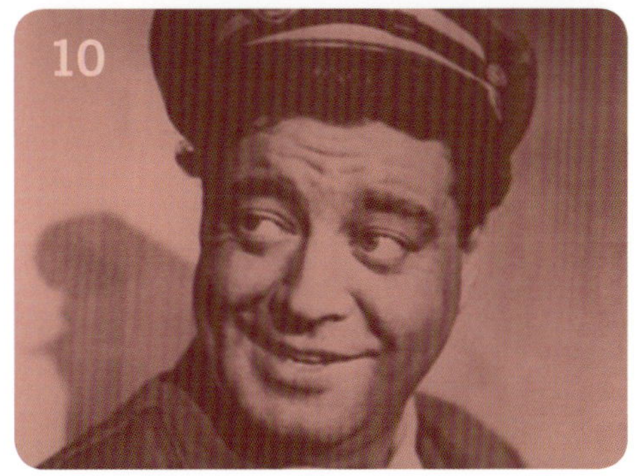

ESOPUS CD #15: **TELEVISION**

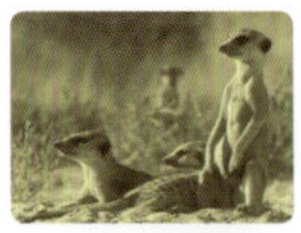

1. STEPHIN MERRITT
"New Theme from *Meerkat Manor*"
Written, performed, and produced by Stephin Merritt
© 2010 Gay and Loud (ASCAP)
Meerkat Manor

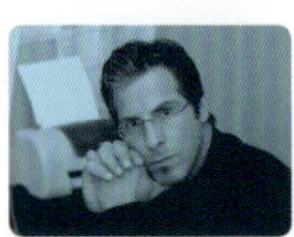

2. THE THIRD WHEEL BAND
"Tell You Twice"
Written and produced by Steph Allen, Ryan Langlois, and Greg Barresi
© 2010 The Third Wheel Band
Cheaters

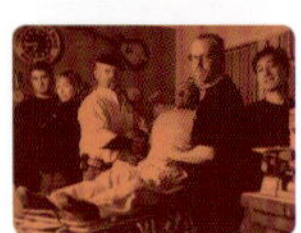

3. ONE RING ZERO
"Busted, Plausible, or Confirmed (The *MythBusters* Song)"
Written, recorded, and performed by Joshua Camp and Michael Hearst
Vocals, theremin, guitars, bass: Michael Hearst
Vocals, accordion, keyboard, sequencing: Joshua Camp
© 2010 One Ring Zero Publishing (BMI)
MythBusters

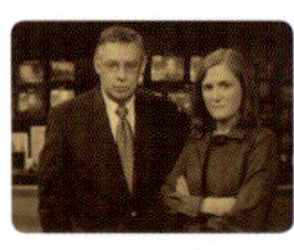

4. RYLAND BOUCHARD
"Hope Rides Alone"
Written, performed, and produced by Ryland Bouchard
© 2010 Ryland Bouchard (BMI)
Democracy Now!

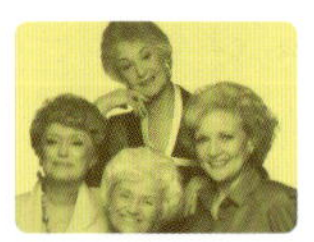

5. CLOUD NOTHINGS
"I Apologize"
Written, performed, and produced by Dylan Baldi
© 2010 DB91
The Golden Girls

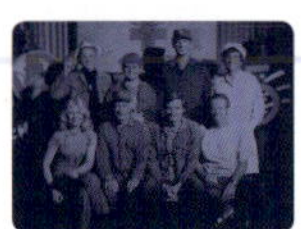

6. ANDREW CEDERMARK
"Still Life with Sour Mash"
Written, performed, and recorded by Andrew Cedermark at home
in August 2010, with singing by Carianne King
© 2010 Andrew Cedermark
M*A*S*H

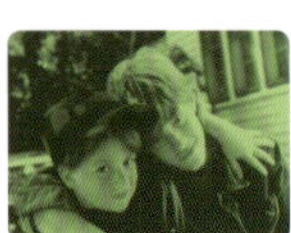

7. FESTIVAL
"Today's Adventure!"
Song and lyrics by Alexis, Lindsay, and Mike Powell
Vocals, percussion: Alexis Powell
Vocals: Lindsay Powell
Vocals, guitar, and bass: Mike Powell
© 2010 make the fun
The Adventures of Pete & Pete

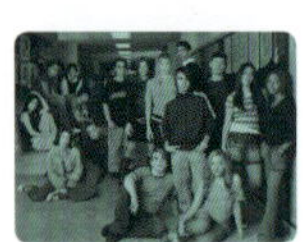

8. AUTRE NE VEUT
"Live for the Baby"
Written and produced by Autre Ne Veut
© 2010 Autre Ne Veut
Degrassi: The Next Generation

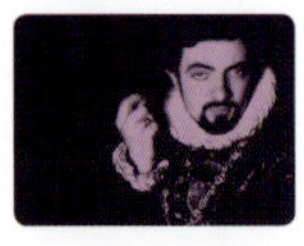

9. DAVID THOMAS BROUGHTON
"Age of Giving"
Recorded, mixed, and not mastered by David Thomas Broughton at home
© 2010 David Thomas Broughton
Blackadder

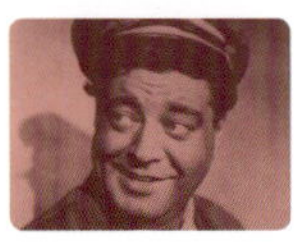

10. LAURIE SCHWARTZ
"There Was Also the Fact that He Was Shaped Like the Moon"
Created and produced by Laurie Schwartz
Guest artists: Dan Minahan, Susan Stone, Josh Patner, Richard Einhorn,
Edoardo Bellando
© 2010 Laurie Schwartz
The Jackie Gleason Show

PHOTO CREDITS: 1. © Discovery Communications, LLC; 2. © Bobby Goldstein Productions, Inc.; 3. © Discovery Communications, LLC; 4. © Steve J. Sherman; 5. © Touchstone Television/NBC Universal; 6. © 20th Century Fox Television; 7. © Wellsville Productions/Nickelodeon; 8. © Epitome Pictures/CTV Television Network; 9. © British Broadcasting Corporation; 10. © Columbia Broadcasting System

Brooklyn-based Adley Atkin is the force behind **Autre Ne Veut**, whose self-titled debut album was released this September on Olde English Spelling Bee.

Ryland Bouchard, the former mastermind of The Robot Ate Me, lives in Knoxville, TN. His albums include *SEEDS* (2008), *Cowboys and Cuckoos* (2009), and the EP *Better This Than Nothing*, which was released by Swim Slowly this February.

David Thomas Broughton released his full-length debut, *The Complete Guide to Insufficiency*, in 2005, and went on to collaborate with chamber ensemble 7 Hertz in 2007. The London-based singer-songwriter's next album is *Outbreeding*.

Charlottesville, VA–based **Andrew Cedermark**, formerly guitarist for Titus Andronicus, released his first full-length solo effort, *Moon Deluxe*, on Underwater Peoples this September.

Cloud Nothings is the musical project of Cleveland-based multi-instrumentalist Dylan Baldi. His eight-song debut, *Turning On*, is out via Bridgetown.

Festival is composed of Alexis, Lindsay, and Mike Powell, who live in Portland, OR; Chicago, IL; and Tucson, AZ respectively. The group's debut album, *Come, Arrow, Come*, was released in 2008 on Language of Stone records.

Los Angeles–based **Stephin Merritt** is best known as the principal singer and songwriter for The Magnetic Fields, whose albums include *69 Love Songs* (1999; Merge) and this year's *Realism* (Nonesuch). Merritt's work as a composer includes the scores for the films *Pieces of April* and *Eban and Charley* and the theatrical musicals *My Life as a Fairytale* and *Coraline*.

Micheal Hearst and Joshua Camp are **One Ring Zero**, the New York–based band whose 2007 album *As Smart As We Are* featured lyrics and songs by writers like Paul Auster, Margaret Atwood, and Jonathan Lethem. The band released *Planets*, a response to the 100th anniversary of Gustav Holst's *The Planets*, earlier this year.

Laurie Schwartz is a composer, curator, and independent-radio producer based in Europe. Her music has been performed at major international venues and festivals, and released on CD by Academy, Edition Zeitklang, Cantate-Musicaphon, and Zeitkratzer.

Based in New York City, **The Third Wheel Band** is a roots-Americana group composed of Steph Allen, Ryan Langlois, and Greg Barresi.